Audi 100

Owners Workshop Manual

by J H Haynes
Member of the Guild of Motoring Writers
and Peter Ward

Models covered:
Audi 100 LS, GL, SE and S Coupe with 1760 cc (107 cu in) or
1871 cc (114 cu in) engine

Covers models with manual and automatic transmission. Does not cover
new Audi 100 4 cyl or 5 cyl models

ISBN 0 85696 500 6

Printed in England *(162-8M5)*

Haynes Publishing Group
Sparkford Nr Yeovil
Somerset BA22 7JJ England

Haynes Publications, Inc
861 Lawrence Drive
Newbury Park
California 91320 USA

Acknowledgements

Thanks are due to Audi NSU Auto Union AG for their assistance with regard to the use of technical material and certain illustrations. The Champion Sparking Plug Company supplied the illustrations showing the various spark plug conditions. The bodywork repair photographs used in this manual were provided by Lloyds Industries Limited who supply 'Turtle Wax', 'Dupli-color Holts', and other Holts range products.

Lastly thanks are due to all those people at Sparkford who helped in the production of this manual. Particularly Brian Horsfall, Les Brazier, Rod Grainger, Andy Legg, Ian Robson and David Neilson.

About this manual

Its aim

The aim of this manual is to help you get the best value from your car. It can do so in several ways. It can help you decide what work must be done (even should you choose to get it done by a garage), provide information on routine maintenance and servicing, and give a logical course of action and diagnosis when random faults occur. However, it is hoped that you will make full use of the manual by tackling the work yourself. On simpler jobs it may even be quicker than booking the car into the garage, and having to go there twice, to leave and collect it. Perhaps most important, a lot of money can be saved by avoiding the costs the garage must charge to cover its labour and overheads.

The manual has drawings and descriptions to show the function of the various components so that their layout can be understood. Then the tasks are described and photographed in a step-by-step sequence so that even a novice can do the work.

Its arrangement

The manual is divided into thirteen Chapters, each covering a logical sub-division of the vehicle. The Chapters are each divided into consecutively numbered Sections and the Sections into paragraphs (or sub-sections), with decimal numbers following on from the Section they are in, eg 5.1, 5.2, 5.3 etc.

It is freely illustrated, especially in those parts where there is a detailed sequence of operations to be carried out. There are two forms of illustration: figures and photographs. The figures are numbered in sequence with decimal numbers, according to their position in the Chapter: eg Fig. 6.4 is the 4th drawing/illustration in Chapter 6. Photographs are numbered (either individually or in related groups) the same as the Section or sub-section of the text where the operation they show is described.

There is an alphabetical index at the back of the manual as well as a contents list at the front.

References to the 'left' or 'right' of the vehicle are in the sense of a person facing forwards in the driver's seat.

Whilst every care is taken to ensure that the information in this manual is correct no liability can be accepted by the authors or publishers for loss, damage or injury caused by any errors in, or omissions from, the information given.

Contents

1972 Audi 100 Coupe S (UK specification)

1973 Audi 100LS four door sedan (North American specification)

Buying spare parts
and vehicle identification numbers

Buying spare parts

Spare parts are available from many sources, for example: VW/Audi garages, other garages and accessory shops, and motor factors. Our advice regarding spare part sources is as follows:

Officially appointed VW/Audi garages - This is the best source of parts which are peculiar to your vehicle and are otherwise not generally available (eg: complete cylinder heads, internal gearbox components, badges, interior trim etc). It is also the only place at which you should buy parts if your car is still under warranty - non-VW/Audi components may invalidate the warranty. To be sure of obtaining the correct parts it will always be necessary to give the storeman your car's engine and chassis number, and if possible, to take the 'old' part along for positive identification. Remember that many parts are available on a factory exchange scheme - any parts returned should always be clean! It obviously makes good sense to go straight to the specialists on your car for this type of part for they are best equipped to supply you.

Other garages and accessory shops - These are often very good places to buy materials and components needed for the maintenance of your car (eg; oil filters, spark plugs, bulbs, fan belts, oils and greases, touch-up paint, filler paste etc). They also sell general accessories, usually have convenient opening hours, charge lower prices and can often be found not far from home.

Motor factors - Good factors will stock all of the more important components which wear out relatively quickly (eg; clutch components, pistons, valves, exhaust system, brake cylinders/pipes/hoses/seals/shoes and pads etc). Motor factors will often provide new or reconditioned components on a part exchange basis - this can save a considerable amount of money.

Vehicle identification numbers

The engine number is stamped on the rear of the block near the clutch housing (photo).

The transmission number is on the strengthening rib of the transmission unit (photo).

The chassis number is stamped at the top of the rear of the engine compartment (photo).

The data plate is forward of the shock absorber mounting on the right-hand side of the engine compartment (photo).

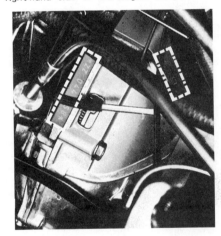

The engine and transmission numbers

Data plate

Chassis number

Routine maintenance

The maintenance tasks listed in this section are basically those recommended by the manufacturer but are supplemented by some additional items which will help to eliminate premature failure of a component or system.

If you have purchased a new Audi 100 you will be entitled to a free service at 300 miles (500 km) and 3000 miles (5000 km); it is strongly recommended that these checks are carried out by your Audi dealer.

1 Weekly, before a long journey or 250 miles (400 km)

1 Check the level of the electrolyte in the battery. If necessary top up to the bottom of the filler tubes using distilled water only.
2 Remove the engine oil dipstick, wipe it clean then replace it. Now remove it again and check the oil level, and if necessary top up using a multigrade engine oil such as Castrol GTX. Do not overfill and never allow the level to fall below the lower line on the dipstick. After replenishing, or if the level is checked after running the engine, allow a minute or two for all the oil to drain into the sump. The dipstick is on the carburettor side of the engine at the rear; the oil filler is on top of the rocker housing (photo).
3 Check the radiator coolant level when cold and top up if necessary to the level mark in the filler neck using an antifreeze and water mixture of the same proportions as being used in the cooling system.
4 Check the level of water in the windscreen washer reservoir and top up if necessary.
5 Check the tyre pressures and adjust if necessary. This should be done when the tyres are cold ie before a run. If checked after a run the pressure will always increase due to the heat generated. The correct values are given in the Specifications section of Chapter 11.
6 Check brake reservoir fluid level and top-up if necessary.
7 Check operation of all external lights and the horn.

2 Every 6000 miles (10000 km)

Carry out the weekly tasks as applicable plus:
1 Spring back the clips on the air cleaner, remove the cover and take out the filter (except Audi 100). Tap the air cleaner on a hard surface then blow through with an airline if at all possible; this is to remove the dust and dirt. Taking great care not to let dirt enter the carburettor, wipe the inside of the air cleaner container to remove the accumulated deposits. The new element can now be fitted and the cover replaced (photo).
2 Check and adjust the tension of the alternator and fan drive belts. Adjust if necessary, until a belt deflection of approximately 0.4 in (10 mm) is obtained when a pressure of 22 lb (10 kg) is applied in the centre of the longest run of the belt. The adjustment procedure is given in Chapters 2 and 10.
3 Check the functioning of the windscreen wipers and washer unit. If necessary adjust the washer jets and renew the wiper blades as described in Chapter 10.
4 Check the battery connections for corrosion and tightness. If corrosion is present it should be removed as described in Chapter 10. Even if no corrosion is present smear the terminals with a little petroleum jelly. Check also the specific gravity since this may give you warning of impending failure, here again the correct values are given in Chapter 10. The battery is located beneath the rear passenger seat squab.

5 Check and adjust the valve rockers if necessary. The correct clearances and procedure are given in Chapter 1.
6 Except where a BHCI electronic ignition system is fitted, clean and adjust the distributor contact points. At the same time lubricate the distributor then carefully wipe clean the distributor cap (inside and out), the plug leads, rotor, coil and suppressor caps. The full procedure for this is given in Chapter 4. On completion arrange for the dwell angle and dynamic timing setting to be checked using electronic equipment.
7 Carefully clean around the spark plugs to prevent any dirt etc from entering the engine, then remove the plugs. Clean them and reset the gaps as described in Chapter 4.
8 Check and adjust the free play in the clutch lever and pedal, and lubricate the cable. Refer to Chapter 5 for details.
9 A container of at least 7 pints (4 litres) capacity will be needed. Wipe around the engine drain plug then remove it and allow the oil to drain into the container. This job is best carried out after a warming up run to allow the oil to thin down a little. Carefully clean the lip of the drain hole, the drain plug and the sealing washer before replacing. The drain plug is located at the rear end of the sump. At the same time renew the oil filter but place a container below it when unscrewing to catch the oil which drips out. When fitting the new filter make sure the contact face on the engine is clean then smear a little engine oil or grease over the seal ring before fitting. Screw the filter on firmly by hand only (photo). The filter is situated on the exhaust side of the engine, just in front of the starter motor.
10 Where manual transmission is fitted, wipe around the filler/level plug before removing it then top up if necessary using a suitable light bodied extreme pressure gear oil of SAE 80 grade, eg Castrol Hypoy Light. This job is simplified a little if oil is dispensed from a plastic container (photo) as available in most accessory shops. Clean the filler/level plug and the sealing lip on the transmission cover before refitting. The plug is situated on the side of the transmission unit, about half way up the side wall towards the rear end.

Where automatic transmission is fitted, again take the precautions of cleaning the filler/dipsticks before removing and refitting. Use a gear oil of SAE 90 EP grade (eg Castrol Hypoy B) for the transmission unit, and an automatic transmission fluid such as Castrol TQ Dextron O. The combined filler/dipsticks are on top of the transmission, the one nearest the engine being for the final drive unit. When checking the automatic transmission fluid level first run the car to warm the fluid up a little. When lukewarm, select N, put the handbrake on with the car on a level surface then start the engine and let it idle. Now remove the dipstick, wipe it clean with a non-fluffy rag then replace it. Withdraw it again and check that the level is between the two marks on the dipstick. Top up as necessary but on no account overfill or allow the level to fall below the lower mark.
11 Carefully check all the rubber boots on the drive shafts and steering gear for damage, and leakage or loss of lubricant. Replace defective parts as necessary.
12 Check and adjust the wheel bearing play as described in Chapter 11.
13 Check the condition of the brake pads and linings, renewing or adjusting (rear brakes only) as required. At the same time check the fluid level in the reservoir (photo) and top up if necessary - do not overfill, or allow the level to fall below the minimum mark. The level will fall as brake wear takes place but if it has dropped drastically, check the system for leakage.
14 Carefully examine all flexible and rigid pipes for cracking and corrosion.
15 Check the tightness of the wheel retaining bolts after removing the hub cap.

16 Carefully examine the tyres for irregular wear patterns. If irregular wear is indicated check the suspension alignment (toe-out, camber, caster and ground clearance) as described in Chapter 11.

17 Check the tightness of all nuts and bolts on the drive shafts, power unit mountings, exhaust flange and clips, front suspension, steering gear and rear axle.

18 Arrange for the headlamp beam alignment to be checked using proper equipment.

19 Using a general purpose light bodied oil such as Castrol Everyman Oil apply a few drops to the handbrake compensator, boot hinges and lock, accelerator linkage and bearings, carburettor linkage, bonnet hinges, catch and release lever cable, door hinges and lock cylinders, and heater linkages.

20 Check and adjust all doors, boot and bonnet lids as necessary.

21 Check that the seat belts and their anchorage points are intact, secure and undamaged.

22 Test drive the car and listen for odd squeaks and rattles. Check that all the instruments, lights, brakes, throttle response etc are satisfactory. On completion of the test leave the car standing for a while, then check for oil and water leaks underneath. Tighten clips, plugs etc as necessary.

RM1.2. Topping up the engine oil

RM2.1. Removing the air cleaner cover

RM2.9. Removing the oil filter

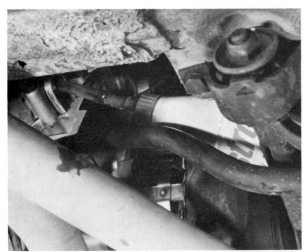

RM2.10. Topping up the transmission oil

RM2.13. The brake fluid reservoir

23 Arrange for your local Audi dealer to check the CO (carbon monoxide) content of the exhaust gases and at the same time make any necessary adjustments.

3   Every 12000 miles (20000 km)

Carry out the previously listed tasks as applicable, plus:
1   Renew the air filter element (except Audi 100).
2   Renew the spark plugs.
3   Renew the distributor contact points (except where a BHCI system is incorporated, in which case they should be checked, and cleaned if necessary - refer to Chapter 4 for details).

4   Every 18000 miles (30000 km)

Carry out the previously listed tasks as applicable, plus:
1   Renew the in-line fuel filter to the fuel pump.
2   Renew the distributor contact points of BHCI systems if their condition warrants it.
3   Where a manual transmission unit is fitted, wipe around the drain plug and drain the contents into a container of at least 3½ pints (2 litres) capacity. This is best carried out after a warming up run to allow the oil to thin down a little. Before refitting the drain plug wipe it clean, and also the sealing faces of the washer and the transmission itself. Replenish using Castrol Hypoy light or an equivalent light bodied SAE 80 EP oil. From October 1975, the gearbox is 'filled for life' and does not require an oil change unless the unit is to be overhauled. Check the level as for earlier gearboxes.

Where automatic tranmission is fitted drain the final drive and transmission separately, using the same procedures as described for manual transmission. Replenish using Castrol Hypoy B (or an equivalent SAE 90 EP gear oil) for the final drive and Castrol TQ Dextron O (or an equivalent automatic transmission fluid) for the transmission unit. When checking the fluid level refer to the procedure given in paragraph 2.10 of Routine maintenance.
4   Replenish the grease in the rear wheel bearings. **Note:** Even if you have not completed 18000 miles the grease should be replenished at intervals of approximately 1 year.

5   Every 24000 miles (40000 km)

Carry out the previously listed tasks as applicable, plus:
1   Renew the air cleaner (complete) on Audi 100 models.

6   Every 60000 miles (100000 km)

1   Renew all seals and flexible hoses in the braking system and renew the fluid. **Note:** Even if 60000 miles have not been completed this task is recommended at intervals of two to three years.
2   Decarbonise the engine, and regrind the valves and seats. Refer to Chapter 1 for details.
3   Overhaul the carburettor.
4   Overhaul the distributor.
5   Overhaul the fuel pump.
6   Check clutch cable for wear and renew if necessary.
7   Check wheel bearings and suspension for wear, renewing as necessary.
8   Overhaul the alternator.
9   Overhaul the starter motor.
10 Renew the timing chain.

Tools and working facilities

Introduction

A selection of good tools is a fundamental requirement for anyone contemplating the maintenance and repair of a motor vehicle. For the owner who does not possess any, their purchase will prove a considerable expense, offsetting some of the savings made by doing-it-yourself. However, provided that the tools purchased are of good quality, they will last for many years and prove an extremely worthwhile investment.

To help the average owner to decide which tools are needed to carry out the various tasks detailed in this manual, we have compiled three lists of tools under the following headings: *Maintenance and minor repair. Repair and overhaul,* and *Special.* The newcomer to practical mechanics should start off with the *Maintenance and minor repair* tool kit and confine himself to the simpler jobs around the vehicle. Then, as his confidence and experience grows, he can undertake more difficult tasks, buying extra tools as, and when, they are needed. In this way, a *Maintenance and minor repair* tool kit can be built-up into a *Repair and overhaul* tool kit over a considerable period of time without any major cash outlays. The experienced do-it-yourselfer will have a tool kit good enough for most repair and overhaul procedures and will add tools from the *Special* category when he feels the expense is justified by the amount of use to which these tools will be put.

It is obviously not possible to cover the subject of tools fully here. For those who wish to learn more about tools and their use there is a book entitled *How to Choose and Use Car Tools* available from the publishers of this manual.

Maintenance and minor repair tool kit

The tools given in this list should be considered as a minimum requirement if routine maintenance, servicing and minor repair operations are to be undertaken. We recommend the purchase of combination spanners (ring one end, open-ended the other); although more expensive than open-ended ones, they do give the advantages of both types of spanner.

Combination spanners - 9, 10, 11, 12, 13 and 17 mm
Adjustable spanner - 9 inch
Engine sump/gearbox/rear axle drain plug key (where applicable)
Spark plug spanner (with rubber insert)
Spark plug gap adjustment tool
Set of feeler gauges
Brake adjuster spanner (where applicable)
Brake bleed nipple spanner
Screwdriver - 4 in long x ¼ in dia (flat blade)
Screwdriver - 4 in long x ¼ in dia (cross blade)
Combination pliers - 6 inch
Hacksaw, junior
Tyre pump
Tyre pressure gauge
Grease gun (where applicable)
Oil can
Fine emery cloth (1 sheet)
Wire brush (small)
Funnel (medium size)

Repair and overhaul tool kit

These tools are virtually essential for anyone undertaking any major repairs to a motor vehicle, and are additional to those given in the *Maintenance and minor repair* list. Included in this list is a comprehensive set of sockets. Although these are expensive they will be found invaluable as they are so versatile - particularly if various drives are included in the set. We recommend the ½ in square-drive type, as this can be used with most proprietary torque wrenches. If you cannot afford a socket set, even bought piecemeal, then inexpensive tubular box spanners are a useful alternative.

The tools in this list will occasionally need to be supplemented by tools from the *Special* list.

Sockets (or box spanners) to cover range in previous list
Reversible ratchet drive (for use with sockets)
Extension piece, 10 inch (for use with sockets)
Universal joint (for use with sockets)
Torque wrench (for use with sockets)
'Mole' wrench - 8 inch
Ball pein hammer
Soft-faced hammer, plastic or rubber
Screwdriver - 6 in long x 5/16 in dia (flat blade)
Screwdriver - 2 in long x 5/16 in square (flat blade)
Screwdriver - 1½ in long x ¼ in dia (cross blade)
Screwdriver - 3 in long x 1/8 in dia (electricians)
Pliers - electricians side cutters
Pliers - needle nosed
Pliers - circlip (internal and external)
Cold chisel - ½ inch
Scriber
Scraper
Centre punch
Pin punch
Hacksaw
Valve grinding tool
Steel rule/straight edge
Allen keys
Selection of files
Wire brush (large)
Axle-stands
Jack (strong scissor or hydraulic type)

Special tools

The tools in this list are those which are not used regularly, are expensive to buy, or which need to be used in accordance with their manufacturers' instructions. Unless relatively difficult mechanical jobs are undertaken frequently, it will not be economic to buy many of these tools. Where this is the case, you could consider clubbing together with friends (or a motorists' club) to make a joint purchase, or borrowing the tools against a deposit from a local garage or tool hire specialist.

The following list contains only those tools and instruments freely available to the public, and not those special tools produced by the vehicle manufacturer specifically for its dealer network. You will find occasional references to these manufacturers' special tools in the text of this manual. Generally, an alternative method of doing the job without the vehicle manufacturer's special tool is given. However, sometimes, there is no alternative to using them. Where this is the case and the relevant tool cannot be bought or borrowed you will have to entrust the work to a franchised garage.

Valve spring compressor
Piston ring compressor
Balljoint separator
Universal hub/bearing puller
Impact screwdriver
Micrometer and/or vernier gauge
Carburettor flow balancing device (where applicable)
Dial gauge
Stroboscopic timing light
Dwell angle meter/tachometer
Universal electrical multi-meter
Cylinder compression gauge
Lifting tackle (photo)
Trolley jack
Light with extension lead

Buying tools

For practically all tools, a tool factor is the best source

since he will have a very comprehensive range compared with the average garage or accessory shop. Having said that, accessory shops often offer excellent quality tools at discount prices, so it pays to shop around.

Remember, you don't have to buy the most expensive items on the shelf, but it is always advisable to steer clear of the very cheap tools. There are plenty of good tools around at reasonable prices, so ask the proprietor or manager of the shop for advice before making a purchase.

Care and maintenance of tools

Having purchased a reasonable tool kit, it is necessary to keep the tools in a clean serviceable condition. After use, always wipe off any dirt, grease and metal particles using a clean, dry cloth, before putting the tools away. Never leave them lying around after they have been used. A simple tool rack on the garage or workshop wall, for items such as screwdrivers and pliers is a good idea. Store all normal spanners and sockets in a metal box. Any measuring instruments, gauges, meters, etc, must be carefully stored where they cannot be damaged or become rusty.

Take a little care when tools are used. Hammer heads inevitably become marked and screwdrivers lose the keen edge on their blades from time to time. A little timely attention with emery cloth or a file will soon restore items like these to a good serviceable finish.

Working facilities

Not to be forgotten when discussing tools, is the workshop itself. If anything more than routine maintenance is to be carried out, some form of suitable working area becomes essential.

It is appreciated that many an owner mechanic is forced by circumstances to remove an engine or similar item, without the benefit of a garage or workshop. Having done this, any repairs should always be done under the cover of a roof.

Wherever possible, any dismantling should be done on a clean flat workbench or table at a suitable working height.

Any workbench needs a vice: one with a jaw opening of 4 in (100 mm) is suitable for most jobs. As mentioned previously, some clean dry storage space is also required for tools, as well as the lubricants, cleaning fluids, touch-up paints and so on which become necessary.

Another item which may be required, and which has a much more general usage, is an electric drill with a chuck capacity of at least 5/16 in (8 mm). This, together with a good range of twist drills, is virtually essential for fitting accessories such as wing mirrors and reversing lights.

Last, but not least, always keep a supply of old newspapers and clean, lint-free rags available, and try to keep any working area as clean as possible.

Spanner jaw gap comparison table

Jaw gap (in)	Spanner size
0.250	¼ in AF
0.275	7 mm
0.312	5/16 in AF
0.315	8 mm
0.340	11/32 in AF; 1/8 in Whitworth
0.354	9 mm
0.375	3/8 in AF
0.393	10 mm
0.433	11 mm
0.437	7/16 in AF
0.445	3/16 in Whitworth; ¼ in BSF
0.472	12 mm
0.500	½ in AF
0.512	13 mm
0.525	¼ in Whitworth; 5/16 in BSF
0.551	14 mm
0.562	9/16 in AF
0.590	15 mm
0.600	5/16 in Whitworth; 3/8 in BSF
0.625	5/8 in AF
0.629	16 mm
0.669	17 mm
0.687	11/16 in AF
0.708	18 mm
0.710	3/8 in Whitworth; 7/16 in BSF
0.748	19 mm
0.750	¾ in AF
0.812	13/16 in AF
0.820	7/16 in Whitworth; ½ in BSF
0.866	22 mm
0.875	7/8 in AF
0.920	½ in Whitworth; 9/16 in BSF
0.937	15/16 in AF
0.944	24 mm
1.000	1 in AF
1.010	9/16 in Whitworth; 5/8 in BSF
1.023	26 mm
1.062	1.1/16 in AF; 27 mm
1.100	5/8 in Whitworth; 11/16 in BSF
1.125	1.1/8 in AF
1.181	30 mm
1.200	11/16 in Whitworth; ¾ in BSF
1.250	1¼ in AF
1.259	32 mm
1.300	¾ in Whitworth; 7/8 in BSF
1.312	1.5/16 in AF
1.390	13/16 in Whitworth; 15/16 in BSF
1.417	36 mm
1.437	1.7/16 in AF
1.480	7/8 in Whitworth; 1 in BSF
1.500	1½ in AF
1.574	40 mm; 15/16 in Whitworth
1.614	41 mm
1.625	1.5/8 in AF
1.670	1 in Whitworth; 1.1/8 in BSF
1.687	1.11/16 in AF
1.811	46 mm
1.812	1.13/16 in AF
1.860	1.1/8 in Whitworth; 1¼ in BSF
1.875	1.7/8 in AF
1.968	50 mm
2.000	2 in AF
2.050	1¼ in Whitworth; 1.3/8 in BSF
2.165	55 mm
2.362	60 mm

A Haltrac hoist and gantry in use during a typical engine removal sequence

Lubrication chart

1 Engine
2 Transmission and final drive
3 Steering rack
4 Wheel bearings
5 Steering ball joints
6 Distributor
7 Drive shaft joints
8 Brake fluid reservoir
9 Battery

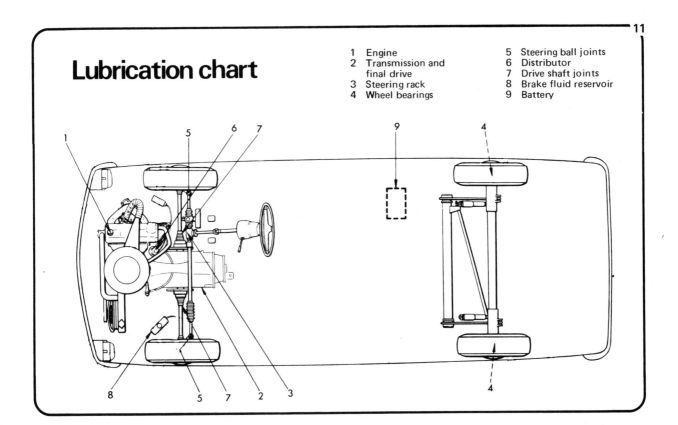

Recommended lubricants

Component	Type of Lubricant or Fluid	Castrol Product
Engine	Multigrade 20W/50 engine oil	Castrol GTX
Transmission and Final Drive	Very light bodied extreme pressure gear oil, SAE 80 EP ...	Castrol Hypoy Light
Automatic Transmission	Automatic transmission fluid of Dexron type ...	Castrol TQ Dexron O
Final Drive (with Automatic Transmission)	Light bodied, extreme pressure gear oil, conforming to specification MIL-L-2105B, SAE 90 EP ...	Castrol Hypoy B
Steering Rack	Liquid transmission grease (eg. Calypsol LS2341 or Klueber ALN 600) ...	—
Wheel bearings	High melting point general purpose Lithium ... base grease	Castrol LM Grease
Steering ball joints	High melting point general purpose Lithium ... base grease with a molybdenum disulphide additive	Castrol MS3 Grease
Distributor Cam and Pivot	High melting point general purpose Lithium ... base grease	Castrol LM Grease
Drive shaft joints	Molykote BR2 grease	—
Brake fluid reservoir	Hydraulic fluid to specifications SAE J1703e ...	Castrol Girling Universal Brake and Clutch Fluid
Cooling system	Anti-freeze	Castrol Anti-freeze
Battery terminals	Petroleum jelly	—

Additionally Castrol Everyman Oil can be used for all general purpose lubrication, such as door locks, hinges, accelerator linkages, etc.

Chapter 1 Engine

For modifications, and information applicable to later models, see Supplement at end of manual

Contents

Specifications

General:

Engine type	4 cylinder, 4 stroke, in-line
Valve arrangement	Overhead
Cooling system	Water cooled
Firing order	1 3 4 2
Engine static timing	T.D.C.
Piston clearance	0.001 in. (0.03 mm)
Oil pump type	Gear
Oil pressure - maximum	85 psi (6 atm)
- minimum	14 psi (1 atm)

Oil filter type	Full flow, renewable canister	
Idle speed	950 + 50 rpm (925 + 75 for U.S.A. models)	
Maximum speed	5800 rpm	
Lubricant type	Multigrade engine oil	
Lubricant capacity	7 pints (4 litres), approximately	

	Audi 100 (before 1972)	Audi 100 Sweden (before 1972)	Audi 100S (before 1972)
Horsepower, DIN ...	80 at 5000 rpm	85 at 5100 rpm	90 at 5500 rpm
SAE ...	90 at 5000 rpm	97 at 5100 rpm	102 at 5500 rpm
Engine code	ZV	ZU	ZX
Fuel grade	Regular	Regular	Premium
Bore	3.208 in. (81.5 mm)	3.208 in. (81.5 mm)	3.208 in. (81.5 mm)
Stroke	3.322 in. (84.4 mm)	3.322 in. (84.4 mm)	3.322 in (84.4 mm)
Capacity	107.401 cu. in. (1760 cc)	107.401 cu. in. (1760 cc)	107.401 cu. in. (1760 cc)
Compression ratio ...	9.1 : 1	9.1 : 1	10.2 - 0.6 : 1
Torque, DIN	100 lb ft (13.8 kgm) at 3000 rpm	100 lb ft (13.8 kgm) at 3000 rpm	104.9 lb ft (14.5 kgm) at 3000 rpm
SAE ...	104.9 lb ft (14.5 kgm) at 3000 rpm	104.9 lb ft (14.5 kgm) at 3000 rpm	112.1 lb ft (15.5 kgm) at 3000 rpm
HP/litre output, DIN	45.5	45.5	51.2
Mean piston speed ...	46.3 ft/sec (14.1 m/sec)at 5000 rpm	46.3 ft/sec (14.1 m/sec) at 5000 rpm	46.8 ft/sec (15.5 m/sec) at 5500 rpm
Mean mechanical pressure at maximum torque	140.5 psi (9.88 kg/cm^2)	140.5 psi (9.88 kg/cm^2)	147.5 psi (10.38 kg/cm^2)
Tappet clearance, warm			
Inlet	0.006 in. (0.15 mm)	0.006 in. (0.15 mm)	0.006 in. (0.15 mm)
Exhaust	0.015 in. (0.40 mm)	0.015 in. (0.40 mm)	0.015 in. (0.40 mm)
Timing (1 mm valve stroke/0 tappet clearance)			
Inlet opens ...	8° BTDC on crankshaft	5° BTDC on crankshaft	8° BTDC on crankshaft
Inlet closes ...	40° ABDC on crankshaft	37° ABDC on crankshaft	40° ABDC on crankshaft
Exhaust opens ...	43° BBDC on crankshaft	39° BBDC on crankshaft	43° BBDC on crankshaft
Exhaust closes ...	7° ATDC on crankshaft	3° ATDC on crankshaft	7° ATDC on crankshaft

	Audi 100LS (before 1972)	Audi 100LS Sweden (before 1972)	Audi 100LS USA (before 1972)
Horsepower, DIN ...	100 at 5500 rpm	100 at 5500 rpm	100 at 5500 rpm
SAE ...	115 at 5500 rpm	115 at 5500 rpm	115 at 5500 rpm
Engine code	ZZ *	ZS	ZY/ZT **
Fuel grade	Premium	Premium	Premium
Bore	3.208 in. (81.5 mm)	3.208 in. (81.5 mm)	3.208 in. (81.5 mm)
Stroke	3.322 in. (84.4 mm)	3.322 in. (84.4 mm)	3.322 in. (84.4 mm)
Capacity	107.401 cu. in. (1760 cc)	107.401 cu.in. (1760 cc)	107.401 cu. in. (1760 cc)
Compression ratio ...	10.2 - 0.6 : 1	10.2 - 0.6 : 1	10.2 : 1
Torque, DIN	110.66 lb ft (15.3 kgm) at 3200 rpm	110.66 lb ft (15.3 kgm) at 3200 rpm	110.66 lb ft (15.3 kgm) at 3200 rpm
SAE ...	120 lb ft (16.5 kgm) at 3200 rpm	120 lb ft (16.5 kgm) at 3200 rpm	120 lb ft (16.5 kgm) at 3200 rpm
HP/litre output, DIN	57	57	57
Mean piston speed ...	46.8 ft/sec (15.5 m/sec) at 5500 rpm	46.8 ft/sec (15.5 m/sec) at 5500 rpm	46.8 ft/sec (15.5 m/sec) at 5500 rpm
Mean mechanical pressure at maximum torque	156 psi (10.95 kg/cm^2)	156 psi (10.95 kg/cm^2)	156 psi (10.95 kg/cm^2)
Tappet clearance, warm			
Inlet	0.006 in. (0.15 mm)	0.006 in. (0.15 mm)	0.009 - 0.002 in. (0.20 - 0.05 mm)
Exhaust	0.015 in. (0.40 mm)	0.015 in. (0.40 mm)	0.015 - 0.002 in. (0.40 - 0.05 mm)
Timing (1 mm valve stroke/ 0 tappet clearance)			
Inlet opens ...	8° BTDC on crankshaft	5° BTDC on crankshaft	5° BTDC on crankshaft
Inlet closes ...	40° ABDC on crankshaft	37° ABDC on crankshaft	37° ABDC on crankshaft
Exhaust opens ...	43° BBDC on crankshaft	39° BBDC on crankshaft	39° BBDC on crankshaft
Exhaust closes ...	7° ATDC on crankshaft	3° ATDC on crankshaft	3° ATDC on crankshaft

* Up to engine number 200 000
** Automatic transmission

	Audi 100LS Switzerland (before 1972)	Audi 100LS Switzerland, Automatic (before 1972)	Audi 100 Coupe'S (before 1972)
Horsepower, DIN ...	107 at 5500 rpm	112 at 5600 rpm	115 at 5500 rpm
SAE ...	115 at 5500 rpm	127 at 5600 rpm	130 at 5500 rpm
Engine code	ZM	ZN	ZP
Fuel grade	Premium	Premium	Premium
Bore	3.228 in. (82.0 mm)	3.307 in. (84.0 mm)	3.307 in. (84 mm)

Stroke	3.322 in. (84.4 mm)	3.322 in. (84.4 mm)	3.322 in. (84.4 mm)
Capacity	107.874 cu. in. (1782 cc)	114.120 cu. in. (1871 cc)	114.120 cu. in. (1871 cc)
Compression ratio ...	10.2 - 0.6 : 1	10.2 - 0.6 : 1	10.2 - 0.6 : 1
Torque, DIN	110.66 lb ft (15.3 kgm) at 3500 rpm	118 lb ft (16.3 kgm) at 3500 rpm	118 lb ft (16.3 kgm) at 4000 rpm
SAE ...	120 lb ft (16.5 kgm) at 3500 rpm	123 lb ft (17.0 kgm) at 3500 rpm	123 lb ft (17.0 kgm) at 4000 rpm
HP/litre output, DIN	60	59.8	61.5
Mean piston speed ...	46.8 ft/sec (15.5 m/sec) at 5500 rpm	46.8 ft/sec (15.5 m/sec) at 5500 rpm	41.6 ft/sec (12.68 m/sec) at 4500 rpm
Mean mechanical pressure at maximum torque	152.9 psi (10.75 kg/cm^2)	156 psi (10.95 kg/cm^2)	156 psi (10.95 kg/cm^2)
Tappet clearance, warm			
Inlet	0.006 in. (0.15 mm)	0.006 in. (0.15 mm)	0.006 in. (0.15 mm)
Exhaust ...	0.015 in. (0.40 mm)	0.015 in. (0.40 mm)	0.015 in. (0.40 mm)
Timing (1 mm valve stroke/ 0 tappet clearance)			
Inlet opens ...	8° BTDC on crankshaft	17° BTDC on crankshaft	17° BTDC on crankshaft
Inlet closes ...	40° ABDC on crankshaft	49° ABDC on crankshaft	49° ABDC on crankshaft
Exhaust opens ...	43° BBDC on crankshaft	48° BBDC on crankshaft	48° BBDC on crankshaft
Exhaust closes ...	7° ATDC on crankshaft	18° ATDC on crankshaft	18° ATDC on crankshaft

	Audi 100, with emission control (1972/73)	Audi 100LS, with emission control (1972/73)	Audi 100 USA, with emission control (1972)
Horsepower, DIN ...	85 at 5100 rpm	100 at 5500 rpm	95 at 5200 rpm
SAE ...	95 at 5100 rpm	115 at 5500 rpm	110 at 5200 rpm
Engine code	ZU	ZZ ***	ZL/ZK **
Fuel grade	Regular (88 octane)	Premium (98 to 99 octane)	Regular (91 octane minimum)
Bore	3.208 in. (81.5 mm)	3.208 in. (81.5 mm)	3.307 in. (84 mm)
Stroke	3.322 in. (84.4 mm)	3.322 in. (84.4 mm)	3.322 in. (84.4 mm)
Capacity	107.401 cu. in. (1760 cc)	107.401 cu. in. (1760 cc)	114.120 cu. in. (1871 cc)
Compression ratio ...	9.0 : 1	10.2 - 0.6 : 1	8.2 - 0.6 : 1
Torque, DIN	100 lb ft (13.8 kgm) at 3000 rpm	110.66 lb ft (15.3 kgm) at 3200 rpm	110.66 lb ft (15.3 kgm) at 3200 rpm
SAE ...	104.9 lb ft (14.5 kgm) at 3000 rpm	119.4 ft lb (16.5 kgm) at 3200 rpm	119.4 lb ft (16.5 kgm) at 3200 rpm
HP/litre output, DIN	48.3	57	51
Mean piston speed ...	46.3 ft/sec (14.1 m/sec) at 5000 rpm	46.8 ft/sec (15.5 m/sec) at 5500 rpm	46.8 ft/sec (15.5 m/sec) at 5500 rpm
Mean mechanical pressure at maximum torque	140.5 psi (9.9 kg/cm^2)	156 psi (10.95 kg/cm^2)	146.5 psi (10.3 kg/cm^2)
Tappet clearance, warm			
Inlet	0.006 in. (0.15 mm)	0.006 in. (0.15 mm)	0.009 - 0.002 in. (0.20 - 0.05 mm)
Exhaust	0.015 in. (0.40 mm)	0.015 in. (0.40 mm)	0.015 - 0.002 in. (0.40 - 0.05 mm)
Timing (1 mm valve stroke/ 0 tappet clearance)			
Inlet opens ...	5° BTDC on crankshaft	5° BTDC on crankshaft	5° BTDC on crankshaft
Inlet closes ...	37° ABDC on crankshaft	37° ABDC on crankshaft	37° ABDC on crankshaft
Exhaust opens ...	39° BBDC on crankshaft	39° BBDC on crankshaft	39° BBDC on crankshaft
Exhaust closes ...	3° ATDC on crankshaft	3° ATDC on crankshaft	3° ATDC on crankshaft

** Automatic transmission
*** From engine number 200001

	Audi 100 USA, with emission control (1973)	Audi 100GL and Coupe' S, with or without emission control (1972/73)
Horsepower, DIN	95 at 5500 rpm	112 at 5600 rpm
SAE	110 at 5500 rpm	129 at 5600 rpm
Engine code	ZL/ZW **	ZJ
Fuel grade	Regular (91 octane minimum)	Premium (98 to 99 octane)
Bore	3.307 in. (84 mm)	3.307 in. (84 mm)
Stroke	3.322 in. (84.4 mm)	3.322 in. (84.4 mm)
Capacity	114.120 cu. in. (1871 cc)	114.120 cu. in. (1871 cc)
Compression ratio	8.2 - 0.6 : 1	10.2 - 0.6 : 1
Torque, DIN	110.66 lb ft (15.3 kgm) at 3200 rpm	118 lb ft (16.3 kgm) at 3500 rpm
SAE	119.4 lb ft (16.5 kgm) at 3200 rpm	126.6 lb ft (17.5 kgm) at 3500 rpm
HP/litre output, DIN	51	60
Mean piston speed	46.8 ft/sec (15.5 m/sec) at 5500 rpm	46.3 ft/sec (14.1 m/sec) at 5000 rpm

Mean mechanical pressure at maximum torque		146.5 psi (10.3 kg/cm^2)	156.5 psi (11.0 kg/cm^2)
Tappet clearance, warm			
Inlet		0.009 - 0.002 in. (0.20 - 0.05 mm)	0.006 in. (0.15 mm)
Exhaust		0.015 - 0.002 in. (0.40 - 0.05 mm)	0.015 in. (0.40 mm)
Timing (1 mm valve stroke/0 tappet clearance)			
Inlet opens		5º BTDC on crankshaft	17º BTDC on crankshaft
Inlet closes		37º ABDC on crankshaft	49º ABDC on crankshaft
Exhaust opens		39º BBDC on crankshaft	36º BBDC on crankshaft
Exhaust closes		3º ATDC on crankshaft	6º ATDC on crankshaft

** Automatic transmission

Cylinder head	in.	mm
Valve seat insert diameter - Inlet	1.555 - 0.0004	39.5 - 0.01
- Exhaust	1.4606 - 0.0004	37.1 - 0.01
Valve seat insert height - Inlet	0.3937 - 0.00354	10 - 0.09
- Exhaust	0.3071 - 0.00354	7.8 - 0.09
Cylinder head bore - Inlet	1.551 + 0.0006	39.4 + 0.016
- Exhaust	1.4567 + 0.0006	37.0 + 0.016
Cylinder head depth - Inlet	0.4921 + 0.0039	12.5 + 0.1
- Exhaust	0.4134 + 0.0039	10.5 + 0.1
Maximum permissible head distortion	0.0016	0.04
Minimum head thickness for reworking	3.5434 - 0.0276	90 - 0.7 m
Valve head diameter - Inlet	1.4961 + 0.0059 − 0.0079	38 + 0.15 − 0.2
- Exhaust	1.2992 + 0.0059 − 0.0079	33 + 0.15 − 0.2
Valve stem diameter - Inlet	0.352 - 0.0006	8.97 - 0.015
- Exhaust	0.35 - 0.0006	8.95 - 0.015
Valve length - Inlet	5.335 - 0.0079	135.5 ± 0.2
- Exhaust	5.3405 - 0.0079	135.65 ± 0.2
Valve cone width - Normal	0.0866 - 0.0118	2.2 - 0.3
- Maximum	0.1378	3.5
Valve seat angle	90º ± 30′	
Maximum permissible valve stem run out	0.00118	0.03
Maximum permissible valve cone run out	0.00118	0.03

Valve guide (brown code)	in.	mm
Outside diameter	0.5512 + 0.001 − 0.007	14 + 0.025 − 0.019
Inside diameter	0.3543 + 0.0009	9 + 0.022
Bore in cylinder head	0.5512 + 0.0007 − 0.0005	14 + 0.018 − 0.013
Valve guide (green code)		
Outside diameter	0.5512 + 0.0008 − 0.0006	14 + 0.021 − 0.014
Inside diameter	0.3543 + 0.0009	9 + 0.022
Bore in cylinder head	0.5512 + 0.0005 − 0.0003	14 + 0.012 − 0.007
Valve guide (white code)		
Outside diameter	0.5512 + 0.0006 − 0.0004	14 + 0.016 − 0.009
Inside diameter	0.3543 + 0.0009	9 + 0.022
Bore in cylinder head	0.5512 + 0.0002	14 + 0.006
Valve guide (Size 1, 1 groove)		
Outside diameter	0.5591 + 0.001 − 0.0004	14.2 + 0.025 − 0.009
Inside diameter	0.3543 + 0.0009	9 + 0.022
Bore in cylinder head	0.5591 + 0.0007	14.2 + 0.018
Valve guide (Size 2, 2 grooves)		
Outside diameter	0.5669 + 0.001 − 0.0004	14.4 + 0.025 − 0.009
Inside diameter	0.3543 + 0.0009	9 + 0.022
Bore in cylinder head	0.5669 + 0.0007	14.4 + 0.018
Minimum guide/cylinder head overlap	0.0003	0.007

Valve seat insert rework dimensions — See illustration in text.

Cylinder block and pistons

Cylinder diameters -   Audi 100, 100S and 100LS:

Cylinder	Piston diameter		Cylinder bore		Honing Code
	in.	mm	in.	mm	
Standard	3.2075	81.47	3.2087	81.50	500
	3.2079	81.48	3.2091	81.51	501
	3.2083	81.49	3.2094	81.52	502
	3.2087	81.50	3.2098	81.53	503
Oversize 1	3.2177	81.73	3.2189	81.76	576
	3.2181	81.74	3.2193	81.77	577
	3.2185	81.75	3.2197	81.78	578
Oversize 2	3.2276	81.98	3.2287	82.01	201
	3.2280	81.99	3.2291	82.02	202
	3.2283	82.00	3.2295	82.03	203
Oversize 3	3.2472	82.48	3.2484	82.51	251
	3.2476	82.49	3.2488	82.52	252
	3.2480	82.50	3.2492	82.53	253

Cylinder diameters -   Audi 100GL and 100 Coupe' S:

Cylinder	Piston diameter		Cylinder bore		Honing Code
	in.	mm	in.	mm	
Standard	3.3063	83.98	3.3075	84.01	401
	3.3067	83.99	3.3079	84.02	402
	3.3071	84.00	3.3083	84.03	403
Oversize 1	3.3161	84.23	3.3173	84.26	426
	3.3165	84.24	3.3177	84.27	427
	3.3169	84.25	3.3181	84.28	428
Oversize 2	3.3260	84.48	3.3272	84.51	451
	3.3264	84.49	3.3276	84.52	452
	3.3268	84.50	3.3280	84.53	453
Oversize 3	3.3457	84.98	3.3469	85.01	501
	3.3461	84.99	3.3472	85.02	502
	3.3465	85.00	3.3476	85.03	503

	in.	mm
Piston ring thickness		
Upper	0.0787 - 0.0004 - 0.0009	2.0 - 0.010 - 0.022
Centre	0.0985 - 0.0004 - 0.0009	2.5 - 0.010 - 0.022
Lower	0.1969 - 0.0004 - 0.0009	5.0 - 0.010 - 0.022
Piston groove height		
Upper	0.0787 + 0.002 + 0.0012	2.0 + 0.05 + 0.03
Centre	0.0985 + 0.002 + 0.0012	2.5 + 0.05 + 0.03
Lower	0.1969 + 0.002 + 0.0012	5.0 + 0.05 + 0.03
Piston ring clearance		
Upper	0.0059	0.15 max.
Centre	0.0059	0.15 max.
Lower	0.0059	0.15 max.
Piston ring gap		
Upper	0.0394	1.0 max.
Centre	0.0394	1.0 max.
Lower	0.0394	1.0 max.
Piston (gudgeon) pin		
Pin diameter	0.9449 - 0.0002	24.0 - 0.005 mm
Pin play	0.0005 to 0.0009	0.012 to 0.023
Permissible pin wear	0.0002	0.005
Connecting rod bushing bore diameter	0.9449 + 0.0007 + 0.0005	24.0 + 0.018 + 0.012
Pin bore in piston	0.9449 + 0.0002 + 0.00004	24.0 + 0.005 + 0.001

	in.	mm
Connecting rod small end bore diameter (without bushing) ...	1.063 + 0.008	27 + 0.021
	1.063 + 0.0035 + 0.002	27 + 0.090 + 0.050
	1.063 + 0.0035 + 0.0011	27 + 0.090 + 0.029
Bushing interference fit	0.0011 to 0.0035	0.029 to 0.09
Maximum permitted variation in bush bore parallelism ...	0.0039 in/3.937 in.	0.1 mm/100 mm

Connecting rods

	in.	mm
Connecting rod bearing shell size		
Standard	1.8898	48
Undersize 1	1.8799	47.75
Undersize 2	1.8701	47.5
Undersize 3	1.8602	47.25
Connecting rod bearing radial play (maximum)	0.0012 to 0.0033	0.030 to 0.084
Connecting rod bearing axial play (maximum)	0.0043 to 0.0091	0.11 to 0.23
Connecting rod bearing wear limits, radial	0.0059	0.15
, axial	0.0118	0.30
Connecting rod weight classification:		

Classification group	Weight (grams)
0	815 - 823
1	823 - 831
2	831 - 839
3	839 - 847
4	847 - 855
5	855 - 863
7	863 - 871
8	871 - 879
9	879 - 887
10	887 - 895
11	895 - 903
12	903 - 911
13	911 - 919
14	919 - 927

Crankshaft

	in.	mm
Bearing play, radial	0.0016	0.04 to 0.10
Thrust bearing play, axial	0.0028 to 0.0075	0.07 to 0.19
Wear limit, radial	0.0071	0.18
Wear limit, axial	0.0079	0.20
Maximum permissible run out	0.0012	0.03
Main bearing journal size	in.	mm
Standard	2.3622 - 0.0016 - 0.0024	60.0 - 0.04 - 0.06
Undersize 1	2.3524 - 0.0016 - 0.0024	59.75 - 0.04 - 0.06
Undersize 2	2.3425 - 0.0016 - 0.0024	59.5 - 0.04 - 0.06
Undersize 3	2.3327 - 0.0016 - 0.0024	59.25 - 0.04 - 0.06
Maximum eccentricity	0.0012	0.03
Big end bearing journal size		
Standard	1.8898 - 0.0016 - 0.0024	48 - 0.04 - 0.06
Undersize 1	1.8799 - 0.0016 - 0.0024	47.75 - 0.04 - 0.06
Undersize 2	1.8701 - 0.0016 - 0.0024	47.5 - 0.04 - 0.06
Undersize 3	1.8602 - 0.0016 - 0.0024	47.25 - 0.04 - 0.06
Maximum eccentricity	0.0012	0.03
Maximum permissible difference between camshaft and crankshaft end float	0.02	0.5

Torque wrench settings:

Note: The torque values quoted in this manual do not include the 'run-down' torque. All screw threads should be lightly oiled or greased prior to assembly. Any contamination of the threads should be removed prior to lubrication.

	lb ft	kgm
Exhaust manifold end plate	14.47 ± 15%	2.0 ± 15%
Starter motor to engine block	43.4 ± 15%	6.0 ± 15%
Exhaust manifold to head	17.4 ± 15%	2.4 ± 15%

Fuel pump to block	12.3 to 15.9	1.7 to 2.2
Thermostat cover	7.2 ± 15%	1.0 ± 15%
Oil pump, block to oil line	7.2 ± 15%	1.0 ± 15%
Valve tappet clearance	10.8 to 36.2	1.5 to 5.0
Heater flange to head	14.5 ± 15%	2.0 ± 15%
Camshaft guide flange	18.1 ± 15%	2.5 ± 15%
Transmission to engine (12 mm)	54.2 ± 15%	7.5 ± 15%
Transmission to engine (10 mm)	32.5 ± 15%	4.5 ± 15%
Transmission to engine (8 mm)	18.1 ± 15%	2.5 ± 15%
Guard rail to block	8.7 ± 15%	1.2 ± 15%
Chain tensioner	8.7 ± 15%	1.2 ± 15%
Rocker lever mounting bolt to head	72.3 maximum	10.00 maximum
Distributor clamping lever to block	14.5 ± 15%	2.0 ± 15%
Clamping screw	2.2 to 3.6	0.3 to 0.5
Thermostat to head	14.5 ± 15%	2.0 ± 15%
Clutch cover plate to flywheel	23.1 ± 15%	3.2 ± 15%
Bearing cap No. 5 to block (8 mm)	23.1 ± 15%	3.2 ± 15%
Bearing cap to block (12 mm)	57.9 ± 15%	8.0 ± 15%
Alternator to holder, holder to block	18.1 to 25.3	2.5 to 3.5
Fan to hub	7.2 ± 15%	1.0 ± 15%
Air guide ring to fan support	14.5 to 18.1	2.0 to 2.5
Fan support to block	32.5 ± 15%	4.5 ± 15%
Camshaft sprocket to camshaft	57.9 ± 15%	8.0 ± 15%
Oil filter	18.1 to 25.3	2.5 to 3.5
Oil pressure switch	10.8 ± 15%	1.5 ± 15%
Upper oil pump body to lower body	7.2 ± 15%	1.0 ± 15%
Oil pump to block	14.5 ± 15%	14.5 ± 15%
Oil check valve	18.1 to 25.3	2.5 to 3.5
Sump to block (6 mm)	5.8 ± 15%	0.8 ± 15%
Sump to block (8 mm)	10.8 ± 15%	1.5 ± 15%
Oil pan plug	28.9 ± 15%	4 ± 15%
Con rod bolt	25.3 to 31.1	3.5 to 4.3
Con rod bolt (later type - see text)	40 to 43	5.5 to 6.0
Pulley to crankshaft	130 to 180	18.0 to 25.0
Pulley to water pump	14.5 ± 15%	2.0 ± 15%
Inlet manifold to head	17.5 ± 15%	2.4 ± 15%
Inlet manifold support	14.5 ± 15%	2.0 ± 15%
Flywheel to crankshaft	65.1 ± 15%	9.0 ± 15%
Timing chain cover	5.8 to 7.2	0.8 to 1.0
Temperature transmitter	7.2 ± 15%	1.0 ± 15%
Engine mounts. Stop to front cross member	18.1 ± 15%	2.5 ± 15%
Engine support to block	30.4 ± 15%	4;2 ± 15%
Engine mount to console	21.7 ± 15%	3.0 ± 15%
Engine support to mount	43.4 − 7.23	6.0 − 1
Locknut to left engine mount	68.7 − 7.23	9.5 − 1
Rear engine mount to transmission	21.7 ± 15%	3.0 ± 15%
Rear cross member to engine mount	30.4 ± 15%	4.2 ± 15%
Rear cross member to body	18.1 ± 15%	2.5 ± 15%
Carburettor to inlet manifold	14.5 ± 15%	2.0 ± 15%
Front oil passage plug	21.7 ± 15%	3.0 ± 15%
Rear oil passage plug	32.5 ± 15%	4.5 ± 15%
Cylinder head plug	57.9 ± 15%	8.0 ± 15%
Timing chain tensioner plug	3.6 to 7.2	0.5 to 1.0
Water pump to block (8 mm)	14.5 ± 15%	2.0 ± 15%
Water pump to block (6 mm)	8.7 ± 15%	1.2 ± 15%
Spark plug	21.7 ± 15%	3.0 ± 15%
Cylinder head to block, in steps (cold)	28.8, 43.4, 57.9 ± 15%	4, 6, 8, ± 15%
(warm)	65.1 ± 15%	9 ± 15%
Valve rocker cover to head	9.4 ± 15%	1.3 ± 15%

1 General description

The engine unit used throughout the Audi 100 range is a four cylinder, four stroke overhead valve design. The engine and gearbox/final drive is rubber mounted and is positioned with the engine ahead of the front axle.

The cylinder block is of cast iron with the main bearing caps bolted in. A tempered steel crankshaft is fitted, with all bearing surfaces induction hardened and ground; end thrust is taken up on the centre bearing. Light alloy pistons with recessed combustion chambers, for greater efficiency, are employed together with a light alloy cylinder head into which is inserted the valve seat inserts and valve guides. For improved efficiency the inlet manifold is heated by the engine coolant.

The range of engine outputs is achieved by the use of differently recessed pistons, by larger cylinder bores, variations in valve timing and different types of carburetter.

2 General note

1 The procedure and methods given in this Chapter have proved to be practicable in the workshop. However it is appreciated that facilities will vary and it will sometimes be necessary to divert from the order given. For example it is not

essential to remove or replace such items as the manifolds or fan support bracket in the order stated; much will depend upon where the job is being carried out and whether a particular side or end of the engine is accessible at the required moment.

2 Many of the major operations listed can be carried out with the engine still fitted in the car provided that certain items are temporarily removed for access purposes. The operations which can be carried out with the engine in-situ are, as follows:

a) Removal and replacement of the cylinder head.
b) Removal and replacement of the sump.
c) Removal and replacement of the big end bearings.
d) Removal and replacement of the pistons and connecting rods.
e) Removal and replacement of the timing chain.
f) Removal and replacement of the engine mountings.
g) Removal and replacement of the oil pump.
h) Removal and replacement of the manifolds and carburettor.
j) Renewal of the crankshaft front oil seal.

3 The major operations below can only be carried out with the engine removed from the car:

a) Removal and replacement of the main bearings.
b) Removal and replacement of the crankshaft.
c) Removal and replacement of the flywheel.
d) Renewal of the crankshaft rear oil seal.
e) Removal and replacement of the camshaft. Note: The camshaft can be removed without removing the engine from the car if the front engine mountings can be disconnected and the engine raised a little to clear the front body crossmember. However, this method makes the whole operation so difficult, that it is probably easier to remove the engine.

PART A – DISMANTLING PROCEDURE

3 Engine (and transmission unit) - removal

1 It is not possible to remove the engine from the car unless the transmission is removed in conjunction with it. Whichever unit is to be dismantled should first have its lubricant drained off.

2 If block and tackle equipment is to be used for removing the engine - remove the engine bonnet. This is not essential if the engine is to be removed from beneath, but does give better accessibility for the little extra work involved. The bonnet is held by two nuts at each hinge, don't forget to disconnect the windscreen washer pipe also.

3 Remove the apron (this is the transverse panel below the front bumper) (photo).

4 Disconnect the battery earth terminal. The battery is underneath the rear seat cushion.

5 Remove the carburettor air cleaner. Cover the carburettor air intake with polythene or something similar to prevent grease and dirt falling inside. The polythene can be taped in position if necessary. Disconnect the intake hoses and vacuum pipe from the air cleaner (photos).

6 Set the heater control to 'Warm', remove the radiator pressure cap then use a socket wrench to remove the drain plug from the radiator.

7 Remove the bleed screw in the heater inlet connection on the bulkhead once the water has started to drain.

8 When draining is completed disconnect all hoses connecting the engine to the heater and radiator (photos).

9 Pull off the filter and inlet pipe to the petrol pump (photo) and suitably blank the hose with a bolt to prevent spillage.

10 If a brake servo is fitted remove the vacuum connection at the inlet manifold (photo).

11 Disconnect the speedometer drive and clutch cable connections (photos).

12 Disconnect the gearshift linkage at the gearbox, (photo) but first mark the relative positions of the splines on the gearshift tube and lever. This is very important since although it would appear that the pinch bolt can only be fitted in one position it is possible to reassemble the mechanism with one spline out of position. At the same time it is necessary to remove the holder through which the tube passes. This is secured to the rear end of

the transmission unit by two nuts.

13 Remove the accelerator linkage at the carburettor, the mounting pivot and link rod. Remove the throttle shaft (photos).

14 If a brake pedal support is available it should be fitted so that the pedal is depressed approximately 1.3/16 in (3 cm). The pedal can otherwise be supported by a wooden block which will permit the 1.3/16 in movement, then a wooden strut used to hold the pedal down against the block. The other end of the strut can be wedged against the seat frame or steering wheel (photo).

15 Separate the brake connection at the union which lies beneath the area in which the throttle shaft was fitted (photo).

16 Remove the right hand engine mounting guard plate (photo).

17 Disconnect all electrical leads (as appropriate) and including earth straps to the temperature transmitter, idle cut-off valve, ignition system, regulator, alternator, starter, oil pressure switch, reverse light switch, carburettor and electric fan. It is a wise precaution to remove the distributor cap complete with leads also (photos).

18 Remove the radiator and cowl - there are two mounts and one stay. It is not necessary to remove the cowl from the radiator (photos).

19 Provided that you are not too limited for working space it will only be necessary to disconnect the engine stop at the front crossmember. However the fan assembly can be removed at this stage if you are at all worried about manoeuvring the engine away from the car once it has been disconnected. If the fan is to be removed it will need to be removed together with support and stop pad (photo).

20 Disconnect the front exhaust pipe at the manifold flange and take off the primary silencer (photo).

21 Disconnect the drive shafts, at the brake discs. Take care not to lose the insulating washer between the flanges (photo).

22 Support each drive shaft flange from the upper wishbone. Whichever method is used, due consideration must be given to their weight since they should not be allowed to fall.

23 Detach the transmission stabilizer from the lower wishbone (photo).

24 The next step will vary according to the particular facilities available. If it is proposed to lift the engine out, consideration must be given to the overall height of the engine, and the height to which it must be raised to clear the front of the car. Whichever method is adopted it is very important that the engine is correctly balanced and for this purpose strategically placed chains appear to be the answer. If it is not possible to lift the engine out, provided that it is possible to take the weight of the engine from above, the method described in the following paragraphs is satisfactory (photos).

25 Slide a trolley jack beneath the car to take the weight of engine and transmission unit. Raise the jack a little then tie the transmission to the crossmember in the engine compartment using a heavy rope. The jack can then be removed to allow better access.

26 Detach the rear transmission mounting at the crossmember then remove the crossmember itself (photo).

27 Take off the twin horns from beneath the left hand engine mounting (photo) then fit the chains from the hoist around the engine mounting.

28 Take the weight off the engine mountings by means of the hoist, then remove the nuts from the mountings where they are attached to the side members. Don't remove the mountings and brackets from the engine at this stage.

29 Remove the rope from the engine compartment crossmember when you are sure that the engine and transmission are properly balanced.

30 Now, carefully lower the engine and transmission to the ground. This will require some manipulation and movement as it is lowered but make sure that when on the ground it is clear of the car.

31 It is now necessary to raise the front end of the car above the engine to allow sufficient clearance for the car to be pushed back, or alternatively, for the engine to be pulled forward.

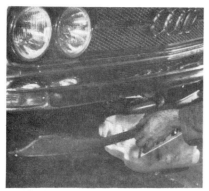

3.3 Removing the sill panel

3.5a The carburettor air cleaner fresh air inlet pipe

3.5b Lifting off the air cleaner

3.8a Engine inlet manifold hoses

3.8b The radiator top hose

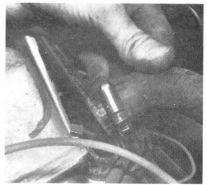

3.8c The hose at the rear end of the cylinder block

3.8d The radiator bottom hose

3.9 The fuel pump inlet pipe

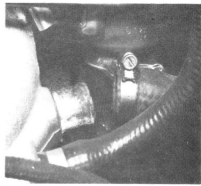

3.10 The brake servo hose

3.11a Disconnecting the clutch cable end

3.11b Disconnecting the clutch cable sleeve

3.12 The gearshift linkage splines

3.13a Removing the accelerator linkage

3.13b Removing the accelerator linkage

3.14 A suitable brake pedal support

3.15 Separating the brake union connection

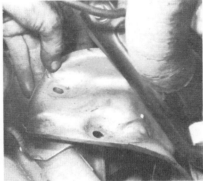

3.16 Removing the engine mount guard plate

3.17a Removing the distributor cap

3.17b Removing the temperature transmitter connection

3.17c The oil pressure switch connection

3.17d The coil/distributor lead

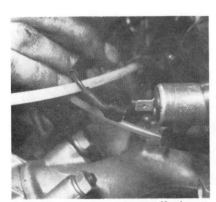

3.17e The carburettor idle cut-off valve connection

3.17f The starter motor connections

3.18a A lower radiator mount

3.18b Lifting out the radiator

3.19 The engine stop pad

3.20 The front exhaust pipe mounting

3.21 Disconnecting the drive shafts

3.23 Removing the transverse stabilizer

3.24a The lifting chains in position

3.24b The lifting chains in position

3.26 Removing the rear transmission mount and crossmember

3.27 The twin horns removed

3.31 The car raised clear of the power unit

4.3 The transmission separated from the engine

6.5 The distributor drive position marked on the block

Lifting can either be done using the chassis frame members or as shown in the photograph. If the latter method is adopted some protective material will be necessary to avoid damage to the car (photo).

4 Separating the transmission unit from the engine

1 Carefully clean the engine/transmission unit - particularly in the area of the engine/bellhousing joint.
2 Carefully support the unit at the engine and transmission ends, then remove the nuts and bolts which hold the two parts together. Note that the starter motor is also removed.
3 Separate the transmission unit from the engine making sure that it is pulled away squarely (photo). This avoids strain on the clutch and main shaft.
4 Note whether the engine/transmission unit dowels are in the transmission bellhousing flange or the engine flange. If one or the other is not going to be refitted to the car the dowels should be put into the part which will be refitted. Alternatively they can be removed for safety but it is imperative that they are fitted when engine and transmission unit are bolted together.
5 Put the transmission safely on one side. If there is to be some delay before any work is done on it, cover it with a polythene sheet.
6 Transfer the engine to a suitable support stand or workbench.

5 Removing the fan, fan support and stop pad (engine out of car)

1 Initially slacken the two screws at the outer end of the fan support and remove the belt from the fan pulley. The fan can now be removed from the support if required.
2 Now remove the three hexagon headed screws at the engine end of the support and lift the support (and fan if applicable), away from the engine.

6 Removing the distributor (engine out of the car)

1 To enable the distributor to be fitted in the correct position, and therefore simplify the timing procedure, it is best to note the position of certain items.
2 First set number one piston at top dead centre (tdc) on the firing stroke, using the crankshaft pulley or flywheel timing marks as appropriate. Now mark the relationship of the rotor to the distributor body and the distributor body to the cylinder block.
3 Now disconnect the pneumatic and electrical connections at the distributor.
4 Take off the distributor, either by removing the screws which secure the fixing bracket or by loosening the pinch bolt.
5 When the distributor has been lifted off, mark the position of the slot in the oil pump drive, noting that it is offset (photo).
6 Refit the distributor cap and put the parts on one side for safety.

7 Removing the alternator (engine out of the car)

1 Slacken all the mounting bolts and nuts, and move the alternator towards the engine to relieve drive belt tension.
2 Remove the fan and alternator drive belts.
3 Disconnect the alternator earth strap then remove all the bolts and lift the alternator away from the engine (photo).
4 Remove the slotted adjusting link.
5 Place the alternator and drive belts on one side to avoid damage.

8 Removing the carburettor (engine out of the car)

1 If you have removed the engine from the car you will have already removed the air cleaner. If this is not the case, the air cleaner should be removed now.
2 Disconnect the water hoses from the automatic choke (if not previously removed) (photo).
3 Detach the idle cut-off valve connections.
4 Disconnect the fuel inlet pipe (photo).
5 Remove the carburettor and its plastic cover. The nuts are difficult to get at so take care not to damage them by using unsuitable spanners (photos).
6 Put the carburettor on one side for safety, preferably wrapped in a polythene bag.

9 Removing the fuel pump (engine out of the car)

1 Remove the fuel outlet pipe at the pump.
2 Remove the two socket headed bolts (photo) and lift off the pump.
3 Put the pump on one side for safety, preferably wrapped in a polythene bag.
Note: On some cars a packing piece is fitted between the fuel pump and engine block. If one has been fitted, it should now be removed and kept with the pump.

10 Removing the water pump and thermostat (engine out of the car)

1 Loosen the lower hose clip on the by-pass hose. (This is the short hose above the water pump pulley).
2 Remove the two hexagon headed screws and take off the thermostat housing.
3 Remove the water pump pulley (photo). It is held by three bolts, and it will probably be necessary to prevent it from moving by wedging a screwdriver between the other bolt heads and the central spigot of the pulley.
4 Remove the hose connecting the water pump to the inlet manifold (photo).
5 Take out the water pump securing screws and put both pump and thermostat on one side. Note the length of the five screws for when replacement is required (photo).

11 Removing the clutch

1 Mark the relative position of the clutch and flywheel with white paint or chalk so that they can be refitted in the same position. This is because they are a balanced assembly.
2 Whilst preventing the flywheel from turning (by jamming the starter ring gear) slacken the clutch pressure plate securing screws cross-wise and evenly, then remove them in the same manner. The pressure plate and friction disc can then be lifted clear (photo).

12 Preparation for engine stripdown

1 If an engine support stand is available, the engine can be fitted to it to facilitate dismantling.
2 If not already carried out, remove the drain plug at the transmission end of the sump and drain off the oil into a suitable container capable of holding at least seven pints. Temporarily replace the drain plug.
3 Remove the oil filter and pressure switch (photo). Remember that some oil will spill out, so place a suitable container beneath it.
4 Thoroughly clean all the exterior surfaces of the engine. To prevent the cleaning solvents entering the oil filter drillings carefully clean this area first and mask it with adhesive tape.

13 Removing the cylinder head

Note: If this operation is to be carried out with the engine in the car it will first be necessary to drain the cooling system, remove

7.3 Removing the alternator

8.2 Removing the choke water pipes

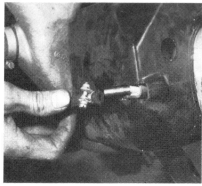

8.4 Removing the fuel pipe at the carburettor

8.5a Removing the carburettor cover

8.5b Removing the carburettor

9.2 Removing the fuel pump

10.3 Removing the water pump pulley

10.4 Disconnecting the water hose from the inlet manifold to the water pump

10.5 The water pump removed from the block

11.2 Removal of the clutch

12.3 Removing the oil pressure switch

13.1 Taking off the rocker cover

the air cleaner, detach the front exhaust pipe, the appropriate water hoses and electrical connections. Removal of the manifolds and carburettor are not essential at this stage but their removal will make the assembly lighter for handling purposes. Where necessary, make reference to the appropriate sections in the manual.

1 Remove the rocker cover (photo).

2 Remove the three nuts holding the exhaust manifold cover and take it off (photo).

3 Unscrew the eight exhaust manifold nuts and detach the manifold from the engine (photo).

4 Remove the eight nuts on the inlet manifold studs and the manifold support bracket nut. Lift away the manifold (photo).

5 Loosen the rocker adjusting nuts sufficiently to allow the rocker arms to be lifted (photo) and the pushrods removed. Put the pushrods on one side and note the order of removal for when replacement is required. A piece of hardboard is useful for this purpose, with holes drilled to accommodate the pushrods.

6 Slacken each cylinder head bolt slightly keeping strictly to the sequence shown (Fig. 1.1). Once the bolts have been slackened they can be removed.

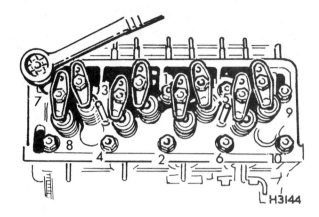

Fig. 1.1. The order of slackening the cylinder head bolts (Sec. 13)

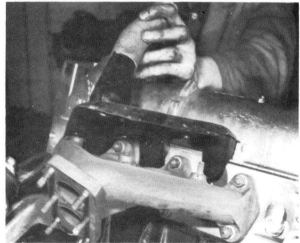

13.2 The exhaust manifold cover being removed

13.3 Removing the exhaust manifold

13.4 Removing the inlet manifold

13.5 Slackening the rocker to permit removal of the pushrods

7   Remove the cylinder head (photo) and put it on one side. If it is not to be dismantled immediately, cover it with polythene.
8   Remove the valve tappets (cam-followers) from the engine and put them with their respective pushrods so that they too can be refitted in their respective locations. Note: This step need not be carried out if the engine block is not to be dismantled further.

---

14 Dismantling the cylinder head

1   Remove the adjusting nuts and bearings from each rocker arm. Keep each rocker arm, bearing and nut together.
2   Compress each valve spring in turn and remove the collets (photo). Keep the collets, spring retainers and springs for each valve together for convenience. (The springs will normally be renewed during any overhaul).
3   Prise off the valve stem oil seals, (photo a) then the spring discs from the inlet valves (photo b) and rotocaps from the exhaust valves (photo c).
4   Do not remove the rocker arm joint studs unless absolutely essential. If they do need to be removed the alignment procedure is given in the section dealing with cylinder head reassembly.
5   Put the valves, seals, spring discs and rotocaps, with their respective rocker arms and pushrods.
6   If it is not intended to carry out any further work immediately put all the parts on one side for safety and cover with polythene.

---

15 Dismantling the engine block - general note

When dismantling the engine, be prepared for a small amount of oil remaining in the crankshaft, connecting rods, sump, oil pump, etc. Keep a supply of clean, non-fluffy rag handy and frequently wipe your hands. It's an impossible task to keep your hands completely clean but tools and small parts are much more easily handled when they are dry.

---

16 Removing the timing chain (including the sump and timing chain cover)

Note: This operation can be carried out with the engine in the car provided that the sump is drained, and the front grille and sill panels are removed. If necessary, make reference to Chapter 12 for the latter items.
1   Remove the sump and oil drain tube (if fitted). Four of the socket head screws are easily removed but for the remaining fifteen it may be necessary to maufacture a tool. This really depends on the contents of your tool box.
2   With the sump removed and out of the way the crankshaft

pulley can be removed (photo). If the engine is out of the car it will almost certainly be necessary to temporarily lock the flywheel ring in position to prevent the crankshaft from turning but do not attempt to jam the crankshaft for this operation. If necessary, remove the flywheel first (see next section) then loosely refit the bolts which can then be used to support a lever whilst undoing the crankshaft pulley nut. If the nut is difficult to remove with the engine in the car, first remove the starter motor and jam the flywheel ring but take extreme care that no damage is done.
3   Unscrew the timing chain cover bolts and remove the cover (photo).
4   On the early type chain tensioner, fold back the tab on the locking device for the chain tensioner hexagon headed plug, then remove the plug. Now insert an 1/8 in AF allen key into the plug hole and turn anti-clockwise to prevent the plug falling out. The chain tensioner and guide plate can now be removed (photo). On the later type, remove the chain tensioner first then press in the slipper and turn it to lock in position.
5   Remove the camshaft sprocket, pulling it off complete with the timing chain (photo).

---

17 Removing the flywheel

1   Mark the position of the flywheel with respect to the crankshaft (photo). They are a balanced assembly and should be refitted in the same relative positions.
2   Temporarily lock the flywheel in position then take out the six bolts and pull the flywheel off.
3   Withdraw the transmission drive shaft guide bearing out of the crankshaft. This may require the use of an extractor.

---

18 Removing the oil pump

1   Take out the two screws which hold the oil line to the block, followed by two screws at the other end on the oil pump.
2   Take off the oil line if considered necessary.
3   Unscrew the hexagon headed bolt retaining the oil pump then carefully lift the pump off (photo). Note that there is a spacer beneath the fixing lug through which the bolt passes.

---

19 Removing the pistons and connecting rods

Note: If this operation is carried out with the engine in the car it will be necessary to remove the sump, oil pump (after draining the oil), and the cylinder head.
1   Remove the big end (connecting rod) bearing caps one at a time (photo). Mark them in a manner which will identify each

Fig. 1.2. The early type timing chain tensioner (Sec. 16)

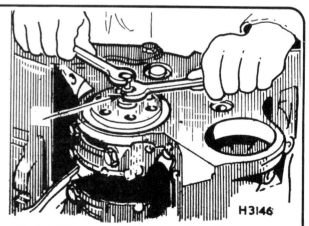

Fig. 1.3. Using an extractor (arrowed) to withdraw the transmission drive shaft guide bearing (Sec. 17)

13.7 Lifting off the cylinder head

14.2 Using the spring compressor

14.3a A valve stem seal

14.3b An inlet valve spring disc

14.3c An exhaust valve Rotocap

16.2 Removing the crankshaft pulley

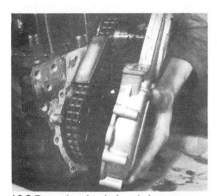
16.3 Removing the timing chain cover

16.4 Removing the later type chain tensioner

16.5 The timing chain being removed

17.1 Alignment marks on the flywheel and crankshaft

18.3 The oil pump removed

19.1 A big end cap being removed

with the connecting rod to which it belongs and which way round it was fitted.

2   Now carefully push each piston/connecting rod assembly up through its bore until it engages from the top of the block. Once the piston rings are clear of the block, the complete piston/connecting rod assembly can be withdrawn. Each piston and connecting rod should now be marked with the number of the cylinder from which it came. Never scratch identification marks on the pistons. If they will not be handled a great deal a soft lead pencil can be used; if they are likely to be handled, masking tape can be used with a number written on it. If only the connecting rods are to be re-used these will need to be marked.

20 Removing the crankshaft

1   Remove the main bearing caps, (photo) again marking them to prevent mix up when they are refitted.
2   Very carefully lift out the crankshaft (photo). Sometimes the main bearing shells stick to the crankshaft, so make sure that they do not drop and become damaged.
3   Carefully remove the oil seal on the flywheel end of the crankshaft, making sure that the outer surface is not damaged.
4   When the crankshaft has been removed, carefully mask the sealing ring surface to prevent damage.
5   Remove the remaining main bearing shells by pressing one end. In this manner they will slide round the bearing housing in the block and can be picked out.
6   Unscrew the oil pressure relief valve. This is in the crankcase cavity of number 4 cylinder (photo). If the valve is to be removed, note whether it has an 18 mm or 20 mm screw thread.

21 Removing the camshaft

Note: If this operation is to be done with the engine in the car it will be necessary to remove the cylinder head and pushrods, and slacken the engine mountings to allow the engine to be moved a little when withdrawing the camshaft.

1   Remove the camshaft guide flange screws and take off the flanges (photo).
2   If the engine has been taken out of the car it is strongly recommended that it is turned on end when withdrawing the camshaft to prevent possible damage to the bearing bushings in the block. If the engine is still in the car, withdraw the camshaft very slowly but first remove the tappets (cam followers) using a suction tool (as used for valve grinding). Whichever method you are adopting fit a screw into the threaded recess on the end of the camshaft to enable it to be pulled out.
3   After removal - as with the other parts of the valve mechanism - keep the cam followers with their respective valves and pushrods.

22 Dismantling the piston and connecting rod assembly

1   First carefully remove the piston rings, sliding them upwards towards the top of the piston. This is facilitated somewhat if an old 0.020 in feeler gauge can be slid behind the ring once one end has been lifted out of the groove.
2   Now remove the internal circlip at one end of the gudgeon pin (photo) and press the pin out. This can normally be done by heating the piston in very hot water and just pressing the pin out by hand. If this method is not successful, again heat the piston in hot water then grip the top of the connecting rod in a vice using suitable jaw clamps to avoid damage. Now very carefully drive out the pin using a suitable drift.
3   Put the parts carefully on one side to avoid damage.

23 Dismantling the oil pump

1   Before dismantling the oil pump, whether for inspection or

20.1 The end main bearing cap being removed

any other reason, it must be appreciated that Audi do not provide replacement parts or dimensions of the various component parts. It must therefore be considered whether to renew the pump regardless of its condition or whether to attempt to make it last for a further spell in service.
2   Unless the car has been operating in extremely adverse conditions it is quite reasonable to assume that the pump can be dismantled for inspection and cleaning (photos) in the same way as for other parts provided that it has not been in use for more than 40000 miles.
3   If a mileage of 40000 has been exceeded, and in any case where it is found necessary to renew items like the crankshaft and bearing shells, the only safe way of approaching the job is to renew the pump regardless.

24 Cleaning and storage

1   You will now have around you a large number of parts which have been removed/dismantled. The next major step is to decide which parts are still serviceable and which are to be renewed. This process takes some time and some preparatory work will be required.
2   Remove all oil and grease deposits using petrol and a bristle paint brush about ½ inch wide. Do this job systematically and don't forget to keep all associated parts together. Make sure that all identification marks are still present after each item has been cleaned. Remove any gasket remnants with a blunt scraper.
3   When the various groups of parts have been cleaned don't leave them lying around to collect dust. Cover each group with polythene - it is well worth the trouble.

PART B – DECARBONISATION – INSPECTION, REPAIR AND RENEWAL OF PARTS

25 Decarbonisation

1   Modern engines, together with modern fuels and lubricants, have virtually nullified the need for the engine to have a 'de-coke' which was common enough only a few years ago. Carbon deposits are formed mostly on the modern engine only when it has to do a great deal of slow speed, stop/start running, for example, in busy traffic and city traffic conditions. If carbon deposit symptoms are apparent, such as pinking or pre-ignition and running on after the engine has been switched off, then a good high speed run on a motorway or straight stretch of road is usually sufficient to clear these deposits out. It is beneficial to

20.2 The crankshaft being lifted out

20.6 The oil pressure relief valve being removed

21.1 The camshaft guide flange

22.2 The internal circlip for the piston pin

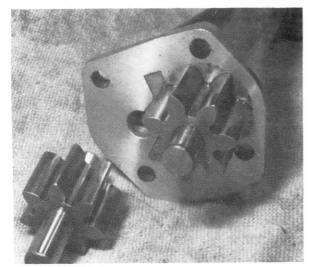

23.2a The oil pump gears

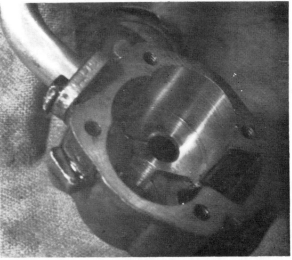

23.2b The interior of the oil pump housing

any motor car to give it a good high speed run from time to time.

2 If the need for decarbonisation only, has been established, the procedure is given in the following paragraphs. In this case, much of the procedure previously described in this Chapter will be irrelevant. However, a list is now given of the items which have to be removed from the engine if decarbonisation only is to be carried out. Instructions for their removal will be found earlier in the chapter.

a) Drain the cooling system.
b) Remove the air cleaner and its associated flexible pipes.
c) Remove the thermostat housing.
d) Remove all the water hoses connected to the cylinder head, carburettor and inlet manifold.
e) Remove the distributor cap and leads.
f) Remove all the electrical connections to the cylinder head.
g) Remove the exhaust manifold at the cylinder head and front exhaust pipe.
h) Remove the carburettor and its fuel pipe.
j) Remove the inlet manifold, taking off the distributor vacuum connection and the brake servo line.
k) Remove the cylinder head.
l) Remove the valves and valve springs.
m) Remove the spark plugs.

2 Assuming the pistons etc have not been removed from the engine, it is most important that the oil and water passages are kept free from the carbon particles which will be freed during decarbonisation. The best way of doing this - although at the same time it is tedious - is to mask the passages with a suitable tape. Alternatively, provided that some care is taken, pieces of non-fluffy rag can be used if they are carefully tucked into the openings.

3 Now raise two of the pistons to the top of the bores and mask off the other two bores in the manner described for the water and oil passages, to prevent the entry of pieces of carbon.

4 Now smear a little grease around the top of the piston when it contacts the cylinder wall to prevent carbon falling down and scratching the polished surface.

5 There are two schools of thought as to how much carbon should be removed from the piston crown. One school recommends that a ring of carbon should be left round the edge of the piston and on the cylinder bore as an aid to ensure low oil consumption. Although this is probably true for early engines with worn bores, on modern engines the thought of the second school can be applied, which is that for effective decarbonisation all traces of carbon should be removed.

6 If all traces of carbon are to be removed proceed as follows: With a blunt scraper carefully scrape away the carbon from the piston crown, taking great care not to scratch the aluminium. Also scrape the carbon away from the surrounding lip of the cylinder wall. When all the carbon has been removed, scrape away the grease which will now be contaminated with carbon particles, taking care not to press any into the bores. Remove the rags or masking tape from the other two cylinders and turn the crankshaft so that the two pistons which were at the bottom are now at the top. Place rag or masking tape in cylinders which have been decarbonised and proceed as before.

7 If a ring of carbon is going to be left round the piston this can be helped by inserting an old piston ring into the top of the bore to rest on the piston and ensure that carbon is not accidentally removed. Check that there are no particles in the cylinder bores.

8 If the engine has been dismantled the same method of carbon removal can be adopted as described in the preceding paragraph. Although it is not quite so important to keep everything clean during the operation, it is, however, necessary to remove the piston rings and carefully clean all the parts afterwards.

9 Cleaning the carbon from the valves is a straighforward operation but take care not to damage the stems by holding them in a vice or clamp. Details of permissible wear limits are given in a later section of this chapter.

10 Now for the cylinder head. Again it will be necessary to mask the oil and water passages, and remove the carbon deposits. With this sort of operation (unless you are experienced) it is advisable to remove the carbon deposits, using a blunt scraper or something like a piece of Formica. The latter is quite hard and with some degree of care this method is perfectly satisfactory. The main point is that on no account should the polished surfaces be scratched. For those who are experienced it is quite in order to liberally lubricate a wire brush with engine oil (provided that the wires are springy and not burred out at the ends) and brush the deposits away. However, if you are in any doubt, use the first method since an error with the second method could prove to be very expensive.

11 It is recommended that spark plugs are renewed unless they have only completed a few thousand miles. If the existing ones are to be re-used they should preferably be cleaned on a sand blasting machine which will remove the deposits more effectively than cleaning by hand.

26 Valve grinding

1 Before the valves and seats are reground it is recommended that they are inspected as detailed later. It is no use trying to grind in faulty valves.

2 The best type of tool for valve grinding is the suction type which can be pressed on to the head of the valve.

3 It will probably be necessary to use a coarse grinding paste to start with followed by a fine paste once all imperfections have been removed. At all times use a back-and-forth motion by rubbing the stem of the suction tool between the fingers and palms of the hands, rotating it slightly every few seconds to assist distribution of the paste. Whilst this operation is continuing, make sure that the grinding paste does not contact the valve stem or abrasion will occur here.

4 When you have finished there should be no signs of imperfection of any sort on the seating faces, which should each have a continuous ring of uniform grey appearance.

5 When the operation is completed it is most important that all traces of the grinding paste are removed before any reassembly work is carried out. The valves can be washed in petrol or paraffin then dried; a cloth moistened with petrol or paraffin will normally clean all the deposits from the cylinder head and the cavity behind the valve head.

27 Inspecting the cylinder head for distortion

1 The maximum permissible distortion of the cylinder head is 0.0016 in (0.04 mm) and for most practical purposes a straight edged ruler and feeler gauge are suitable. The procedure is as follows: Lay the edge of the ruler across the width of the cylinder head, in five or six different positions, along the length of the cylinder head face. The edge of the ruler should be 100% in contact with the surface of the head. However, if daylight is seen between the edge of the rule and the head surface, it indicates that high or low spots (distortion) are present. In this case find the thickest feeler blade which will pass between the head and ruler, where daylight is seen - if the clearance exceeds 0.0016 in (0.04 mm) the distortion of the cylinder head is beyond acceptable limits. Repeat this process on the longitudinal face of the head; the ruler used should have a flat edge larger than the head. The same tolerances apply.

2 An alternative method, and more accurate too if the facilities are available, is to lightly coat an inspection surface plate with engineers blue then gently slide the head over it. Ideally it should pick up traces of the blue all over but if only local pick up occurs, a high spot exists. This can be measured using a dial gauge. 0.0016 in (0.04 mm) is the maximum degree of distortion acceptable, if the head is to be refitted.

3 Where excessive distortion of the cylinder head exists it may be possible to have a very small amount of metal skimmed from the head surface to restore flatness. Alternatively, the distorted cylinder head can be replaced by a new unit - these may be available on an exchange basis.

28 Inspecting valves and valve guides

1 Carefully examine the end of the valve stem for any signs of indentation caused by the valve rocker arm. Whilst it is permissible to grind the end of the valve a very small amount, it is unlikely that the general condition of the valve will be satisfactory if excessive wear exists here.

2 Carefully examine the seating area of each valve for fitting and/or burning, especially the exhaust valves. If the pitting is very slight, the marks can be removed by grinding but if there is excessive pitting, replacement valves should be fitted, as it is just not worth attempting to grind the old ones to this extent.

3 Carefully examine the valve stem and guide for wear. Whilst a micrometer can be used on the valve stem to detect wear, there is no simple way of measuring the internal surfaces of the guides. In cases such as this a certain amount of discretion has to be used but a good guide is that if the valve can be rocked in the guide, renew the valves. If the new valve can still be rocked in the guide, the guide needs renewing also (see later sections).

29 Inspecting valve seat inserts

1 Carefully examine the sealing face of the insert for pitting and burning, especially the exhaust valve inserts. If the pitting is very slight, the marks can be removed by grinding but if there is excessive pitting arrangements should be made for new inserts to be fitted (see next section).

2 At the same time as checking the condition of the sealing face of the insert, also check for cracks in the insert and in the cylinder head material between the inlet and exhaust valves. On early cars there were instances of cracks occuring but later models have a slightly modified head which precludes this type of damage.

3 If the pitting or burning of the valve seats is not too deep, but at the same time would require a lot of valve grinding to bring it to a satisfactory condition it is recommended that an Audi dealer or an approved cylinder head specialist is contacted to discuss the possibility of recutting the seats (see the next section also).

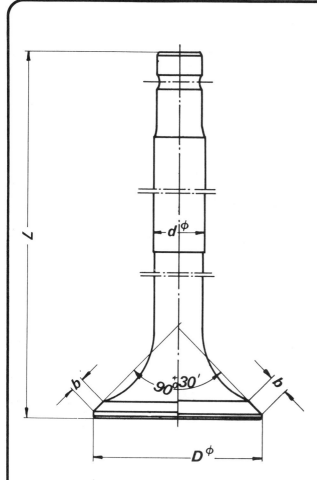

FIG. 1.4. VALVE REWORK DIMENSIONS (SEC. 28)

L = overall length
d = diameter of stem
D = diameter of head
b = minimum cone width
b, = maximum cone width

Fig. 1.5. Checking the valve stem run-out (Sec. 28)

Fig. 1.6. The circlip in position in the groove in the valve guide (Sec. 29)

30 Renewal of valve guides and valve seat inserts

1   Renewal of valve guides and valve seats is a job which should undoubtedly be entrusted to an Audi dealer or an approved cylinder head specialist. It is not a job that can be carried out with makeshift equipment.

2   If either the valve guides or the seat inserts require renewal (as judged from the previous inspection) it is well worthwhile considering renewal in pairs. It is almost certain that if only one part is renewed excessive bedding in or seat recutting will have to be carried out. There is also good reason to assume that if one part is in such a poor state that renewal is required the condition of the other part cannot be very satisfactory.

3   Where the pitting of existing seats is not too severe an Audi dealer or cylinder head specialist may recommend the seats being recut. This is satisfactoy provided that the dimensions in the illustrations (Figs. 1.7 and 1.8) can be maintained.

Note: With any of the above operations, new valves should be fitted. These must, of course, be ground in as described earlier in this section.

31 Inspecting cylinder bores

1   The cylinder bores must be examined for taper, ovality, scoring and scratches. Start by carefully examining the top of the cylinder bores. If they are at all worn a very slight ridge will be found on the thrust side. This marks the top of the piston ring travel. The owner will have a good indication of the bore wear prior to dismantling the engine, or removing the cylinder head. Excessive oil consumption accompanied by blue smoke from the exhaust is a sure sign of worn cylinder bores and piston rings.

2   Measure the bore diameter just under the ridge with a micrometer and compare it with the diameter at the bottom of the bore, which is not subject to wear. If the difference between the two measurements is more than 0.003 in (0.08 mm) then it will be necessary to fit special piston rings or to have the cylinders rebored and fit oversize pistons and rings. If no micrometer is available remove the rings from a piston and place the piston in each bore in turn about ¾ inch below the top of the bore. If an 0.005 inch (0.127 mm) feeler gauge can be slid between the piston and the cylinder wall on the thrust side of the bore then remedial action must be taken. Oversize cylinder bores are listed at the beginning of this chapter.

3   If it is decided that remedial action is required, the work should be carried out by an Audi dealer or a reboring specialist. When reboring is necessary new pistons will be required (see next section). These should be supplied by the dealer to match the bore size. The engine block has a boring code stamped just behind the right hand engine mounting strut and it is recommended that this is altered to suit the oversize bore.

32 Inspecting the pistons and piston rings

Note: If it is found necessary to replace pistons it must be ascertained whether the centre piston ring groove has a chamfer on its lower wall. If no chamfer is present it may be necessary to fit a new set of pistons incorporating the chamfered type of piston ring - when the earlier type stocks are depleted. The chamfered wall type piston also has a different oil scraper ring. Pistons and rings must be all of one type.

1   Worn pistons and rings can usually be diagnosed when the symptoms of excessive oil consumption and low compression occur and are sometimes, though not always, associated with worn cylinder bores. Compression testers that fit into the spark plug holes are available and these can indicate where low compression is occuring. Wear usually accelerates the more it is left so when the symptoms occur early action can possibly save the expense of a rebore.

2   Another symptom of piston wear is piston slap — a knocking noise from the crankcase not to be confused with big end

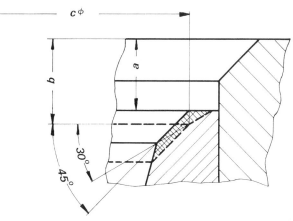

FIG. 1.7. INLET VALVE SEAT INSERT REWORK DIMEN-SIONS (SEC. 30)

a   =   0.9846 in. (2.5 mm) minimum
b   =   1.1811 in. (3 mm) maximum
c   =   1.4724 in. (37.4 mm) diameter

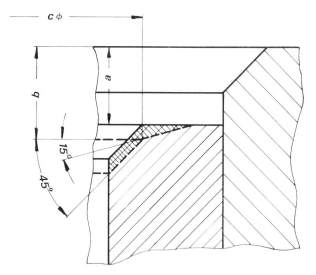

FIG. 1.8. EXHAUST VALVE SEAT INSERT REWORK DIMENSIONS (SEC. 30)

a   =   0.1063 in. (2.7 mm) minimum
b   =   0.126 in. (3.2 mm) maximum
c   =   1.276 in. (32.4 mm) diameter

Fig. 1.9. Cylinder bore wear measurement using a dial gauge (Sec. 31)

bearing failure. It can be heard clearly at low engine speed when there is no load (idling for example) and is much less audible when the engine speed increases. Piston wear usually occurs in the skirt or lower end of the piston and is indicated by vertical streaks in the worn area which is always on the thrust side. It can also be seen where the skirt thickness is different.

3   To check for piston wear, measure the diameter at about 0.63 in (16 mm) from the top of the piston. If the wear exceeds 0.00158 in (0.04 mm), even if the bore is not to be rebored, the pistons must be renewed. Piston sizes are listed in the Specifications section.

4   At the same time as checking for wear, carefully examine the piston crown for signs of cracking or other damage. If any is present the piston must be renewed.

5   Check the wear between the edges of the piston rings and the wall of the ring groove. The maximum permissible gap is 0.0059 in (0.15 mm). If this is exceeded new pistons will be required.

6   Fit each piston ring in turn into the top of the cylinder bore to which it belongs.

7   Measure the gap between the ends of the rings. The maximum permissible is 0.0394 in. (1 mm). If this is exceeded, new rings and possibly a rebore cylinder block will be required. In cases such as this it is best to discuss the problem with a specialist in this field. It may be possible to fit 'stepped' top rings to a piston to restore performance with partially worn pistons and bores.

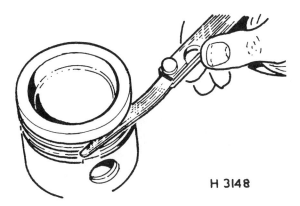

Fig. 1.10. Measuring the piston ring in the groove (Sec. 32)

---

33 Inspecting the gudgeon pins

1   The minimum permissible gudgeon pin diameter is 0.9445 in (23.99 mm) and if this dimension is too small the pin must be renewed. A micrometer is satisfactory for carrying out a check of this type.

---

34 Inspecting the connecting rods

1   Big end bearing failure is accompanied by a noisy knocking from the crankcase and a drop in oil pressure.

2   Bearings which have not broken up, but are badly worn will give rise to low oil pressure and some vibration, also a light knocking may be heard when the engine is first started. The bearings should be matt grey in colour. With lead-indium bearings, should a trace of copper colour be noticed the bearings are badly worn as the lead bearing material has worn away to expose the indium underlay. Renew the bearings if they are in this condition or if there is any sign of scoring or pitting - if there is any doubt about their condition, renew the bearings anyway.

3   The best method of checking the small end bearing is to use a gudgeon pin which is known to be satisfactory. If the pin can be fitted by pushing it in without any effort, the small end bearing must be renewed.

Note: If connecting rod assemblies part number 059 105 401B are fitted as replacements they must be renewed in sets and fitted with the identification markings (arrowed) towards the camshaft. The nuts for this version must be tightened to 40 to 43.4 lb ft (5.5 to 6 kgm).

   If connecting rods have to be renewed note the weight class number on the cap and fit replacement parts of the nearest available number.

Fig. 1.11. Measuring the piston ring in the bore (Sec. 32)

---

35 Inspecting the crankshaft and main bearings

1   Failure of the main bearings is accompanied by vibration (which can be quite severe as the engine speed rises and falls), and a drop in oil pressure. Excessive wear of this type can result from low oil pressure or contaminated oil - which will also give rise to scoring of the crankshaft journals and big end bearing shells.

2   Carefully examine all the bearing surfaces for cracking,

scoring, corrosion or obvious signs of wear. If any defects are present the bearings must be replaced in sets and the crankshaft journals reground. Since it is a major job to renew main bearings, if you are in any doubt or if the bearings have been in service for more than 30000 miles, it is safest to renew them.

3 Check the crankshaft journal sizes using a micrometer in various positions around each journal. The journal sizes and limits of ovality are listed in the Specifications section.

4 Temporarily fit the crankshaft to the block and fit the bearing caps. Now measure the crankshaft end float, using feeler gauges between the sides of the bearings and the crankshaft webs to check the clearance. The acceptable limits of wear and play are given in the Specifications section.

5 Now temporarily fit the connecting rods to the crankshaft and remove the side float in the same way as for the main bearings. Again refer to the Specifications section for the acceptable limits of wear and play.

6 If excessive crankshaft end float is found (paragraphs 4 and 5) new bearing shells will be required even if they are otherwise satisfactory.

FIG. 1.12. LATER TYPE CONNECTING ROD ASSEMBLY (SEC. 34)

a   Complete assembly
b   Nut
c   Bolt
    Identification markings arrowed

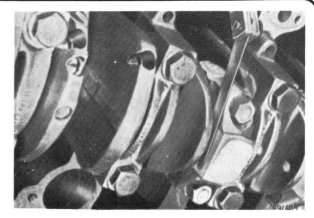

Fig. 1.13. Measuring crankshaft/main bearing axial play (Sec. 35)

Fig. 1.14. Measuring big end/crankshaft axial play (Sec. 35)

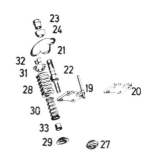

FIG. 1.15. CAMSHAFT AND VALVES (SEC. 34)

1 Camshaft	19 Push rod guide
2 Camshaft sprocket	20 Push rod guide
3 Timing chain	21 Rocker arm
4 Pin	22 Mounting bolt
5 Guide flange	23 Adjusting nut
6 Lock washer	24 Bearing
7 Hex. head screw	25 Inlet valve
8 Plain washer	26 Exhaust valve
9 Stretch screw	27 Rotocap, exhaust
10 Guide rail	valve
11 Chain tensioner	28 Outer valve spring
12 Lock plate	29 Spring retainer,
13 Plug	intake valve
14 Lock plate	30 Inner valve spring
15 Hex. head screw	31 Spring retainer
16 Hex. head screw	32 Valve collet
	33 *Valve seal

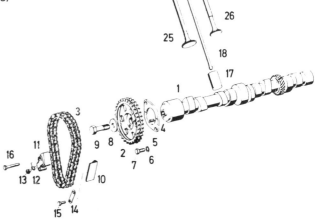

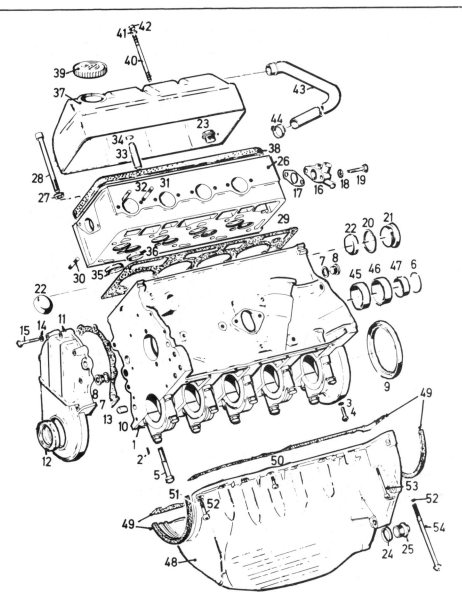

FIG. 1.16. CYLINDER BLOCK AND HEAD COMPONENTS (SEC. 34)

1 Engine block	14 Plain washer	27 Plain washer	40 Stud
2 Dowel pin	15 Hex. head screw	28 Socket head cap screw	41 Seal
4 Socket head screw	16 Flange	29 Gasket, cylinder head	42 Hex. nut
5 Hex. head screw	17 Gasket	30 Stud	43 Vent hose
6 Plug, rear camshaft	18 Washer	31 Stud	44 Clip
bearing	19 Hex. head screw	32 Stud	48 Sump
7 Seal	20 Seal	33 Valve guide	49 Gasket (set)
8 Plug	21 Plug	34 Snap ring	50 Socket head screw
9 Shaft seal (flywheel end)	22 Cap, engine block	35 Valve insert (inlet)	51 Socket head screw
10 Dowel pin	23 Cap, cylinder head	36 Valve insert (exhaust)	52 Washer
11 Timing housing cover	24 Seal	37 Rocker cover	53 Socket head screw
12 Shaft seal	25 Plug	38 Gasket	54 Socket head screw
13 Gasket	26 Cylinder head	39 Plug	

36 Inspecting timing chain, chain tensioner and sprocket

1   Any timing chain which has been used for a period exceeding 60000 miles (100000 km) should be renewed. Only chains which have straight links may be used.

2   If an existing chain is to be reused carefully inspect it for damage and/or slackness in the linkages. Fit the chain to the sprockets and check for a good firm fit between the sprocket teeth.

3   Check the sprocket teeth for wear and deformation. Renew any worn or damaged parts.

4   Examine the sliding surface of the chain tension slipper and the rubber based guide rail. If any obvious wear is present renew the parts without hesitation.

5   Check the condition of the chain tensioner spring. If it is distorted or broken this too, must be renewed.

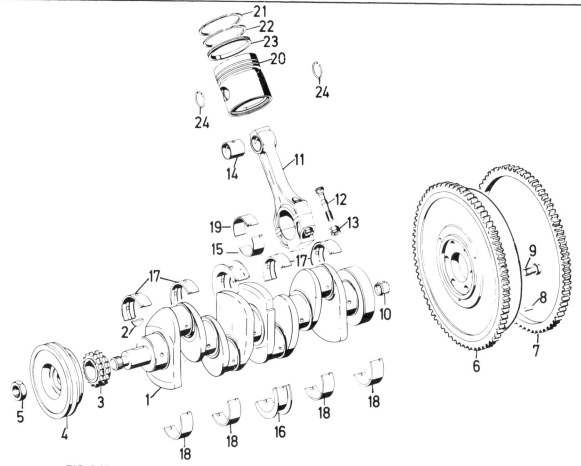

FIG. 1.17. CRANKSHAFT, BEARINGS, CONNECTING RODS, PISTONS AND RINGS (SEC. 34)

1 Crankshaft	7 Starter gear	13 Nut	19 Con rod bearing shell, half
2 Woodruff key	8 Dowel pin	14 Bushing	20 Piston
3 Crankshaft sprocket	9 Hex. head screw	15 Thrust bearing shell, upper half	21 Top ring
4 Pulley	10 Needle bearing	16 Thrust bearing shell, lower half	22 Middle ring
5 Hex. nut	11 Con rod	17 Main bearing shell, upper half	23 Bottom ring
6 Flywheel	12 Con rod bolt	18 Main bearing shell, lower half	24 Circlip

PART C – REASSEMBLY PROCEDURE

37 General note

1 Although some of the parts which have been removed will show no apparent wear or damage, don't be misled into thinking that they are necessarily satisfactory. The best example of this is probably the valve springs: it is seldom that they appear to be unsatisfactory until compared with new ones. It will then be found that they are a bit shorter and can be compressed a little more easily.

2 With gaskets the same sort of thing applies. They can sometimes appear to be satisfactory but as a general rule they should be renewed even if they have only been used for a short time.

3 A little discretion can be used with O-rings and oil seals. However, if they have completed a considerable mileage, alway renew them for safety's sake.

4 Split pins, tab washers and self locking nuts. Although a little discretion can be used with self locking nuts, the general rule for split pins and tab washers is that they should never be used more than once.

5 Where an engine has had major working parts replaced it is necessary to use a special running-in oil and filter (Part no. 059 115 561) for the first 300 to 450 miles (500 to 700 km), following which the normal type of filter and oil can be used.

type of filter and oil can be used.

6 Whenever cylinder bores have been ground oversize, the housing code number should be stamped on the cylinder block in the position shown. A list of the code numbers is given in the Specifications section at the beginning of the Chapter.

7 Whenever the connecting-rod (or big-end) bearings are renewed it is important that new nuts and special bolts are used.

Fig. 1.18. The correct type of connecting rod bolt (Sec. 37)

38 Refitting the crankshaft and main bearings

1   Initially replace the oil pressure relief valve.
2   Refit each main bearing shell in the cylinder block taking note of the identification markings if the same shells are being used again. Note that the centre bearing shell is shouldered and that all shells on the block are grooved on their bearing face.
3   Refit the shells in the main bearing caps (photos) noting the identification marks (if applicable).
4   Apply a little engine oil to the bearing faces in the block (photo) then carefully lay the crankshaft in position.
5   Rotate the crankshaft once or twice to spread the oil, then fit the bearing boss/shells into their respective positions (photo).
6   Lightly pinch up the bearing cap bolts then fit the oil seal on the flywheel end of the crankshaft. A great deal of care must be exercised here to prevent the seal from being damaged. It should be fitted using a suitable tool to pull it into position using the flywheel bolt holes on the end of the crankshaft, or alternatively - very carefully pressed in by working around the periphery (photo).
7   The bearing caps can now be tightened to the correct torque in two steps starting at number 1 bearing (photo).

39 Refitting the pistons and connecting rods

1   When refitting the piston rings always make sure that the word "Top" on the ring is uppermost, and that the ring gaps are spaced radially at intervals of 120° Note: If the pistons have not yet been fitted to the connecting-rods it is recommended that this latter step is carried out first as described in the following paragraph.
2   With the piston rings removed from the piston, heat the piston in water to a temperature of around 70°C to facilitate fitment of the gudgeon pin (The gudgeon pin should be liberally lubricated). Very carefully dry all the parts afterwards then refit the internal circlip. If there is any doubt about its condition it should be renewed. Note that the arrow on the piston crown must point towards the front of the car when finally assembled. If the later type connecting rods are being used make sure that when they are assembled to the piston it will be in such a way that the bosses on the bearing caps are towards the camshaft.
3   Refit the shell bearings to the connecting-rods and bearing caps, (photo) according to their respective markings (if appropriate).
4   Squirt some engine oil on the bearing surfaces and on the cylinder bore walls, then, using a suitable piston ring clamp (photo) insert the pistons and connecting-rods into the cylinders working from the cylinder head end (photo). Some rotation of the crankshaft will be required during this operation but when all piston connecting-rod assemblies have been fitted and the bearing caps attached the cap nuts can be tightened to the correct torque (photo) (see Specifications).

40 Refitting the camshaft and timing chain

1   Smear a little engine oil over the camshaft journals and cams then very carefully fit it into position (photo). This can be done with the engine in a vertical or horizontal position but take care not to damage the cams or journals in any way.
2   With the camshaft fitted into the block, fit the guide flange, followed by the camshaft and crankshaft sprockets. If necessary the crankshaft sprocket can be heated to a temperature of around 70°C to facilitate fitment. Note the Woodruff key on the crankshaft sprocket and the dowel pin on the camshaft sprocket.
3   Temporarily fit the bolt to the camshaft sprocket.
4   Now measure the end float of both the crankshaft and camshaft. If the difference between the two end floats is greater than 0.02 in (0.5 mm), when measured from the end face of the block to the outer face of the sprocket tooth ring, the appropriate sprocket should be renewed. (If the engine has been

dismantled completely, the sprockets will have already been inspected and renewed if necessary).
5   Now remove the camshaft sprocket bolt, fit the chain guide rail and fit the timing chain to the crankshaft sprocket with number 1 piston at top-dead-centre (tdc).
6   Rotate the camshaft as necessary then refit the chain and sprocket so that the notch (indentation) on the sprocket aligns with the notch in the guide rail (photo).
7   Fit the camshaft sprocket bolt and torque tighten it as required (see Specifications).
8   The chain tensioner can now be fitted and once this is done the slipper can be released either by turning the plunger with an allen key or turning the slipper as it is being fitted. Depress the slipper two or three times to ensure that it is spring loaded against the chain.
9   If the engine is in the car, replace the tappets (cam followers) and pushrods followed by the timing chain cover and cylinder head. Finally, check the engine alignment. These latter operations are described fully later in this Chapter.

41 Refitting the oil pump

1   The oil pump with its associated pipe can be refitted easily but don't forget the spacer beneath the fixing lug. When fitting the pump it is necessary to correctly align the offset slot with the markings on the block where the distributor is mounted.
2   When everything is satisfactorily aligned the hexagon headed screws can be refitted.

42 Refitting the timing chain cover, crankshaft front oil seal and sump

1   The crankshaft front oil seal can be renewed with the engine fitted by prising the old seal out with a screwdriver then carefully driving in a new seal. Liberally smear the seal with a general purpose grease, particularly in the groove. Where an engine has been dismantled carefully press the oil seal into the timing chain cover then refit the cover to the engine using a new gasket. The cover can then be torque tightened crosswise.
2   Fit the sump gaskets (photo) using a little general purpose grease to hold them in position. At the same time fit the rubber or cork inserts into the end grooves (photo).
3   Seal the ends of the gaskets with a little universal gasket cement such as golden Hermetite. Note that the gasket at the starter motor end does not require sealing or sticking since it is self adhesive.
4   The sump cover can now be replaced (photos), torque tightening the screws crosswise. As with removal of these screws

FIG. 1.19. MEASURING THE END FLOAT OF THE CAMSHAFT (SEC. 40)

e   *Crankshaft sprocket*

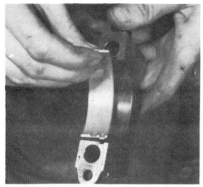

38.3a Fitting a main bearing shell in the bearing cap

38.3b The main bearing caps ready for fitment

38.4 The bearing shells being lubricated

38.5 Fitting the main bearing caps

38.6 The flywheel oil seal being positioned

38.7 Torque tightening the main bearings

39.3 Fitting a big end bearing shell

39.4a Fitting a piston ring compressor or clamp

39.4b Sliding in the piston and connecting rod

39.4c Torque tightening the big end bearings

40.1 Refitting the camshaft

40.6 Aligning the camshaft sprocket notch

42.2a The sump gasket ends

42.2b The end groove seal on the sump

42.4a Refitting the sump

42.4b The sump bolts loosely fitted

43.1a Refitting a valve

43.1b Assembling an exhaust valve spring

43.1c Assembling an inlet valve spring

43.3 Compressing the valve spring to fit the collets

44.2 Driving on the flywheel

it may be necessary to make up a tool to fit the socket head screws.

5   Finally refit the oil drain plug and oil pressure switch, making sure that the sealing washers are intact and clean.

43 Reassembling the cylinder head

1   To avoid confusion it may be found preferable to refit all the exhaust valves or all the inlet valves at the same time (photo). The assembly procedure is more or less the same but don't forget that below the oil seal on the valve stem a rotocap is fitted for the exhaust valves (photo) and a spring retainer is fitted on the inlet valves (photo).

2   When refitting the valve stem seals take care not to damage them as they are slid over the groove at the end of the valve stem.

3   Using a suitable valve spring compressor, compress the valve springs (photo) just sufficiently to allow the upper spring retainers and split collets to be fitted. The spring compressor can then be removed.

4   Repeat the operation for the remaining valves on the cylinder head.

5   Pushrod guides and rockers may be loosely fitted at this stage but will require final positioning and adjustment after refitting the cylinder head to the block.

44 Refitting the crankshaft pulley and flywheel

1   Refit the flywheel to the engine, taking note of the identification markings made during dismantling.

2   The flywheel can be driven into position using a heavy piece of wood as shown in the photograph, but make sure that all the

bolts can be fitted properly.

3 When the bolts are torque tightened (photo) it will probably be necessary to lock the flywheel in position (photo). The latter will definitely be necessary for the following step.

4 Now fit the crankshaft pulley at the front end of the block, noting that it is located by a Woodruff key, and torque tighten the nut.

5 If the engine mounting brackets were removed, or if a new block is being used, this is a convenient time to refit them.

6 Refit the oil drain tube (if applicable) to the outlet behind the crankshaft pulley.

45 Refitting the cylinder head

1 First insert the cam followers into their respective positions (photo) if not already fitted.

2 Now position the cylinder head gasket on the block (photo); there is no need to worry about which side goes uppermost because it will only fit one way If you have any trouble keeping it in position use a little general purpose grease (not gasket cement) to hold it stationary.

3 Give a good squirt of engine oil to the cylinder walls to provide lubrication for the piston rings on initial engine start up.

4 Now carefully lift the cylinder head into position (photo) and fit the bolts loosely to prevent movement.

5 The head can now be torque tightened in steps as shown in the specifications section (photo) make sure that you keep strictly to the sequence shown in the illustration (Fig. 1.20).

46 Refitting the water pump (engine out of the car)

1 Refit the water pump to the block (photo). If necessary a little general purpose grease can be used to hold the gasket in position, but do not use gasket cement.

2 Torque tighten the screws to the values given in the specifications section.

47 Refitting the alternator (engine out of the car)

1 When refitting the alternator (photo) don't forget the rubber mounts on the top bracket. Lightly tighten the nuts, final adjustment will need to be carried out after the fan belt and water pump pulley are fitted.

Note: Always fit the long bolt so that the thread is facing forward to facilitate removal when fitted in the car.

2 Don't forget to connect the alternator earth strap to the block also (photo).

48 Refitting the thermostat and housing (engine out of the car)

1 After fitment of the water pump the thermostat housing and water pump/thermostat hose can be fitted (photo).

2 Now fit the thermostat into position making sure that the bridge piece is fore and aft along the line of the engine (photo).

3 When replacing the cover make sure that the O-ring is undamaged.

49 Refitting the fuel pump (engine out of the car)

1 Refitting the fuel pump is a straightforward job. If a thick spacer was originally fitted between the pump and the block, this must be refitted. Otherwise just the gasket is used.

50 Refitting the distributor (engine out of the car)

1 Refit the distributor (and clamp plate if previously removed) (photo) taking great care that the body and drive are correctly

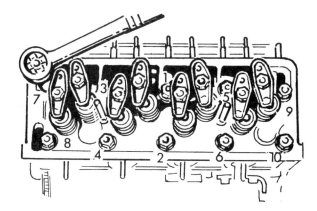

Fig. 1.20. The order of tightening the cylinder head bolts (Sec. 45)

aligned with the identification marks made earlier.

2 With the distributor in position, rotate the crankshaft and check that when number one piston is at top dead centre on its firing stroke, the distributor rotor is pointing to number one electrode in the cap. (If there is any doubt about whether number one position is on its firing stroke at top dead centre, this operation can be carried out after setting the valve/rocker clearances).

3 If the distributor contacts have been renewed, or are now about to be renewed, refer to Chapter 4 for the correct procedure. Note. If the contacts are known to have completed 6000 miles (10000 km) (or 18000 miles for BHCI electronic ignition systems) they should be renewed or refaced.

51 Refitting the inlet manifold and carburettor

1 Using new gaskets at each inlet port, reassemble the inlet manifold to the cylinder block (photo). It is important to remember that there are two supports to be fitted for the carburettor air cleaner, one at studs 2 and 3, the other at studs 6 and 7 (photo). Torque tighten the nuts to the value stated in the specifications section.

2 Now fit the carburettor using a new manifold/carburettor gasket (photo). The third air cleaner support is fitted to the two studs furthest away from the cylinder block before torque tightening the nuts.

3 Reconnect the hose between the water pump and the inlet manifold.

4 Replace the plastic cover (where applicable) over the carburettor.

5 Reconnect the fuel pump/carburettor feed pipe.

6 Reconnect the vacuum pipe between the inlet manifold and the distributor advance and retard mechanism.

52 Refitting the exhaust manifold

1 Position new manifold gaskets at each port making sure that the beaded edge faces outwards (photo). If gaskets with a small cutout are fitted they should be fitted with the cutout downwards. Gaskets which have one straight section in the port hole should be fitted with the straight edge uppermost. Now fit the manifold (photo).

2 Torque tighten the manifold in position to the valves shown in the specifications section. Don't forget the pressed steel cover to which the air cleaner is connected.

53 Valve/rocker adjustment

1 Fit the valve pushrods into their respective positions making sure that they are running through the cutaways in the pushrod guide plates.

44.3a Torque tightening the flywheel securing bolts

44.3b A suitable flywheel locking device

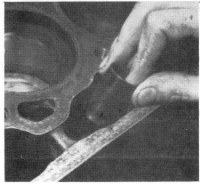
45.1 A cam follower being refitted

45.2 Positioning the cylinder head gasket

45.4 Refitting the cylinder head

45.5 Torque tightening the cylinder head

46.1 Refitting the water pump

47.1 Repositioning the alternator

47.2 The alternator earth strap

48.1 The thermostat housing

48.2 Fitting the thermostat into the housing

50.1 Refitting the distributor

51.1a Refitting the inlet manifold

51.1b One of the air cleaner supports

51.2 Refitting the carburettor

52.1a The exhaust manifold gaskets in position

52.1b The exhaust manifold being fitted

53.3 Adjusting the valve/rocker gaps

53.6 Refitting the rocker cover

54.3 The hose support clip being fitted

55.2 Refitting the fan drive belt

55.3 Refitting the alternator drive belt

56.3 Using the transmission mainshaft to align the clutch plate

57.2a The lifting cables for the engine

2 Tighten the rocker a little to correctly position the pushrods then, making sure that they are free to move within the guide plates tighten the latter in position.

3 The rocker adjustment nuts can now be tightened up and the valve clearance adjusted to 0.004 in (0.10 mm) for the inlet valves and 0.014 in (0.35 mm) for the exhaust valves (photo). These are basic settings for a cold engine, and will require checking and possibly adjusting after an initial warming up run on the car later on.

4 The valve clearance on number 1 cylinder should be adjusted when the rocker arms of number 4 cylinder overlap ie at the point when both rocker arms move in different directions at the same time (in balance). Number 2 cylinder valve clearances should be adjusted when number 3 cylinder rockers overlap, number 3 cylinder when number 2 rockers overlap and number 4 when number 1 rockers overlap. If difficulty is encountered when turning the crankshaft the spark plugs can be temporarily removed. Counting from the timing cover end of the engine, inlet valves are numbered 1-3-5-7, and exhaust valves 2-4-6-8.

5 When all the valves have been adjusted, squirt a little engine oil over all the moving parts of the valve gear. This is to make sure that they are lubricated when the engine is started initially.

6 Finally refit the rocker cover (photo).

54 Refitting the water pump pulley, hoses, etc (engine out of the car)

1 Refit the water pump pulley.

2 Refit the hose between the carburettor choke heater and the inlet manifold, noting that the choke connection furthest from the cylinder block connects to the manifold connection furthest from the cylinder block.

3 Refit the hose union at the rear (clutch) end of the cylinder head using a new gasket. Don't forget the hose support clip (photo).

4 Reconnect the remaining carburettor choke connection to the hose union which has just been fitted.

55 Refitting the fan support bracket, stop and drive belts (engine out of the car)

1 Refit the fan and its support bracket to the cylinder block but before positioning the bolts make sure that the engine stop pad is in position.

2 Before tightening the fan/bracket adjustment bolts, fit the fan drive belt (photo) and tension it as described in Chapter 2. Check the adjustment again after tightening the bolts at the fan.

3 Refit the alternator drive belt and adjust it for the same free movement as for the fan drive belt (photo).

56 Refitting the clutch

1 Unless a new clutch has been fitted, make sure that the pressure plate assembly is replaced in the original position relative to the flywheel.

2 Before fitting the pressure plate make sure that the clutch disc is fitted so that the longest part of the central spigot is facing towards the cylinder block.

3 Align the assembly on to the flywheel but do not tighten the fixing screws until the clutch disc is correctly centralised. For this purpose a suitable tabular spanner, a piece of round bar or the transmission unit mainshaft can be used (photo)

4 Torque tighten the nuts to the values shown in the specifications section.

57 Refitting the engine to the transmission

1 Support the transmission unit on the bench using wooden blocks - so that it can be moved as required.

2 Lift the engine using the right hand (exhaust side) engine mounting bracket and the fan support bracket, as near the engine as possible (photos).

3 Carefully lift the engine, making sure that the chains do not foul any of the engine components (such as the carburettor) and lift it towards the transmission.

4 Move the engine and transmission slightly as necessary and bring the two units together. The last half inch or so may be difficult until the dowels and transmission main shaft line up. The two units can finally be drawn together using the bolts. Don't allow the weight of the engine or transmission to be carried on the gearbox main shaft. Fit the clutch cable adjustment bracket.

5 Note the special bolt used for fitting the starter motor at its lower lug (photo).

6 Refit the oil filter.

58 Refitting the engine and transmission to the car

1 Place the engine and transmission on the floor in front of the car and remove the chains.

2 Raise the front of the car using the same protective packing as used when removing the engine and transmission, then with the car handbrake off carefully move the car and portable hoist forwards over the engine. Alternatively the engine can be slid

57.2b The lifting cables for the engine

57.5 The special bolt for the starter motor

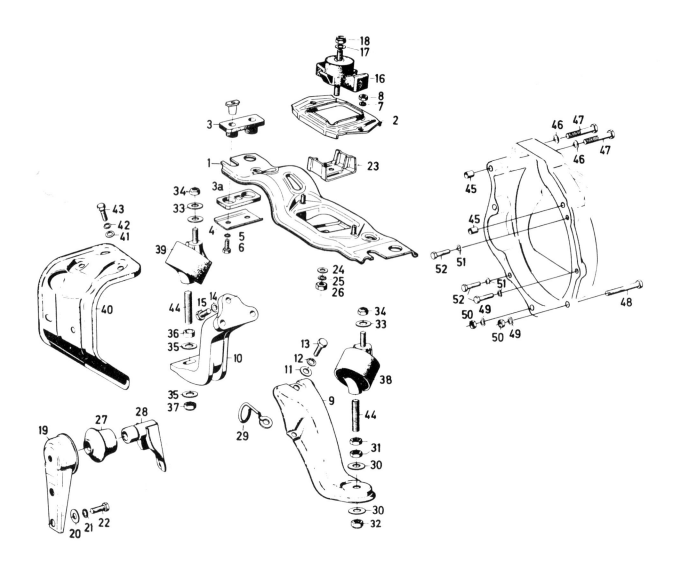

FIG. 1.21. MOUNTING PARTS (SEC. 58)

1 Cross member	14 Plain washer	27 Stop pad, front	40 Guard
2 Stop plate	15 Hex. head screw	28 Holder, stop pad	41 Plain washer
3 Insulating plate, upper	16 Power plant bearing, rear	29 Holder, oil drain hose, front	42 Lock washer
3a Insulating plate, lower	17 Plain washer	30 Plain washer	43 Hex. head screw
4 Washer	18 Lock nut	31 Hex. nut	44 Stud
5 Lock washer	19 Stop, front	32 Lock nut	45 Dowel sleeve
6 Hex. head screw	20 Plain washer	33 Plain washer	46 Washer
7 Lock washer	21 Lock washer	34 Lock nut	47 Hex. head screw
8 Nut	22 Hex. head screw	35 Plain washer	48 Hex. head screw
9 Engine support, left	23 Stop bracket	36 Spacer	49 Washer
10 Engine support, right	24 Plain washer	37 Locknut	50 Hex. nut
11 Plain washer	25 Lock washer	38 Power plant bearing left	51 Washer
12 Lock washer	26 Hex. nut	39 Power plant bearing right	52 Hex. head screw
13 Hex. head screw			

under the car.

3 Taking a great deal of care, slowly lower the car down over the engine making sure that the engine support lugs on the chassis do not foul.

4 Now refit the hoist chains to the engine using the support brackets, passing the rear (right hand or exhaust side) chain around the end of the cylinder head.

5 Carefully lift the engine, turning as necessary and support the

weight temporarily with a trolley jack.

6 The transmission end can be manoeuvred into position once the front end is aligned with the mountings.

7 Now fit the rear mounting cross member to the car and the transmission to the crossmember.

8 Assemble the front engine mountings, not forgetting the engine mounting guard plate on the right hand side.

59 Checking the alignment of the engine and transmission

1 Having fitted the engine and transmission into the car it is now necessary to check its alignment.

2 Check the distance between each brake disc and the inner edge of the lower wishbone pivot, using a ruler (photo). The distance must be equal to within 0.08in (2 mm); any correction required must be made at the mounting crossmember.

3 Now check the distance between the sides of the crankshaft pulley and the edges of the chassis frame side members using a tape measure (photo). The maximum permissible deviation is 0.08 in (2 mm) and adjustment should be made at the supports.

4 Position the stop on the front transverse chassis frame member so that the rubber pad locates without being placed under tension. If new engine/transmission mounts have been fitted the stop should be pulled downwards 0.12 to 0.2 in (3 to 5 mm) to allow for settlement of the rubber mounts. Tighten the stop in the required position.

5 Place a straight edge across the lower wishbone pivot at its forward bush and measure the height from each of the shoulders on the transmission. The maximum difference must not exceed 0·16 in (4 mm). Adjustment can be made at the left-hand mount by altering the position of the nuts at the engine bracket below the mount. Adjustment at the right-hand mount may only be made by fitting a different thickness spacer. These are available in thicknesses of 0.2, 0.28 and 0.36 in (5,7 and 9 mm).

6 After any corrections have been made at any of the points above, recheck all the alignment settings.

7 Refit the twin horns below the left-hand engine mounting.

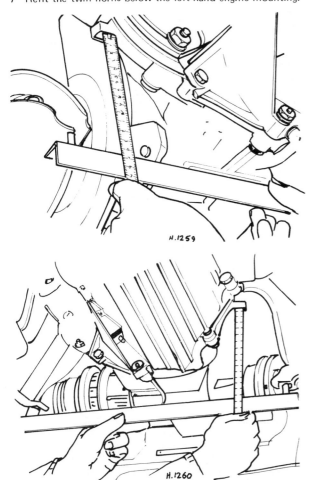

Fig. 1.22. Power unit height measurement (Sec. 59)

59.2 Checking the alignment of the power unit after refitting to the car

59.3 Checking the alignment of the power unit after refitting to the car

60 Refitting the gearchange linkage

1 Fit the gearshift tube through the holder, then assemble the holder to the transmission unit using the two uppermost rear studs.

2 Assemble the gearshift tube lever and intermediate lever to the transmission gearshift lever.

3 Refit the gearshift tube lever to the gearshift tube making sure that the splines are correctly aligned. This is a two man job since it will need one person to manipulate the gear lever from inside the car and thus move the gearshift tube backwards and forwards.

61 Refitting the clutch cable

1 Refit the clutch cable and fit it to the operating lever.

2 Fit the outer cable ends to the bracket and adjust such that there is a total free pedal travel of 0.59 to 0.78 in (15 to 20 mm).

3 Further details of clutch adjustment are detailed in Chapter 5.

62 Refitting the radiator and associated hoses

1 Install the radiator, making sure that when it is correctly fitted, the rubber fan cover sits flat against the cowl around its complete circumference.
2 Reconnect the top and bottom radiator hoses to the thermostat housing and lower water pump connection respectively. The latter connection has an intermediate coolant pipe fitted.
3 Reconnect the two heater hoses. The upper hose (the one with the bleed valve) is connected to the carburettor inlet manifold. The lower hose is connected to the union at the rear end of the cylinder head.

63 Refitting the remaining items in the engine compartment

1 Reconnect the engine earth strap between the crossmember at the rear of the engine and the engine block. Make sure that the surfaces are clean and free from rust or other corrosion.
2 Reconnect the accelerator linkage at the carburettor, then fit the clip in place for security.
3 Reassemble the spring loaded ball and socket joint at the bulkhead end of the carburettor linkage.
4 Reconnect the hydraulic brake connections at the union on the bulkhead, running the flexible hose below the accelerator linkage rod.
5 Refit the brake pedal support.
6 Refit the distributor cap and spark plug leads.
7 Reconnect the leads to the water temperature sensor at the rear of the cylinder head, to the ignition coil, carburettor idle shut off valve, oil pressure switch, reverse light leads, distributor, starter motor (photo) and alternator.
8 Reconnect the fuel pipe and in-line filter to the fuel pump.
9 Reconnect the speedometer drive to the transmission.
10 Reconnect the brake servo pipe to the inlet manifold.
11 Refit the air cleaner to the three mounting brackets, making sure that the rubber gasket is correctly positioned on the carburettor.
12 Reconnect the air intake hose, the warm air intake hose, the engine breather hose and the vacuum unit suction pipe to the inlet manifold.
13 Refit the sill panel.
14 Refit the engine bonnet and re-connect the windscreen washer hose. Adjust the bonnet position as necessary using the free movement at the hinge lugs.

64 Refitting the drive shafts, transverse stabilizer and exhaust pipe

1 Reconnect the drive shafts at the brake discs. It is essential to refit the insulating washer which must be undamaged. Tighten the bolts to the value given in the specifications torque section.
2 Refit the transverse stabilizer bar to the rear arm of the lower wishbone. Tighten the bolts to the correct torque.
3 Reconnect the front exhaust pipe and primary silencer. Make sure that all the fixing straps are reconnected.

65 Preparation for engine start-up

1 Before topping up the lubrication and cooling systems, have a last look round for loose hose connections, brake hose unions, transmission and engine sump plugs, etc.
2 Whilst keeping an eye on the fluid level, bleed the braking system as described in Chapter 9.
3 Replenish the engine sump and transmission units with the recommended type and quantity of lubricant.
4 Fill the radiator with an antifreeze and water (or corrosion inhibitor and water) mixture of the recommended proportions (see Chapter 2.)

63.7 The starter motor connections being refitted

5 Reconnect the battery earth strap and replace the rear seat.

66 Engine start-up and test run

1 Start the car engine in the usual manner. There may be some difficulty in starting because enough fuel to fill the carburettor float chamber will need to be sucked from the tank.
2 Check that all the warning lights, main lights and direction indicators are fully functional.
3 Run the engine at fairly high speed with the heater bleed valve open. This may be closed when the coolant is seen to flow out, but don't forget to keep an eye on the level in the radiator, and also, for any signs of leakage.
4 Carry on running the car engine like this until the thermostat opens, which is indicated by a sudden drop in the coolant level, then top up again to the base of the filler neck.
5 When the engine has fully warmed up check, and adjust if necessary, the valve/rocker clearances. The correct clearance for a warm engine is given in the specifications section.
6 As soon as is practically possible after the initial engine run arrange for the dynamic ignition timing to be checked, and adjusted if necessary.
7 Finally recheck the coolant level, the engine and transmission oil levels and the brake fluid level. Also check the tightness of the cooling system hose clips.
8 Now test run the car to make sure that everything is working satisfactorily. On the initial run it is advisable to check after a mile or two that there is no water or oil splashing about beneath the bonnet.

PART D – USA VERSION DIFFERENCES

67 General note

As previously stated there are a number of differences between the engines which comply with the European emission control requirements and those which comply with the USA requirements. These differences are listed under the various sections in the manual and reference should always be made to the appropriate section for any special instructions when carrying out repairs.

68 Double port inlet manifold (1971 models)

1 The double port inlet manifold was introduced to permit preheating of the fuel from stage 1 of the carburettor. The stage 1 fuel port is preheated from the engine coolant in the manifold, whilst the second fuel port allows the stage 2 fuel to be separately guided to the engine. This system ensures maximum atomization of the fuel/air mixture.

2 The stage 1 port is not round, but the correct gasket has a round opening. This is, in fact correct and must not be interfered with.

3 In cases of gasket damage or where fuel is found in the depression of the inlet manifold, a paper gasket part number 059 129 799 should be fitted each side of the existing flange gasket.

4 The maximum carburettor/intake manifold nut torque is 11 ± 0.7 lb ft (1.5 ± 0.1 kgm).

FIG. 1.24. SECTIONAL VIEW OF DOUBLE PORT INLET MANIFOLD (SEC. 68)

c   Carburettor
d   Fuel port, stage 1
e   Pre-heating port, stage 1
f   Fuel port, stage 2

FIG. 1.23. DOUBLE PORT INLET MANIFOLD AND GASKET (SEC. 68)

a   Stage 1 port   b   Gasket

PART E — FAULT DIAGNOSIS

69 General note

1 The items listed in this Section cannot be considered to be the only ones which might give trouble. However, the list is as comprehensive as is practically possible and should save a lot of time and trouble in the event of breakdown, failure to start, unsatisfactory running, etc. Even if you are unable to rectify the fault at the roadside, the information given will perhaps enable you to continue motoring for a while knowing that you can carry out the repairs later.

Many of the items listed, eg. fuel and ignition faults are not directly associated with the engine section of the manual. However, reference needs to be made to them in this Section and, where diagnosis shows them to be responsible, further reference should be made to the relevant Section.

70 Fault finding table - Engine

Symptom	Reason/s	Remedy
No current at starter motor	Discharged or defective battery	Charge or replace battery. Push-start car in an emergency.
	Loose or corroded battery terminals	Tighten or clean the terminals.
	Defective ignition switch or broken wiring	Temporarily by-pass the existing wiring with another lead.
	Engine earth strap disconnected	Check and retighten strap.
Current at starter motor	Jammed starter motor drive pinion	Place car in gear and rock to and fro. If the fault still persists, remove the starter.
	Defective starter motor	Remove and recondition.
No spark at spark plug	Ignition leads damp or wet	Wipe dry the distributor cap and ignition leads.
	Ignition leads to spark plugs loose	Check and tighten at both spark plug and distributor cap ends.

Symptom	Reason/s	Remedy
	Shorted or disconnected low tension leads	Check the wiring on the low tension terminals of the coil and to the distributor.
	Dirty, incorrectly set, or pitted contact breaker points	Clean and adjust the contacts.
	Faulty condenser	Check contact breaker points for arcing, remove and fit new.
	Defective ignition switch	By-pass switch with wire.
	Ignition leads connected wrong way round	Remove and replace leads to spark plugs in correct order.
	Faulty coil	Remove and fit new coil.
	Contact breaker point spring earthed or broken	Check spring is not touching metal part of distributor. Check insulator washers are correctly placed. Renew points if the spring is broken.
No fuel at carburettor float chamber or at jets	No petrol in petrol tank	Refill tank!
	Vapour lock in fuel line. (In hot conditions or at high altitude)	Blow into petrol tank, allow engine to cool, or apply a cold wet rag to the fuel line.
	Blocked float chamber needle valve	Remove, clean, and replace.
	Fuel line filter blocked	Remove, clean, and replace.
	Choked or blocked carburettor jets	Dismantle and clean.
	Faulty fuel pump	Remove, overhaul and replace.
Excess of petrol in cylinder or carburettor flooding	Wet plugs due to excessively rich mixture	Remove and dry spark plugs or with wide open throttle, push-start the car.
	Float damaged or leading or needle not seating	Remove, examine, clean and replace float and needle valve as necessary.
	Float lever incorrectly adjusted	Remove and adjust correctly.
Fuel/air mixture leaking from cylinder	Burnt out exhaust valves	Remove cylinder head, renew defective valves.
	Sticking or leaking valves	Remove cylinder head, clean, check, and renew valves as necessary.
	Worn valve guides and stems	Remove cylinder head and renew valves and valve guides.
	Weak or broken valve springs	Remove cylinder head, renew defective springs.
	Blown cylinder head gasket. (Accompanied by increase in noise)	Remove cylinder head and fit new gasket.
	Worn pistons and piston rings	Dismantle engine, renew pistons and rings.
	Worn or scored cylinder bores	Dismantle engine, rebore, renew pistons and rings.
Incorrect adjustments	Ignition timing wrongly set	Check and reset ignition timing.
	Contact breaker points incorrectly gapped	Check and reset contact breaker points.
	Incorrect valve clearances	Check and reset clearances.
	Incorrectly set spark plugs	Remove, clean, and regap.
	Carburation too rich or too weak	Tune carburettor/s for optimum performance.
Carburation and ignition faults	Dirty contact breaker points	Remove, clean, and replace.
	Fuel filters blocked causing top end fuel starvation	Dismantle, inspect, clean, and replace all fuel filters.
	Distributor automatic balance weights or vacuum advance and retard mechanisms not functioning correctly	Overhaul distributor.
	Faulty fuel pump giving top end fuel starvation	Remove, overhaul, or fit exchange reconditioned fuel pump.
Oil being burnt by engine	Badly worn, perished or missing valve stem oil seals	Remove, fit new oil seals to valve stems.
	Excessively worn valve stems and valve guides	Remove cylinder head and fit new valves and valve guides.
	Worn piston rings	Fit oil control rings to existing pistons or purchase new pistons.
	Worn pistons and cylinder bores	Fit new pistons and rings, rebore cylinders.
	Excessive piston ring gap allowing blow-by	Fit new piston rings.
	Piston oil return holes choked	Decarbonise engine and pistons.

Symptom	Reason/s	Remedy
Oil being lost due to leaks	Leaking oil filter gasket	Inspect and fit new gasket as necessary.
	Leaking top cover gasket	Inspect and fit new gasket as necessary.
	Leaking timing case gasket	Inspect and fit new gasket as necessary.
	Leaking sump gasket	Inspect and fit new gasket as necessary.
	Loose sump plug	Tighten, fit new gasket if necessary.
Unusual noises from engine	Worn valve gear. Noisy tapping from top cover.	Check valve clearances.
	Worn big end bearing. Regular heavy knocking	Fit new bearings, and crankshaft if necessary.
	Worn timing chain (rattling from front of engine)	Fit new timing chain.
	Worn main bearings. (Rumbling and vibration)	Fit new bearings, and crankshaft if necessary.
	Worn crankshaft. (Knocking, rumbling and vibration)	Regrind crankshaft, fit new main and big end bearings.

71 Checking cylinder compression pressures

1 In cases of inadequate engine power or faulty running a very useful diagnostic check can be carried out by checking the cylinder pressures. This should only be carried out once the engine has reached normal operating temperature.

2 A suitable pressure tester should be fitted to each spark plug hole in turn with the remaining plugs removed.

3 Now crank the engine (about ten times is sufficient) with the accelerator pedal floored and note the pressure. With a fully charged battery the following values should be obtained:-

Engine	Compression ratio	Pressure
80 DIN HP	9.1 : 1	128 to 170 psi (9.0 to 12.0 atm)
90 DIN HP	10.2 : 1	142 to 185 psi (10.0 to 13.0 atm)
100 DIN HP	10.2 : 1	142 to 148 psi (10.0 to 13.0 atm)

4 The maximum permissible difference between cylinders is 30 psi (2.0 atm).

5 If any deviations from these figures are recorded, first check the valve/rocker clearances.

6 If these are satisfactory, spray a little engine oil into each spark plug hole to assist the piston rings in sealing. If no improvement occurs worn valves or a blowing cylinder head gasket are indicated. If an improvement is obtained, faulty piston rings or a worn cylinder bore are indicated.

Chapter 2 Cooling, heating and exhaust systems

For modifications, and information applicable to later models, see Supplement at end of manual

Contents

Specifications

Cooling system

Type	Pressurised with water pump and fan
Pump type	Centrifugal, belt driven from engine
Fan type	8 bladed, belt driven from engine
Radiator cap blow-off pressure	12.8 ± 1.42 psi (0.9 ± 0.1 atii)
Radiator cap inward relief pressure	0.57 to 1.14 psi (0.04 to 0.08 atii)
Cooling system leak test pressure	14.22 psi (1 atii)
Thermostat begins to open	83º C (181º F) approximately
fully open	93º C (199º F) approximately
Coolant capacity	13.2 pints (7.5 litres, 16 US pints) approximately
Radiator type	Cross contra-flow

Note: Some cars for the US market have a five bladed electric fan which switches on at a coolant temperature of 92º C (197º F) and switches off at 82º C (180º F). On early models the switch is fitted in the bottom of the radiator; for 1973 models it is located beneath the alternator, in the water pump/radiator connecting tube.

Heating system

Type	Fresh air, blower assisted
Heating medium	Engine coolant
Maximum airflow with blower	413.2 cu. ft/min (11.7 m^3/min) at 90 mph
Maximum airflow without blower	293.1 cu. ft/min (8.3 m^3/min) at 90 mph
Blower ventilator diameter	6.77 in. (172 mm)
Blower blade diameter	6.61 in. (168 mm)
Number of blades	5
Blower regulator resistance	5.4 ohm, variable
Voltage	5.0 to 13.0 volts
Current	1.7 to 5.3 amps
Speed	1160 to 1500 rpm

Exhaust system
The system comprises:-

a. Front 'siamese' exhaust pipe
b. Primary silencer and pipe
c. Final silencer
d. Tailpipe
e. Tailpipe extension

Torque wrench settings

	lb ft	kgm
Exhaust manifold end plate	14.47	2.0
Thermostat cover	7.2	1.0
Heater flange to cylinder head	14.5	2.0
Thermostat to cylinder head	14.5	2.0
Fan to hub	7.2	1.0
Air guide ring to fan support	14.5 to 18.1	2.0 to 2.5
Fan support to engine block	32.5	4.5

Temperature transmitter	...	...	...	...	...	7.2	1.0
Water pump to engine block (8 mm)		...	...	...	...	14.5	2.0
Water pump to engine block (6 mm)		...	...	...	...	8.7	1.2
Heater nut (6 mm)	...	...	...	...	...	3.6	0.5
Coolant drain plug	...	...	...	...	...	10.8	1.5
Radiator strut hex. head screw	...	...	...	...	5.1	0.7
Radiator rubber bearing nut	...	...	...	...	13.0	1.8
Fan to flange hex. head screw	...	...	...	...	7.2	1.0
Stop screw, hex. head (8 mm)	...	...	...	...	18.1	2.5
Water pump pulley	...	...	...	...	...	7.2	1.0

All torque values are ± 15% except where otherwise specified.

1 General description

1 With the exception of the USA models manufactured prior to 1973, the cooling system of all models is similar and is conventional in form. Points to note are the water heated induction manifold and automatic choke, although the latter item is not fitted to any USA models from 1972 onwards. The main difference in the cooling circuit for the pre - 1973 USA models is the repositioned thermostat to the induction manifold. This allows very rapid warming up owing to the radiator being by-passed until the thermostat opens. For 1973 the USA cooling circuit reverted to the European version with the exception of the water heated automatic choke which was still not used, and the addition of an electric fan.

2 Water for the heater is tapped from the engine block and is routed through a heat exchanger and back to the pump. Heating is basically by air and is ducted into the car via an exterior intake forward of the base of the windscreen. When the heater is not in use and ventilation only is required, the heat exchanger is by-passed. A booster fan is provided to give heating or ventilation whilst the car is stationary or at low speed. Air distribution to the car interior is through slots at the top of the instrument panel, variable direction louvres on either side of the instrument panel and vents in the foot area. Slots are provided at window height on the rear side panels to permit airflow through the car.

3 The only special note regarding the exhaust system is for when replacements are required. Since there are differences between the various models, the exact type must be specified.

2 Checking the cooling system for leaks

1 If leakage is suspected from the cooling system there are two basic checks which can be carried out. However, make sure that the coolant level is definitely going down appreciably since there

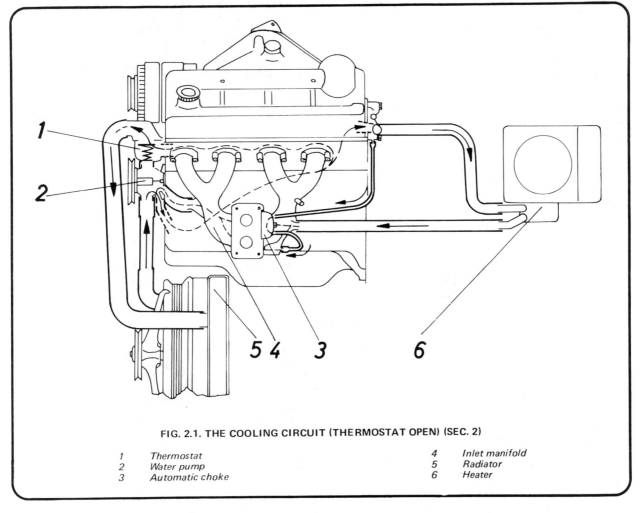

FIG. 2.1. THE COOLING CIRCUIT (THERMOSTAT OPEN) (SEC. 2)

1	Thermostat		4	Inlet manifold
2	Water pump		5	Radiator
3	Automatic choke		6	Heater

will be some drop in level when comparing hot with cold.

2   There is one very important thing to remember when checking the cooling system, and it is that since the system is pressurised it has the effect of raising the boiling point of the coolant. Therefore if the radiator cap is suddenly removed it can cause a pressure drop in the system and the hand can be scalded as steam and boiling water escape.

3   Whenever the cap needs to be removed from a hot system, always use a thick cloth to cover and hold the cap then turn the cap slowly to the first stop until the pressure has equalized (ie the hissing has stopped). The cap can now be depressed slightly and turned further, then removed. If the system has been boiling, keep well clear of the radiator filler because it is possible for air locks to occur which will suddenly release gushes of very hot water.

4   To test the cooling system for leaks, a proprietary hand pump specially manufactured for the purpose should be used. When a pressure of 14.22 psi is applied there should be no pressure drop over a period of 1 to 2 minutes. Make sure that when fitting the pump the coolant level is correct and the sealing lip on the filler neck is clean. It may be necessary to apply pressure two ir three times to trace the leaking coolant.

5   To check the pressure relief valve in the radiator cap it can be tested using the hand pump also. The blow-off pressure should be 12.8 $\pm$ 1.42 psi.

6   To test the inward relief valve or vacuum valve remove the radiator cap from the engine, press the sides of the top coolant hose together and then refit the radiator cap. When the hose is released it should return to its correct shape and air should be heard entering the system via the valve in the cap.

3   Draining the cooling system

1   To drain the cooling system, initially place a container of adequate size beneath the radiator drain plug.

2   Set the the centre heater control lever at warm.

3   Remove the radiator cap and open the bleed valve screw on the upper of the two hoses (this one goes to the heater).

4   Using a socket spanner remove the radiator drain plug and allow all the water to drain.

5   Before refitting the plug, make sure that the washer is clean and intact, and the sealing surface on the radiator is clean.

4   Flushing the cooling system

1   With the passage of time, sludge tends to build up in the cooling system. If this is severe, one of the proprietary brands of flushing compounds can be used to clear the system.

2   Since most manufacturers recommend that the antifreeze is renewed at least every other year, it is advisable to flush through the system at this time.

3   Flushing agents need not be used unless trouble is suspected but it is a good idea to run water straight through the radiator first from the top and out of the drain hole, and then reverse the process by holding a hose against the drain hole and letting water flow from the filter. Alternatively the bottom radiator hose can be removed and water forced in through the orifice.

5   Filling the cooling system

1   Before refilling the cooling system, give all the hoses and hose clips a good checkover. With time the clips tend to relax slightly and hoses deteriorate. Renew any suspect hoses.

2   If antifreeze is to be added reference should be made to the table to determine the correct strength required.

3   If antifreeze is not to be added a suitable inhibitor should be used. However, no harm is done by leaving antifreeze in the system during the summer without the use of an inhibitor.

4   Before filling the system set the heater lever at warm and open the bleed screw on the heater hose.

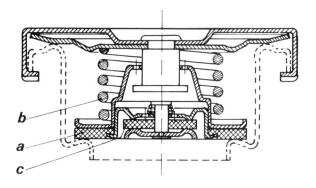

FIG. 2.2. SECTIONAL VIEW OF THE RADIATOR PRESSURE CAP (SEC. 2)

a   *Pressure relief valve*
b   *Spring*
c   *Inward relief valve or vacuum valve*

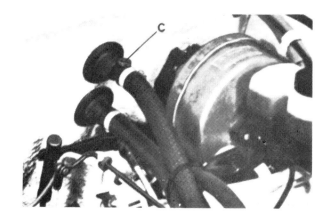

Fig. 2.3. Cooling system bleed valve (c) (Sec. 3)

Fig. 2.4. Radiator drain plug (a) (Sec. 3)

5   Add the coolant until it is seen to seep from the bleed screw, then tighten the screw.

6   Now run the engine at a fast idle speed, checking the level periodically. With the engine cold the coolant level should be at the base of the filler neck.

7   Check all the hose connections for signs of coolant leakages.

Antifreeze required	Protection down to
4.6 pints (2.6 litres)	-20°C (-4° F)
5.2 pints (3 litres)	-25°C (-13°F)
5.8 pints (3.3 litres)	-30°C (-22°F)
6.2 pints (3.6 litres)	-35°C (-31°F)

Only use a good quality antifreeze such as Castrol antifreeze.

6   Heater - removal, dismantling and refitting

1   Initially drain the engine coolant as described elsewhere in this section.

2   Disconnect the battery earth strap (the battery in underneath

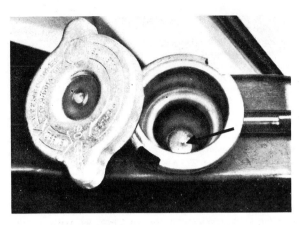

Fig. 2.5. The radiator filler cap and neck (Sec. 5)

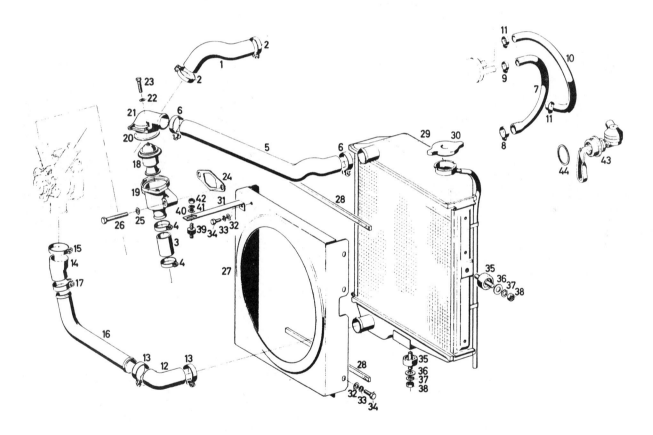

FIG. 2.6. THE RADIATOR, THERMOSTAT AND ASSOCIATED HOSES (SEC. 5)

1 Hose	12 Coolant hose	23 Hex. head screw	34 Hex. head screw
2 Clip	13 Clip	24 Gasket	35 Rubber bearing
3 Water hose	14 Coolant hose	25 Plain washer	36 Plain washer
4 Clip	15 Clip	26 Hex. head screw	37 Washer
5 Coolant hose	16 Coolant pipe	27 Cowl	38 Hex. nut
6 Clip	17 Clip	28 Seal	39 Metal/rubber bearing
7 Heater line	18 Thermostat	29 Radiator	40 Plain washer
8 Clip	19 Housing thermostat	30 Cap	41 Washer
9 Clip	20 Seal	31 Strut	42 Hex. nut
10 Coolant hose	21 Cover, thermostat housing	32 Plain washer	44 Seal
11 Clip	22 Washer	33 Washer	

the rear seat cushion).

3 Remove the bleed screw completely from the upper heater hose, taking care not to damage the seal.

4 Slacken both heater hose clips and pull off the hoses.

5 If it is necessary to remove the blower motor guard, the metal tabs need to be folded back and the guard lifted off.

6 Remove the passenger's side knee protection. This is held on with seven self tapping screws; the one at the side of the driver's parcel shelf also has a locking nut which can be reached after opening the glove compartment lid.

7 Remove the driver's side knee protection. This is held on by three self tapping screws.

8 Remove both self tapping screws and washers which hold the instrument panel trim to the lower part of the heater.

9 Pull off the instrument panel trim and (where applicable) the centre shelf.

10 Carefully prise open the spring clips which are used to retain the heater control cables for the foot area flap (right hand), windshield flap (left hand) and heater valve(left hand). Also unhook the right angled end fittings.

11 Pull off the plug connecter (brown lead) from the heater controls and the red lead which is connected to the emergency warning light switch.

12 Working from the passenger side remove the two nuts and washers, and the self tapping screw, and ease the heater downwards.

13 Remove the heater from the car to a suitable work bench if further work is to be carried out.

14 The heater body can be removed from the heat exchanger after initially removing the nut which holds the heater valve linkage bracket, and then disconnecting the heater valve plunger rod.

15 The heater body upper and lower halves are clipped together. These clips can be prised carefully off then the two halves separated. If necessary a blunt knife edge or similar tool can be used to separate the two parts; when separated the top half can be lifted off.

16 The heat exchanger can now be lifted out of the lower part of the body.

17 If it is required to check the heater for leakage, blank one of the connecting pipes and apply an air pressure of 14 psi to the other connection. The whole heat exchanger can then be immersed in a container of water and any leakage noted. On completion the item must be dried using an air line.

18 The blower motor can, easily, be removed from the top half of the body by removing the two electrical connections (they cannot be interchanged) and springing back the four clips which secure the motor body.

Note. Since the fan assembly is shrunk on to the motor shaft, and balanced to reduce vibration and increase bearing life, it must not be removed from the motor.

19 When refitting the blower motor and fan blade assembly note that the spring clips locate in slots in the cover plate at the fan end. It will be necessary to juggle the motor around to align it.

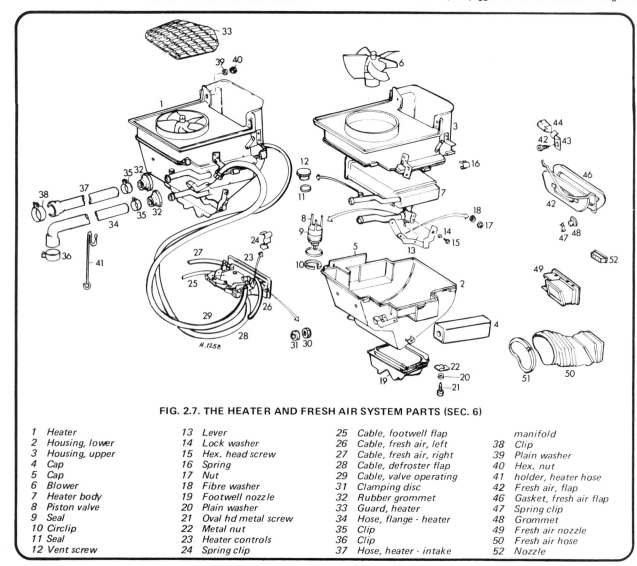

FIG. 2.7. THE HEATER AND FRESH AIR SYSTEM PARTS (SEC. 6)

1	Heater	13	Lever	25	Cable, footwell flap		manifold
2	Housing, lower	14	Lock washer	26	Cable, fresh air, left	38	Clip
3	Housing, upper	15	Hex. head screw	27	Cable, fresh air, right	39	Plain washer
4	Cap	16	Spring	28	Cable, defroster flap	40	Hex. nut
5	Cap	17	Nut	29	Cable, valve operating	41	holder, heater hose
6	Blower	18	Fibre washer	31	Clamping disc	42	Fresh air, flap
7	Heater body	19	Footwell nozzle	32	Rubber grommet	46	Gasket, fresh air flap
8	Piston valve	20	Plain washer	33	Guard, heater	47	Spring clip
9	Seal	21	Oval hd metal screw	34	Hose, flange - heater	48	Grommet
10	Circlip	22	Metal nut	35	Clip	49	Fresh air nozzle
11	Seal	23	Heater controls	36	Clip	50	Fresh air hose
12	Vent screw	24	Spring clip	37	Hose, heater - intake	52	Nozzle

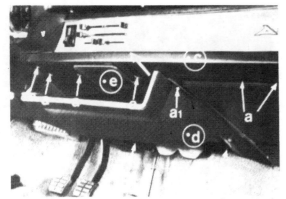

FIG. 2.8. PASSENGER'S SIDE KNEE PROTECTION (SEC. 6)

a   *Self tapping screws*
a₁ *Self tapping screw with locking nut*
b   *Self tapping screws*
c   *Right knee protection*
d   *Instrument panel trim*
e   *Ashtray*

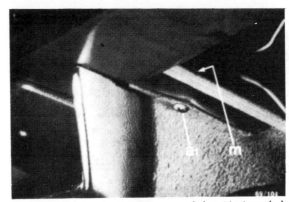

Fig. 2.9. Close-up of self-tapping screw (a₁) and locknut (m) (Sec. 6)

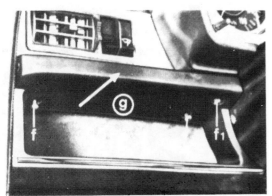

FIG. 2.10. DRIVER'S SIDE KNEE PROTECTION (SEC. 6)

f   *Self tapping screws*
f₁ *Self tapping screw*
g   *Knee protection*

Fig. 2.11. Prising open the spring clip (a) (Sec. 6)

Fig. 2.12. Heater fixing nuts (a) and self tapping screw (b) (Sec. 6)

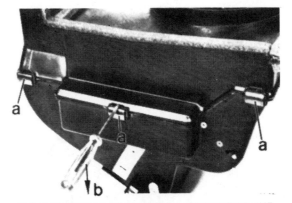

FIG. 2.13. SEPARATING THE TWO HALVES OF THE HEATER BODY (SEC. 6)

a   *Spring clips*
b   *Prising tool (eg. screwdriver)*

It can only be fitted in one position.

20 Fit the blower into the upper part of the housing, prise back the blades slightly and refit the securing clips.

21 Reconnect both motor leads.

22 Check that the Prestic seal between the two halves of the body and the foam padding around the top are intact. Replace or tidy this up as necessary.

23 Mate the two halves of the body together and refit the spring clips. This operation may require the use of circlip pliers with a cranked end to spread the clips apart.

24 The heater can now be refitted to the car.

25 Reconnect the hooked ends of the heater control cables which were removed.

26 Place the heater control levers in the OFF position then fit new spring clips for the control cable sleeves. It is essential that the cable sleeves project at least 0.2 in (5 mm) beyond the spring clip.

27 When each of the above cables is connected, check the operation of the foot area flap, windshield flap and heater valve plunger rod.

28 The remaining items can now be refitted in the reverse order to removal.

29 On completion the coolant can be added and the system bled until free of air.

---

7 Heater valve - replacement

---

1 The heater valve can be replaced whilst in the vehicle after removing the knee protection between the steering column and the heater (see previous section).

2 Remove the hexagon headed screw which holds the heater valve to the heater, and the nut on the linkage.

3 Prise the plunger rod out of the lever.

4 Have a suitable container at hand to catch the coolant then remove the circlip from the end of the heater valve.

5 Remove the retaining plate, seal, O-ring and washer by pulling them off over the plunger rod.

6 Remove the small circlip then take out the washer and seal.

7 Clean the metal parts including the bore of the heater valve.

8 Renew all the rubber parts and coat them lightly with Molykote 1104 grease, together with the bore of the valve.

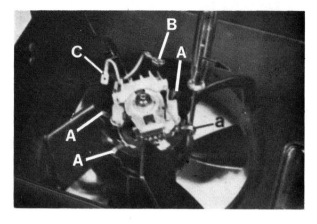

FIG. 2.14. THE BLOWER MOTOR (SEC. 6)

a   Springs
b   Connecting lead
c   Connecting lead

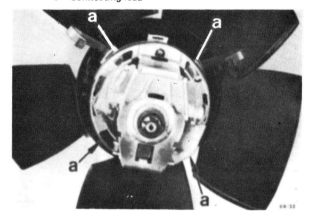

Fig. 2.15. Motor housing cover plate slots (a) (Sec. 6)

FIG. 2.16. COMPONENT PARTS OF THE HEATER VALVE (SEC. 7)

a = Circlip	c = Seal	e = Washer
b = Retaining plate	d = O-ring	f = Lock washer

g = Washer
h = Seal
i = Valve rod and plunger

9   If either of the circlips has been damaged during removal it should be renewed.
10 Reassemble the heater valve in the reverse order to removal.
11 On completion add the coolant and bleed the system free of air.

8   Foot area nozzle - replacement

1   The foot area nozzle can be removed with the heater in the car by unscrewing the two self tapping screws on the front of the lower half of the heater body.

9   Heater controls - removal and installation

1   Remove the battery earth strap, both knee protections and the instrument panel trim as previously described.
2   Take out the ashtray by depressing the spring.
3   Remove the three screws which retain the ashtray. Remove the holder.
4   Disconnect the red and brown leads from the ashtray holder.
5   Remove all the knobs from the control levers.
6   Prise off the clips which hold the cable sleeves.
7   Prise off the clamping discs which hold the assembly to the instrument panel. Ease the assembly away from the panel and pull it downwards.
8   Remove the electrical connections from the heater controls.
9   Remove the control cable sleeves from their clip fixings. Some of the clips have a barb on the end which fits into the elongated slot in the fixing bracket. To release the cable sleeve the barbed end is pressed towards the other end of the slot and released. The other clips are fitted with the barb over the end of the bracket, in which case this end is pulled out to release the barb.
10 Should it be necessary to remove fresh air flap cables first remove the spring clips (see previous paragraph) on the metal plate of the bulkhead below the instrument panel on each side.
11 Remove the eyelet from the flap operating bracket when the flap cable is removed.
12 Before any controls are reinstalled, check the operation of the heater. Both lower heater controls additionally operate the blower motor. At the first notch the blower runs at half speed and at the second notch, full speed. If necessary, the sliding contact may be bent slightly to achieve satisfactory operation.

13 The heater controls can now be fitted in the reverse order to removal. Make sure that new control cable clips are fitted, and that the cable is furthest away from the barbed end of the clip and at least 5 mm of outer sleeve is projecting beyond the clip. Fit the electrical connections as shown in the illustration and note the cutaway in the heater control light socket which the projection on the bulb holder will need to connect with.
14 The control assembly can now be fitted back on to the instrument panel. For this operation it may be necessary to compress the instrument panel and heater control assembly together to enable the clamping discs to be fitted. Always use new clamping discs for this particular operation.

10 Fresh air flap, nozzle and hoses - removal and installation

1   To remove the fresh air flap disconnect the bowden cable from the bracket.
2   Remove the two self tapping screws then take off the flap, bracket and both bearings.
3   Check that the Bowden cable seal and the sealing strip around the flap are intact. Renew or re-stick the seals in place as necessary.

FIG. 2.17. THE HEATER CONTROLS (SEC. 9)

a   Fresh air control, left side
b   Fresh air control, right side
c   Temperature control lever
d   Blower and flow control for windscreen
e   Blower and flow control for footwell

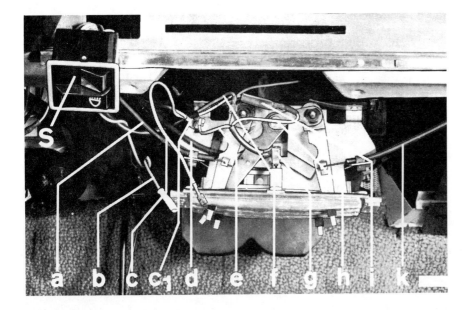

**FIG. 2.18. HEATER CONTROLS
– REMOVAL (SEC. 9)**

a = Bowden cable, left fresh
        air flap
b = Brown lead - to resistor for
        blower motor
c = Brown lead - to cigarette
        lighter (ground)
c₁ = Brown lead - to heater
        controls
d = Bowden cable, heater valve
e = Brown lead - heater control
        illumination
f = Red lead - to cigarette
        lighter
g = Heater control light
h = Yellow/red lead - heater con-
        trol illumination
i   = Coupling, heater control
        illumination connection
k = Bowden cable, right fresh
        air flap
S = Parking light and high beam
        (dip beam) switch
        Tail fog light switch (opt-
        ional extra for fog lights)

4 When replacing the flap make sure that the bowden cable is still slightly tensioned to prevent the flap from rattling. Adjust the cable sleeve as necessary.

5 To remove the side window demist nozzles (the smaller of the two) a pair of pliers or the hooked end of a piece of stiff wire can be used.

6 The adjustable fresh air nozzle can be removed by carefully prising off with a pair of thin bladed screwdrivers or similar.

7 When refitting the fresh air nozzles, note the differences between left and right. This also applies to the hoses.

8 Fit the hose in position first, initially sliding it over the bent-up edge of the bulkhead. Make sure that the seal is securely fitted all round.

9 Now fit the nozzle and again make sure that the seal is intact. If the spring clips are damaged they should be renewed. Guide the hose as necessary until the seal on the nozzle is over the hose outlet.

11 Radiator - removing and refitting

1 Initially drain the radiator coolant as described earlier in this Chapter.

2 Loosen the hose clip at the top of the radiator and pull off the hose.

3 Remove the hexagon headed screw on the stay which is connected to the cowl. Slacken the nut at the other end then swing the stay out of the way.

4 Remove the bottom hose connection at the base of the radiator.

5 Unscrew the nut on the bottom rubber bearing bracket. Note that a flat washer and spring washer are fitted.

6 Now slacken the nut on the rubber bearing which is half way up the radiator on the engine side. Do not lose the large washer.

7 Lift out the radiator, complete with the cowl.

8 The cowl is fitted to the radiator with six hexagon headed screws, spring and flat washers. These can now all be removed.

9 With the radiator removed, any necessary repairs can be carried out. Although in some cases a cracked radiator can satisfactorily be repaired using a resin binding material such as Cataloy, it is generally more satisfactory to solder it. If you have not got the facilities at hand a well equipped garage will repair it at moderate cost.

10 Use an air line to blow the grease and dirt from the air passages. If this is not available a stiff brittle paint brush can be used.

11 It is a good idea to flush through the radiator with a hose

pipe while it is out of the car, to remove any sludge deposits.

12 When the cowl is to be refitted to the radiator check that the rubber buffer strips are intact.

13 The radiator and cowl can now be refitted to the car in the reverse order to removal.

14 Finally check that the rubber seal of the fan cover is correctly fitted all the way round the circumference of the lip on the cowl.

12 Fan - removing and refitting

1 Loosen the two hexagon headed screws which secure the air guide ring to the fan support, then remove the fan belt.

2 Take out the three screws at the other end of the fan support then move the fan and support away from the engine and out of the engine compartment.

3 The fan can be removed by folding back the three tabs on the washer and removing the three screws. The fan can now be pulled off. When replacing it is important that a new tab washer is used.

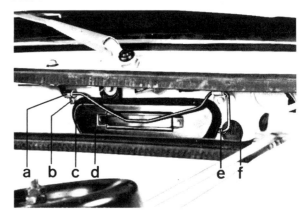

FIG. 2.19. FRESH AIR FLAP (SEC. 10)

a = Fresh air flap bearing
b = Self tapping screw
c = Flap seal
d = Fresh air flap and bracket
e = Bowden cable and eyelet
f = Seal, Bowden cable

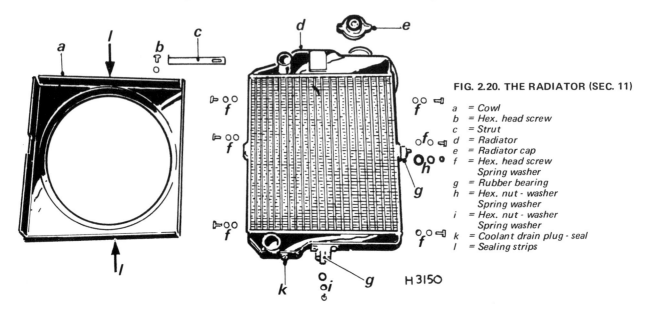

FIG. 2.20. THE RADIATOR (SEC. 11)

a = Cowl
b = Hex. head screw
c = Strut
d = Radiator
e = Radiator cap
f = Hex. head screw
  Spring washer
g = Rubber bearing
h = Hex. nut - washer
  Spring washer
i = Hex. nut - washer
  Spring washer
k = Coolant drain plug - seal
l = Sealing strips

H 3150

4   If the air guide ring, bearing or pulley need to be renewed they cannot be renewed as separate items. It's a case of renewing all or nothing.

5   Before refitting the fan, check that the pad at the engine end of the fan support is in good condition. Renew as necessary.

6   When refitting the fan to the car, first press the stop pad on to the stop then slide the fan support in from the side.

Note. If the fan support is found to be under tension after refitment, the fixing screws of the stop should be slackened and the engine alignment checked as detailed in Chapter 1.

7   Adjust the fan belt tension so that with a pressure of approximately 22 lb (10 kg) there is a deflection of the belt of approximately 0.4 in (10 mm).

13 Thermostat - removing and refitting

1   Initially drain the engine coolant as described previously in this Chapter.

2   Take out the two screws and spring washers holding the cover in position and take out the thermostat.

3   The thermostat can be checked by heating it in water. It should commence to open at about 83°C (181°F) and be fully open at about 93°C (199°F).

4   Before refitting the thermostat back into the housing carefully clean around the lip in the housing where it is to be seated.

5   Also check and clean the cover and body where the O-ring seal is fitted.

6   When fitting the thermostat into the housing make sure that the bridge piece is fore and aft along the line of the engine.

7   Finally replace the cover.

8   If it is necessary to remove the complete housing, first remove the two hose connections then take out the screws which hold the housing to the engine. Use a new gasket when refitting.

14 Water pump - removing and refitting

1   Initially drain the engine coolant as detailed previously in this Chapter.

2   Remove the nut holding the alternator pulley then pull off the pulley. Remove the drive belt.

3   Remove the nut and bolt on the alternator pivot bracket

adjacent to the water pump pulley.

4   Loosen the hose clip then pull off the hose at the base of the water pump.

5   Remove the thermostat (complete) from the engine by removing the two fixing screws and taking off the hose from the water pump.

6   Remove the water pump pulley. For this operation it will be necessary to hold the pulley temporarily whilst the screws are slackened. Do not lose the spring washers.

7   Carefully prise off the pulley using two levers or screwdrivers.

8   Take off the one remaining hose.

9   Remove the five hexagon headed screws retaining the water pump. Note their relative sizes and length. Do not lose the spring washers.

10 Remove the mounting plate and water pump.

Note: The water pump should not be dismantled for repair, but exchanged for a factory overhauled or new item if faulty.

11 Replacement of parts is straightforward but, it is important that new gaskets are used for the water pump and thermostat.

12 When refitting the drive belt it should be tensioned so that with a load of approximately 22 lb (10 kg) there is a deflection of approximately 0.4 in (10 mm) on the longest run between pulleys.

15 Exhaust system - removing and refitting

1   To remove the front exhaust pipe slacken the clip just forward of the primary silencer.

2   Remove the six Thermag nuts connecting the front pipe to the manifold.

3   The front exhaust pipe can now be removed from the car.

4   The primary silencer can be removed by loosening the clip at the inlet side of the final silencer then removing the retaining strap just aft of the primary silencer (photo).

5   The primary silencer can now be removed from the car, complete with its connecting pipe.

6   To remove the final silencer, first slacken the clip at its outlet and take off the tailpipe by removing the two retaining straps at the outlet end.

7   The two retaining straps on the final silencer can now be removed and the silencer taken off.

8   When refitting the parts it is recommended that new clips are used and a new gasket is fitted between the front exhaust pipe

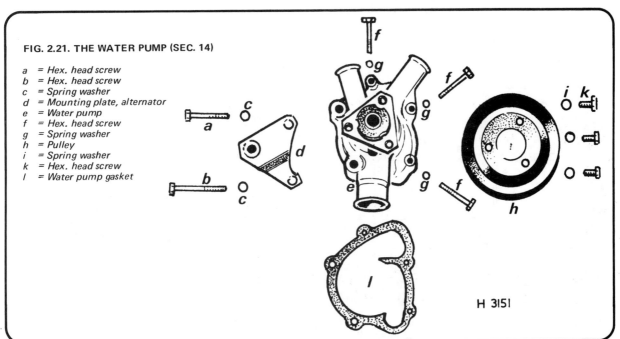

FIG. 2.21. THE WATER PUMP (SEC. 14)

a = Hex. head screw
b = Hex. head screw
c = Spring washer
d = Mounting plate, alternator
e = Water pump
f = Hex. head screw
g = Spring washer
h = Pulley
i = Spring washer
k = Hex. head screw
l = Water pump gasket

H 3151

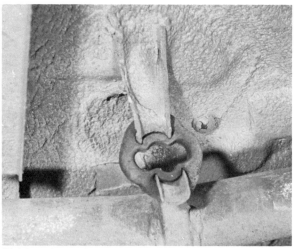

15.4 An exhaust pipe retaining strap

and the manifold unless it can be positively established that they are in a satisfactory condition. Make sure that the rubber pad is fitted above the tailpipe to prevent it from rattling against the underframe.

Note: When ordering replacement parts for the exhaust system, full details regarding the particular vehicle model must be supplied since several types are in use. From 1975 exhaust systems are aluminium coated.

16 Cooling systems on USA versions

1   The main differences between the European and USA versions are described in the introduction to this Chapter.
2   With the belt driven fan versions, replacement of parts can be carried out as detailed for the European versions. Although the thermostat is fitted to the inlet manifold the procedure for replacing parts has not been changed.
3   Where an electric fan is fitted the fan support is held on to the radiator cowl by three hexagon headed bolts.
4   The electric fan sensor is fitted at the base of the radiator on early models, but for 1973 models was re-sited in the connecting tube between the radiator and water pump, beneath the alternator.

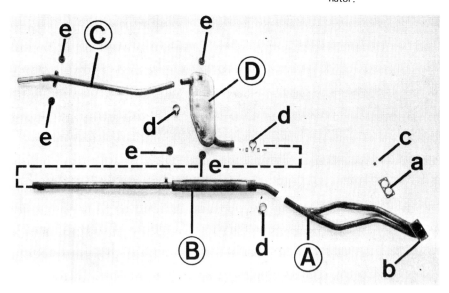

FIG. 2.22. THE EXHAUST SYSTEM (SEC. 15)

A   exhaust pipe, front
B   primary silencer with pipe
C   tailgate
D   final silencer
a   gasket
b   flange
c   Thermag hex. nuts
d   clip with washers, hex. head screw, washer and hex. nut
e   retaining strap

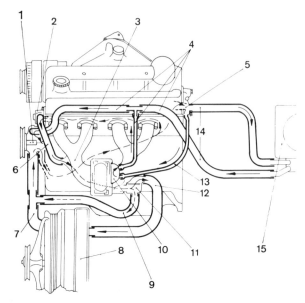

FIG. 2.23. THE COOLING CIRCUIT, PRE-1972 USA VERSIONS (SEC. 16)

1   Water pump
2   Flange, front of cylinder head
3   Inlet manifold
4   Return line, heater and automatic choke
5   Flange, rear of cylinder head
6   Connecting line to inlet manifold
7   Radiator circuit from radiator to water pump
8   Radiator and fan (or electric fan)
9   Bypass line from inlet manifold to water pump
10 Preheating, automatic choke
11 Thermostat, inlet manifold
12 Radiator circuit
13 Automatic choke circuit
14 Heater circuit
15 Heater

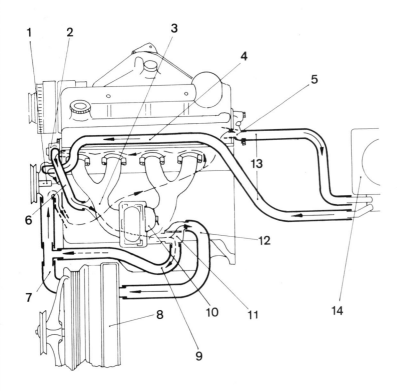

FIG. 2.24. THE COOLING CIRCUIT, 1972 USA VERSIONS (SEC. 16)

1   Water pump
2   Flange, front of cylinder head
3   Inlet manifold
4   Return line, heater
5   Flange, rear of cylinder head
6   Connecting line to inlet manifold
7   Radiator circuit to water pump
8   Radiator and electric fan
9   Bypass line from inlet manifold to water pump
10 Electric automatic choke
11 Thermostat (in inlet manifold)
12 Radiator circuit
13 Heater circuit
14 Heat exchanger (heater)

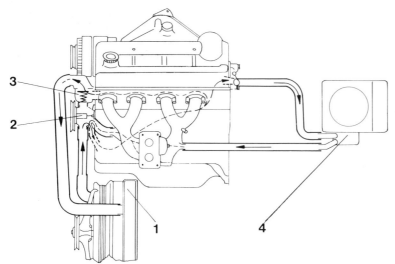

FIG. 2.25. THE COOLING CIRCUIT, 1973 USA VERSIONS (SEC. 16)

1   Radiator
2   Water pump
3   Thermostat
4   Heat exchanger (heater)

Fig. 2.26. Fan sensor (a) on 1973 USA versions (Sec. 16)

17 Fault finding table - Cooling, heating and exhaust systems

Symptom	Reason/s	Remedy
Heat generated in engine not being successfully disposed of by radiator	Insufficient water in cooling system	Top up radiator.
	Fan belt slipping. (Accompanied by a shrieking noise on rapid engine acceleration)	Tighten fan belt to recommended tension or replace if worn.
	Radiator core blocked or radiator grille restricted	Reverse flush radiator, remove obstructions.
	Bottom water hose collapsed, impeding flow	Remove and fit new hose.
	Thermostat not opening properly	Remove and fit new thermostat.
	Ignition advance and retard incorrectly set (Accompanied by loss of power, and perhaps, misfiring)	Check and reset ignition timing.
	Carburettor/s incorrectly adjusted (mixture too weak	Tune carburettor/s.
	Exhaust system partially blocked	Check exhaust pipe for constrictive dents and blockages.
	Oil level in sump too low	Top up sump to full mark on dipstick.
	Blown cylinder head gasket. (Water/steam being forced down the radiator overflow pipe under pressure)	Remove cylinder head, fit new gasket.
	Engine not yet run-in	Run-in slowly and carefully.
	Brakes binding	Check and adjust brakes if necessary.
Too much heat being dispersed by radiator	Thermostat jammed open	Remove and renew thermostat.
	Incorrect specification thermostat fitted allowing premature opening of valve	Remove and replace with new thermostat which opens at a higher temperature.
	Thermostat missing	Check and fit correct thermostat.
Leaks in system	Loose clips on water hoses	Check and tighten clips if necessary.
	Top, bottom, or by-pass water hoses perished and leaking	Check and replace any faulty hoses.
	Radiator core leaking	Remove radiator and repair.
	Thermostat gasket leaking	Inspect and renew gasket.
	Radiator pressure cap spring worn or seal ineffective	Renew radiator pressure cap.
	Blown cylinder head gasket. (Pressure in system forcing water/steam down overflow pipe)	Remove cylinder head and fit new gasket.
	Cylinder wall or head cracked	Dismantle engine, dispatch to engineering works for repair.
	Engine core plug leaking	Fit new core plug.

Chapter 3 Fuel system and carburation

For modifications, and information applicable to later models, see Supplement at end of manual

Contents

Specifications

Carburettor ... ... Solex		
Model	Audi 100 (before 1972)	Audi 100S (before 1972)	Audi 100 (1972/73, with emission control)

	Audi 100 (before 1972)	Audi 100S (before 1972)	Audi 100 (1972/73, with emission control)
Carburettor type ...	Downdraught	Downdraught	Downdraught
Carburettor model and number	35 PDSIT-5, E 16107	35 PDSIT-5, E 16108	35 PDSIT, E 16785
Venturi	27	27	27
Main jet	X147.5	X147.5	X137.5
Air correction jet ...	70	70	100
Idle fuel jet	g55 (in cut-off valve)	g55 (in cut-off valve)	g50 (in cut-off valve)
Idle air jet bore ...	160	160	180
Injection rate per stroke	1.25 ± 0.15 cc	1.25 ± 0.15 cc	1.15 ± 0.15 cc
Choke gap	3.5 ± 0.1 mm (0.138 ± 0.004 in.)	3.5 ± 0.15 mm (0.138 ± 0.004 in.)	4.2 ± 0.15 mm (0.165 ± 0.006 in.)
Throttle gap	1.7 ± 0.1 mm (0.067 ± 0.004 in.)	1.7 ± 0.1 mm (0.067 ± 0.004 in.)	1.0 ± 0.05 mm (0.043 ± 0.001 in.)
Bimetallic spring ...	10 x 0.38 x 470 mm long	10 x 0.38 x 470 mm long	10 x 0.38 x 470 mm long
Float needle valve ...	1.75 (with ball)	1.75 (with ball)	1.75 (with ball)
Float valve seal ...	0.5 mm	0.5 mm	0.5 mm
Float weight ...	7.3g	7.3g	7.3g
Fuel level	11.5 to 13.5 mm (0.452 to 0.531 in.)	11.5 to 13.5 mm (0.452 to 0.531 in.)	13 to 15 mm (0.511 to 0.590 in.)
CO content at idle ...	4% since mid 1969 previously 4.5%	4% since mid 1969 previously 4.5%	1.5 ± 0.2%

Model	Audi 100 Sweden (before 1972)		Audi 100LS (before 1972)	
Carburettor type ...	Downdraught, two stage		Downdraught, two stage	
Carburettor model and number	32 TDID, E16647		32/35 TDID, E16279/E16710 *	
	Stage 1	Stage 2	Stage 1	Stage 2
Venturi	24	27	24	27
Main jet	X125	X145	X125 **	X145
Air correction jet ...	160	120	160 **	100
Idle fuel jet	g50 (in cut-off valve)	50 (idle reserve)	g55 (in cut-off valve)	50 (idle reserve)
Idle air jet bore ...	155	100 (idle reserve)	140	100 (idle reserve)
Injection rate per stroke	1.3 + 0.15 cc		1.65 + 0.15 cc	
Choke gap	3.0 ± 0.15 mm (0.118 ± 0.006 in.)		2.8 ± 0.15 mm (0.110 ± 0.006 in.)	
			3.0 ± 0.15 mm (0.118 ± 0.006 in.) *	

Throttle gap	1.6 ± 0.1 mm (0.063 ± 0.004 in.)	1.6 ± 0.1 mm (0.063 ± 0.004 in.)
Bimetallic spring ...	8 x 0.36 x 470 mm long	8 x 0.38 x 470 mm long
Float needle valve ...	2.0	2.0
Float valve seal ...	2 mm	2 mm
Float weight	7.3g	7.3g
Float level		15.5 to 17.5 mm (0.610 to 0.689 in.)
CO content at idle ...	1 ± 0.2%	4% since mid 1969, previously 4.5%
Air passage jet, (throttle closed)	0130 to 0160	0130 to 0160
Opening tem. of thermo start valve *** ...	-5 to -10° C	-5 to -10° C
Outlet jet (throttle) ***	1.4 mm	1.4 mm
Air jet (cover) *** ...	0.8 mm	0.8 mm
Fuel jet (float chamber) ***	1.1 ± 0.1 mm	1.0 mm

* Automatics
** X120 and 150 respectively, up to Engine No. ZZ 016 348
*** Starting aid

Model	Audi 100LS Sweden (before 1972)		Audi 100LS USA (before 1972)	
Carburettor type ...	Downdraught, two stage		Downdraught, two stage	
Carburettor model and number	32 TDID, E16629/E16646 *		32 TDID, E16240B	
	Stage 1	Stage 2	Stage 1	Stage 2
Venturi	24	27	22	27
Main jet	X125	X145	X102.5	X140
Air correction jet ...	140	100	120	100
Idle fuel jet	g50 (in cut-off valve)	50 (idle reserve)	g47.5 (in cut-off valve)	50 (idle reserve)
Idle air jet bore ...	190	100 (idle reserve)	130	100 (idle reserve)
Injection rate per stroke	1.3 + 0.15 cc		'slow' min. 1.3 + 0.15 cc 'fast' 0.6 to 0.95 cc	
Choke gap	3.0 ± 0.15 mm (0.118 ± 0.006 in.)		3.2 ± 0.2 mm (0.126 ± 0.008 in.)	
Throttle gap ...	1.6 ± 0.1 mm (0.063 ± 0.004 in.)		1.4 ± 0.1 mm (0.055 ± 0.004 in.)	
Bimetallic spring ...	8 x 0.36 x 470 mm long		8 x 0.36 x 470 mm long	
Float needle valve ...	2.0		2.0	
Float valve seal ...	2 mm		0.5 mm	
Float weight	7.3g		7.3g	
Float level	15.5 to 17.5 mm (-.610 to 0.689 in.)		14.0 ± 1 mm (0.551 ± 0.040 in.)	
CO content at idle ...	1 ± 0.2%		1 ± 0.2%	
Air passage jet (throttle closed)	0130 to 0160		0100 to 0130	
Opening temp. of thermo start valve *** ...	−5 to −10° C		−5 to −10° C	
Outlet jet (throttle) ***	1.4 mm		1.4 mm	
Air jet (cover) *** ...	0.8 mm		0.8 mm	
Fuel jet (float chamber) ***	1.1 + 0.1 mm (injection tube 45*)		1.0 mm (injection tube 50)	

* Automatics
*** Starting aid

Model	Audi 100LS Switzerland (before 1972)		Audi 100LS Switzerland Automatic (before 1972)	
Carburettor type ...	Downdraught, two stage		Downdraught, two stage	
Carburettor model and number	32/35 TDID, E16279		32/35 TDID, E16681	
	Stage 1	Stage 2	Stage 1	Stage 2
Venturi	24	27	24	28
Main jet	X125 **	X145	X120	X135
Air correction jet ...	160 **	100	130	100
Idle fuel jet	g55 (in cut-off valve)	50 (idle reserve)	g55 (in cut-off valve)	50 (idle reserve)
Idle air jet bore ...	140	100 (idle reserve)	155	100 (idle reserve)
Injection rate per stroke	1.8 ± 0.15 cc		1.6 ± 0.15 cc (slow)	
Choke gap	2.8 ± 0.15 mm (0.110 ± 0.006 in.)		3.2 ± 0.15 mm (0.126 ± 0.006 in.)	
Throttle gap ...	1.6 ± 0.1 mm (0.063 ± 0.004 in.)		1.6 ± 0.1 mm (0.063 ± 0.004 in.)	
Bimetallic spring ...	8 x 0.36 x 470 mm long		8 x 0.36 x 470 mm long	
Float needle valve ...	2.0		2.0	
Float valve seal ...	2 mm		2 mm	
Float weight	7.3g		7.3g	
Float level	15.5 to 17.5 mm (0.610 to 0.689 in.)		15.5 to 17.5 mm (0.610 to 0.689 in.)	
CO content at idle ...	4% since mid 1969, previously 4.5%		4% since mid 1969, previously 4.5%	
Air passage jet (throttle closed)	0130 to 0160		0130 to 0160	

Opening temp. of thermo start valve ***	−5 to −10º C
Outlet jet (throttle) ***	1.4 mm
Air jet (cover) *** ...	0.8 mm
Fuel jet (float chamber) ***	1.1 + 0.1 mm

** X120 and 150 respectively, up to Engine No. ZZ 016 348
*** Starting aid

Model	Audi 100 Coupe' S (before 1972)	Audi 100LS (1972/73, with emission control)
Carburettor type ...	Two downdraught, two stage	Downdraught, two stage
Carburettor model and number	32/35TDID, E16048 (front) E16049 (rear)	32/35 TDID, E16842/E16843*

	Stage 1 ****	Stage 2 ****	Stage 1	Stage 2
Venturi	24	28	24	27
Main jet	X120	X130	X125	X140
Air correction jet ...	120	100	150	100
Idle fuel jet	50 (in cut-off valve)	50 (idle reserve)	g50 (in cut-off valve)	50 (idle reserve)
Idle air jet bore ...	140	100 (idle reserve)	190	100 (Idle reserve)
Injection rate per stroke	0.9 + 0.15 cc		1.3 + 0.15 cc (slow) 0.87 + 0.1 cc (fast)	
Choke gap	2.5 + 0.15 mm (0.098 + 0.006 in.)		3.5 + 0.15 mm (0.138 + 0.006 in.)	
Throttle gap ...	0.65 + 0.05 mm (0.025 + 0.001 in.)		1.05 + 0.05 mm (-.006 + 0.001 in.) 1.2 + 0.05 mm (0.047 + 0.001 in.)*	
Bimetallic spring ...	8 x 0.36 x 470 mm long		8 x 0.36 x 470 mm long	
Float needle valve ...	2.0		2.0	
Float valve seal ...	1.5 mm		2 mm	
Float weight	7.3g		7.3g	
Float level ...	15.5 to 17.5 mm (0.610 to 0.689 in.)		15.5 to 17.5 mm (0.610 to 0.689 in.)	
CO content at idle ...	4% since mid 1969, previously 4.5%		1.5 + 0.2 %	
Air passage jet (throttle closed)	0130 to 0160		0130 to 0160	

* Automatics
**** Applicable to front and rear carburettors.

Model	Audi 100GL and 100 Coupe' S (1972/73, with emission control)	Audi 100 USA (1972/73, with emission control)
Carburettor type ...	Downdraught, two stage	Downdraught, two stage
Carburettor model and number	32/35 TDID, E16844/E16845*	32/35 TDID, E16849/E16850*

	Stage 1	Stage 2	Stage 1	Stage 2
Venturi	24	28	24	28
Main jet	X127.5	X135	X127.5/125*	X135
Air correction jet ...	140	110	150	100
Idle fuel jet	g50 (in cut-off valve)	50 (idle reserve)	g57.5 (in cut-off valve)	50 (idle reserve)
Idle air jet bore ...	190	100 (idle reserve)	155	100 (idle reserve)
Injection rate per stroke	1.6 + 0.15 cc (slow) 0.87 + 0.1 cc (fast)		min. 1.3 + 0.5 cc (slow) 0.6 to 0.95 cc (fast)	
Choke gap	3.5 + 0.15 mm (0.138 + 0.006 in.)		3.5 + 0.15 mm (0.138 + 0.006 in.)	
Throttle gap ...	1.1 + 0.05 mm (0.043 + 0.001 in.) 1.3 + 0.05 mm (0.051 + 0.001 in.)*		1.45 + 0.05 mm (0.057 + 0.001 in.) 1.7 + 0.1 mm (0.067 + 0.004 in.)*	
Bimetallic spring ...	8 x 0.36 x 470 mm long		8 x 0.38 x 470 mm long	
Float needle valve ...	2.0		2.0	
Float valve seal ...	2 mm		2 mm	
Float weight ...	7.3g		7.3g	
Float level	15.5 to 17.5 mm (0.610 to 0.688 in.)		15.5 to 17.5 mm (0.610 to 0.688 in.)	
CO content at idle ...	1.5 + 0.2%		1.0 + 0.2%	
Air passage jet (throttle closed)	0130 to 0160		0130 to 0160	
Opening temp. of thermo start valve*** ...	−5 to −10º C*		−5 to −10º C*	
Outlet jet (throttle) ***	1.4 mm*		1.4 mm *	
Air jet (cover) ***	0.8 mm *		0.8 mm	
Fuel jet (float chamber) ***	1.0 + 0.1 mm *		1.0 + 0.1 mm *	

* Automatics
*** Starting aid

Model	Audi 100LS (1972/73, without emission control)		Audi 100GL and 100 Coupe' S (1972/73, without emission control)	
Carburettor type ...	Downdraught, two stage		Downdraught, two stage	
Carburettor model and number	32/35 TDID, E16679/E16710 *		32/35 TDID, E16912/E16913 *	
	Stage 1	Stage 2	Stage 1	Stage 2
Venturi	24	27	24	28
Main jet	X125	X145	X120	X135
Air correction jet ...	160	100	130	100
Idle fuel jet ...	g55 (in cut-off valve)	50 (idle reserve)	g55 (in cut-off valve)	50 (idle reserve)
Idle air jet bore ...	140	100 (idle reserve)	155	100 (idle reserve)
Injection rate per stroke	1.65 ± 0.15 cc		1.6 ± 0.15 cc (slow) 0.85 ± 0.1 cc (fast)	
Choke gap	2.8 ± 0.15 mm (0.110 ± 0.006 in.) 3.0 ± 0.15 mm (0.118 ± 0.006 in.) *		3.5 ± 0.15 mm (0.138 ± 0.006 in.)	
Throttle gap	1.6 ± 0.1 mm (0.063 ± 0.004 in.)		1.1 ± 0.05 mm (0.043 ± 0.001 in.) 1.3 ± 0.05 mm (0.051 ± 0.001 in.) *	
Bimetallic spring ...	8 x 0.38 x 470 mm long		8 x 0.36 x 470 mm long	
Float needle valve ...	2.0		2.0	
Float valve seal ...	2 mm		2 mm	
Float weight	7.3g		7.3g	
Float level	15.5 to 17.5 mm (0.610 to 0.688 in.)		15.5 to 17.5 mm (0.610 to 0.688 in.)	
CO content at idle ...	—		—	
Air passage jet (throttle closed		0130 to 0160		0130 to 0160
Opening temp. of thermo start valve *** ...	−5 to −10º C *		−5 to −10º C *	
Outlet jet (throttle) *** ...	1 mm *		1.4 mm *	
Air jet (cover) *** ...	0.8 mm *		0.8 mm *	
Fuel jet (float chamber) ***	1.0 + 0.1 mm *		1.0 mm *	

* Automatics
*** Starting aid

Air cleaner

Type								
Audi 100 ...	...	...	...	...	...	...	...	Disposable
Other models ...	...	...	...	...	...	...	...	Replaceable paper element

Fuel pump

Type ...	...	...	...	...	...	...	...	...	Solex, diaphragm
Operation ...	...	...	...	...	...	...	...	...	Pushrod from camshaft
Pump stroke ...	...	...	...	...	...	...	...	...	0.197 in. (5 mm)
Fuel pump delivery pressure	...	...	...	...	...				3.55 psi (0.25 kg/cm^2) maximum
delivery rate, per hour	...	...	...						9.4 gallons (34 litres, 11.3 US gallons) at 2000 strokes/minute
Float needle valve opening pressure	...	...	...						7.1 to 8.5 psi (0.5 to 0.6 kg/cm^2)

Fuel tank capacity ... ...   12.8 gallons (58 litres, 15.3 US gallons) approximately

Fuel octane requirement ... ...   Refer to Chapter 1 Specifications

1 General description

Although carburettors of many different part numbers are fitted throughout the Audi 100 range, they fall into two basic categories. These are the single stage carburettor fitted to the 100 and 100S, and the two stage fitted to all other models. The latter type is virtually two carburettors in one, the second stage coming into operation when the first stage throttle is open more than two thirds; the choke is only operative on the first stage. A more detailed description of the respective types is given under the appropriate heading later in this Chapter.

The fuel pump and tank for European cars are conventional in form. Differences applicable to the USA versions are described later in the Chapter.

2 Fuel tank sender unit - removal and replacement

1 Lift the carpeting in the floor of the boot.
2 Remove the electrical connections from the gauging unit.
3 Remove the gauging unit mounting screws then lift the unit out of the tank manipulating the float lever as necessary.

4 When replacing the unit always fit a new gasket.

3 Fuel tank - removal and replacement

1 Remove the carpeting from the floor of the boot.
2 Remove the electrical connections from the gauging unit.
3 Loosen the hose clip on the fuel inlet pipe.
4 Remove the mounting screws around the tank circumference.
5 Disconnect the tank breather hose and fuel inlet hose.
6 Drain the contents of the fuel tank.
7 Remove the fuel feed pipe to the fuel pump.
8 Lift out the tank.
9 Replacement is the reverse of removal, but first fit a new Prestic seal, 7 mm wide around the underside of the mounting face.

4 Fuel pump - description of operation

1 The fuel pump (photo) is plunger operated from an eccentric on the camshaft. As the pushrod moves up, fuel in the cavity is pumped out of the outlet valve. On the down stroke the

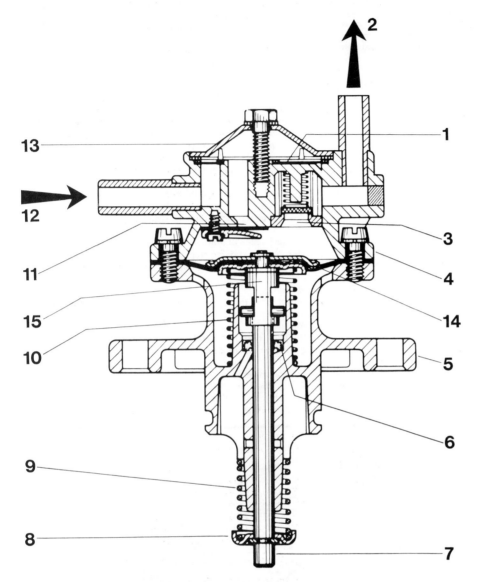

FIG. 3.1. SECTIONAL VIEW OF THE FUEL PUMP (SEC. 4)

1   Filter
2   Fuel outlet
3   Outlet valve
4   Pump upper part
5   Pump lower part
6   Oil scraper ring
7   Pushrod
8   Spring retainer
9   Spring
10 Spring
11 Inlet valve
12 Fuel inlet
13 Cover
14 Diaphragm
15 Coupling

4.1 The fuel pump

small non-return valve in the outlet port closes and more fuel is sucked into the cavity above the diaphragm. When maximum delivery pressure is attained, an override spring on the pushrod compresses and prevents movement of the diaphragm.

---

5   Fuel pump - checking delivery pressure on car

1   Fuel pump performance can be checked using one of the commercially available sets of equipment if there is any doubt about its performance.

2   The pipe connections from the equipment should be connected to the fuel pump outlet and carburettor inlet and the equipment raised to carburettor height.

3   Now, with the engine running at approximately 2000 rev/min, a pressure of 2.85 to 4.27 psi (0.2 to 0.3 kg/cm^2) should be obtained.

4   Now switch off the engine and check that there is a delay before the pressure falls away.

5   Start the engine again and check the pressure at which the float needle valve opens. This should be between 7.1 and 8.5 psi (0.5 and 0.6 kg/cm^2).

6 Fuel pump - removal and overhaul

1   Take off the two fuel pipes and remove the two fixing bolts. If there is a spacer below the pump this must be refitted when the pump is installed.

2   Clean the exterior of the pump and mark both halves at the flange to enable the parts to be refitted in the same positions.

3   Remove the screws around the flange and separate the two parts of the pump.

4   Working on the top part of the pump only, it should be possible to blow in fuel at the inlet but not possible to suck out fuel. It should also be possible to suck out fuel at the outlet, but not blow in fuel. If either valve is found to be faulty in this test, the upper part of the pump must be renewed.

5   To gain access to the parts in the top of the pump, remove the cover screw. The filter and seals can then be inspected.

6   Turning your attention to the lower half of the pump, compress the spring and remove the circlip.

7   Separate the parts and carefully remove the diaphragm and pushrod assembly from the pump body.

8   Carefully inspect the diaphragm for cracks and the spring for wear. Renew any damaged or suspect parts.

9   Check the mating surfaces of the two halves of the pump for distortion.

10 When reassembling the pump take great care that the diaphragm is not rucked or twisted and make sure that the top and bottom halves are correctly aligned. Tighten the screws crosswise.

11 Now check the pump performances by connecting pipes to the inlet and outlet. Dip the inlet pipe into a fuel container and raise the pump about 20 ins (50 cm) above it. Operate the pump at about one stroke per second and check that fuel is delivered before thirty strokes have been completed.

7 32 TDID two stage carburettor - description of operation

A Cold starting

1   The automatic choke will set itself once the accelerator pedal has been floored; the actual position of the choke depends upon the temperature of the bi-metallic spring.

2   After releasing the accelerator pedal, the stop lever rests on the highest step of the stepped washer (or cam) and the throttle butterfly is held open slightly by the connecting rod.

3   Once the engine has started, manifold depression causes the diaphragm and diaphragm rod to be pulled downwards and thus opens the choke butterfly a little against the force of the bi-metallic spring. With this movement, the stepped washer also moves since it is connected to the diaphragm rod follower by a spring and therefore allows the stop lever to move down a step and so reduce the idling speed.

4   The choke will gradually begin to open, its position being determined by the closing force of the bi-metallic spring and opening force of the manifold depression. At the same time the stop lever is moving step by step down the stepped washer until the idling speed is at its minimum.

B Idling

1   At idle, the suction below the butterfly causes the fuel to flow from the main jet to the idle jet, and air is drawn in via the idle air bore.

2   The mixture then enters the inlet manifold via a drilling below the idle mixture regulating screw.

C Transition

1   As the throttle is opened beyond the idle position, the butterfly clears the bypass bores and increases the amount of fuel/air mixture which enters the engine. Thus a smooth

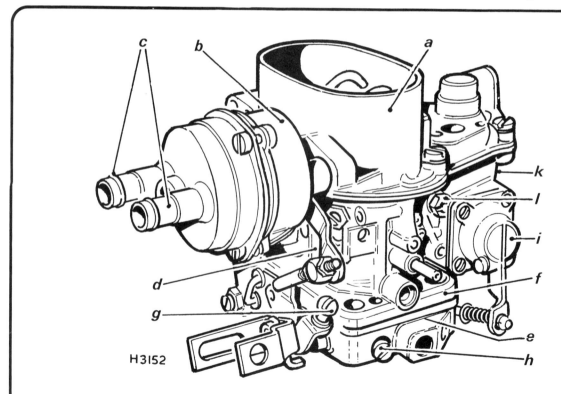

H3152

FIG. 3.2. 32 TDID TWO STAGE CARBURETTOR (SEC. 7A)

a Cover	d Mixing chamber	g Idle screw	k Float housing
b Automatic choke	e Throttle	h Mixture screw (idle)	l Idle jet (or idle cut-off
c Water connections	f Insulator	i Accelerator pump	valve)

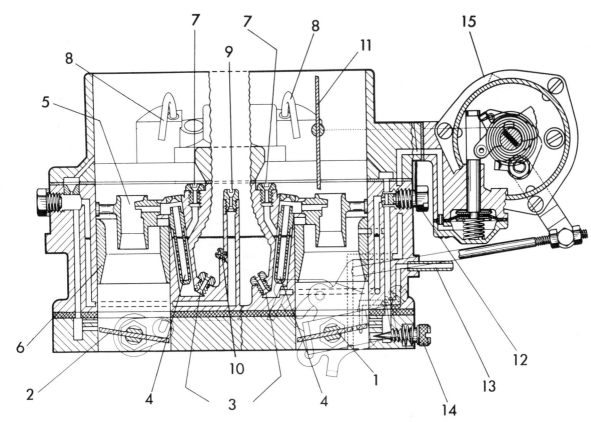

FIG. 3.3. SECTIONAL VIEW OF 32 TDID CARBURETTOR (SEC. 7A)

1 Stage 1 throttle	5 Outlet arm and atonizer	9 Breather jet	12 Idle jet
2 Stage 2 throttle	6 Venturi	10 Stage 2 transfer jet	13 Distributor vacuum connection
3 Main jet	7 Air correction jet	(idle reserve)	14 Idle mixture screw
4 Mixing tube	8 Enrichment tube	11 Choke butterfly	15 Automatic choke

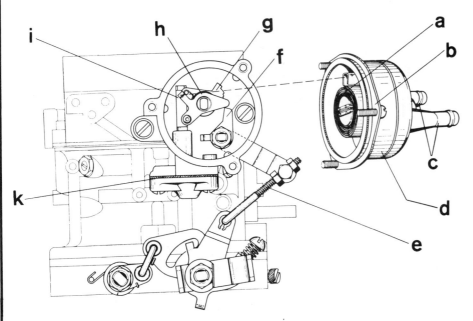

FIG. 3.4. AUTOMATIC CHOKE OF 32 TDID CAR-BURETTOR (SEC. 7A)

a Bi-metallic spring
b Retaining ring
c Water connections
d Choke cover
e Connecting rod
f Stop lever
g Stepped washer (cam)
h Follower
i Diaphragm rod
k Diaphragm

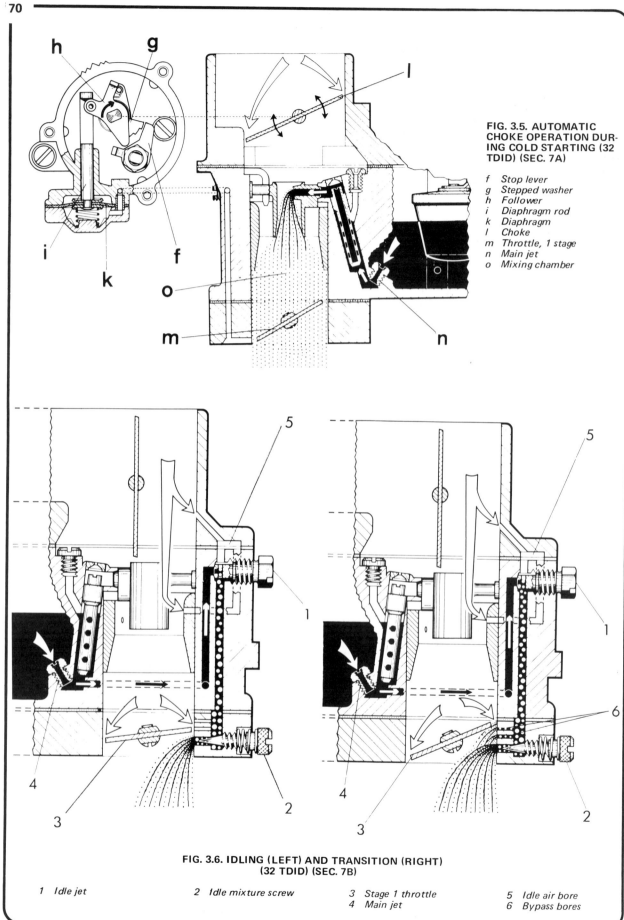

FIG. 3.5. AUTOMATIC CHOKE OPERATION DURING COLD STARTING (32 TDID) (SEC. 7A)

f   Stop lever
g   Stepped washer
h   Follower
i   Diaphragm rod
k   Diaphragm
l   Choke
m   Throttle, 1 stage
n   Main jet
o   Mixing chamber

FIG. 3.6. IDLING (LEFT) AND TRANSITION (RIGHT)
(32 TDID) (SEC. 7B)

| 1 Idle jet | 2 Idle mixture screw | 3 Stage 1 throttle | 5 Idle air bore |
| | | 4 Main jet | 6 Bypass bores |

transition from idle to normal operation is obtained.

2 The same transition system with bypass bores exists in the second stage of the carburettor.

D Normal operation

1 As the throttle is opened wider, the air velocity in the venturi increases and air is drawn in from the bore in the outlet arm.

2 Fuel flows into the mixing tube, air enters via the air correction jet and the mixture is passed to the atomizer in the outlet arm.

3 Stage two operates in the same manner. Stage two automatically comes into operation when the stage one throttle is open more than two thirds.

E Accelerating

1 During acceleration, the sudden inflow of air swamps the main jet fuel flow and tends to provide a weak mixture. Therefore a diaphragm operated accelerator pump operates and injects fuel into the air stream to temporarily enrichen the mixture.

F Full load enrichment

1 At full load and high speed the inlet airflow tends to weaken the mixture. Therefore an enrichment tube is fitted, which acts as a jet pump, and fuel is drawn out by the incoming airflow.

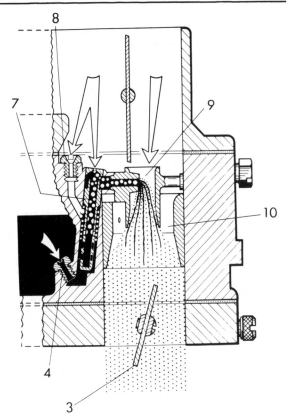

FIG. 3.7. NORMAL OPERATION (32 TDID) (SEC. 7D)

3 Throttle butterfly
4 Main jet
7 Mixing tube
8 Air correction jet
9 Outlet arm with atomizer
10 Venturi

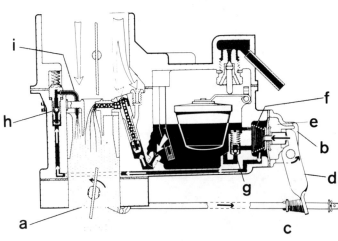

FIG. 3.8. ACCELERATING (32 TDID) (SEC. 7D)

a Throttle butterfly
b Delivery pump
c Pump rod and spring
d Pump lever
e Pump diaphragm
f Diaphragm spring
g Ball valve (suction valve)
h Ball valve (pressure valve)
i Injection tube

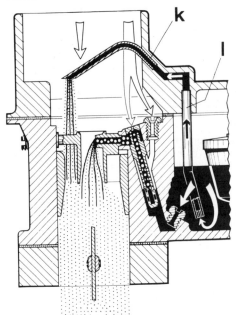

FIG. 3.9. FULL LOAD ENRICHMENT (32 TDID) (SEC. 7D)

k Enrichment tube
l Connecting tube

8 32 TDID carburettor - check and adjustments

A Checking the float level

1 Remove the air cleaner, then the hose connections from the choke.

2 Disconnect the fuel hose and remove the five screws which retain the top of the carburettor.

3 Disconnect the pump linkage by removing the circlip (not the hexagon nuts).

4 Take off the carburettor top half and invert it on a working surface.

5 Check that the float height, as measured from the upper edge of the float bead to the surface of the carburettor flange, is in accordance with the specification requirements at the beginning of the Chapter.

6 Adjust if necessary by carefully bending the float lever tab.

7 Reassemble the carburettor.

B Checking the pump injection rate

1 Run the engine to fill the float chamber then remove the carburettor from the car.

2 Turn back the throttle idle screw fully then place a container beneath the venturi of stage 1.

3 Keeping the carburettor level operate the throttle ten times over its full range of travel and check that the amount of fuel delivered meets the specification requirements (Note. If the carburettor cover is removed for this operation, first depress the injection tube spring).

4 The injection rate can be corrected if necessary by adding washers between the spring and lever to increase, or removing washers to decrease the rate.

5 If the specified rate cannot be obtained, dismantle the pump and renew the parts as necessary.

6 Check that a good jet of fuel is squirted out of the injection tube and that the tube is pointing directly into the increasing throttle butterfly gap. Slight bending of the injection tube is permissible.

C Checking the automatic choke

1 Remove the carburettor from the car and mark the position of the choke housing with respect to the body.

2 Remove the choke cover and bi-metallic spring, noting the insulator between the cover and the body.

3 Check all the parts for wear and damage, and lightly lubricate them.

4 Check the choke gap by pressing the diaphragm rod down to the stop whilst holding the follower against the stop in the closed position. Now check that the gap between the choke and the housing wall meets the specification requirements. The pin on the follower can be bent if necessary to meet the requirements.

5 When checking the throttle gap, first close the choke so that the stop lever is on the highest step of the stepped washer. Adjust the connecting rod if necessary to make any correction.

6 When reassembling the choke always ensure that the eyelet on the bi-metallic spring engages above the arm of the follower.

D Adjusting the idle

1 This is to be carried out on the car with the engine at normal running temperature, and with the ignition system satisfactorily set and adjusted.

2 Adjust the idle to 950 rev/min then screw in the mixture control screw until the engine runs erratically (too weak a mixture).

3 Turn back the screw approximately 1/8 turn until the engine runs smoothly. If this is turned back too far the mixture will be over-rich (indicated by 'hunting' and a sooty exhaust gas). When carrying out the adjustments it is useful to rev the engine a little after each setting.

4 After completion of the aforementioned, the system should be checked on an exhaust system analyser to check for carbon monoxide content.

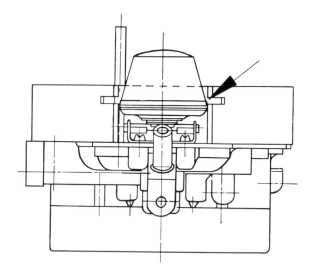

Fig. 3.10. Checking the float height (32 TDID) (Sec. 8A)
Float bead upper edge arrowed

FIG. 3.11. INJECTION RATE ADJUSTMENT (32 TDID)
(SEC. 8B)

b Injection (accelerator) pump lever

FIG. 3.12. NOTING THE CHOKE HOUSING POSITION
(32 TDID) (SEC. 8C)

a Standard notch alignment with large tooth
b Standard notch alignment with large tooth
c Cover retaining screws
D Insulator

FIG. 3.13. CHECKING THE CHOKE GAP (32 TDID)
(SEC. 8C)

i   Measuring gauge (eg. twist drill)

FIG. 3.14. CHECKING THE THROTTLE GAP (32 TDID)
(SEC. 8C)

o   Measuring gauge (eg. twist drill)

9   35 PDSIT - 5 single stage carburettor - description of operation

1   The operation of this single stage carburettor is identical to that described for the 32 TDID carburettor except that any references to the second stage should be ignored.

10   35 PDSIT - 5 carburettor - checks and adjustments

A   Checking the fuel level.
1   Initially run the engine for about one minute to fill the float chamber.
2   Remove the air cleaner and fuel hose.
3   Take out the five screws which retain the top of the carburettor.
4   Disconnect the pump linkage by removing the circlip (not the hexagon nuts).
5   Now hold a finger over the fuel inlet pipe to prevent further fuel entering the float chamber, and lift off the cover and gasket.
6   Check the fuel level using a depth gauge. The correct value is given in the specifications section. Fuel level may be adjusted if necessary by fitting fibre washers beneath the needle valve.

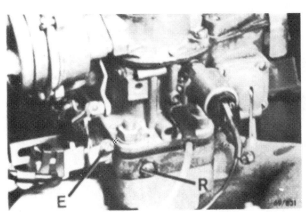

FIG. 3.15. ADJUSTING THE IDLE (32 TDID) (SEC. 8D)

E   Idle speed adjustment
R   Idle mixture adjustment

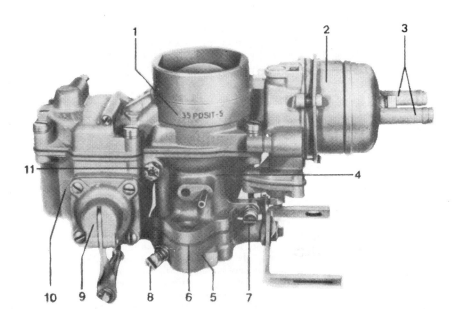

FIG. 3.16. 35 PDSIT - 5
SINGLE STAGE CARBURE-
TTOR (SEC. 9)

1   Carburettor cover
2   Automatic choke
3   Water connections
4   Mixing chamber
5   Throttle
6   Gasket
7   Idle screw
8   Idle mixture screw
9   Accelerator pump
*10 Float housing, sometimes
     fitted with idle cutoff
     valve*
11 Idle jet

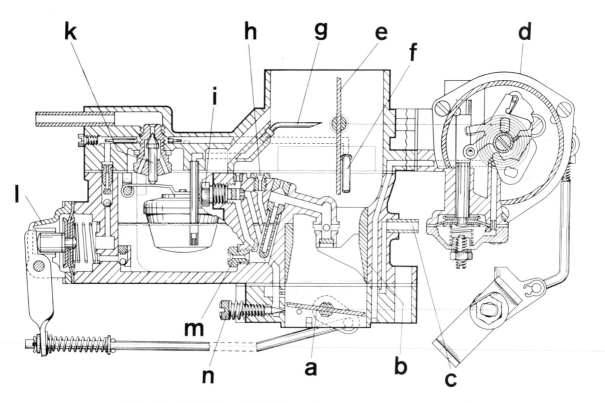

FIG. 3.17. SECTIONAL VIEW OF 35 PDSIT - 5 CARBURETTOR (SEC. 9)

a	Throttle butterfly	d	Automatic choke	h	Air correction jet	m	Main jet
b	Venturi	e	Choke	i	Idle jet	n	Idle mixture control
c	Connecting tube, ignition	f	Injection tube	k	Float needle valve		screw
	control	g	Enrichment tube	l	Accelerator pump		

B Checking the pump injection rate

1 With the carburettor cover still removed, turn back the idle adjustment screw.

2 Now fit a plastic tube over the accelerator pump orifice in the body with the other end of the tube in a measuring cylinder.

3 Operate the pump to first fill the tube then repeat the operation over the full range of travel ten times. Check that the injection rate meets the specification requirements.

4 The injection rate can be corrected if necessary by adding washers between the spring and lever to increase, or removing washers to decrease the rate.

5 If the specified rate cannot be obtained, dismantle the pump and renew the parts as necessary.

6 Bend the injection tube if necessary to align the injection stream with the opening throttle gap.

C Checking the automatic choke

1 Refer to the procedure set out for the 32 TDID carburettor decribed previously.

D Adjusting the idle

1 Refer to the procedure set out for the 32 TDID carburettor described previously.

---

11 35 PDSIT air/mixture control, single stage carburettor - description of operation

A Automatic choke

The operation of the automatic choke under cold starting conditions is the same as that for the 32 TDID and 35 PDSIT - 5 carburettors previously described.

B Idle and air mixture control system

1 The idle air/fuel mixture is produced in the air/mixture section of the carburettor. Here fuel is taken from the float chamber via the additional fuel jet, is mixed with air entering at point B and passes to the air mixture control bore (4a) as an air/fuel mixture (Fig. 3.21).

2 Fuel is also passed to the mixture tube recess via the main jet and is metered at the idle fuel jet, the actual quantity of fuel depending upon idle speed. It is then emulsified with metered air from the idle air bore and, after regulation by the idle mixture control screw, flows into the air mixture bore with the air/fuel mixture.

3 The air/fuel mixture from the idle and air control systems is metered by the air mixture control screw. Therefore the idle speed can be regulated by this screw without altering the composition of the idle mixture.

C Transition

Refer to the section for the 32 TDID carburettor.

D Partial load enrichment

1 At idle, there is a relatively high suction in the vacuum bore due to its positioning in the intake tube of the throttle. In this condition, the vacuum piston is sucked upwards and the enrichment valve is closed under spring pressure.

2 As the throttle is opened, (ie partial load), the suction decreases and allows the piston to fall. The enrichment valve is then pushed open and allows fuel into the enrichment tube recess and therefore enriches the air/fuel mixture in the main jet system.

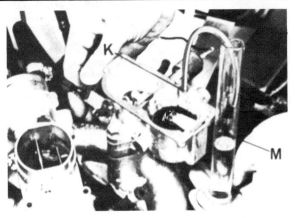

Fig. 3.18. Using a depth gauge to measure the fuel level on a 35 PDSIT - 5 carburettor (Sec. 10A)

FIG. 3.19. CHECKING THE PUMP INJECTION RATE ON A 35 PDSIT - 5 CARBURETTOR (SEC. 10B)

K   Plastic tube
M   Measuring cylinder

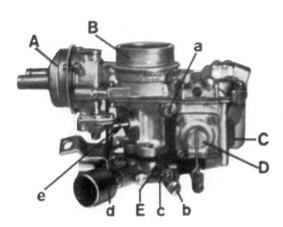

FIG. 3.20. 35 PDSIT AIR/MIXTURE CONTROL, SINGLE STAGE CARBURETTOR (SEC. 11A)

A   Automatic choke
B   Carburettor cover
C   Carburettor housing
D   Accelerator pump

E   Throttle
a   Idle jet
b   Air control screw
c   Mixture control screw

d   Mixture cut off valve
e   Vacuum connection
f   Fuel inlet
g   Plug, main jet

h   Retaining screw, venturi
i   Stop screw (sealed) for throttle
k   Automatic choke connecting rod
l   Throttle lever

FIG. 3.21. IDLE AND AIR/MIXTURE CONTROL ON THE 35 PDSIT CARBURETTOR (SEC. 11B)

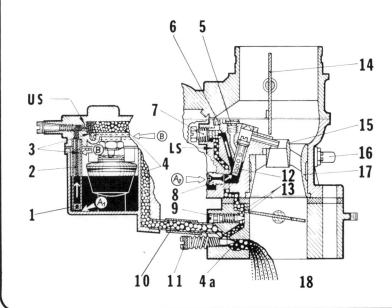

1   Additional fuel jet
2   Riser
3   Air bores for air mixture
4   Air mixture bore
5   Air correction jet
6   Idle air bore
7   Idle fuel jet
8   Main jet
9   Idle mixture screw
10 Connecting tube
11 Air mixture control screw
12 Mixture tube
13 Bypass bores
14 Choke
15 Outlet and atomizer
16 Vacuum connection
17 Venturi
18 Throttle
A   Fuel
B   Air
LS Idle control system
US Air/mixture control system

E Full load enrichment

1 Under full load condition, fuel is sucked out of the enrichment tube. According to the velocity of the incoming air (ie the position of the throttle) the suction in the enrichment tube lifts the floating needle from its seat and allows varying amounts of fuel into the incoming air stream. This is a progressive enrichment dependant upon the degree of throttle opening.

F Accelerating

Refer to the section for the 32 TDID carburettor.

---

13 32/35 TDID air control, two stage carburettor - description of operation

---

1 The only differences between the operation of this carburettor and 32 TDID previously described, is the idle control system. The fuel for the idle control system first passes through the main jet and is then metered by the idle fuel jet. It then enters the inlet manifold via the idle mixture control screw orifice. Air only is fed to the air/fuel mixture produced in the idle control system, the amount being regulated by the air control screw.

---

12 35 PDSIT carburettor - checks and adjustments

---

1 Owing to the fact that it is essential to adjust this type of carburettor using special equipment and facilities, no adjustments or dismantling are permissible.

2 If carburation troubles are experienced, the appropriate remedial action and adjustment must be carried out by an Audi dealer or a properly equipped carburettor specialist.

FIG. 3.22. PARTIAL AND FULL LOAD ENRICHMENT ON THE 35 PDSIT CARBURETTOR (SEC. 11D)

20	Enrichment valve
20a	Enrichment valve spring
21	Float chamber
22	Float
23	Fuel inlet
24	Float needle valve
25	Vacuum piston, operating rod and spring
26	Needle valve
27	Vacuum bore
28	Ventilation bore
29	Enrichment tube
30	Riser
A	Fuel
B	Air

2 The operation is otherwise similar to the 32 TDID carburettor described previously.

---

14 32/35 TDID carburettor - checks and adjustments

---

1 Owing to the fact that it is essential to adjust this type of carburettor using special equipment and facilities, no adjustments or dismantling are permissible.

2 If carburation troubles are experienced, including the balancing of twin carburettors on the Coupe's where applicable, remedial action and adjustment must be carried out by an Audi dealer or a properly equipped carburettor specialist.

FIG. 3.23. 32/35 TDID AIR CONTROL, TWO STAGE CARBURETTOR (SEC. 13)

A	Automatic choke
B	Carburettor cover
C	Carburettor housing
D	Accelerator pump
E	Throttle
7	Air control screw
8	Mixture control screw
9	Vacuum connection
11	Idle cut off valve
12	Stage 1 enrichment tube
13	Stage 2 enrichment tube
14	Stage 1 throttle adjustment screw

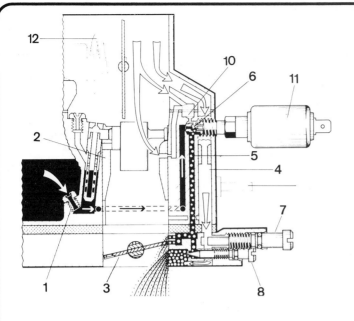

FIG. 3.24. IDLE CONTROL SYSTEM OF THE 32/35 TDID CARBURETTOR (SEC. 13)

1   Main jet, stage 1
2   Venturi, stage 1
3   Throttle, stage 1
4   Idle air control bore
5   Idle mixture bore
6   Idle fuel jet
7   Air control screw
8   Idle mixture control screw
9   Vacuum connection
10   Idle air bore
11   Electric cut off valve
12   Enrichment tube, stage 1
13   Main jet, stage 1

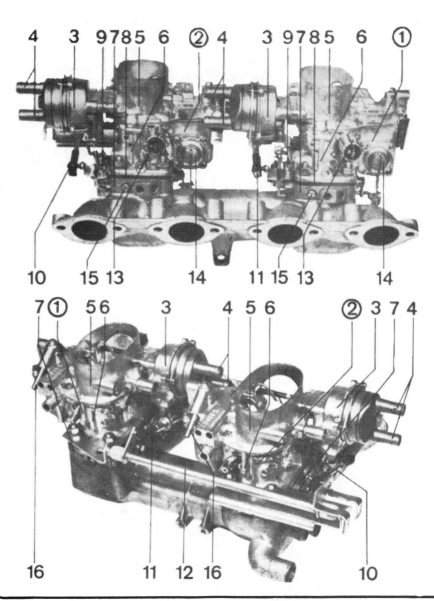

FIG. 3.25. TWIN 32/35 TDID CARBURETTORS FITTED TO THE EARLY MODELS OF THE COUPE' S (SEC. 13)

1   32/35 carburettor, front
2   32/35 carburettor, rear
3   Automatic choke
4   Water connections
5   Carburettor cover
6   Mixture chamber, stage 1 and 11
7   Throttle
8   Gasket
9   Idle control screw
10   Linkage, rear carburettor
11   Connecting linkage, front carburettor
12   Carburettor connecting rod
13   Idle cut off valve with idle jet
14   Delivery pump
15   Idle mixture control screw
16   Fuel inlet tube

15 Air cleaners

1   The air cleaner on the Audi 100 is a 'throw-away' item. It must be removed from its three attachment points at intervals of 24000 miles (40000 km) and a complete new filter fitted.
2   Other models have a replaceable paper element which is accessible after springing back the clips which retain the cover.
3   Incorporated in the air cleaner inlet tube there is a vacuum unit on some models. This is connected to a thermo control valve on the inlet manifold which will open the fresh (cold) air intake flap and close the warm air intake at temperatures above 30°C (86°F). Below these temperatures the thermo-control valve sucks the flap in the intake closed and warm air is drawn in from above the exhaust manifold.
4   The vacuum unit can be removed from the air cleaner after first depressing the retaining spring carefully.

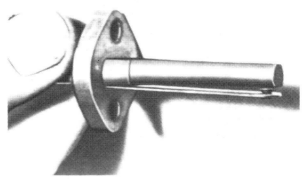

Fig. 3.26. Thermo control valve (Sec. 15)

16 Fuel system (USA models) - description

1   Cars supplied for the USA market up till the end of 1971 have a non-vented fuel tank cap. When the fuel in the tank expands it can flow to the expansion container in the upper left hand corner of the boot.
2   Fumes from the fuel tank and the expansion container are absorbed by a container of activated carbon to prevent discharge to the atmosphere. This container is in the engine compartment.
3   A connecting line is made between the carbon container and the air cleaner. As air enters the air cleaner, it passes through the vapour saturated carbon which is consequently cleaned.
4   It is important that all hose clips are kept tight in order to maintain optimum efficiency of the system.
5   For 1972 systems a fuel return was added into the connecting pipe between the fuel pump and the carburettor with a return line to the fuel tank. At low throttle openings the manifold depression opens the valve and passes excess fuel back to the tank. At low depression values, ie wide throttle openings the valve remains closed.
6   For 1973 this system was replaced by a three way adaptor, with a calibrated orifice (or insert) in the tank return line.
Note. In cases of a defective fuel return valve the system should

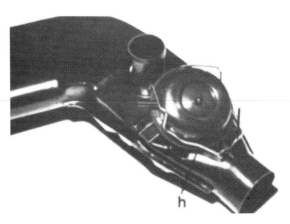

Fig. 3.27. Retaining springs (h) on vacuum unit (Sec. 15)

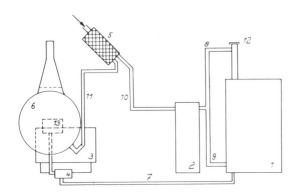

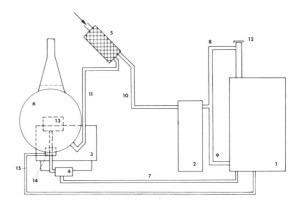

FIG. 3.28. DIAGRAMMATIC REPRESENTATION OF USA FUEL SYSTEMS (SEC. 16)
(LEFT) UP TO THE END OF 1971; (RIGHT) FOR 1972 MODELS

1   Fuel tank
2   Expansion container
3   Engine
4   Fuel pump
5   Activated carbon container
6   Air cleaner
7   Fuel line from tank to fuel pump
8   Breather line from filler neck to expansion container
9   Breather line from tank to expansion container
10 Breather line from activated carbon container
11 Connecting line from activated carbon container to filter
12 Cap, fuel tank
13 Carburettor - inlet manifold line
14 Fuel return valve
15 Fuel line from return valve to tank

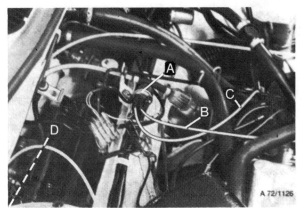

FIG. 3.29. RETARDED IGNITION CUT-OFF (SEC. 16)

a   Cut-off valve
b   Vacuum line to carburettor
c   Vacuum line to distributor
d   Switch

be modified to the later type which will also mean plugging the suction line at the manifold with solder.

7   Exhaust gas re-circulation was also introduced for USA model automatics in 1973. With this system exhaust gas is fed in the inlet manifold via the exhaust gas filter and exhaust gas recirculation (EGR) valve. Due to the positioning of the suction tapping on the carburettor, which controls the EGR valve, feed back only takes place at partial throttle openings.

8   Cars with manual transmission for 1973 are fitted with a switch operated solenoid valve. This operates on fourth gear only, and prevents hesitant operation at moderate throttle openings by venting the vacuum line to ambient and thereby preventing retardation of the ignition.

17 32/32 TDID idle air control carburettor (USA models) description of operation

1   The operation of this carburettor is similar to that described for the 32/35 TDID carburettor fitted to European models (see previously).

2   There is however a vacuum connection tapped into the pressure relief bore above the throttle butterfly to control the advanced ignition timing of the twin box distributor under partial load conditions.

3   Also, in addition to the normal choke control, there is a thermo-starting valve which comes into operation at temperatures below 5°C. At these low temperatures the thermo-start valve cone is closed and additional fuel is drawn via the fuel jet to the air stream. At higher temperatures, or after the electrically heated element within the thermo-start valve has heated up, the valve opens, thereby equalising the suction at each end of the enrichment tube. The additional fuel delivery is thereby interrupted.

18 32/35 TDID carburettor (USA models)

This carburettor is similar to the 32/32 TDID carburettor previously described with the exception of an electrically operated automatic choke. It was introduced in 1972 as a standard fitment for USA models.

19 Carburettor adjustments (USA models)

1   Owing to the fact that it is essential to adjust carburettors using special equipment and facilities in order to satisfy the exhaust emission regulations, no adjustments or dismantling are permissible.

2   If carburation trouble is experienced, remedial action and adjustment must be carried out by an Audi dealer or a properly equipped carburettor specialist.

20 Air cleaner (1971 USA models)

A flap is incorporated in the air cleaner inlet which partially shuts off the intake of fresh air at low engine speeds or when idling. This is to ensure that air for the carburettor tends to be drawn from the downstream side of the flap, to which side the crankcase fumes are delivered. The fumes are therefore re-circulated through the carburettor and burnt by the engine.

21 Air cleaners (other USA models)

1   For information regarding other air cleaners refer to the section dealing with European models.

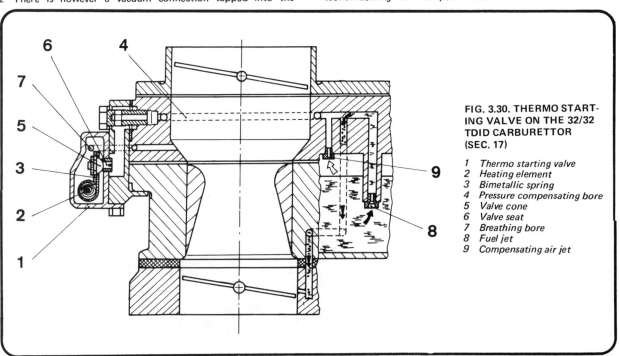

FIG. 3.30. THERMO START-ING VALVE ON THE 32/32 TDID CARBURETTOR (SEC. 17)

1   Thermo starting valve
2   Heating element
3   Bimetallic spring
4   Pressure compensating bore
5   Valve cone
6   Valve seat
7   Breathing bore
8   Fuel jet
9   Compensating air jet

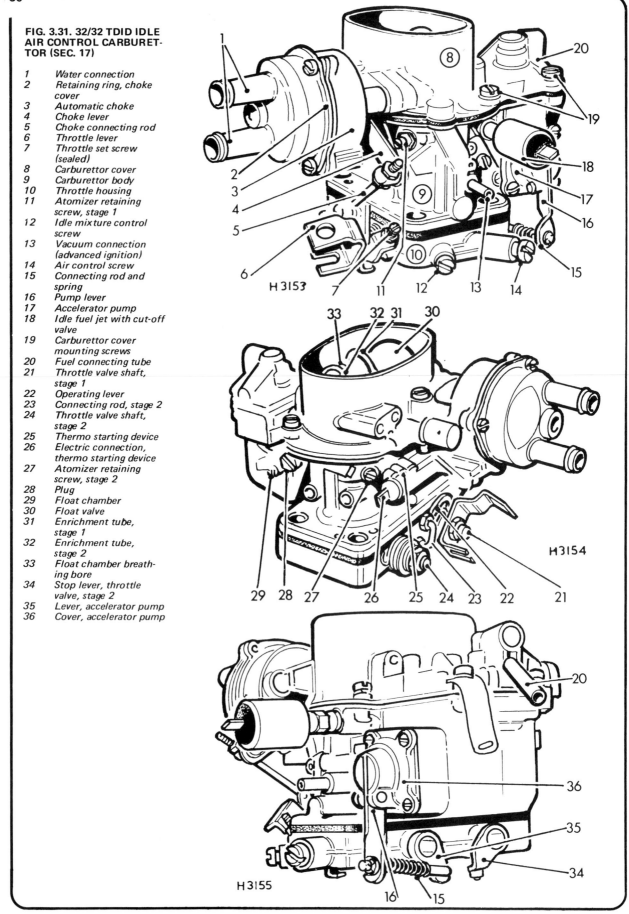

FIG. 3.31. 32/32 TDID IDLE AIR CONTROL CARBURETTOR (SEC. 17)

1   Water connection
2   Retaining ring, choke cover
3   Automatic choke
4   Choke lever
5   Choke connecting rod
6   Throttle lever
7   Throttle set screw (sealed)
8   Carburettor cover
9   Carburettor body
10   Throttle housing
11   Atomizer retaining screw, stage 1
12   Idle mixture control screw
13   Vacuum connection (advanced ignition)
14   Air control screw
15   Connecting rod and spring
16   Pump lever
17   Accelerator pump
18   Idle fuel jet with cut-off valve
19   Carburettor cover mounting screws
20   Fuel connecting tube
21   Throttle valve shaft, stage 1
22   Operating lever
23   Connecting rod, stage 2
24   Throttle valve shaft, stage 2
25   Thermo starting device
26   Electric connection, thermo starting device
27   Atomizer retaining screw, stage 2
28   Plug
29   Float chamber
30   Float valve
31   Enrichment tube, stage 1
32   Enrichment tube, stage 2
33   Float chamber breathing bore
34   Stop lever, throttle valve, stage 2
35   Lever, accelerator pump
36   Cover, accelerator pump

H 3153

H3154

H 3155

22 Fault finding table - Fuel system and carburation

Symptom	Reason/s	Remedy
FUEL CONSUMPTION EXCESSIVE		
Carburation and ignition faults	Air cleaner choked and dirty giving rich mixture	Remove, clean and replace air cleaner.
	Fuel leaking from carburettor, fuel pump, or fuel lines	Check for, and eliminate, all fuel leaks. Tighten fuel line union nuts.
	Float chamber flooding	Check and adjust float level.
	Generally worn carburettor	Remove, overhaul and replace.
	Distributor condenser faulty	Remove, and fit new unit.
	Balance weights or vacuum advance mechanism in distributor faulty	Remove, and overhaul distributor.
Incorrect adjustment	Carburettor incorrectly adjusted	Tune and adjust carburettor (where permitted)
	Mixture too rich	
	Idling speed too high	Adjust idling speed.
	Contact breaker gap incorrect	Check and reset gap.
	Valve clearances incorrect	Check rocker arm to valve stem clearances and adjust as necessary.
	Incorrectly set spark plugs	Remove, clean, and regap.
	Tyres under-inflated	Check tyre pressures and inflate if necessary.
	Wrong spark plugs fitted	Remove and replace with correct units.
	Brakes dragging	Check and adjust brakes.
INSUFFICIENT FUEL DELIVERY OR WEAK MIXTURE DUE TO AIR LEAKS		
Dirt in system	Partially clogged filters in pump and fuel line	Remove and clean filters.
	Dirt lodged in float chamber needle housing	Remove and clean out float chamber and needle valve assembly.
	Incorrectly seating valves in fuel pump	Remove, dismantle, and clean out fuel pump.
Fuel pump faults	Fuel pump diaphragm leaking or damaged	Remove, and overhaul fuel pump.
	Gasket in fuel pump damaged	Remove, and overhaul fuel pump.
	Fuel pump valves sticking due to petrol gumming.	Remove, and thoroughly clean fuel pump.
Air leaks	Too little fuel in fuel tank (Prevalent when climbing steep hills)	Refill fuel tank.
	Union joints on pipe connections loose	Tighten joints and check for air leaks.
	Split in fuel pipe on suction side of fuel pump	Examine, locate, and repair.
	Inlet manifold to block or inlet manifold to carburettor gasket leaking	Test by pouring oil along joints - bubbles indicate leak. Renew gasket as appropriate.

Chapter 4 Ignition system

For modifications, and information applicable to later models, see Supplement at end of manual

Contents

Specifications

Distributor

Distributor type	Bosch (type varies with model)
Condenser	0.23 to 0.35 microfarad (not fitted to 1973 USA models)
Advance mechanism	Centrifugal and vacuum
Distributor contact gap	0.016 in. (0.4 mm)
Distributor rotation	Anti-clockwise
Dwell angle	50 + 3° (55.5% + 3.5%)
Firing order	1 3 4 2
Ignition timing, degrees	30° BTDC at 3000 rev/min, vacuum disconnected on crankshaft (dynamic)
100LS, USA	9° ATDC at idle, vacuum connected and 27 + 3° on crankshaft at 2500 rev/min, without vacuum
100 USA, 1972	8° ATDC at idle, vacuum connected and 27 + 3° on crankshaft at 2500 rev/min, without vacuum
100 USA, 1973	8° ATDC at idle, vacuum connected and 30 + 3° on crankshaft at 2750 rev/min, without vacuum
Ignition timing (static)	TDC
Ignition coil	Bosch (type varies with model)
Coil primary resistance	1.7 to 2.1 ohm (0.12 to 0.15 for 1973 USA models)
Series resistor	0.9 + 0.1 ohm (not fitted to 1973 USA models)

Note: The Audi 100 USA models for 1973 are fitted with the BHCI (battery - high voltage - condenser - ignition) system.

Spark plugs

	Audi 100 (pre-1972) Audi 100S & LS Audi 100 Sweden (pre 1972)	Audi 100LS USA, Sweden, Switzerland (all pre 1972) Audi 100 USA (1973)	Audi 100LS Auto Switzerland (pre 1972) Audi 100 Coupe'S (pre 1972)	Audi 100 (1972/73) Audi 100 USA (1972)	Audi 100GL & Coupe' S (1972/73)
Bosch	W 200 T 30	W 225 T 2	W 240 T 2	W 200 T 30	W 240 T 2
Beru	200/14/3A	225/14/3A	240/14/3	200/14/3A	240/14/3
Champion	N4	N7Y	N3	N8Y	N6Y
Bosna (Yugoslavia) ...	FE 80	FE 80	FE 80	FE 80	FE 80

Spark plug gap

Standard ignition system	0.028 in (0.7 mm)
BHCI ignition system	0.035 in (0.9 mm)

Position of No. 1 cylinder	Nearest radiator

1 General description

1 The ignition system fitted as standard equipment to the Audi 100 range - with the exception of 1973 Audi 100 USA models - is of conventional design, being similar to the systems used in practically all modern cars.

This system comprises the ignition switch, ignition coil, the distributor (which is driven at half engine speed) and spark plugs. The basic operation of the system can be summarised as follows:

For simplicity let us consider the system to be divided into two separate halves, the low tension (LT) and the high tension (HT). The LT side comprises the primary winding of the ignition coil, the ignition switch, the contact breaker, the condenser and the associated wiring to make the connections to and from the battery. The HT side is made up of the secondary winding of the ignition coil, the distributor cap and rotor, the spark plugs and their connecting leads.

As the distributor cam rotates, the contacts will be closed for a period of time. During this time, current will flow in the primary winding of the coil (which is only a transformer anyway) but due to its self inductance, which opposes current flow, a magnetic field is not set up immediately; hence there is no secondary induced voltage worth considering. As the cam rotates further, the contacts will open and at this instant of time a spark will try to jump the contact gap as the magnetic field in the coil rapidly collapses and current starts to flow again. This spark is absorbed by the condenser which then rapidly discharges back through the primary coil winding and speeds the collapse of the field.

Now, at the time when the contacts opened the distributor rotor had turned to a position which effectively connected the secondary winding of the coil to a particular spark plug, and since there is now a continuous secondary circuit the decaying magnetic field induces a voltage in the secondary coil winding. This voltage is in the order of 15000 to 18000 volts and is sufficient to enable a spark to jump across the spark plug electrode gap. The distributor contacts will now close again as the cam rotates further and the cycle is repeated for the next spark plug.

Now that we have looked at some of the fundamental points of the ignition circuit we need to consider some of the refinements that are required for correct timing under all conditions. For efficient combustion of the petrol/air mixture a spark is required just before the piston reaches top-dead-centre (TDC), since there is a time lag between the spark occurring and development of the full force of the mixture burning. Unfortunately, this time lag varies with engine speed and load, so two devices are used to alter the timing of the spark. These are the centrifugal advance and retard mechanism which advances the point of ignition as engine speed increases and the vacuum advance and retard which depends on the inlet manifold depression (or suction) for its operation. Where there is a relatively low depression, for example hill climbing with a wide throttle opening, the mechanism will rotate the contact assembly in the distributor in the direction of cam rotation, thus delaying or retarding the spark. Conversely, with a car cruising at a moderately fast speed on level surfaces there will be an increase in manifold depression and a tendency for a more advanced spark.

On the Audi cars, a series resistor is added in the primary circuit of the ignition coil to limit the current flow and internal heat generated. Except for the very early cars, this resistor is by-passed during the starting sequence in order to produce a bigger magnetic field and spark when it is most needed.

2 Although adequate for most needs, the system described in Section 1 does have its shortcomings. For this reason the battery high voltage condenser ignition (BHCI) system is used on the 1973 versions of the Audi 100 USA. This has the advantage of a higher HT voltage (20000 to 25000 volts) which does not vary with engine speed, a larger permissible spark plug electrode gap which gives a more intensive spark, no sparking at the contact breaker points, a more precisely timed spark and, due to its lower dynamic internal resistance, is less sensitive to any leakage resistance at the spark plug.

The principle of operation is that a condenser within the electronic control is charged to between 350 and 400 volts. When the distributor contacts open, the electronic control fires a thyristor (a semi-conductor device which can loosely be described as a gate or switch), which in turn causes the capacitor to discharge via the primary winding of the coil. A voltage is induced in the secondary winding and a spark is produced at the plug electrodes. The centrifugal and vacuum advance and retard mechanisms are retained but there is no necessity for a condenser connected across the contact breaker points since this part of the circuit no longer switches the highly inductive primary coil voltage.

Note 1
With the BHCI system there is a danger to life if the ignition switch is operated and the leads or terminals to the coil are touched, when the coil has been removed and there is a defective condenser.

Note 2
Where a BHCI system has recently been in use and the ignition switch is then removed from the circuit, an electric shock could result from touching terminal A.

Note 3
A modification has been introduced to BHCI systems, where there is a tendency for the engine to 'run on' after the ignition has been switched off. This comprises a diode plug to be inserted in lead 61 from the alternator at the existing WECO plug (diode plug part No 059 905 371). This item is standard equipment from chassis No 80 21 122 696.

2 Ignition coil and series resistor - checking

A Early version, starter motor without terminal 16.
1 Disconnect the lead on the resistor which connects with the distributor (terminal f).
2 Connect an ammeter of low internal resistance, and which can register up to 5 amps dc between terminal f and a good earth point on the chassis.
3 Connect a dc voltmeter capable of registering 12 volts between the ignition switch terminal on the coil and a good earth point on the chassis.
4 With the ignition switched on, the voltage should be not less than 11 volts and the current approximately 3.8 to 4.8 amps, decreasing as the coil warms up.
5 Operate the starter motor and check that the voltage does not fall below 9 volts.
6 If the voltage is low in the above checks, this could be due to a discharged battery, corroded battery terminals or high resistance connections. These points should all be checked.
7 If the ammeter reading is high, or does not read at all, a fault in the coil or resistor is indicated.
8 To check the coil secondary winding first reconnect the wiring, then remove the central HT lead from the distributor cap. Operate the starter with the lead 0.3 to 0.4 in (8 to 10 mm)

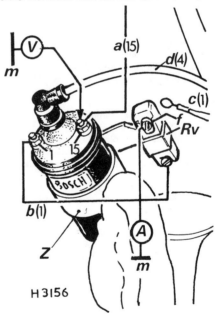

H 3156

FIG. 4.1. IGNITION COIL CHECKING, STARTER MOTOR WITHOUT TERMINAL 16. PRIMARY WINDING CHECKS (SEC. 2A)

Z	Coil
Rv	Series resistor
a	Ignition switch terminal
b	Resistor/coil connecting lead
c	Lead from distributor
d	HT connection
F	Distributor connection terminal
m	Chassis earth
A	Ammeter
V	Voltmeter

from a good earth point and check for a continuous sparking as
the engine rotates.
Note. Make sure the hands and leads are dry, or an electric shock
will result.
9 If there is no spark at paragraph 8 first check the contacts for
adjustment and the condition of their faces, then the connections to the condenser and internal wiring.
10 If there is still no spark, and all the wiring connections etc.
are satisfactory, a fault in the coil or condenser is indicated.
These will need checking by a car electrical specialist.

B Later version, starter motor with terminal 16
1 To check the primary winding disconnect the lead on the coil
which connects with the distributor, then connect an ammeter
between the coil terminal and a good earth point on the chassis.
The ammeter must be suitable for reading at least 5 amps dc.
2 Connect a dc voltmeter capable of registering 12 volts
between a good earth point on the chassis and the resistor
terminal which is connected to the ignition switch.
3 With the ignition switched on the voltage should be not less
than 11 volts and the current approximately 3.8 to 4.8 amps,
decreasing as the coil warms up.
4 Operate the starter motor and check that the voltage does
not fall below 9 volts.
5 If the voltage is low in the above checks, this could be due to
a discharged battery, corroded battery terminals or high
resistance connections. These points should all be checked.
6 If the ammeter reading is high, or does not read at all, a fault
in the coil or resistor is indicated.
7 To check the secondary windings, refer to paragraphs 8
onwards of part A of this section.

3 Distributor

A Removal and replacement
1 Initially remove the air cleaner then remove the distributor
cap by springing back the retaining clips.
2 Disconnect the green lead to the ignition coil and carefully
take off the vacuum connection.
3 Remove the distributor complete with the bracket by
undoing the two hexagon headed screws. This may need carefully prising off because the rubber O-ring tends to stick.
4 If there is any need to remove the bracket from the distributor, carefully mark its position to prevent altering the
ignition timing when refitting.
5 When refitting the distributor to the car, lightly lubricate the
O-ring then turn the rotor carefully to align the offset drive.
6 Finally replace the cap.

B Contact breaker - contact removal and adjustment
1 With the distributor cap removed (see part A) pull off the
rotor and remove the plastic petrol protection cap. (photo).
2 Pull off the insulated connection at its junction with the
condenser and green coil lead.
3 Unscrew the slotted retaining screw on the contact baseplate
and lift out the contacts.
4 When refitting contacts to the distributor, first lightly smear
the cam surfaces and fixed contact pivot pin with a
molybdenum disulphide grease then apply a very small quantity
of high melting point grease (approximately equivalent to one
match head) to the angle on the contact breaker lever (arrowed)
(Fig. 4.4).
5 Refitting the contacts is a reversal of the removal sequence.
When fitted set them so that with the lever on top of one of the
peaks of the cam, the gap is 0.016 in (0.4 mm). This is achieved
by putting the car into top gear and moving it slightly to turn
the cam then slackening the contact fixing screw and inserting a
feeler gauge between the contacts. To facilitate movement of the
contacts a screwdriver can be inserted in the groove in the
contact plate and turned (photos).

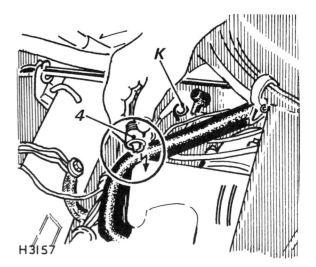

**FIG. 4.2. IGNITION COIL CHECKING, STARTER MOTOR
WITHOUT TERMINAL 16. SECONDARY WINDING CHECKS
(SEC. 2A)**

4   HT lead
K   Distributor cap centre connection

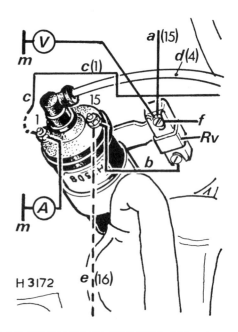

**FIG. 4.3. IGNITION COIL CHECKING, STARTER MOTOR
WITH TERMINAL 16. PRIMARY WINDING CHECKS
(SEC. 2B)**

Rv   Series resistor
a   Ignition switch terminal
b   Resistor/coil connecting lead
c   Lead from distributor
d   HT connection
e   Starter motor connection terminal
f   Series resistor terminal
m   Chassis earth
A   Ammeter
V   Voltmeter

3.B1 The distributor with the rotor and cap removed

3.B5(a) Checking the contact gap with a feeler gauge

3.B5(b) Using a screwdriver to adjust the contacts

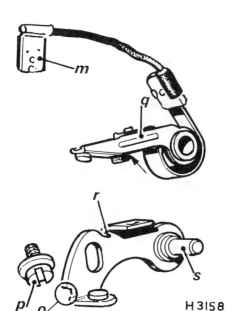

H 3158

FIG. 4.4. THE DISTRIBUTOR CONTACTS (SEC. 3B)

m	Flat plug connection
o	Groove
p	Screw

q	Contact breaker lever
r	Contact plate
s	Pin

C Condenser - removal

1 Remove the distributor cap then take out the condenser retaining screw.
2 Disconnect the insulated lead inside the distributor, then take off the condenser complete with plastic spacer.
3 There is no reliable and simple method for checking the condenser. If the correct equipment is not available the condenser should be tested by an approved car electrical specialist.

D Contact cleaning and refacing

1 Contacts can be cleaned using a petrol moistened rag.
2 In time, the contact faces deteriorate as a deposit is built up on one and a pitting occurs on the other. These are best refaced on an oil stone, but it is important to remember that the contact faces must be flat and parallel, or very slightly domed when fitted. Do not grind away at an angle. If possible remove all the deposits and pitting; this is particularly important in the case of the deposits.
3 After refacing, clean the contacts (paragraph 1) then refit to the distributor.
4 Finally make the necessary adjustments as previously described.

4 Spark plugs

1 Only use spark plugs of a recommended type. Not only will performance be impaired if unsatisfactory types are used but serious engine damage can also result.
2 Always maintain the correct electrode gaps. If any adjustments are to be made, only bend the outer (earth) electrode - never the middle one. It is permissible to carefully file the end of the central electrode when cleaning.
3 When spark plug cleaning is required, arrange for the work to be carried out by a garage which has a suitable sand blasting and performance testing machine. This method of cleaning is far more effective than a wire brush and at the same time performance can be checked under high pressure conditions.
4 Before refitting the spark plugs to the car, make sure that the electrode gaps are properly set (see specifications), and that the insulators and screw threads are clean. Apply a drop of engine oil to the screw threads before refitting to the car.

5 HT leads and suppressor caps

1 HT leads are normally supplied complete with connecting caps, and this type should always be used in preference to others.
2 The leads can be checked using a suitable ohmmeter, whereupon the following values should be obtained.

Type a lead (spark plug lead = 1.4k ohms $\pm$ 20%.
Type b lead (coil to distributor) = negligible resistance.
Type c lead (spark plug lead) = 6k ohm, comprising 1k ohm in the adaptor and 6k ohm in the plug cap.
Type d lead (coil to distributor) = 2k ohm, comprising 1k ohm in the adaptor and 6k ohm in the plug cap.

3 Any leads which show signs of cracking or other deterioration should always be renewed. The same applies to the connecting caps.
Note: On 1973 USA models, special heat resistant leads and ceramic caps are used.

6 Static ignition timing

1 Static engine timing should only be carried out as a means of initial setting prior to dynamic setting. Whilst it is permissible to run an engine after static timing only, it is essential that dynamic checking and adjustment is carried out at the earliest possible time.
2 Initially check the condition of the distributor contacts and check the adjustment.
3 Now put the car into fourth gear with the handbrake off and turn the engine until the zero mark on the flywheel or crankshaft pulley (as appropriate) aligns with the notch (photo).

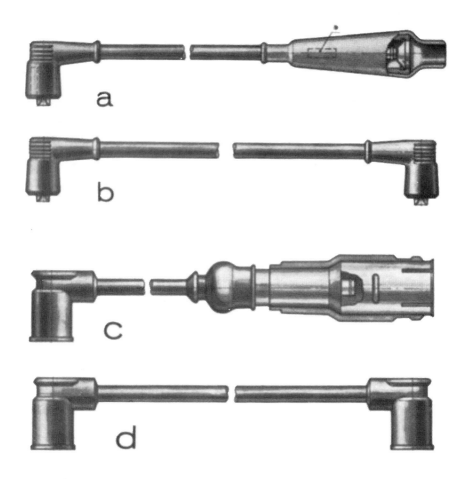

Fig. 4.6. Different types of HT leads which have been used (see text) (Sec. 5)

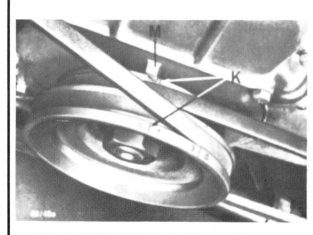

FIG. 4.7. TIMING MARKS ON THE CRANKSHAFT
PULLEY (SEC. 6)

M   Zero mark
K   Notch

6.3 Align the zero mark with the notch

4 At this point the distributor contacts should be just commencing to open. This can be checked, if necessary, by connecting a 12 volt test lamp between the ignition terminal 1 and the chassis earth. When the contacts open the lamp will illuminate, and vice versa, if the ignition is switched on.

5 Adjust the distributor if necessary by slackening the pinch bolt and turning the distributor body slightly.

7 Dynamic ignition timing

1 Dynamic ignition timing can only be carried out using electronic test equipment and is therefore beyond the scope of this manual.

2 In cases where ignition timing is to be checked first set the static timing then arrange for a car electrical specialist to carry out the dynamic timing.

8 Ignition retarding for low octane fuels

1 In the case of engines which require a high octane fuel there will be a tendency for the engine to 'pink' if lower grade fuels have to be used in an emergency.

2 In this instance only, the ignition timing should be retarded by an amount equal to one degree on the crankshaft for every octane unit below 98 eg 95 octane is three degrees.

9 Twin box distributor fitted to 1971 USA models

1 A Bosch twin box distributor was introduced in 1971 in order to provide improved idling. Two vacuum connections are provided, one going to each side of the vacuum unit diaphragm.

2 The connection on the outer side of the vacuum unit goes to the carburettor, and the connection on the underside goes to the inlet manifold.

3 The distributor contacts, rotor, caps, leads and condenser are similar to those of other models. Reference should therefore be made to the earlier sections in this Chapter for further information.

10 Ignition system - fault finding and symptoms

By far the majority of breakdowns and running troubles are caused by faults in the ignition system either in the low tension or high tension circuits.

There are two main symptoms indicating ignition faults: Either the engine will not start or fire, or the engine is difficult to start and misfires. If it is a regular misfire, ie the engine is only running on two or three cylinders the fault is almost sure to be in the secondary, or high tension circuit. If the misfiring is intermittent, the fault could be in either the high or low tension circuits. If the car stops suddenly, or will not start at all, it is likely that the fault is in the low tension circuit. Loss of power and overheating, apart from faulty carburation settings, are normally due to faults in the distributor or incorrect ignition timing.

11 Fault diagnosis - engine fails to start

1 If the engine fails to start and the car was running normally when it was last used, first check there is fuel in the petrol tank. If the engine turns over normally on the starter motor and the battery is evidently well charged, then the fault may be in either the high or low tension circuits. First check the HT circuit. **Note** - If the battery is known to be fully charged, the ignition light comes on, and the starter motor fails to turn the engine **check the tightness of the leads on the battery terminals** and also the secureness of the earth lead to its **connection to the body.** It is quite common for the leads to have worked loose, even if they look and feel secure. If one of the battery terminal posts gets very hot when trying to work the starter motor this is a sure indication of a faulty connection to that terminal.

2 One of the commonest reasons for bad starting is wet or damp spark plug leads and distributor. Remove the distributor cap. If condensation is visible internally, dry the cap with a rag and also wipe over the leads. Replace the cap.

3 If the engine still fails to start, check that current is reaching the plugs, by disconnecting each plug lead in turn at the spark plug end, and hold the end of the cable about 3/16 inch away from the cylinder block. Spin the engine on the starter motor.

4 Sparking between the end of the cable and the block should be fairly strong with a strong regular blue spark. (Hold the lead with a glove, to avoid electric shock). If current is reaching the plugs, then remove them and clean and regap them. The engine should now start.

5 If there is no spark at the plug leads, take off the HT lead from the centre of the distributor cap and hold it to the block as before. Spin the engine on the starter once more. A rapid

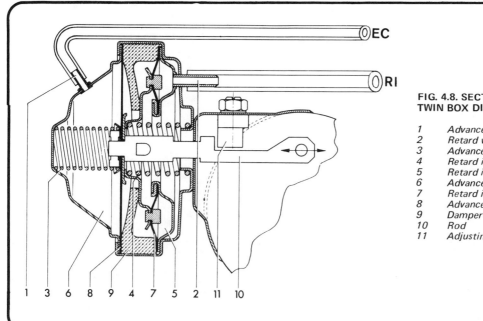

FIG. 4.8. SECTIONAL VIEW OF THE TWIN BOX DISTRIBUTOR (SEC. 9)

1	Advance vacuum connection (EC)
2	Retard vacuum connection (RI)
3	Advance ignition spring
4	Retard ignition spring
5	Retard ignition vacuum chamber
6	Advance ignition vacuum chamber
7	Retard ignition diaphragm
8	Advance ignition diaphragm
9	Damper
10	Rod
11	Adjusting eccentric (sealed)

succession of blue sparks between the end of the lead and the block indicates that the coil is in order and that the distributor cap is cracked, the rotor arm is faulty or the carbon brush in the top of the distributor cap is not making good contact with the spring on the rotor arm. Possibly the points are in bad condition. Clean and reset them as described in this Chapter.

6   If there are no sparks from the end of the lead from the coil check the connections at the coil end of the lead. If it is in order start checking the low tension circuit.

7   Use a 12v voltmeter or a 12v bulb and two lengths of wire. With the ignition switched on and the points open, test between the low tension wire to the coil and earth. No reading indicates a break in the supply from the ignition switch. Check the connections at the switch to see if any are loose. Refit them and the engine should run. A reading shows a faulty coil or condenser or broken lead between the coil and the distributor.

8   Take the condenser wire off the points assembly and with the points open, test between the moving point and earth. If there is now a reading then the fault is in the condenser. Fit a new one and the fault is cleared.

9   With no reading from the moving point to earth, take a reading between earth and the CB or − terminal of the coil. A reading here shows a broken wire which will need to be replaced between the coil and distributor. No reading confirms that the coil has failed and must be replaced, after which the engine will run once more. Remember to refit the condenser wire to the points assembly. For these tests it is sufficient to separate the points with a piece of dry paper while testing with the points open.

12 Fault diagnosis - engine misfires

1   If the engine misfires regularly, run it at a fast idling speed. Pull off each of the plug caps in turn and listen to the note of the engine. Hold the plug cap in a dry cloth or with a rubber glove as additional protection against a shock from the HT supply.

2   No difference in engine running will be noticed when the lead from the defective circuit is removed. Removing the lead from one of the good cylinders will accentuate the misfire.

3   Remove the plug lead from the end of the defective plug and hold it about 3/16 inch away from the block. Restart the engine. If the sparking is fairly strong and regular the fault must lie in the spark plug.

4   The plug may be loose, the insulation may be cracked, or the points may have burnt away giving too wide a gap for the spark to jump. Worse still, one of the points may have broken off. Either renew the plug, or clean it, reset the gap and then test it.

5   If there is no spark at the end of the plug lead, or if it is weak and intermittent, check the ignition lead from the distributor to the plug. If the insulation is cracked or perished, renew the lead. Check the connections at the distributor cap.

6   If there is still no spark, examine the distributor cap carefully for tracking. This can be recognised by a very thin black line running between two or more electrodes, or between an electrode and some other part of the distributor. These lines are paths which now conduct electricity across the cap thus letting it run to earth. The only answer is a new distributor cap.

Measuring plug gap. A feeler gauge of the correct size (see ignition system specifications) should have a slight 'drag' when slid between the electrodes. Adjust gap if necessary

Adjusting plug gap. The plug gap is adjusted by bending the earth electrode inwards, or outwards, as necessary until the correct clearance is obtained. Note the use of the correct tool

Normal. Grey-brown deposits, lightly coated core nose. Gap increasing by around 0.001 in (0.025 mm) per 1000 miles (1600 km). Plugs ideally suited to engine, and engine in good condition

Carbon fouling. Dry, black, sooty deposits. Will cause weak spark and eventually misfire. Fault: over-rich fuel mixture. Check: carburettor mixture settings, float level and jet sizes; choke operation and cleanliness of air filter. Plugs can be re-used after cleaning

Oil fouling. Wet, oily deposits. Will cause weak spark and eventually misfire. Fault: worn bores/piston rings or valve guides; sometimes occurs (temporarily) during running-in period. Plugs can be re-used after thorough cleaning

Overheating. Electrodes have glazed appearance, core nose very white – few deposits. Fault: plug overheating. Check: plug value, ignition timing, fuel octane rating (too low) and fuel mixture (too weak). Discard plugs and cure fault immediately

Electrode damage. Electrodes burned away; core nose has burned, glazed appearance. Fault: pre-ignition. Check: as for 'Overheating' but may be more severe. Discard plugs and remedy fault before piston or valve damage occurs

Split core nose (may appear initially as a crack). Damage is self-evident, but cracks will only show after cleaning. Fault: pre-ignition or wrong gap-setting technique. Check: ignition timing, cooling system, fuel octane rating (too low) and fuel mixture (too weak). Discard plugs, rectify fault immediately

Chapter 5 Clutch

Contents

Specifications

Type	Single plate, diaphragm spring, cable operated
Pressure plate type	Fichtel and Sachs MF 215
Clutch disc type	15 PSD with torsion damper
Clutch disc lining	Beral K66
Thickness of new disc (unloaded)	0.37 to 0.405 in. (9.4 to 10.3 mm)
Thickness of disc with 1056 lb (480 kg) load	0.35 ± 0.012 in. (8.9 ± 0.3 mm)
Minimum permissible thickness of worn disc (loaded)	0.276 in. (7 mm)
Clutch release travel	0.315 + 0.04 in. (8 + 1 mm)
Maximum permissible re-adjustment for worn disc	0.315 in. (8 mm) approximately
Clutch pressure	1080 to 1235 lb (490 to 560 kg)
Release pressure at 0.315 in. (8 mm) release travel	275 lb (125 kg) approximately
Clutch play at pedal	0.6 in. (15 mm) approximately
Profile of internal splines	24 x 2.5

Torque wrench settings

	lb ft	kg m
Pressure plate mounting screws	24.6 to 27.5	3.4 to 3.8
8 mm hexagon nut	10.85	1.5

1 General description

A diaphragm type single plate clutch is fitted to all Audi 100 models which have a manually operated gearbox. The clutch is cable operated and a ball bearing release is fitted.

Note: From transmission No 528 345 ZE onwards, a centrally guided clutch release bearing is fitted. Until depletion of stocks, if a new transmission is fitted to a car with the earlier type fittings, the original clutch pressure plate can be used if the clutch release shaft is removed and exchanged for the former type. Alternatively, and after depletion of stocks, the new type pressure plate must be installed.

2 Clutch - removal, inspection and replacement

1 In order to do any work on the clutch assembly it is necessary to first remove the engine and transmission from the car. This operation, together with removal of the clutch plate from the engine, is given in Chapter 1.

2 Using a stiff dry paint brush, dust the clutch friction plate and the pressure plate assembly. Take care not to inhale the dust - it may be harmfully irritating to the lungs.

3 Carefully examine the clutch friction plate for signs of distortion, burning or oil impregnation. If any of these faults are evident a new plate must be fitted.

4 Examine the internal splines of the friction plate for damage and wear. The plate can be fitted to the gearbox mainshaft to check for sloppiness. If this is present, (make sure that it is not the mainshaft at fault) the plate should be renewed.

5 Check the thickness of the clutch friction plate. A new friction plate should be 0.37 to 0.4 in (9.4 to 10.3 mm) thick. If the old friction plate is worn to within 1/32" of the rivet heads, it should be renewed.

6 If suitable workshop facilities are available, new linings can be riveted on. If this is done, the linings should be riveted on, one side at a time, then a run-out check carried out. The latter operation will require a special alignment tool which can be centred in a lathe. The maximum permissible run-out is 0.019 in (0.5 mm).

7 Examine the clutch pressure plate for scoring, loose rivets and damaged diaphragm spring leaves. If any fault is evident on this assembly it must be renewed as a whole - there is no workshop repair scheme.

8 Later versions of the clutch pressure plate have a release shaft with a centrally guided bearing. It is therefore essential that any replacement pressure plate fitted is of the correct type. Note: If a replacement transmission is fitted to the car the earlier type pressure plate can be used if the clutch release shaft mechanism is connected to the earlier type. The alternative is to use the later type clutch pressure plate.

9 When fitting the clutch assembly to the car it is essential that it is centred correctly. The full procedure is given in Chapter 1.

3 Clutch operating lever - removal and adjustment

1 The clutch operating lever can be removed, after disconnecting the cable, by removing the bolt and then withdrawing the lever from the splines.

2 When replacing the lever, or if adjustment for any other

reason is required, set the lever so that a dimension of 6.3 in (160 mm) is obtained between the tip of the lever hook and the clutch cable mounting bracket.

4 Clutch withdrawal mechanism - removal and reassembly

1 Prise out the springs which hold the clutch release (thrust) bearing, and put the bearing on one side for safety.
2 Prise off the release shaft spring from the leg of the operating fork.
3 Remove the screw and washer at each end of the release shaft which secures the eccentric bearing to the transmission casing.
4 Slide the release shaft towards the operating lever side of the transmission and remove the eccentric bearing at the other end.
5 Now slide the lever back, remove the other eccentric bearing and take out the lever.
6 When refitting the eccentric bearings make sure that the thinnest wall is facing forwards (ie towards the clutch housing).

5 Clutch cable - removal and adjustment

1 If the clutch cable is to be removed from the car, it is first necessary to remove the protective knee padding. Details of this procedure are given in Chapter 2 under 'heater removal.'
2 To remove the cable, loosen the two adjusting nuts at the clutch end of the cable, then slip the cable out of the bracket.
3 The cable can now be unhooked at the clutch pedal and operating lever.
4 Slacken the locknut holding the eyelet at the pedal end, then remove both the eyelet and the locknut.

5 Withdraw the complete cable from the engine compartment side, taking care that the washer and bush behind the bulkhead are not lost.
6 Replacement of the cable is a reversal of the removal sequence.
7 Check that the clutch operating lever setting is correct (see previous section), then by means of the adjusting nuts at the mounting bracket, take up the cable adjustment until there is a free pedal travel of 0.59 to 0.78 in (15 to 20 mm).

6 Clutch (and brake) pedal removal

1 Remove the protective knee padding and instrument panel trim as detailed in Chapter 2 under 'heater removal.'
2 Remove the lock clip from the pedal shaft.
3 Unhook the springs from the ends of the pedal levers.
4 Loosen the locknut on the swivel joint on the brake pedal then remove the ES pin.
5 Withdraw the pedal shaft.Note: If the pedal shaft has been fitted from the heater side it will be necessary to remove the heater as described in Chapter 2.
6 Unhook the clutch cable and remove the pedal.
7 Screw the brake plunger into the swivel joint until the brake pedal can be removed.
8 The procedure for replacement is the reverse of that for removal, but new pedal bushes should always be used.
9 After reassembly, the swivel joint on the brake pedal can be adjusted by turning the brake plunger until the pedal rests on the rubber pad. This should provide a free movement of approximately 0.039 in (1 mm) between the piston rod and the piston or 0.196 in (5 mm) at the brake pedal.

FIG. 5.1. CLUTCH OPERATING LEVER ADJUSTMENT (SEC. 3)

a Lever
b Mounting bracket
c Pinch bolt
X Dimensions of 6.3 in (160.0 mm)

Fig. 5.2. The clutch withdrawal mechanism (Sec. 4)

Fig. 5.3. Later type clutch pressure plate (Sec. 4)

Fig. 5.4. Early type clutch pressure plate (Sec. 4)

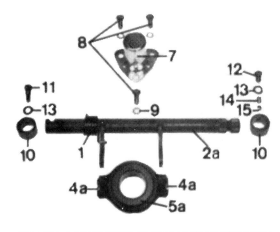

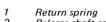

FIG. 5.5. LATER TYPE CLUTCH RELEASE SHAFT (SEC. 4)

1   Return spring, release shaft
2a Release shaft assembly
4a Spring
5a Bearing, centrally guided
7   Guide sleeve
8   Hex. head screw
9   Lockwasher
10 Guide bushing, release shaft
11 Hex. head stud
12 Hex. head screw
13 Washer
14 Spring
15 Pressure pin

FIG. 5.6. EARLY TYPE CLUTCH RELEASE SHAFT (SEC. 4)

1   Return spring
2   Release shaft assembly
4   Spring
5   Bearing
10 Guide sleeve, release shaft
11 Hex. head stud
12 Hex. head screw
13 Washer
14 Spring
15 Pressure pin

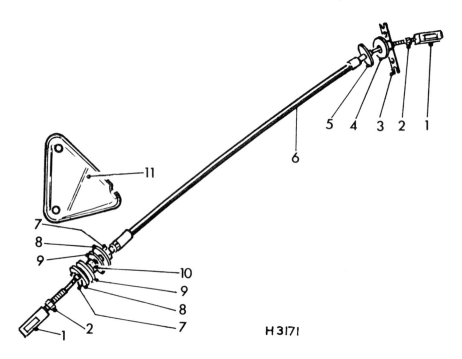

H 3171

FIG. 5.7. COMPONENT PARTS OF THE CLUTCH CABLE (SEC. 5)

1 Threaded eyelet	4 Bushing	7 Hex. nut	10 Bushing
2 Hex. nut	5 Washer	8 Washer	11 Mounting bracket
3 Bulkhead	6 Cable	9 Rubber washer	

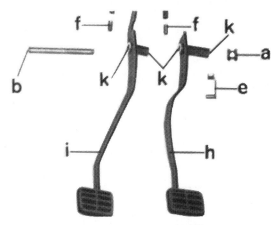

FIG. 5.8. THE CLUTCH AND BRAKE PEDALS (SEC. 6)

a	Lock clip
b	Shaft
e	ES pin
f	Spring with sleeve
h	Brake pedal
i	Clutch pedal
k	Bushing

FIG. 5.9. PEDAL ADJUSTMENT (SEC. 6)

c	Nut
d	Swivel joint
g	Brake plunger
h	Brake pedal
l	Rubber pad

7 Clutch squeal - diagnosis and cure

1 If on taking up the drive or when changing gear, the clutch squeals this is sure indication of a badly worn clutch release bearing. As well as regular wear due to normal use, wear of the clutch release bearing is much accentuated if the clutch is ridden or held down for long periods in gear, with the engine running. To minimise wear of this component the car should always be taken out of gear at traffic lights or for similar hold ups.

2 It may be found that if the clutch release bearing is very badly worn due to lack of lubrication or overheating a different type of noise, being of a more harsh or grinding nature, may be experienced.

3 The clutch release bearing is not an expensive item and it is recommended that it always be renewed during a major clutch overhaul.

8 Clutch slip - diagnosis and cure

1 Clutch slip is a self evident condition which occurs when the clutch friction plate is badly worn, the release arm free travel is insufficient, oil or grease have got onto the flywheel or pressure plate faces, the pressure plate itself is faulty or the cable is incorrectly adjusted.

2 The reason for clutch slip is that, due to one of the faults listed above, there is either insufficient pressure from the pressure plate, or insufficient friction from the friction plate to ensure solid drive.

3 If small amounts of oil get into the clutch, they will be burnt off under the heat of clutch engagement, in the process gradually darkening the linings. Excessive oil on the clutch will burn off leaving a carbon deposit which can cause bad slip, or fierceness, spin and judder.

4 If clutch slip is suspected, and cconfirmation of the condition is required, there are several tests which can be made:

a) With the engine in 2nd or 3rd gear and pulling lightly up a moderate incline, sudden depression of the accelerator pedal may cause the engine to increase its speed without any increase in road speed. Easing off on the accelerator will then give a definite drop in engine speed without the car slowing.

b) Drive the car at a steady speed in top gear and braking with the left leg, try to maintain the same speed by depressing down on the accelerator. Providing the same speed is maintained a change in the speed of the engine confirms that slip is taking place.

c) In extreme cases of clutch slip the engine will race under normal acceleration conditions.

9 Clutch spin - diagnosis and cure

1 Clutch spin is a condition which occurs when the operating cable is incorrectly adjusted, the release arm free travel is excessive, there is an obstruction in the clutch (either on the primary gear splines or in the operating lever itself) or oil may have partially burnt off the clutch linings and left a resinous deposit which is causing the clutch disc to stick to the pressure plate or flywheel.

2 The reason tor clutch spin is that due to any, or a combination of, the faults just listed, the clutch pressure plate is not completely freeing from the centre plate, even when the clutch pedal is fully depressed.

3 If clutch spin is suspected, the condition can be confirmed by extreme difficulty in engaging first gear from rest, difficulty in changing gear, and very sudden take-up of the clutch drive at the fully depressed end of the clutch pedal travel as the clutch is released.

4 Check the operating lever free travel and that the cable is correctly adjusted.

5 If these points are checked and found to be in order, then the fault lies internally in the clutch, and it will be necessary to remove the clutch for examination.

10 Clutch judder - diagnosis and cure

1 Clutch judder is a self-evident condition which occurs when the gearbox or engine mountings are loose or too flexible; when there is oil on the faces of the clutch friction plate; or when the clutch pressure plate has been incorrectly adjusted.

2 The reason for clutch judder is that due to one of the faults just listed, the clutch pressure plate is not freeing smoothly from the friction disc, and is snatching.

3 Clutch judder normally occurs when the clutch pedal is released in 1st or reverse gears, and the whole car shudders as it moves backwards or forwards.

4 If the above points are all satisfactory, check also for wear in the final drive unit and drive shaft couplings.

Chapter 6 Manual transmission

For modifications, and information applicable to later models, see Supplement at end of manual

Contents

Specifications

Type	Two shaft, constant mesh with Porsche synchronization		
Type reference	083		
Speeds	Four forward, one reverse		
Gear type	Helical tooth		
Gear ratios:	Audi 100	Audi 100S and LS	Audi 100GL and Coupe' S
Final drive	37 : 9	35 : 9	37 : 10
First gear	34 : 10	34 : 10	34 : 10
Second gear	35 : 18	35 : 18	35 : 18
Third gear	34 : 25	34 : 25	34 : 25 reinforced
Fourth gear	29 : 30	29 : 30	29 : 30
Reverse gear	31 : 10	31 : 10	31 : 10

Release shaft diameter	20 mm (0.787 in.)
Stub axle diameter	35 mm (1.378 in.)
Synchronization size	75 mm (2.95 in.)
Gearshift travel	12 mm (0.472 in.)
Lubricant	SAE 80 hypoid transmission fluid (eg. Castrol Hypoy Light)
Capacity	3.5 pints (2 litres, 4.2 US pints)

Mainshaft

	in.	mm
Maximum permissible run-out	0.00078	0.02
Oil slinger flange to bearing shoulder	13.16	334.5

Selector rod stop pins:
Reverse and first/second	0.67	17
First/second and third/fourth	0.46	11.7

Drive pinion:
End play	0.0039	0.1

Speedometer drive needle bearing:
Depth	2.22 ± 0.008	56.5 ± 0.2 mm

Differential bearings:
End float	0.0039	0.1 mm

Selector springs:
Reverse	1.1614	29.5
First/second	1.3386	34.0
Third/fourth	1.0236	26.0

Torque wrench settings

	lb ft	kg m
* Stub axle nut	18 to 23.8	2.5 to 3.3
* Differential flange nut	18 to 23.8	2.5 to 3.3
* Transmission cover nut	18 to 23.8	2.5 to 3.3
* End cover nut/screw	18 to 23.8	2.5 to 3.3
Shift rod cover screw	5.78 to 7.23	0.8 to 1.0
Reverse operating lever	21.7 to 28.9	3.0 to 4.0
Crownwheel - differential housing screw	50.6	7.0
Drive pinion nut	72.3 to 79.5	10.0 to 11.0
Caliper stud	28.9 to 36.1	4.0 to 5.0
Oil filler/level screw	21.7 to 25.3	3.0 to 3.5
Oil drain screw	21.7 to 25.3	3.0 to 3.5
Mainshaft needle bearing screw	2.9 to 4.3	0.4 to 0.6
Speedometer drive bush	25.3 to 28.9	3.5 to 4.0
Reverse switch	25.3 to 28.9	3.5 to 4.0
Clutch release shaft set screw	7.23 to 10.85	1.0 to 1.5
Steering lock plug	4.3 to 6.5	0.6 to 0.9

* As from transmission No. 218940 the tensile strength of these nuts was changed from 6G to 8G and the studs from 8G to 10K. During repair it is essential that studs and nuts of the new type are used.

1 General description

The manual transmission used for the Audi 100 series is a two-shaft unit with an integral differential assembly, and incorporates a Porsche synchronization system. All gears are helically toothed and, with the exception of reverse, are in constant mesh - the clutch bodies are fixed to the gear wheels.

The final drive unit is a conventional type and is incorporated in the transmission housing.

Note 1: Following the introduction of the engine oil guard and centrally guided clutch release bearing, it has become necessary to provide exchange transmission units, when required, to the latest standard.

Note 2: If it is required to renew the third or fourth speed gears, replacement of either must be in pairs only.

Note 3: If the first, second or reverse speed gears are to be renewed, the main shaft must be renewed also. The main shaft cannot be renewed without these gears.

2 Dismantling the transmission - cautionary note

1 The information given in this Chapter describes the method of stripping and rebuilding the transmission unit. By practical experience it has been proved that there are no real obstacles to be overcome provided that no major parts are to be removed.

2 It is strongly recommended that before any dismantling is carried out, the reader familiarises himself with the notes included in this section since, unless a straightforward strip and rebuild is carried out, checking backlash of the crownwheel and pinion, and end float of the drive pinion will pose a problem.

3 If there is reason to suppose that replacement of major parts will be necessary, first consult your Audi dealer. He will advise you as to what stage the rebuilding can go before the checks are carried out. It will then be necessary for these checks to be carried out by the dealer who will also then complete some of the rebuilding.

4 The full rebuild procedure is given later in the chapter and can be referred to where it is unnecessary to carry out the aforementioned checks and adjustments.

3 Dismantling the transmission - preliminary operations

1 Remove the engine and transmission unit from the car as detailed in Chapter 1 and separate the two major assemblies.

2 Carefully clean the outside of the transmission unit with petrol or proprietary solvents, taking care that none is allowed to contact the clutch thrust bearing.

3 Remove the reversing light switch (photo).

4 Remove the brake calipers and associated hydraulic pipes from each side in turn (photos).

5 Remove the retaining spring clips from the clutch release bearing using a screwdriver or similar (photo). Put the bearing to one side for safety.

6 If it is necessary to remove the clutch release shaft and bearings, the procedure is given in Chapter 5.

7 Remove the speedometer drive bush (photo).

4 Shift rod - removal, dismantling and reassembly

1 Remove the three hexagon headed screws which retain the shift rod cover, after marking its relative position on the shift rod (photo) then carefully drive out the rod and cover from the other end (photo).

2 If the shaft seal is faulty it can be prised out and a new one fitted using a small amount of a multi-purpose grease such as Castrol LM.

3 Remove the hexagon headed plug from the shift rod cover and take out the washer, spring and plunger.

4 The shaft can now be taken out of the cover and, if necessary, the oil seal renewed.

5 When reassembling the shift rod, it is important to use a sealant such as golden Hermetite on all the sealing surfaces and screws.

3.3 Removing the reversing light switch

3.4a Removing the brake calipers and discs

3.4b Removing the brake calipers and discs

3.5 Removing the clutch release bearing

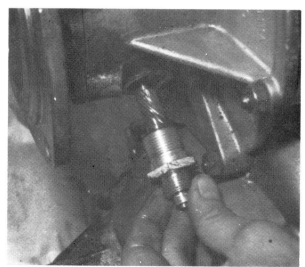

3.7 Removing the speedometer drive bush

4.1a Marking the shift rod position

4.1b Withdrawing the shift rod

5 Stub axles - removal, dismantling and reassembly

1 By working through the two holes in the stub axle flange remove the four nuts and washers from the mountings.

2 Obtain two 12 mm bolts each of about 5¼ in (135 mm) in length and locally relieve the diameter at the end. This is to prevent thread damage on the stub axle flange should the bolt threads be damaged.

3 Fit the bolts through the stub axle flange in such a way that they rest on the two bosses on the transmission casing then carefully and evenly tighten them to withdraw the stub axle (photo).

4 If it is required to remove the bearings, use a universal extractor to pull off each bearing and flange in turn.

5 It is recommended that the shaft seals are replaced, even if there is no apparent fault. These can be prised out of the flanges. Before fitting new seals, fill the space between the inner and outer lips with a multi-purpose grease such as Castrol LM.

6 Examine the bearings, as they are before cleaning. If there is any sign of rough running or slackness they should be replaced without hesitation. With rough running bearings the damage will already have occurred so although cleaning them may give an apparent cure, they will not last.

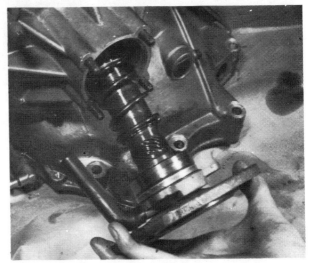

5.3 Removing the stub axle

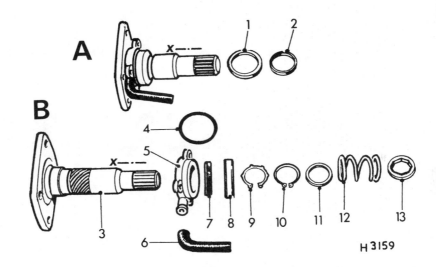

FIG. 6.1. THE STUB AXLES
(SEC. 5)

A   Stub axle, left
B   Stub axle, right
1   Washer
2   Washer
3   Stub axle, right with speedometer drive
4   Cord seal
5   Flange
6   Drain hose
7   Shaft seal
8   Grooved ball bearing
9   Circlip
10   Circlip
11   Washer
12   Spring
13   Thrust washer

H 3159

7 It is essential that cord seals are renewed irrespective of whether any other parts have been renewed.

8 When reassembling, make sure that the bearing is fitted with the lettering on the race facing towards the transmission unit. Take care that the outer race of the bearing is not loaded during fitment. All sliding surfaces on the axle shaft should be lightly coated with Molykote G or LM348 during this assembly stage.

9 The stub axles can now be reassembled to the transmission unit in the reverse order to that in which they were removed.

6 Transmission end cover - removal and replacement

1 Remove the three hexagon headed screws and four nuts from the transmission end cover. Note the relative screw lengths for when replacement is required. Remove the lock washers.

2 Take off the end cover (photo) and note the gasket thickness and number of shims fitted (photo). Replacement gaskets are supplied in three different thicknesses and the correct thickness must be used.

3 Before replacing the end cover remove all traces of gasket material from both the end cover and the transmission cover.

4 When replacing the shims they can be held in position if

necessary using a little multi-purpose grease.

5 When the end cover is in position coat the screw threads with golden Hermetite after first ensuring that they are clean. Use new lock washers on the screws and studs.

7 Differential flange and transmission cover - removal

1 Remove the end cover as described in the previous section.

2 Remove the nine hexagonal nuts which secure the differential flange to the cover.

3 Using a hide or plastic mallet tap all round the flange to break the seal, then carefully and evenly pull it away from the transmission cover (photo).

4 Remove the three springs noting their relevant lengths (photo), ie reverse spring is 1.16 in (29.5 mm), first/second spring is 1.34 in (34 mm) and third/fourth spring is 1.02 in (26 mm).

5 Either by tipping the transmission, or by using the magnetic oil drain plug, remove the three stop pins. Note: If the stop pins are of the old type, (ie without a flat surface running parallel to the major axis), they must either be modified or discarded and the new type used. If rework is carried out, the flat surface must

6.2a Removing the end cover and shim

6.2b Removing the end cover drive pinion shim

6.2c Removing the end cover mainshaft shim

7.3 Removing the differential flange

7.4 The selector rod springs

7.7 Removing the nut from the drive pinion

7.9a Removing the transmission cover

7.9b The transmission gear clusters

7.10 The differential assembly being removed

8.1 Removing the circlip from the mainshaft

8.2a Removing the mainshaft bearing

8.2b Taking out the mainshaft

be parallel to the axis and all burrs carefully removed (see Fig. 6.2.)

6 Using an appropriate tool, and working from inside the differential housing, move the reverse gear selector rod (top) and third gear selector rod (bottom) outwards to lock the drive pinion.

7 Fold back the tab on the nut fitted to the end of the pinion shaft, then unscrew the nut (photo).

8 Take off the nine nuts and washers which retain the transmission cover. Carefully drive out the upper dowel from the case.

9 Using an aluminium drift carefully and evenly drive off the end cover and gear clusters. Lift the end cover and gear clusters out, then lay them carefully on one side (photos).

10 Lift the differential assembly out (photo) and put it on one side. If it is not to be worked on immediately, place it in a polythene bag.

8 Mainshaft - removal, dismantling and reassembly

1 Remove the circlip and washer from the mainshaft at the bearing in the transmission cover (photo).

2 Using a suitable bearing extractor which will fit the screw thread in the mainshaft, draw out the mainshaft bearing (photo). It will be necessary at the same time for an assistant using a rubber or plastic hammer to drive the bearing out from the clutch end. The mainshaft can now be removed (photo).

3 If it is required to remove the third and fourth speed gears from the shaft it will be necessary to use a suitable press capable of exerting loads of 10 to 12 tons.

4 Assuming that this work is to be proceeded with, it will be necessary to remove the oil slinger from the mainshaft. It is not possible to remove this item intact and it will therefore be destroyed in the removal process. The slinger can be cut or torn using pliers but whatever happens do not scratch the ground surface of the mainshaft in the area where the slinger is fitted.

5 Remove the circlip, shim and needle cage (or needle sleeve) from the mainshaft then place the mainshaft on the press.

6 Remove the fourth speed gear (the largest one) and inner race of the needle bearing.

7 In a similar manner the third speed gear can be removed after removing the circlip (later models only).

8 Clean all the component parts and carefully inspect the

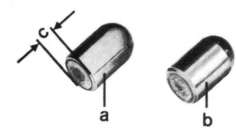

FIG. 6.2. THE STOP PINS (SEC. 7)

a New type pin
b Old type pin
c Dimension 0.295 - 0.004 in. (7.5 - 0.1 mm)

mainshaft and second gears. If the latter is unserviceable the mainshaft must be renewed complete with the gear.

9 Place the mainshaft on vee blocks at the bearing positions shown in the illustration (Fig. 6.3) and measure the total amount of run-out at the point where the oil slinger is fitted. The maximum permissible run-out is 0.00078 in (0.02 mm).

Note: Should it be found necessary to replace the mainshaft complete with second speed gear, or the third or fourth speed gear, it is essential that the mating gear on the drive pinion is replaced since they are machine lapped in pairs to ensure silent operation.

10 Carefully examine the rolling surfaces of the race and check that each roller is free spinning. If any heat discolouration is present the race should be renewed even though it may appear satisfactory in other respects. If the needles and cage require renewal it is essential that the inner bearing is also renewed.

11 The mainshaft can now be reassembled but it is positively necessary to establish whether there will need to be any renewal of gears on the drive pinion. If the first, second or reverse gears on the pinion require renewal it will be necessary to renew the mainshaft; if the third or fourth gears on the pinion require renewal, the mating mainshaft gear must also be renewed.

12 If it is not intended that the mainshaft will be reassembled immediately all the component parts must be kept together and covered with polythene for protection.

13 When reassembly is started, the first item to be fitted is the

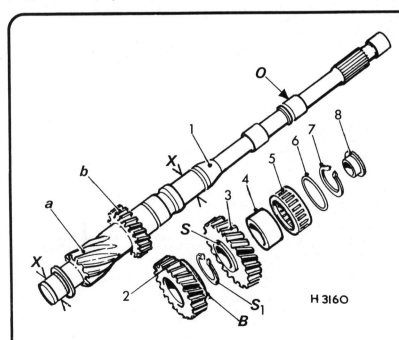

FIG. 6.3. THE MAINSHAFT AND GEARS (SEC. 8)

1 Main shaft
2 Gear, 3rd speed
3 Gear, 4th speed
4 Needle bearing (inner race not available separately)
5 Needle (not available separately)
6 Shim
7 Circlip
8 Oil slinger
a Gear, reverse and 1st speed
b Gear, 2nd speed
S1 Circlip
X Bearing positions for vee blocks during run-out checks
O Measure the run-out here

H 3160

third speed gear. Heat it in an oil bath at a temperature of about 100°C (212°F) then press it on to the mainshaft so that the collar is towards the clutch end.

14 If the transmission is of the type where a circlip is used to secure the gear, it should be fitted now.

15 Heat the fourth speed gear to a similar temperature and press this on too, with the collar away from the clutch end (ie towards the third speed gear). Now fit the needle cage, shim and circlip.

16 Again using an oil bath, heat the inner ring of the needle bearing to approximately 150°C (302°F). To fit it to the mainshaft a tube of 1.18 in (30 mm) inside diameter and 12.6 in (320 mm) length will be required, but great care must be exercised to ensure that it is fitted squarely. Because the mass of the ring is very small the whole operation must be carried out as quickly as possible or the heat will be lost. A pair of grips can be used to pick up the hot ring but on no account must the bearing surface be damaged.

17 Fit the oil slinger to the mainshaft next with the flange towards the clutch end of the shaft. It must be fitted so that the dimension from the outer surface of the slinger flange (ie the surface towards the clutch end of the mainshaft) to the bearing shoulder at the first speed gear end of the shaft is 13.16 in (334.5 mm). In this position the collar of the oil slinger will be positioned in such a way that its centre is immediately above the groove in the shaft.

18 With the oil slinger correctly positioned, use a flat nose punch and indent four positions, each disposed radially, at 90° around the mainshaft groove circumference. Make sure that the shaft is adequately supported during this step.

19 Now put the assembled mainshaft on one side for safety and cover with polythene until it is required.

9 Drive pinion - removal, dismantling and reassembly

1 Slide the reverse gear selector rod partly out of the transmission cover towards the differential end so that a depth of 0.51 in (13 mm) (approximately) is measured from the end cover face to the other end of the rod. The reverse gear selector rod is the lowest one with the transmission cover in the inverted position.

2 Slide the first/second speed selector rod (the middle one) in the same direction until it engages in second gear.

3 Slide the third/fourth speed selector rod to the idle position as described previously for the reverse gear selector rod (see Paragraph 1).

4 Now carefully drive out the drive pinion, lift it away from the cover and lay it on one side (photos).

5 Take off the selector rods one at a time. Take care not to lose the stop pins. The pin length for the reverse and first/second

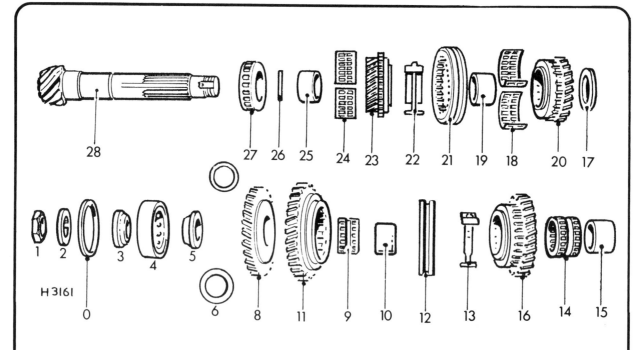

FIG. 6.4. THE DRIVE PINION AND GEARS (SEC. 9)

0	Shim	16	2nd speed gear assembly - synchronizing ring faces 1st speed gear
1	Hex. nut		
2	Lock plate with projection	17	Thrust washer with projection
3	Four point bearing inner race	18	Needle cage - two part
4	Four point bearing outer race and cage	19	Needle bearing inner race (27.35 mm long)
5	Four point bearing inner race	20	3rd speed gear assembly - synchronizing ring faces 4th speed gear
6	Shim (end play) - available in various thicknesses		
7	Shim (gear play) - available in various thicknesses	21	Operating sleeve with short threads
8	Reverse gear - collar facing four point bearing	22	Guide sleeve - shrunk on - wider collar faces 4th speed gear
9	Needle cage - one part	23	4th speed gear assembly - synchronizing ring faces 3rd speed gear
10	Needle bearing inner race (27.35 mm long)		
11	1st speed gear assembly - synchronizing ring faces 2nd speed gear	24	Needle cage - two part
12	Operating sleeve with short threads	25	Needle bearing inner race (25.35 mm long)
13	Guide sleeve with internal threads	26	Spacer
14	Needle cage - one part	27	Roller bearing inner race
15	Needle bearing inner race (27.35 mm long)	28	Drive pinion

9.4a Removing the drive pinion

9.4b The drive pinion and selector rods

gears is 0.67 in (17 mm) and for the first/second and third/fourth gears is 0.46 in (11.7 mm).

6 Using a suitable extractor and with the drive pinion vertical - roller race uppermost, pull off the first speed gear assembly together with the reverse gear (photo), shims and four point bearing inner race. Lay the parts carefully on one side.

7 Remove the needle cage (photo) and operating sleeve from the guide sleeve.

8 Now remove the second speed gear assembly together with the needle bearing inner race and the guide sleeve (see Paragraph 10, following).

9 Take off the next needle cage.

10 Using a suitable method remove the needle bearing inner race, thrust washer with projection, third speed gear assembly, operating sleeve, guide sleeve and fourth speed gear assembly. Depending upon the equipment available it may be necessary to carry out this job in stages or together with the second speed gear (photo).

11 The two, two-part needle cages, can now be taken off followed by the upper of the two remaining inner races (photo).

12 Unless a suitable press is available you will not be able to dismantle any further. If a press is available carefully press off the remaining inner race, spacer and roller bearing. Take care that press loads are not applied to the ends of the rollers, but to the cages. Note that the last inner race to be removed is 0.998 in (25.35 mm) long whilst the three others are each 1.077 in (27.35 mm) long.

13 Carefully clean and inspect all the component parts. Examine all the running surfaces of the needle and roller bearings for scoring and signs of heat discolouration. Look for wear and chipping of the teeth of the gears, particularly on the synchronization rings. If it is considered necessary to replace the synchronization rings reference should be made to the next section before reassembly of the drive pinion. Remember that if gears are renewed the mating gears on the mainshaft, or the mainshaft itself, will also have to be renewed.

14 If there is to be any delay before rebuilding the drive pinion, the parts should be put on one side and protected with a polythene covering.

15 When reassembly is to be commenced, initially heat the roller bearing inner race to about 100°C (212°F) in an oil bath and press it on to the drive pinion.

16 Then press on the short needle roller inner race.

17 Fit a two-part needle cage in position, then slide on the fourth speed gear assembly with the helical gearing facing towards the pinion end.

18 Heat the guide sleeve to approximately 150°C (302°F) in an oil bath and fit it so that the wider collar faces towards the pinion end. If a press is used for this operation do not apply pressure to the key profiles.

19 Slide on the operating sleeve.

20 Drive on a needle bearing inner race using a suitable tubular sleeve.

21 Fit the remaining two-part needle cage in position and slide on the third speed gear assembly so that the synchronizing ring is facing towards the pinion end (photo).

22 Now fit the thrust washer with the projecting tongue engaged in the long spline of the drive pinion (photo).

23 The second speed gear assembly can now be fitted (photo) together with the needle bearing inner race and the needle cage.

24 Slide on the guide sleeve and operating sleeve followed by the inner race and needle cage.

25 Now fit the first speed gear assembly with the synchronizing ring towards the second speed synchronizing ring (photo) and the reverse gear with the collar towards the four point bearing (photo).

26 Now press the complete assembly together ensuring that there is no spacing between any of the guide sleeves and needle races.

27 Stand the assembled drive pinion on a surface plate, pinion gear downwards then set up a suitable dial gauge and measure the difference in height between the end face of the pinion splines and the face of the collar on the reverse gear. This is to measure the thickness of shim required.

28 Whatever the height difference is, subtract 0.004 in (0.1 mm) and select a shim of this size. Replacement shims are supplied in steps of 0.1 mm over the range 0.2 to 1.0 mm. If an exact shim size is not available the nearest possible size should be used.

29 Now put the assembled shaft to one side to avoid damage and protect it with a polythene covering.

10 Synchronization gears - removing and refitting

A First speed gear

1 Remove the circlip and take out the synchronization parts.

2 Discard the circlip since the slightest burrs or deformation will impair correct synchronization.

3 Examine the parts for damage and wear, particularly on the teeth, and renew all defective or suspect parts.

9.6 Removing the reverse and first speed gears

9.7 Removing the needle cage

9.10 Removing the second and third speed gears

9.11 The limit to which dismantling of the drive pinion can be done without a press

9.21 Fitting the two part needle cage

9.22 The thrust washer engaged in the long spline

9.23 Refitting the second speed gear assembly

9.25a The guide sleeve, operating sleeve and first gear being fitted

9.25b The reverse gear being fitted

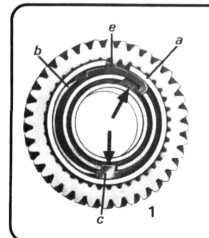
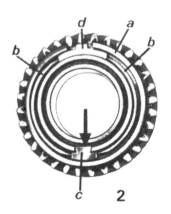

FIG. 6.5. SYNCHRONIZATION GEARS AFTER REMOVING THE CIRCLIP (SEC. 10)

1   Gear, 1st speed
2   Gear, 2nd to 4th speed
a   Synchronizing ring
b   Lock
c   Stop
d   Key
e   Key

4 When reassembling, make sure that the parts are correctly positioned as shown in the illustration (Fig. 6.5).

5 Don't forget to use a new circlip when reassembling and fit it in such a way that the end without the projection is fitted in the groove first of all. The other end (with the projection) then needs to be lifted slightly and spread a little. It can then be pressed down and snapped into the groove. Always use circlip pliers which fit properly to avoid damaging the circlip and thus rendering it useless.

Note: The later type first speed gear is similar to the second, third and fourth (see following section).

B Second, third and fourth speed gears.

1 Take out the circlip and synchronization parts as described for the first speed gears. Although the procedures and technique are the same the component parts are different.

2 Examine the parts for damage and wear, particularly on the teeth, and renew all defective or suspect parts. Don't forget to discard the old circlip and use a new one for reassembly.

3 Reassembly is carried out in the reverse order to removal, following the technique used for the first speed gear.

11 Differential assembly - dismantling and reassembling

1 Remove the tapered roller bearing inner races from each side of the differential assembly using a commercial two prong extractor, There are cutaways in the differential housing to enable the prongs to be fitted.

2 Drive out the tubular key using a 3/16 in diameter punch.

3 Now carefully drive out the differential pinion shaft.

4 The pinions can now be eased out of the large window in the differential housing and placed on one side.

5 The bevel gears can now be taken out of the housing in the same manner.

6 Lay out all the parts carefully so that they can be cleaned and inspected. Carefully examine the roller bearings for heat discolouration, scoring etc., if any is present, the bearings and outer races (one each in the differential flange and the transmission cover) will need renewal. If there is wear on the crownwheel it will need to be removed as described in the following paragraphs, and renewed together with the drive pinion.

7 To remove the crownwheel, initially slacken the eight retaining bolts in opposite pairs, then remove them.

8 The crownwheel can then be removed by driving the differential housing against a hard wooden block.

9 All mating surfaces must be carefully cleaned prior to reassembly.

10 Heat the new crownwheel in an oil bath to a temperature of approximately 80°C (176°F) then rest it on two blocks of wood; the housing assembly can then be driven on from above using two bolts for guidance. Finally tighten down the bolts in crosswise order to a torque of 50.6 lb ft (7 kgm).

11 To continue the reassembly, or start if the crownwheel has not needed replacement, heat the tapered roller bearings in an oil bath to approximately 100°C (212°F) then press on using a tool which does not apply load slowly to the roller cage.

12 The differential assembly can now be placed on one side, protected with a piece of polythene, until required.

12 Reverse gear and selector rod - removal and refitting

1 Remove the hexagon headed screw and washer on the top of the transmission cover.

2 Pull out the reverse gear selector rod, after removing the lever pivot screw, followed by the lever and selector fork (photo).

3 Carefully take out the two stop plungers.

4 If it is necessary to renew the reverse gear, the shaft can be pressed out and the gear removed together with the bushing.

5 If it is necessary to renew the four point bearing outer race, an inner race should be temporarily fitted in place and a tube with an inside diameter of 2.75 in (70 mm) used as a base. Using a suitable tool the bearing can then be pressed out.

6 Before replacing any components carefully clean and inspect the cover. Look for any cracks and general deformation; both inside and out.

7 To renew the four point bearing, heat the transmission cover in an oil bath to about 80°C (176°F). Press in the new bearing so that the lettering is towards the drive pinion using a tool which does not apply a load to the balls.

8 If the reverse gear has been removed it can now be refitted with its bush.

13 Transmission case - replacement of parts

A Drive pinion roller bearing outer race.

1 Remove the dowel pin which locates in the groove of the roller bearing outer race. This must first be removed then the outer race can be driven out.

2 The new outer race can then be driven in but take care that the groove in the outer race is located beneath the dowel pin and that the larger dimension from the groove to the side of the ring is inserted into the transmission casing first.

3 Make sure the outer race is fully pressed home, then fit the dowel pin with the groove uppermost.

Fig. 6.6. The differential assembly (Sec. 11)

12.2 The reverse gear selector rod being removed

B   Mainshaft needle bearing outer race.

1   If not already accomplished, remove the stud from the top of the transmission cover which holds the main shaft needle bearing outer race in position (where applicable).

2   Using an appropriate tool drive out the needle bearing outer race together with the seal and bushing, working from the clutch end of the transmission cover.

3   When refitting the outer race to the transmission cover note that the blind hole in the outer race **must** line up with the relieved diameter at the end of the stud, and therefore a great deal of care must be taken (where applicable). Although it is possible to fit the outer race at normal ambient temperatures it is advisable to cool it by packing it in dry ice for about five to ten minutes. The driving tool can also be cooled at the same time.

4   When the outer race is correctly positioned clean the threads of the stud and then coat them with golden Hermetite before refitting (where applicable).

C   Mainshaft seal and bushing (transmission dismantled)

Note: Whenever any transmission repairs are carried out the mainshaft seal should always be renewed.

1   Drive out the seal and bush working from the clutch end of the transmission cover.

2   Using a suitable tool drive in the bush until it is approximately 0.197 in (5 mm) below the upper surface of the bore.

3   Now fit the seal with the lip inside the transmission cover until it is flush with the upper surface of the bore.

D   Mainshaft seal (transmission removed but not dismantled)

1   Carefully prise out the old seal using a screwdriver or similar item.

2   Lubricate a new seal with glycerine then slide it over the mainshaft in such a way that the sealing lip is facing into the transmission.

3   Using a suitable tubular drift carefully drive in the seal until it is flush with the transmission casing.

E   Left hand brake caliper studs

1   If it is necessary to remove the left hand brake caliper studs a bolt extractor, or alternatively two nuts locked against each other, should be used.

2   When the new studs are ready for fitment degrease all screw threads in the transmission cover and on the studs then apply a coating of Loctite Activator grade N.

3   Now apply a coating of Loctite Binder grade AAV (or alternatively Omnifit type 250, red) to the threads of the studs and torque tighten them as specified. Unless heat can be applied to the transmission cover, 48 hours should be allowed to to lapse (24 hours if Omnifit is used) before the full locking strength is achieved. The studs should be fitted so that the upper edge is approximately 0.02 in (0.5 mm) below the mating surface for the brake caliper.

F   Right hand brake caliper stud

1   There is only one stud on the right hand side but the removal and replacement procedure is the same as for the left hand side.

---

14 Backlash and end float - checking and adjusting

---

1   As stated in the cautionary note at the beginning of the Chapter, checks and adjustments are required during the assembly stages of the transmission if major parts such as bearings, gears, drive pinion etc have been renewed. These checks are considered to be even beyond a workshop manual of this type and will therefore need to be carried out by a properly equipped Audi dealer.

---

15 Transmission unit - reassembly

---

1   Install the reverse gear into the transmission cover as shown

in the photograph, then fit the reverse shaft through the transmission cover. Make sure that the locating pin is correctly aligned with the slot and that the shaft is pressed fully home.

2   Slide the stop plungers into their respective positions. The 0.669 in (17 mm) long plunger is for the first/second speed selector rod (ie the middle one, viewed from inside the transmission cover) and the 0.461 in (11.7 mm) one is for the third/fourth speed selector rod (ie the one to the left of the middle one, viewed from inside the transmission cover).

3   Fit the reverse selector rod into the transmission cover (photo) complete with its selector fork. At the same time it will be necessary to fit the reverse operating lever in such a way that it rests against the selector rod and the selector fork in the groove in the reverse gear. The pivot screw will need to be fitted carefully when this step is completed, then tightened to the torque value stated in the specifications.

4   Make sure that the four point bearing is pressed fully into the transmission cover, using the shim if necessary. If the bearing has been removed or renewed it must be fitted with the lettering towards the pinion.

5   The next step is to select the correct thickness gasket for the end cover. This is best done by ensuring the dimension between the end face of the cover and the outer face of the four point bearing shim, and selecting the gasket as follows:

Dimension	Gasket thickness
0.0039 to 0.0059 in	0.00787 + 0.00197 in
(0.1 to 0.15 mm)	(0.2 + 0.05 mm)
0.00629 to 0.00709 in	0.00984 + 0.00197 in
(0.16 to 0.18 mm)	(0.25 + 0.05 mm)
0.00748 to 0.00866 in	0.0118 + 0.00197 in
(0.19 to 0.22 mm)	(0.3 + 0.05 mm)
0.00906 to 0.0102 in	0.016 + 0.00197 in
(0.23 to 0.28 mm)	(0.4 + 0.05 mm)

6   When the gasket has been selected, place it on one side, for use later on.

7   Fit the first/second speed and third/fourth speed selector rods on the assembled drive pinion as shown in the photograph.

8   Put the first/second speed operating sleeve in second and the reverse selector rod in idle.

9   Slide the pinion and selector rod into the transmission cover, and whilst doing so, press the third/fourth speed operating sleeve towards the cover slightly. This will allow the stop plunger to engage in the groove in the third/fourth speed selector rod.

10 Fit the inner race of the four point bearing, the locking plate and then the nut (photo). Torque tighten the nut then bend up the locking tab.

11 Install the assembled mainshaft into the transmission cover, working at a slight angle (photo).

12 Now carefully press the grooved bearing into the transmission cover (photo) - make sure that the circlip is in the groove.

13 When the bearing is fully home fit the circlip to the end of the mainshaft (photo).

14 Fit the differential assembly into the main transmission case (photo).

15 Align the drive pinion selector rod and operating sleeve so that the third and reverse gears are locked in mesh.

16 Make sure that the mating faces of the transmission casing and transmission cover are clean then lightly smear with a non-setting gasket cement such as golden Hermetite. Note that no gasket is required.

17 Fit the assembled transmission cover to the transmission casing (photo) taking extreme care that the mainshaft does not damage the lip of the seal at the clutch end of the casing.

18 Fit the dowels, followed by the nuts and torque tighten them, (see Specifications).

19 By working through the shift rod opening set the selectors to the idle position.

20 If the tapered roller bearing was removed from the differential flange it should now be refitted with the appropriate shims. Note: The bearing will only normally have been removed if backlash has had to be adjusted following the renewal of major

15.1 The reverse gear in the transmission cover

15.3 The selector rod and plunger

15.7 The assembled pinion ready for fitment

15.10 The four point bearing, locking plate and nut

15.11 Fitting the mainshaft to the transmission cover

15.12 Fitting the grooved bearing

15.13 Fitting the circlip to the end of the mainshaft

15.14 The differential in position

15.17 Fitting the assembled cover to the casing

parts. In this case the appropriate thickness shims will have been selected. Always fit the thickest shims first to prevent damage to the thinner ones if they need to be removed.

21 Now use a new O-ring which has been lightly lubricated with a general purpose grease and fit it to the differential flange.

22 Fit the selector rod plungers and springs in the positions from which they were removed (photo).

23 Install the roller bearing outer race locating pin (if previously removed) in such a way that the machined groove is visible.

24 Fit the differential flange to the transmission casing (photo), torque tightening the nuts crosswise.

25 Assemble the stub axle to the transmission unit, making sure that the drain hoses are positioned in such a way that they will be lowermost when installed in the car (photo). If necessary the thrust washers can be stuck to the circlip using a viscous grease.

26 Torque tighten the nuts crosswise working through the hole

in the flange (photo).

27 Fit the end cover, gasket and bearing shims (photo). Make sure that the three hexagon headed screws are clean and dry, then lightly coat their threads with a non-setting sealant such as golden Hermetite.

28 Now replace the reverse light switch plunger followed by the switch (photos). Make sure that the seal is intact and clean.

29 Refit the speedometer drive (photo).

30 The next step is to fit the shift rod cover and screws (photo). Make sure that all the items are clean then apply a non-setting gasket cement to the screw threads and sealing face of the cover. Note that there is a bracket for the brake pipe union fitted to the screw nearest the transmission cover (photo).

31 Reassemble the gearshift linkage at the other end of the shift rod, making sure that the position marks are correctly aligned.

32 Refit the brake caliper to the transmission housing whilst

15.22 The selector springs and plungers

15.24 The differential flange being fitted

15.25 A stub axle being fitted. Note the speedometer drive above the circlip

15.26 Torque tightening the stub axles

15.27 The gasket and shims in position before fitting the end cover

15.28a The reverse light switch plunger

15.28b The reverse light switch

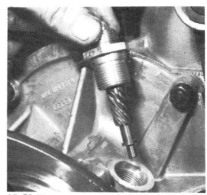

15.29 The speedometer drive being re-fitted

15.30a The shift rod cover being fitted

15.30b The brake pipe union bracket on the shift rod cover

15.32 The brake calipers being re-fitted

locating the brake discs over the stub axles (photo). Torque tighten the nuts on the studs.

33 Refit the clutch release bearing.

34 If considered more convenient, the transmission lubriciant can be added at this stage before reassembling to the power unit.

35 The procedure for fitting the transmission unit to the engine, and refitting both to the car is given in Chapter 1.

16 Adjusting gearshift lever on transmission - column change models

1 Adjust the selector lever so that dimension "d" (refer to Fig.6.7) is 1.929 ± 0.039 in (49 ± 1 mm) when it is in line with the holder.

2 With neutral selected, dimension "f" must be 3.307 in (84 mm), which gives an angle of 23° as measured between the stud on the transmission cover and the centre of the screw on the shift lever.

3 Now check that with second gear selected there is a dimension of 0.118 in (3 mm) between the shift lever and the transmission case.

17 Adjusting gearshift lever on transmission - floor change models

1 Select third or fourth speed on the transmission then adjust the lever in such a way that when it is approximately vertical, with the transmission installed or horizontal, the shaft rod projects through the lever bore by 0.04 to 0.06 in (1.0 to 1.5 mm) approximately.

Note: A special alignment gauge is obtainable for this adjustment but provided that you accept a certain amount of 'trial and error' adjustment, the gauge is not essential.

FIG. 6.7. ADJUSTING THE GEARSHIFT — COLUMN CHANGE MODELS (SEC. 16)

a Hex. nut	c Holder	(49 ± 1 mm)	f Dimension 7.24 in. (84 mm)
b Selector lever	d Dimension 1.929 ± 0.039 in. e Shift lever		g Dimension 0.12 in. (3 mm)

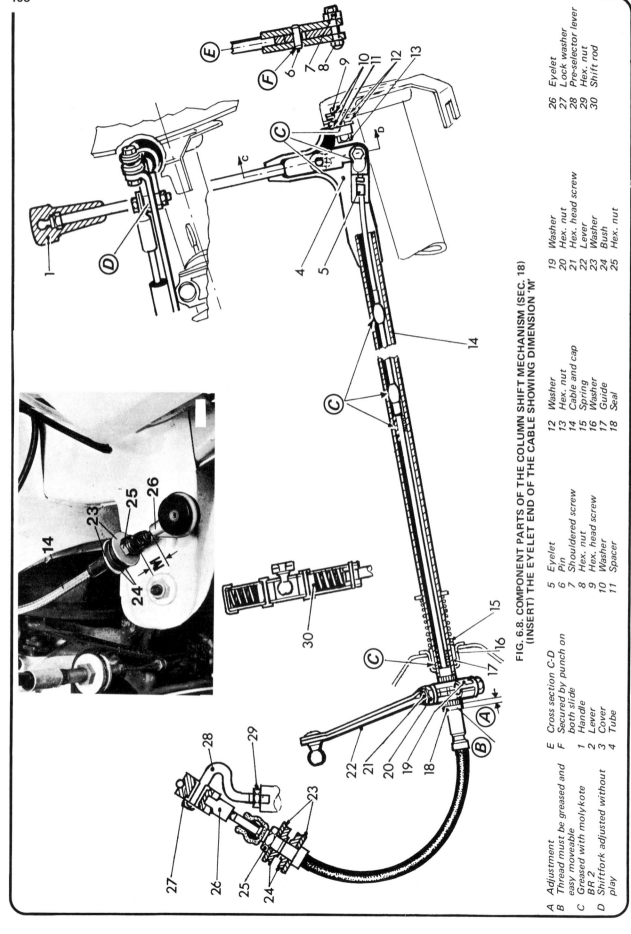

FIG. 6.8. COMPONENT PARTS OF THE COLUMN SHIFT MECHANISM (SEC. 18)
(INSERT) THE EYELET END OF THE CABLE SHOWING DIMENSION 'M'

A	Adjustment	E	Cross section C-D	5	Eyelet	12	Washer	19	Washer	26	Eyelet
B	Thread must be greased and easy moveable	F	Secured by punch on both slide	6	Pin	13	Hex. nut	20	Hex. nut	27	Lock washer
C	Greased with molykote	1	Handle	7	Shouldered screw	14	Cable and cap	21	Hex. head screw	28	Pre-selector lever
	BR 2	2	Lever	8	Hex. nut	15	Spring	22	Lever	29	Hex. nut
D	Shiftfork adjusted without play	3	Cover	9	Hex. head screw	16	Washer	23	Washer	30	Shift rod
		4	Tube	10	Washer	17	Guide	24	Bush		
				11	Spacer	18	Seal	25	Hex. nut		

18 Steering column gearshift cable - replacement

1 Initially remove the instrument panel padding and knee protection (as described for removal of the heater in Chapter 2, and the steering wheel and column casing as described in Chapter 8).

2 Disconnect the cable at the base of the gearshift handle.

3 Disconnect the lever at the shift rod on the transmission.

4 Note the distance "M" (see Fig. 6.8) between the eyelet and the end of the cable cover, and reset this distance when re-assembling.

5 Disconnect the cable at the shift rod cover then prise off the locking device on the eyelet/selector lever junction.

6 Unscrew the eyelet from the cable, then take the cable out of the tube.

7 When reassembling with a new cable, in addition to the distance "M" in paragraph 4 of this Section, set a dimension of 0.1575-0.04 in (4.0-1.0 mm) at point "A" in the illustration. Before the cable is fitted to the tube, apply a little general purpose grease with a molybdenum disulphide additive (eg Castrol MS3) to the sliding surfaces, and before making the connections at each end, (after fitment) make sure that there are no kinks by pushing the cable backwards and forwards two or three times.

8 The connections on the ends of the cable can now be refitted followed by the steering wheel and column casing, then the knee protection padding.

19 Fault finding table - Manual Transmission

Symptom	Reason/s	Remedy
Weak or ineffective synchromesh	Synchronizing rings worn, split or damaged	Dismantle and overhaul transmission.
Jumps out of gear	Broken gearchange fork rod spring	Dismantle and replace spring.
Excessive noise Lack of maintenance	Incorrect grade of oil in transmission or oil level too low Needle roller bearings worn or damaged Gear teeth excessively worn or damaged	Drain, refill, or top up with correct grade of oil. Dismantle and overhaul transmission. Dismantle and overhaul transmission.
Excessive difficulty in engaging gear. Clutch not fully disengaging	Clutch adjustment incorrect	Adjust clutch correctly.

Chapter 7 Automatic transmission

For modifications, and information applicable to later models, see Supplement at end of manual

Contents

Specifications

Torque converter

Type	Hydrodynamic three element, with the stator mounted on a one way, roller - type clutch
Type reference	003
Torque converter multiplication ratio	2.2 : 1 to 0.84 : 1, infinitely variable
Transmission fluid	Castrol TQ Dexron (R)
Capacity (including gearbox)	1.3 gallons (6 litres, 1.6 US gallons)
Quantity required for fluid changing	0.7 gallons (3 litres, 0.8 US gallons)

Final drive unit

Gears	Gleason
Crownwheel	41 teeth
Pinion	11 teeth
Ratio	3.727 : 1
Lubricant	SAE 90 EP gear oil (SAE 80 EP for Arctic climates)
Capacity	0.3 gallons (1.4 litres, 0.4 US gallons)

Gearbox

Type	Planetary, with hydraulically operated brake bands and multi-disc clutches
Annulus gear	84 teeth
Small planetary pinions	16 teeth
Large sun gear	51 teeth
Large planetary pinions	35 teeth
Small sun gear	30 teeth

Gear ranges:	Gearbox	Overall
First	2.65	9.877
Second	1.59	5.926
Third	1.00	3.727
Reverse	1.80	6.709

Torque wrench settings

	lb ft	kg m
Brake caliper stud in transmission case	32.55	4.5
Speedometer bushing in transmission case, front	23.85	3.3
Stub axle, left front, to transmission case	19.5	2.7
Oil drain (Hypoid oil), transmission case, front	21.65 to 26.75	3.0 to 3.7
Instrument connection plug	8.67	1.2
Operating lever, parking lock	14.23	2
Lever, cable to transmission case	2.6	0.36
Vacuum unit to transmission case	18.1	2.5
Oil strainer to valve body	2.6	0.36
Oil drain. Planet gear (Automatic transmission fluid) ...	9.4	1.3
Oil pan to transmission case	6.65	0.92
Drive plate to converter	21.65 to 25.3	3.0 to 3.5

1 General description

1 The automatic transmission unit comprises three assemblies housed in a common casing. These are the torque converter, the housing of which is directly coupled to the engine; the final drive unit which incorporates the differential assembly; and the planetary gearbox with its hydraulically operated multi-disc clutches and brake bands. This latter assembly houses the oil pump, coupled to the torque converter housing and therefore driven at engine speed, which supplies automatic transmission fluid (ATF) to the planetary gears, hydraulic controls and torque converter. The ATF also acts as a lubricant, cooling fluid and torque transfer medium. The final drive unit is separately lubricated with SAE 90 grade hypoid oil.

2 The torque converter is of the hydro-dynamic type and is similar in principle to that found in most automatic transmission systems. Torque multiplication ratio varies over the range 2.2:1 to 0.84:1 (approximately), the maximum value being obtained with the vehicle stationary, transmission engaged and the engine running at full throttle. As the road speed increases, the multiplication ratio falls to a minimum of around 0.84:1 and the engine torque is the same as the torque converter output (or turbine shaft) torque. This is known as the coupling point, and the torque converter is now operating only as a hydro-dynamic coupling. At this point engine speed is in the order 2600 rpm at full throttle and turbine shaft speed 2180 rpm. The design of the torque converter is such that as engine speed increases further, the angle of flow of ATF leaving the turbine causes the stator to turn on its one-way clutch which reduces even further the input/output speed difference until a maximum efficiency in the order of 96% is achieved. It is in this latter range that upward gear changing takes place under normal driving conditions when full throttle is being used.

3 The torque converter alone is inadequate for the provision of tractive effort over the complete range of driving conditions, hence the need for the gearbox driven from the turbine shaft. By the use of a planetary gearbox, forward gear changes can be made without interrupting power flow since all gears are in constant mesh. This changing is achieved by the hydraulically

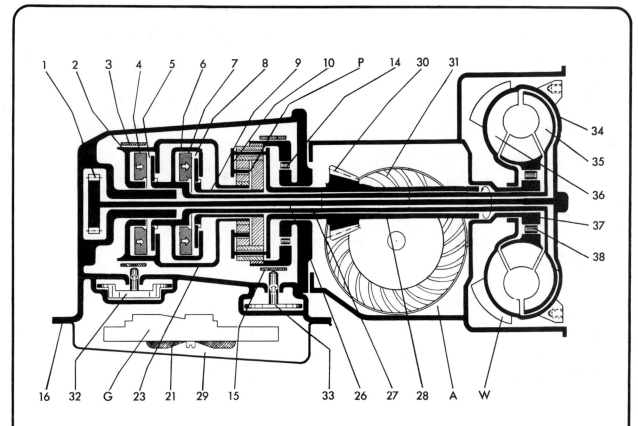

FIG. 7.1. SCHEMATIC DIAGRAM OF THE AUTOMATIC TRANSMISSION (SEC. 1)

1 Oil pump	15 1st gear and reverse brake band	29 Oil pan (automatic transmission fluid)
2 Clutch drum	16 Transmission case	30 Drive pinion
3 2nd gear, brake band	17 Control valve (main)	31 Crown wheel
4 Piston, direct and reverse clutch	18 Valve body	32 Piston, 2nd gear brake band
5 Direct and reverse clutch	19 Separator plate	33 Piston 1st gear and reverse brake band
6 Forward clutch drum with ball valve	20 Transfer plate	34 Torque converter housing
7 Piston, forward clutch	21 Oil strainer	35 Turbine
8 Forward clutch	22 Spring, valve	36 Impeller
9 Forward clutch hub	23 Drive shell	37 Stator support
10 Planetary gear carrier	24 Large planetary pinion	38 One-way clutch
11 Small sun gear	25 Large sun gear	P Planetary gears
12 Small planetary pinion	26 Oil pump shaft	G Transmission control - valve body
13 Annulus	27 Turbine shaft	A Differential - final drive
14 1st gear one-way clutch	28 Drive pinion shaft	W Torque converter

operated multi-disc clutches and brake bands which can hold or release, for example, sun gears, the planetary gear carrier or annulus gear.

4 Gear change timing is primarily a function of road speed (via the centrifugal governor) and engine load (via the vacuum operated primary throttle valve). This can be overridden however, by the kickdown control to provide maximum acceleration, and by the use of the selector lever to hold a particular gear.

5 Although the final drive unit fitted is peculiar to the automatic transmission system, it is conventional, with the drive pinion shaft coupled to the planetary gear carrier.

6 It is sometimes necessary to leave a car 'in gear' with the brakes off. With automatic transmission systems there is no direct coupling between the driven road wheels and the engine, as with manual gearboxes, so the engine cannot be used as a braking device when the car is stationary. On Audi automatic transmission, a parking lever locks into the planetary gear carrier whenever the selector lever is at "P".

Note: Owing to the complexity of the automatic transmission, dismantling should not be attempted by anyone not a specialist in this field. This chapter is limited to removal and replacement of the transmission unit (with the engine in the car), serviceability checks, fault finding and minor fault rectifications.

2 Automatic transmission unit - removal, engine remaining in the car

1 Remove the oval head screws which secure the apron (the apron is the transverse panel beneath the front bumper). Take off the apron and put it safely on one side to avoid damage.

2 Take out the screws holding the front grille and trim, noting the relevant screw lengths for the time when they are to be replaced. Remove the grille and put it safely on one side.

3 Fit an 8 mm x 10 cm (or equivalent size) bolt through the engine holder, stop pad and stop to hold the engine in position once the mountings have been loosened. Fit a nut and washer.

4 If a pedal support is available it should be fitted to the brake pedal in such a way that the pedal is depressed approximately 1 3/16 in (3 cm). Otherwise the pedal should be supported by a wooden block which will permit the 1 3/16 in movement, then a wooden strut made to hold the pedal down against the block. The other end of the strut can be wedged against the seat frame or steering wheel.

5 Remove the brake hoses from the pipelines noting which is which for the time when replacement is required (f1 will be reconnected to e1 - see Fig.7.5).

6 Disconnect the accelerator linkage and push the bush out of the support bracket in the direction of the right angled end of the accelerator link rod.

7 Disconnect the front exhaust pipe at the exhaust manifold, then the primary silencer. If the manifold/exhaust pipe gasket is completely undamaged, put it on one side for re-use; if it is damaged or there is any doubt about its condition, it must be renewed.

8 Remove the engine oil filter and starter motor. (see Chapters 1 and 10).

9 Disconnect each drive shaft in turn at the stub axle and temporarily suspend each from the upper wishbone. This will require two strut hooks which can be made from mild steel rod 9½ in long x 0.2 in dia. (240 cm x 5 mm). If other methods are used to tie the drive shafts to the wishbones, due consideration must be given to their weight.

10 Disconnect the transverse stabilizer bar on each lower wishbone.

11 Unscrew the selector cable holder, then disconnect the cable from the selector lever at the transmission. Remove the holder by pulling it over the bolt.

12 Next, place a workshop lift, trolley jack or similar beneath the transmission. Now disconnect the crossmember and power unit mountings at the body and support.

13 Remove the engine mount guard then left and right

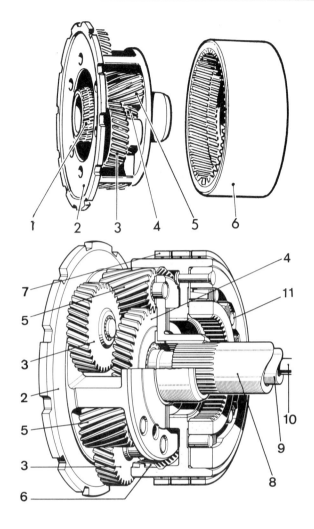

FIG. 7.2. THE PLANETARY GEARBOX (SEC. 1)

1	Small sun gear
2	Planetary gear carrier
3	Large planetary pinions
4	Large sun gear
5	Small planetary pinions
6	Annulus gear
7	1st gear and reverse brake band
8	Drive pinion
9	Turbine shaft
10	Drive shaft, oil pump
11	Roller type one-way clutch

mountings. Note: the position of the left mount is fixed and must not be altered.

14 Insert a 10 mm x 20 cm (or equivalent size) bolt through each mounting hole and fit a nut and washer.

15 Lower the engine and transmission until the weight is taken by the two bolts.

16 Disconnect the vacuum hose either at the T-adaptor or at the vacuum unit; take care that the latter item is not distorted in any way.

17 By working through the starter motor aperture loosen the torque converter housing from the engine drive plate gear ring. This will require a socket wrench with a splined adaptor to suit the three 8 mm fixing screws.

18 Undo the engine/transmission fixing nuts and bolts (quantity 7).

19 Carefully ease the transmission unit rearwards to clear the bolts and dowels then lower it, and immediately carry on to

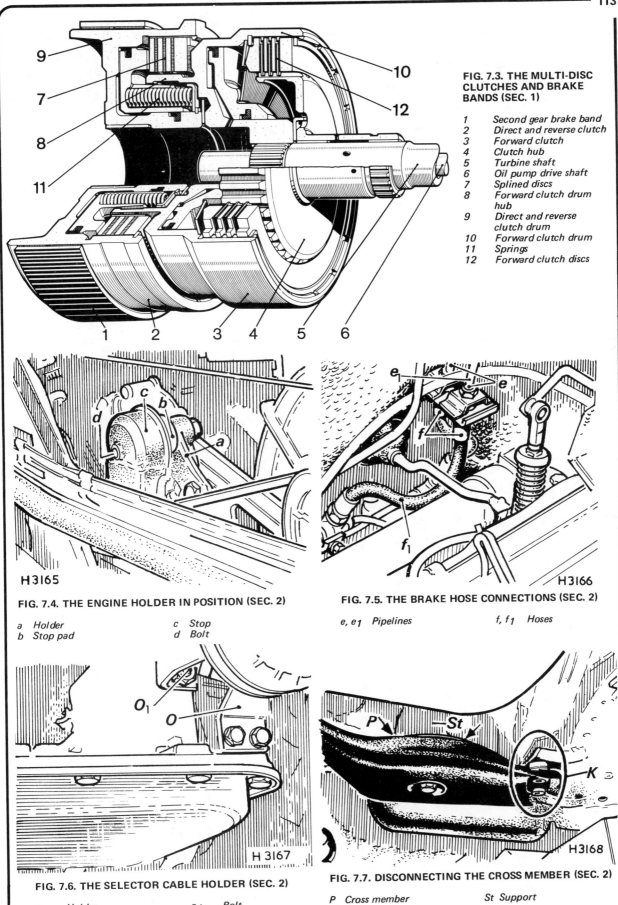

FIG. 7.3. THE MULTI-DISC CLUTCHES AND BRAKE BANDS (SEC. 1)

1 Second gear brake band
2 Direct and reverse clutch
3 Forward clutch
4 Clutch hub
5 Turbine shaft
6 Oil pump drive shaft
7 Splined discs
8 Forward clutch drum hub
9 Direct and reverse clutch drum
10 Forward clutch drum
11 Springs
12 Forward clutch discs

H3165

FIG. 7.4. THE ENGINE HOLDER IN POSITION (SEC. 2)

a Holder
b Stop pad
c Stop
d Bolt

H3166

FIG. 7.5. THE BRAKE HOSE CONNECTIONS (SEC. 2)

e, e₁ Pipelines   f, f₁ Hoses

H 3167

FIG. 7.6. THE SELECTOR CABLE HOLDER (SEC. 2)

o Holder   o₁ Bolt

H3168

FIG. 7.7. DISCONNECTING THE CROSS MEMBER (SEC. 2)

P Cross member   St Support
K Body

Fig. 7.8. The bolt (B) fitted to the mounting bracket (Sec. 2)

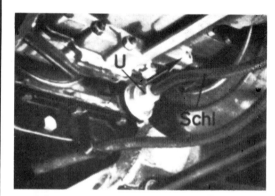

FIG. 7.9. DISCONNECTING THE VACUUM UNIT HOSE (SEC. 2)

Schl   Hose
T   T-adaptor
U   Vacuum unit

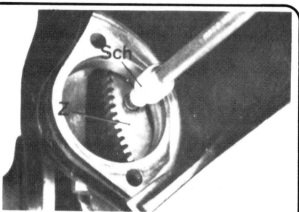

FIG. 7.10. LOOSENING THE TORQUE CONVERTER HOUSING (SEC. 2)

Sch   Splined adaptor
Z   Drive plate gear ring

FIG. 7.11. PREVENTING THE TORQUE CONVERTER FROM MOVING (SEC. 2)

Ha   Holding device

FIG. 7.12. TURNING THE SELECTOR LEVER FOR CABLE ADJUSTMENT (SEC. 3)

1   Cable
2   Clamping screw
3   Selector lever

30 - 104   Device for turning the selector lever

paragraph 20.

20 Fit a suitable device to the transmission housing to prevent movement of the torque converter. This tool **must** stay in position at all times during transit and storage. It is fitted by being moved in the direction of the arrows (see Fig.7.11) and removed in the reverse manner (dotted arrows).

21 Note whether the locating dowels have come away with the transmission unit. If they have, they will need to be removed and fitted to the engine if the same transmission unit is not to be refitted to the car.

3 Automatic transmission unit - replacement

1 To refit the transmission unit it will need to be eased into position and the torque converter holder removed at the last possible moment to prevent it from moving.

2 Bolt the engine and transmission together then reassemble the torque converter to the engine drive plate gear ring.

3 Refit the vacuum hose.

4 Raise the engine/transmission unit and refit the mountings - ensuring that the projection engages in the groove in the mount. Do not tighten the bolts fully. Refit the guard.

5 Reconnect the crossmember and power plant mounting to the body and support. Do not fully tighten the nuts.

6 Recheck the alignment of the engine/transmission as detailed in Chapter 1 - correct if necessary. Finally tighten all the mounting bolts and nuts.

7 Refit the selector cable holder and reassemble the cable to selector lever.

8 Refit the stabilizer to the wishbones.

9 Reconnect the drive shafts.

10 Replace the starter motor and oil filter.

11 Refit the front exhaust pipe and primary silencer.

12 Reconnect the accelerator linkage, bush and the connecting rod and shaft. Refit the brake hoses to the pipelines.

13 Remove the brake pedal support.

14 Refit the grille and apron.

15 Bleed the brakes as detailed in Chapter 9.

4 Selector lever cable adjustment

1 To adjust the selector lever cable, select "P" then fit the cable through the clamping screw.

2 Turn the selector lever in the direction of the arrow until it

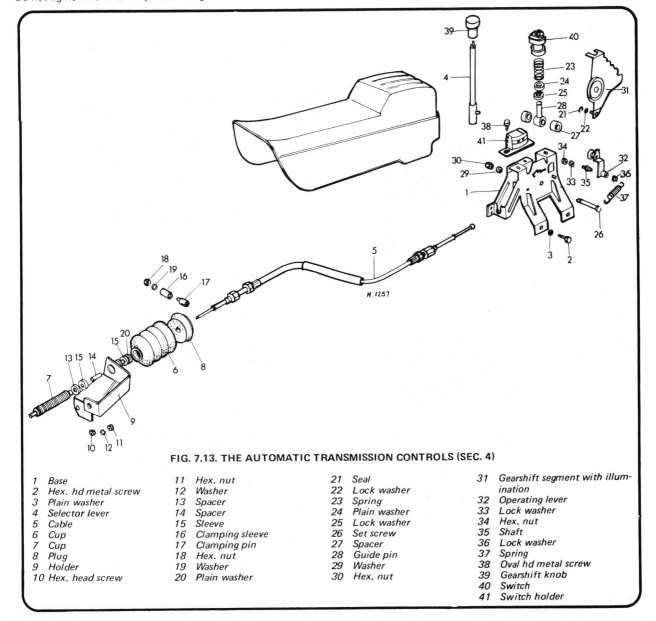

FIG. 7.13. THE AUTOMATIC TRANSMISSION CONTROLS (SEC. 4)

1 Base	11 Hex. nut	21 Seal	31 Gearshift segment with illumination
2 Hex. hd metal screw	12 Washer	22 Lock washer	
3 Plain washer	13 Spacer	23 Spring	32 Operating lever
4 Selector lever	14 Spacer	24 Plain washer	33 Lock washer
5 Cable	15 Sleeve	25 Lock washer	34 Hex. nut
6 Cup	16 Clamping sleeve	26 Set screw	35 Shaft
7 Cup	17 Clamping pin	27 Spacer	36 Lock washer
8 Plug	18 Hex. nut	28 Guide pin	37 Spring
9 Holder	19 Washer	29 Washer	38 Oval hd metal screw
10 Hex. head screw	20 Plain washer	30 Hex. nut	39 Gearshift knob
			40 Switch
			41 Switch holder

reaches the stop. The clamping screw must now be tightened. Some degree of caution must be exercised during this operation since accurate setting prolongs the life of the transmission.

3 With the handbrake on and "P" still selected, start the engine.

4 Move the selector lever towards "D" and note the point at which the engine speed commences to fall off.

5 Now move the selector lever towards "R" and again note the point at which the engine speed commences to fall off.

6 The distance from "N" to "D" and "N" to "R" must be equal, and the speed must fall off before either position is reached. If necessary readjust the selector lever cable to achieve this setting.

5 Replacing the engine drive plate

1 Initially remove the automatic transmission unit as detailed in Section 2 of this Chapter.

2 Removal of the drive plate is straightforward after taking out the six bolts and washers.

3 When refitting the drive plate to the crankshaft a dimension of 0.71 + 0.028 in (18 + 0.7 mm) must be maintained from the end face of the engine block to the outer face of the drive plate. Shim between the crankshaft and the drive plate, if necessary, to achieve this requirement.

6 Replacing the centering collar

1 Initially remove the automatic transmission unit as detailed in Section 2 and the engine drive plate as detailed in Section 5.

2 Using an extractor, remove the old centering collar.

3 Cool the new centring collar and locally heat the block and crankshaft using a portable electric heater/blower.

4 Drive in the new collar with a suitable drift until it bottoms in the hole.

7 Adjusting the 'kickdown' switch setting

1 The correct adjustment of the 'kickdown' switch is achieved

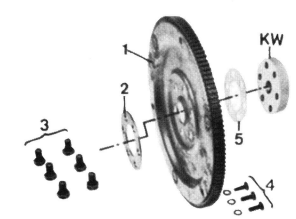

FIG. 7.14. THE ENGINE DRIVE PLATE (SEC. 5)

1	Drive plate	4	Hex. head bolts and
2	Washer		washers
3	Hex. head bolts	5	Shim if required
		KW	Crankshaft

FIG. 7.15. MEASURING THE DISTANCE FROM THE DRIVE PLATE TO THE END FACE OF THE BLOCK (SEC. 5)

1	Drive plate	a	Measured distance

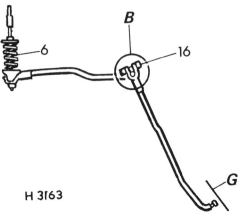

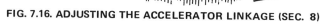

FIG. 7.16. ADJUSTING THE ACCELERATOR LINKAGE (SEC. 8)

3	Socket	16	Hex. head screw	B	Adjustment	C	Ball and socket
6	Spring	18	Ball head	G	Accelerator pedal	X	Setting dimension

when there is a clearance of 0 to 0.011 in (0 to 0.5 mm) between the switch operating leaf spring and spring loaded cap on the accelerator pedal.

2 When the pedal is depressed beyond its normal full travel position, the switch must immediately operate. This will be indicated by an audible click from the switch.

3 A small amount of adjustment can be made by repositioning the switch on its bracket.

8 Adjusting the accelerator linkage

1 Floor the accelerator pedal and prop it in this position.

2 Slacken the pinch screw on the accelerator linkage then set the throttles fully open.

3 Tighten the pinch screw in this position, ensuring that the coil spring is not fully compressed. Release the pedal prop.

4 Now disconnect the ball and socket linkage then floor the accelerator pedal. In this position the socket should be 0.39 to 0.59 in (10 to 15 mm) higher than the ball.

5 Reset the position of the socket on the connecting rod if necessary.

9 Adjusting the vacuum unit (primary throttle pressure)

1 Adjustment will be required if the gearshift timing is incorrect (see next section), or if the vacuum unit or oil seal have been replaced.

2 Disconnect the vacuum unit hose and blank it with a suitable bolt.

3 Remove the blanking plug from the transmission housing and

FIG. 7.17. ADJUSTING THE VACUUM UNIT (SEC. 9)

A   Blanked vacuum hose connection
B   Pressure gauge connection
30 - 106 Adjusting tool

connect a pressure gauge capable of reading at least 50 psi (3.5 kg/cm^2).

4 With the handbrake on, "N" selected and the engine running at about 1000 rpm, adjust the hexagon socket inside the vacuum unit, until a pressure of 48.36 psi (3.4 kg/cm^2) is recorded.

5 Stop the engine, disconnect the pressure gauge, refit the blanking plug and carefully reconnect the hose to the vacuum unit.

10 Gearshift timing

Shift	1 – 2		2 – 3		3 – 2		2 – 1		2 – 1 manual	
	above	below	above	below	above	below	above	below	above	below
Idle rpm	950 ± 50	950 ± 50	950 ± 50	950 ± 50	950 ± 50	950 ± 50	950 ± 50	950 ± 50	950 ± 50	950 ± 50
mph (kmh)	11(17)	13(21)	15(24)	17(28)	12(20)	11(17)	9(15)	7(11)	20(32)	18(29)
Full throttle rpm	2845 to 2540	3050 to 3230	3225 to 3410	4745 to 5075	3180 to 3525	2560 to 2680	2640 to 2755	2320 to 2375	5940 to 6670	3740 to 4150
mph (kmh)	19(30)	21(33)	54(87)	58(94)	39(62)	34(54)	16(25)	14(22)	47(75)	41(66)
Kickdown rpm	3220 to 3630	4940 to 5740	3715 to 3925	5640 to 5980	5296 to 5595	5295 to 5330	4420 to 5230	2955 to 3370	—	—
mph (kmh)	34(55)	40(64)	65 (105)	70(112)	65(104)	61 (98)	36(58)	30(48)	—	—

Note: Kickdown may occur within the rpm range listed, but must occur below the lower value.

2 Cars from Chassis No. 82 31 001 810 onwards

Shift	Model	1 – 2 max.	1 – 2 min.	2 – 3 max.	2 – 3 min.	3 – 2 max.	3 – 2 min.	3 – 1 max.	3 – 1 min.	2 – 1 max.	2 – 1 min.
mph (kmh)	100 LS	13.5 (21.8)	11.7 (18.7)	18 (28.9)	15.9 (25.6)	— —	— —	5.2 (8.4)	0.6 (1.0)	— —	— —
	100 LS USA	13.5 (21.8)	11.7 (18.7)	18 (28.9)	15.9 (25.6)	— —	— —	5.2 (8.4)	0.6 (1.0)	— —	— —
Zero throttle	100 Coupe' S & GL	13.5 (21.8)	11.7 (18.7)	18 (28.9)	15.9 (25.6)	— —	— —	5.2 (8.4)	0.6 (1.0)	— —	— —
mph (kmh)	100 LS	27.5 (44.2)	20.9 (33.6)	58.3 (93.9)	53.6 (86.2)	36.4 (58.5)	31.1 (50.1)	— —	— —	18.1 (29.2)	16.2 (26.1)
Full throttle	100 Coupe' S & GL	29.1 (46.8)	21.5 (34.6)	60.7 (97.7)	55.9 (90.0)	40.3 (64.9)	35.2 (56.6)	— —	— —	18.8 (30.3)	17 (27.3)
mph (kmh)	100 LS	40.1 (64.5)	33.4 (53.8)	68.2 (109.8)	63 (101.4)	64.2 (103.4)	59.6 (96.0)	— —	— —	35.9 (57.7)	28.6 (46.1)
	100 LS USA	40.1 (64.5)	33.2 (53.4)	68.1 (109.6)	62.9 (101.3)	63.8 (102.7)	59.4 (95.6)	— —	— —	35.7 (57.4)	28.5 (45.9)
Kickdown	100 Coupe' S & GL	41.9 (67.5)	35.5 (57.2)	70.7 (113.8)	65.7 (105.7)	67.2 (108.2)	62.9 (101.2)	— —	— —	38.2 (61.5)	31.4 (50.6)

The figures are taken from design calculations.

11 Checking the operation of the automatic transmission

1 Before any performance checking or fault diagnosis is carried out it is absolutely essential that the engine idle setting, ignition timing, carburettor settings, accelerator linkage, gearshift cable, transmission fluid level, 'kickdown' switch setting, etc are all correct.

2 Visually check the vacuum unit for damage, and replace if necessary.

3 Check and rectify any leakage from the transmission or final drive.

4 Check for loose or missing mounting bolts.

5 Check the tranmission fluid level, If it has a burnt smell it indicates burnt friction linings which will require specialist repair. If the fluid is dirty it can cause malfunction of the governor or valves and must therefore be renewed.

6 Provided that there is no obvious damage to the transmission, test drive the car under all conditions and note particularly the gearshift timing (Section 10 of this Chapter). All changes should be made rapidly with no interruption of power flow. If the engine speed suddenly increases after a change has been made a slipping clutch or brake band is indicated.

7 **Stall test:** Connect an external electronic tachometer to the engine; select "N" then start the engine. Apply both foot and handbrakes, select "D" then briefly depress the accelerator pedal and check that a stall-speed of 1900 to 2000 rpm can be obtained. Note: Due to the heat generated this test must be carried out in the shortest possible time. If the correct stall-speed cannot be obtained a fault in the one-way clutch or first speed clutch is indicated.

8 **Pressure test:** This test need only be carried out if satisfactory results have not been obtained from the previous checks and tests.

9 Run the engine until the normal operating temperature is reached then connect a pressure gauge capable of reading 0 to 300 psi (0 to 20 kg/cm^2) to the main pressure test point beneath the brake line mounting clip, after removing the clip and blanking plug.

10 Remove the primary throttle pressure blanking plug and connect a pressure gauge capable of reading 0 to 50 psi (0 to 3.4 kg/cm^2).

11 Run the pressure gauges and hoses into the car (passenger side) so that they can be observed from the driving position. Make sure that they will not chafe against the road or a tyre.

FIG. 7.18. PRESSURE TEST (SEC. 11)

A Brake line mounting clip
a Main pressure test point
b Primary throttle pressure test point

12 Disconnect the vacuum unit hose and blank it with a suitable bolt.

13 Apply the handbrake, select "N" then run the engine at an idle speed of approximately 1000 rpm. The primary throttle pressure should be 48.36 psi (3.4 kg/cm^2); adjust if necessary as described in Section 9 of this Chapter. When the correct primary throttle pressure is obtained, check that the main pressure is 129.43 $\pm$ 2.13 psi (9.1 $\pm$ 0.15 kg/cm^2).

14 Reconnect the hose to the vacuum unit, and check that the primary throttle pressure is 5.7$\pm$1.42 psi (0.4$\pm$0.1 kg/cm^2) and the main pressure is 36.98$\pm$2.13 psi (2.6$\pm$0.15 kg/cm^2).

15 At an idle speed of approximately 1000 rpm and "R" selected, check that the main pressure is 100.98$\pm$7.11 psi (7.1$\pm$0.5 kg/cm^2).

16 With the footbrake, additionally, applied, "R" selected and the accelerator pedal floored for the minimum practicable time, check for a main pressure of 213.35 to 284.47 psi (15 to 20 kg/cm^2).

17 With the footbrake still applied, select "D", floor the accelerator pedal, and check for a primary throttle pressure of 46.93$\pm$1.42 psi (3.3$\pm$0.1 kg/cm^2) and a main pressure of 126.59$\pm$2.13 psi (8.9$\pm$0.15 kg/cm^2). Again, the time taken for this test should be as short as possible.

18 Release the brakes, select "D" and road test the car. The main pressure, at a road speed above 19 mhp (30 kmh), should be 88.2$\pm$1.42 (6.2$\pm$0.1) at full throttle.

19 If any of these requirements are not satisfied, and you are satisfied that the fluid level is correct, there are no leakages and that all adjustments have been properly made - an internal fault is indicated. This will require specialist attention.

12 Fault finding table - Automatic transmission

Symptom	Reason/s	Remedy
No drive at any selector position	a) Fluid level too low b) Broken drive plate c) Pump or drive defective d) Final drive or planetary gear set broken	a) Add fluid as required. Check for leaks. b) Specialist repair. c) Specialist repair d) Specialist repair.
No drive at any forward selection	Forward clutch defective	Specialist repair.
Vehicle does not move unless accelerator pedal has been pumped several times	a) Fluid level incorrect	a) Add fluid as required. Check for leaks.
Jerky on acceleration. Gearshifts erratic. Noisy in reverse	b) Selector lever cable adjustment incorrect	b) Adjust cable.
No power transmission in 1st gear when coasting or in reverse when accelerating	1st and reverse brake bands or pistons defective	Specialist repair.
No power transmission in 3rd or reverse. Transmission fluid smells burnt and is discoloured	Direct and reverse clutch plates burnt, or piston seals faulty Selector lever cable adjustment incorrect	Check selector cable adjustment. If this is satisfactory a Specialist repair is required.
Changes into 3rd gear only	Governor dirty or sticking	Specialist repair.
Insufficient power in reverse. Direct and reverse clutches slipping	Incorrect selector lever cable adjustment or dirty transmission fluid	Adjust selector cable. Test pressure as described in Section 11.
Transmission remains in 1st gear	Governor faulty	Specialist repair.
Gear changing jerky and at too high an engine speed	Fluid level low	Add fluid as required. Check for leaks.
Erratic power transmission	a) Fluid level low b) Selector lever cable incorrectly adjusted	a) Add fluid as required. Check for leaks. b) Adjust selector lever cable.
No power in 1st gear with D selected	1st gear clutch defective	Specialist repair.
No power in 2nd gear with 2 or D selected	2nd gear brake band or piston faulty	Specialist repair.
Delay before engagement	a) Fluid level incorrect b) Fluid pressure incorrect due to faulty vacuum unit or incorrect adjustment c) Friction linings worn or burnt d) Internal leakage	a) Check fluid level. b) Replace or adjust vacuum unit. c) Specialist repair. d) Specialist repair.
Gear changing at too low a speed	a) Incorrectly adjusted or damaged vacuum unit b) Governor or valve body faulty c) Leakage in transmission	a) Replace or adjust vacuum unit. b) Specialist repair. c) Specialist repair.

Symptom	Reason/s	Remedy
Gear changing at too high a speed	a) Vacuum unit faulty or hose leaking b) Vacuum unit incorrectly adjusted or damaged c) Governor or valve body faulty	a) Replace vacuum unit or hose b) Replace or adjust vacuum unit. c) Specialist repair.
No shift to 3rd gear with D selected	a) Governor or valve body faulty b) Direct and reverse clutch faulty (if no shift at 'R' either)	a) Specialist repair. b) Specialist repair.
Harsh engagement when selector lever is moved from 'N' to any other selection	a) Idle speed set too high b) Vacuum unit faulty or hose leaking	a) Adjust idle speed. b) Replace vacuum unit or hose.
Car 'creeps' excessively when idling	Idle speed set too high	Adjust idle speed.
Kickdown not operating	a) Incorrect throttle linkage or kickdown switch setting b) Electrical fault (wiring, solenoid, switch) c) Dirt in valve body	a) Adjust. b) If necessary, repair switches and wiring. However, if the switches and wiring are satisfactory, a Specialist repair will be required. c) Specialist repair.
Poor acceleration and low maximum road speed	a) Fluid level low b) Torque converter faulty c) Brake bands or clutches slipping	a) Check fluid level. Check for leaks. b) Specialist repair. c) Specialist repair.
Poor acceleration and screeching noise in transmission	a) Torque converter one-way clutch slipping b) 1st gear one-way clutch slip	a) Specialist repair. b) Specialist repair.
Grating noise from torque converter. Fluid is of a brassy colour	Torque converter thrust washer worn	Specialist repair.
Oil consumption, and possibly smoke from exhaust	a) Vacuum unit faulty b) Oil seals on governor or pinion faulty	a) Replace. b) Specialist repair.
Transmission oil discoloured and smells burnt	Clutch plates or brake bands burnt	Specialist repair.
Oil leak at housing breather	Fluid leak into final drive	Specialist repair
Parking lock defective	a) Incorrect selector lever cable adjustment b) Operating lever broken	a) Adjust. b) Specialist repair.
Heavy fluid spillage	Torque converter leaking	Specialist repair.
Final drive noisy	Incorrect adjustment or worn bearings	Specialist repair.

Chapter 8 Steering

For modifications, and information applicable to later models, see Supplement at end of manual

Contents

Specifications

Steering gear	Rack and pinion (some models have a vibration damper fitted)
Steering column	Divided, with universal joint and Hardy disc or Audi safety steering or telescopic column.
Turning circle	11.2 m (36 ft 9 in.)
Coupe' S	11 m (36 ft 1 in.)
Track circle	10.2 m (33 ft 5¾ in.)
Coupe' S	10.1 m (33 ft 1½ in.)
Steering ratio (straight ahead)	21.6 : 1
(full lock)	14.4 : 1
Turns, lock-to-lock	3.88
Steering wheel height adjustment (Coupe'. S)	40 mm (1.575 in.)
Toe-out	0º to −20' (0 to 2 mm, 0 to 0.8 in.)
Lubricant	Liquid transmission grease (eg. Calypsol LS 2341 or Klueber ALN 600 or equivalent)
Approximate capacity	250 cc

Torque wrench settings

	lb ft	kg m
Track rod to track rod lever	26	3.6
Track rod to rack	50.6	7.0
Front ball and socket joint to track rod	10.1	1.4
Mount to steering gear	18.1	2.5
Steering gear to body	24.6	3.4
Steering tube to steering joint	7.9	1.1
Hardy disc	12.6 ± 1.8	1.75 ± 0.25
Steering tube to pinion	18.1	2.5
Steering outer tube to body	18.1	2.5
Steering wheel	36.2	5.0

1 General description

The steering gear is a progressive ratio rack and pinion system with, in some cases, a vibration damper. The universal joint and Hardy disc was replaced by the first safety steering system from chassis No 80/81 01 026 044(LHD) or 80/81 01 028 447 (RHD); this was subsequently replaced by a modified safety steering system from chassis No 80 11/81 11 058 476 (100 LS), 80 11/81 11 051 453 (100 S), 80 11/81 11 051 736 (100). Telescopic steering was fitted from chassis No 80 11/81 11 047 071 (100 LS USA) 80 11/81 11 047 868 (100 LS and S Sweden) 80 11/81 11 055 755 (100 Sweden), 81 11 055 794 (100 Coupe' S). A modified steering rack was introduced for the new safety steering and telescopic steering, and cannot be interchanged with the earlier type.

2 Steering column - removal and replacement

1 Take off the battery earth lead, then remove the instrument panel trim.
2 Prise off the steering wheel pad at the central leg.
3 Unscrew the nut which retains the steering wheel and pull the wheel off.
4 Remove the two screws which retain the slip ring and take off the earth connection.
5 Remove the screws which hold in the steering column casing.
6 Remove the washers from the central column, noting that the thickest one is lowermost with the notch facing downwards.
7 Where a column gear change is fitted, take off the change lever at the pivot.
8 Take off the column tube from the bracket on the

Fig. 8.1. Removing the steering wheel pad (b) (Sec. 2)

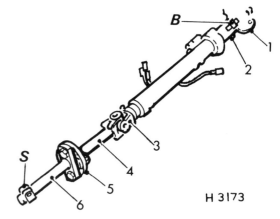

H 3173

FIG. 8.2. THE HARDY DISC STEERING COLUMN (SEC. 2)

1 *Tube*   5 *Hardy disc*
2 *Column*   6 *Tube*
3 *Steering joint*   B *Indicator self cancelling*
4 *Intermediate shaft*   *device*
                                 S *Clip*

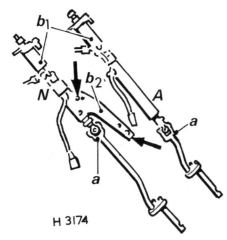

H 3174

FIG. 8.3. SAFETY STEERING COLUMN (SEC. 2)

A   *Former version*   b₁   *Steering tube*
N   *Later version*   b₂   *Steering bracket*
a   *Steering joint*   *Fitting holes are arrowed*

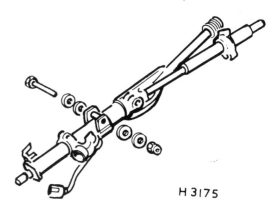

H 3175

Fig. 8.4. Telescopic steering (Sec. 2)

instrument panel.

9 Remove the multi-function steering column switch and disconnect the white lead (see Chapter 10 for details).

10 Disconnect the leads from the ignition switch noting the positions of particular colours.

11 Remove the clip securing the column to the pin, at the lower end.

12 Loosen the column tube mounting beneath the instrument panel.

13 Replacement is a reversal of the removal procedure, but with the telescopic type steering it is important to make sure that the support tube is correctly located in the rubber bearing and that the groove in the rubber cover which rubs against the column tube in filled with a suitable transmission grease.

3 Steering gear (without damper)

A Removing and dismantling

1 If the steering column has not previously been removed, it should be loosened at its mountings and disconnected at the pinion.

2 Disconnect the track rods at the steering knuckle as described in Section 7 of this Chapter.

3 Loosen the steering gear mounts then raise the assembly up through the engine compartment.

4 Take off the rubber boot from the steering gear.

5 Fold back the tab on the lock plate and unscrew the track rod.

6 After removal of the track rod, the stop ring can be removed from the tube.

7 The track rod end can now be removed from the track rod.

8 Remove the retaining rings from the ball joint assembly and take out the ball end.

Note: The steering gear cannot be repaired. If damaged or worn it should be replaced by a new or exchange unit.

B Reassembly and refitting

1 When reassembling the ball joint always use new retaining rings, and fill the rubber cover using a general purpose grease with a molybdenum disulphide additive (eg Castrol MS3).

2 Reassemble the track rods to the steering gear and fit the assembly to the car. Note the position of the mounts and maintain the dimension X at 16.22 in (412 mm) (see Fig.8.6). Do not connect the track rod ends.

3 Connect the steering column and check that the same amount of total movement of the rack can be obtained in both directions.

4 Set the rack to the mid position of its travel and the road wheels to the straight ahead position, then fit the track rods.

5 Adjust the toe-out as described in Chapter 11.

6 If adjustment to the direction indicator cancelling device is required, slacken the Allen screws and set the stop to the centre of the opening with the road wheels in the straight ahead

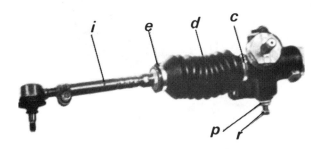

FIG. 8.5. PART OF THE STEERING RACK, SHOWING
ONE TRACK ROD (SEC. 3A)

c   Clip   i   Track rod
d   Boot   p   Locking nut
e   Clip   r   Screw

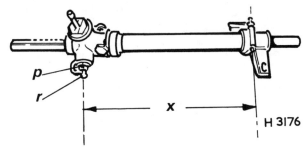

FIG. 8.6. REFITTING THE STEERING GEAR (SEC. 3B)

p   Locking nut   x   Dimension 16.22 in.
r   Screw   (412 mm)

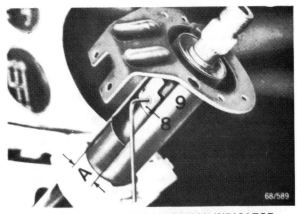

FIG. 8.7. ADJUSTING THE DIRECTION INDICATOR
CANCELLING DEVICE (SEC. 3B)

A   Centre of the opening   8   Allen screw
                             9   Column tube

position.
7   Finally refit the steering column to the car.

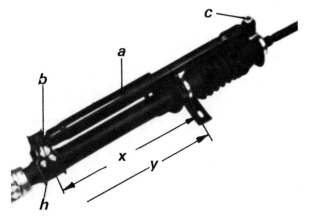

FIG. 8.8. THE STEERING GEAR WITH THE DAMPER
(SEC. 4)

X   Setting dimension 11.3 in. (287 mm)
Y   Dimension from centre of pinion adjustment screw
    16.22 in. (412 mm)
a   Damper
b   Screw, spring washer and nut
c   Screw and spring washer
h   Clip

4   Steering gear (with damper)

1   The same basic instructions apply as for the non-damped
steering with regard to removal, dismantling, reassembling and
refitting. It is, however, necessary to remove the damper before
taking off the steering gear.
2   As with the other type of steering system, the assembly
cannot be repaired. It must be replaced by a new or exchange
unit.

5   Adjustment of the steering rack assembly

1   If excessive free play occurs in the steering rack assembly
after a considerable period in service,   first slacken the locknut
on the underside of the track (below the pinion), then tighten
the screw a little.
2   In this way a considerable amount of wear can be
compensated for but on no account tighten the screw to a
torque greater than 10.42 lb in (12 kg cm).
3   After adjustment has been made, tighten the locknut whilst
ensuring that the screw remains stationary.

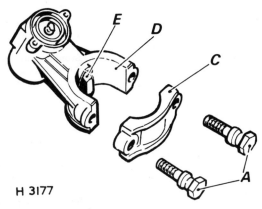

H 3177

FIG. 8.9. THE COMPONENTS OF THE STEERING LOCK
AND IGNITION SWITCH (SEC. 5)

a   Sheer head screws   d   Lock, upper section
c   Lock, lower section   e   Lock pin

6 Steering lock and ignition switch - removal and refitting

1 Remove the steering wheel and wheel trim as described earlier in this Chapter.
2 Drill into the sheer head screws which retain the two halves of the lock, then use a stud extractor to remove the screws.
3 Separate the parts of the new lock, assemble them to the column then tighten the sheer head screws.
4 If only the lock is to be renewed, the steering column will need to be detached first. The lock can then be unscrewed and the new one fitted. Note the locating slot and key on the mating parts.

7 Track rod outer ball joints - inspection, removal and refitting

1 After a considerable period of time, wear is bound to occur in the track rod outer ball joints. Although the joint itself is protected by a rubber boot, this deteriorates with age and results in a loss of grease and ingress of road dirt and water.
2 To check for wear, arrange for an assistant to rotate the steering wheel vigorously in each direction. Watch the ball joints and if any up and down or side to side movement is detected, excessive wear is indicated which should be attended to without delay.
3 If wear is detected, jack the front of the car up with the rear wheels chocked and the handbrake on, then remove the relevant front wheel.
4 Remove the split pin and castellated nut from the shank of the ball joint then slacken the pinch bolt on the track rod. Measure the amount of screw thread visible at the end of the track rod to aid alignment when refitting.
5 It may be possible to remove the ball joint by heavy hammer blows on the side of the steering knuckle. If this method fails don't try to drive the tapered shank out by hitting the screw thread end because the end threads will burr over. This will prevent the eventual withdrawal because it will not pass through the tapered hole in the knuckle. This will also preclude fitting the nut temporarily if you need to use the car to enable a proper steering ball joint separator to be purchased.
6 If you have to purchase a steering ball joint separator (and remember that it is quite likely to be used again in the future) the whole job will be simplified since the joint is pressed out by

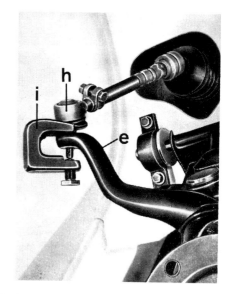

FIG. 8.10. TRACK ROD OUTER BALL JOINT REMOVAL (SEC. 7)

e   Steering knuckle
h   Ball joint
i   Extractor

the screw on the extractor. Now unscrew the ball joint from the track rod.
7 Before fitting the new joint make sure that the tapers on the joint and steering knuckle are clean.
8 Now screw the ball joint on to the track rod the required amount (see paragraph 4 of this section).
9 Fit a new rubber boot - first fill it with molybdenum disulphide grease - then secure it with two new clamping rings.
10 Fit the castellated nut and secure it with a new split pin.
11 Tighten the pinch bolt on the track rod and then either repeat the procedure on the other side of the car or check the toe-out as described in Chapter 11. This latter check is most important whether one or both ball joints have been renewed.

8 Fault finding table - Steering *

Symptom	Reason/s	Remedy
Steering feels vague, car wanders and floats at speed	Tyre pressures uneven Dampers worn	Check pressures and adjust as necessary. Renew dampers.
General wear or damage	Steering gear ball joints badly worn Suspension geometry incorrect Steering mechanism free play excessive	Fit new ball joints. Check and rectify. Adjust or overhaul steering mechanism.
Stiff and heavy steering	Tyre pressures too low	Check pressures and inflate tyres.
Lack of maintenance or accident damage	No oil in steering gear No grease in steering and suspension ball joints. Front wheel toe-out incorrect Suspension geometry incorrect Steering gear incorrectly adjusted too tightly Steering column badly misaligned	Top up steering gear. Clean nipples and grease thoroughly. Check and reset toe-out. Check and rectify. Check and re-adjust steering gear. Determine cause and rectify. (Usually due to bad repair after severe accident damage, and difficult to correct).

* Also refer to the Fault finding table in Chapter 11.

Chapter 9 Braking system

For modifications, and information applicable to later models, see Supplement at end of manual

Contents

Specifications

Front brakes

	Audi 100	Audi S, LS and GL	Audi Coupe' S
Discs:			
Diameter	280 mm (11.02 in.)	280 mm (11.02 in.)	291 mm (11.45 in.)
Pad area (each) ...	26.25 cm^2 (1.59 $in.^2$)	26.25 cm^2 (1.59 $in.^2$)	26.25 cm^2 (1.59 $in.^2$)
Effective braking area	105 cm^2 (6.407 $in.^2$)	105 cm^2 (6.407 $in.^2$)	105 cm^2 (6.407 $in.^2$)
Disc maximum thickness Tolerance	0.02 mm (0.00078 in.)	0.02 mm (0.00078 in.)	0.02 mm (0.00078 in.)
Disc maximum run-out	0.2 mm (0.0078 in.)	0.2 mm (0.0078 in.)	0.2 mm (0.0078 in.)
Pad type	Jurid 215	Jurid 215	Jurid 215

Rear brakes

Drums:			
Diameter	200 mm (7.87 in.)	200 mm (7.87 in.)	200 mm (7.87 in.)
Shoe width ...	40 mm (1.575 in.)	40 mm (1.575 in.)	40 mm (1.575 in.)
Effective braking area	292 cm^2 (16.92 $in.^2$)	292 cm^2 (16.92 $in.^2$)	292 cm^2 (16.92 $in.^2$)
Lining type ...	Jurid 132 (K3)	Jurid 132 (K3)	Jurid 132 (K3)

General

Maximum power ratio:			
Front	57.28	87.83	87.83
Rear	6.26	9.60	9.60
Equivalent braking effect			
Loaded	83%	94%	94%
Unloaded ...	93%	76%	76%
Applied pedal pressure:			
Loaded	45 kg (99.2 lb)	36 kg (79.4 lb)	36 kg (79.4 lb)
Unloaded ...	36 kg (79.4 lb)	17 kg (37.5 lb)	17 kg (37.5 lb)
Brake fluid type	To specification SAE J 1703e (eg. Castrol Girling Universal Brake and Clutch Fluid)		
Approximate capacity	0.4 litres (0.7 pints, 0.845 US pints)		

Modified brake system for 100 USA and 100 Automatics for Europe (except Sweden) (From chassis No. 21 089 628)

Technical data (where different)	
Brake disc diameter, front	291 mm (11.45 in.)
Pad surface	37.5 cm^2 (5.81 $in.^2$)
Pad thickness, new	12.5 mm (0.49 in.)
Effective braking area, front	150 cm^2 (23.25 $in.^2$)
Brake disc thickness	10.5 mm (0.413 in.)

	lb ft	kg m
Disc maximum run-out	0.1 mm (0.004 in.)	
Disc minimum thickness	9.0 mm (0.35 in.)	
Pad type	Jurid 224FE (USA, Ferodo 1 D 330)	
Lining type	Jurid 334	
Brake pressure governor with locking device	BRMS	
Pad thickness control	Ceramic transmitter (USA only) and indicator light in instrument panel.	

Torque wrench settings

	lb ft	kg m
Caliper to transmission	68.7 + 7.23	9.5 + 1
Drive shaft to transmission	73.8 ± 3.62	10.2 ± 0.5
Brake lines to master cylinder mountings	7.96 ± 10%	1.1 ± 10%
Bracket to transmission mountings	15.2	2.1
Brake line to brake hose, front	7.96 ± 10%	1.1 ± 10%
Adaptor to bracket mountings	7.233 - 1.45	1 - 0.2
Brake hose to adaptor to transmission mountings	8.68 + 20% - 10%	1.2 + 20% - 10%
Brake line to transmission mountings	7.96 ± 10%	1.1 ± 10%
Brake line to transmission mountings with nut of transmission flange	7.233 - 1.45	1 - 0.2
Brake line to brake hose, rear, mountings	8.68 + 20% - 10%	1.2 + 20% - 10%
Brake hose to adaptor to rear axle mountings	8.68 + 20% - 10%	1.2 + 20% - 10%
Adaptor to bracket to rear axle mountings	7.233 - 1.45	1 - 0.2
Brake line to adaptor, rear axle, mountings (left and right) ...	7.96 ± 10%	1.1 ± 10%
Brake line to rear axle to wheel cylinder mountings (left and right)	8.68 + 20% - 10%	1.2 + 20% - 10%
Bracket to transmission mountings	7.233 - 1.45	1 - 0.2
Clip to caliper mountings	7.233 - 1.45	1 - 0.2
Breather nipple to wheel cylinder	1.45 to 2.53	0.2 to 0.35

1 General description

All models in the Audi 100 range are equipped with an hydraulic twin-circuit braking system and, with the exception of the 100, an engine operated Teves T51/349 vacuum power brake device (Servo). The handbrake is cable operated and acts on the rear wheels only.

In the unlikely event of failure of the vacuum system, or braking with the engine switched off, the braking effect will not deteriorate although heavier pedal pressure will be required. If either the front or rear brake systems fail (particularly the front), an increase in pedal travel can be expected together with a reduction in braking efficiency.

Note 1: During any servicing operations on the car great care must be excercised to prevent contamination of the brake pads, particularly by oils, additives, paints, adhesives, etc.

Note 2: If the car is to be stored for periods in excess of one month, it is recommended that the brake pads and discs are covered, the fluid level is topped up as necessary, and the handbrake is left in the OFF position with the wheels chocked.

Note 3: The maximum shelf life for rubber seals and hoses is 2 years; parts which have been stored for this period of time or longer should not be used. A 1 year shelf life is permitted for cylinders and calipers, following which they should be dismantled, cleaned in methylated spirits then dried with compressed air. Prior to reassembly they should be lightly coated with ATE cylinder paste or a similar compound.

Storage of parts should be in a dry, dust-free room at temperatures of −10°C to +20°C (+14°F to +68°F), with protection from direct sunlight and sources of heat. Any parts, which have been removed from their original packages, should be stored in dry polythene bags; open bores should be blanked with rubber plugs.

2 Care of the braking system

1 As the braking system is somewhat hidden away, it is all too easy to forget about it, even though its importance cannot be overstressed.

2 Apart from the normal maintenance and checks of the brake pads and linings it is important to remember that the fluid and rubber parts (ie seals and flexible hoses) deteriorate with time.

3 There are separate sections in this Chapter which deal with the various overhaul, repair and replacement procedures, but there is one further point which must be highlighted. This is renewal of the brake fluid.

4 Unless you have reason to overhaul one item only, it is wise to renew all the rubber seals, the flexible hoses and brake fluid at the same time.

5 The brake fluid can be renewed by bleeding it completely from the system then replenishing with new fluid. Methylated spirit can be used to flush the system if necessary but it must be removed completely before refilling with hydraulic fluid.

3 Braking system checks

A Fluid level

1 The brake fluid level must be maintained between the "MAX" and "MIN" markings on the reservoir body.

2 Any topping up should be done using fluid of the correct specification only, eg Castrol Girling Universal Brake and Clutch Fluid.

3 If an excessive drop in fluid level is noted always examine the system carefully for leakage.

4 A periodic slight drop in fluid level will occur as the front brake mechanism compensates for pad wear.

5 When new brake pads are fitted, the fluid level in the reservoir will rise. This should not be allowed to overflow - as it

Fig. 9.1. The brake master cylinder reservoir (Sec. 3A)

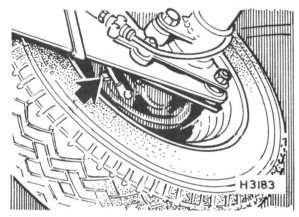

Fig. 9.2. The inspection window (arrowed) in the back plate on late models (Sec. 3B)

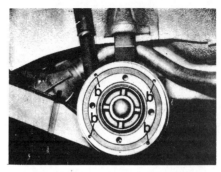

Fig. 9.3. The inspection holes in the earlier brake drums (Sec. 3B)

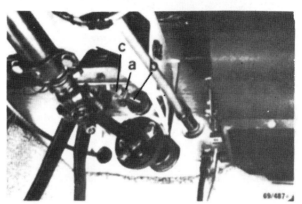

FIG. 9.4. THE BRAKE ROD/PISTON PLAY (SEC. 4)

a Locking nut　　　　　c Swivel joint
b Piston rod

will cause damage to the paintwork - but should be syphoned off. On no account use the car with the fluid level too high.

B Brake pads and linings

1 Wear on the brake pads can be expected to be greater than that on the linings, due to the higher sliding velocities on the friction surfaces, reduced friction area and increased brake pressures.

2 Brake pads must be renewed when the pad thickness is worn down to a minimum of 5/64 in (2 mm).

3 Brake shoe linings must be renewed before they have worn down to the level of the rivet heads. Where bonded linings are fitted, the minimum permissible thickness is 0.8 in (1.0 mm).

4 If brake pads have become impregnated with oil, or have deep cracks through to the backplate, they must be renewed. This also applies to pads which have been completely detached from the backplate.

5 Brake pads which show signs of unequal wear should not be interchanged with others in the same system in an attempt to balance the wear. They must remain in the position in which they were run in.

6 On late model cars there is a small inspection window in the rear brake backplate for inspection of the brake lining thickness. The window is protected by a rubber plug which must always be in place when the car is being used. Other cars have four small inspection holes in the brake drum which are visible once the road wheel has been removed.

4 Braking system adjustment

1 The front brakes are self adjusting and therefore do not require attention of this sort.

2 The first step is to adjust the brake pedal travel which will require removal of the instrument panel trim. This operation is

described in Chapter 2 as a prelude to removal of the heater.

3 Check the play between the brake piston rod and piston, and adjust if necessary until 0.039 in (1 mm) is achieved (This is approximately equal to 0.2 in (5 mm) at the brake pedal). Adjustment can be made by loosening the locknut behind the swivel joint which connects with the brake pedal, and turning the piston rod. Tighten the locknut afterwards.

4 Now check that the fluid level in the reservoir is correct and jack up the car.

5 Ensure that the front brake pads are of adequate thickness and that the pad retaining pins, lock pins and springs are in good condition.

6 Using a 17 mm AF ring or socket spanner tighten both adjusters on the rear brake backplates until the linings are firmly contacting the rim. When viewed from the axle side of the backplate the right hand adjuster should be turned clockwise and the left hand one anticlockwise.

7 Now turn each adjuster back a little until the wheel can just be rotated, without the linings touching the drum.

8 Repeat the operation for the other rear wheel in a similar manner.

9 Check the brake fluid level and pump the pedal a few times to check that the linings clear the drums properly.

10 Lower the car to the ground and briefly test the car for braking efficiency.

5 Handbrake adjustment

1 Initially carry out the adjustment procedure detailed in the previous paragraph.

2 Check that all the handbrake cables are freely moveable. Remove any encrusted dirt.

3 Pull on the handbrake and check that at the first or second notch, both rear brakes commence to engage. On the third or

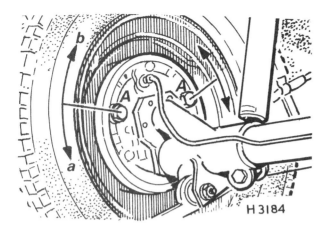

FIG. 9.5. ADJUSTING THE REAR BRAKES (SEC. 4)

A   Adjuster
a   Direction to lock the shoes
b   Direction to release the shoes

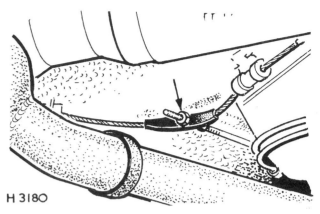

Fig. 9.6. The handbrake compensator (arrowed) (Sec. 5)

fourth notch the brakes should be fully engaged.

4   Adjustment can be made by altering the position of locknut on the metal bridge piece (compensator).

5   Operate the brake lever several times after adjustment to check that the linings clear the rear wheels.

6   If adjustment cannot be achieved as described above the brake cable will need to be renewed as described later in this Chapter.

***

6   Bleeding the braking system (manual transmission)

1   Before any brake bleeding is carried out always make sure that there are no leaks in the system, otherwise you are wasting your time. Any overhaul, repair or adjustment should be completed prior to the bleeding process.

2   You will need a supply of new brake fluid (eg Castrol Universal Girling Brake and Clutch Fluid) (photo), a jam jar, a length of rubber tubing to fit the bleed nipple and which will reach the bottom of the jar, a spanner to fit the bleed nipple (7 mm AF) and an assistant.

3   Check the fluid level in the reservoir and pour about ½ in (13 mm) of fluid in the jam jar (photo).

4   Commencing at the wheel furthest from the master cylinder, which is the left rear for right hand drive cars, slacken the bleed nipple about half a turn (photo) and with the rubber tube connected, bleed into the jar. Your assistant must floor the brake pedal sharply and hold it down whilst you tighten the nipple. The pedal can then be released slowly, the nipple loosened and the procedure repeated. When fluid free of bubbles

is seen to emerge from the bleed tube the nipple can be finally tightened. At all times it is extremely important that there is an adequate supply of fluid in the reservoir; this will need to be topped up several times during the bleeding process.

5   Repeat the procedure for the other brakes in turn, working progressively nearer to the master cylinder.

6   On completion, operate the brake pedal several times, check that all dust caps have been replaced and that the fluid level is correct.

7   Finally road test the car to check for braking efficiency.

Note: Do not reuse brake fluid which has been bled from a system since it will most probably contain air and moisture.*
* Brake fluid is hygroscopic.

***

7   Bleeding the braking system (automatic transmission)

1   The same principle and method of bleeding are applicable as for manual transmissions but the order of bleeding is completely different.

2   Bleeding should be carried out in the order given below
    1   Right upper caliper
    2   Left upper caliper
    3   Right lower caliper (outer)
    4   Right lower caliper (inner)
    5   Left lower caliper (outer)
    6   Left lower caliper (inner)
    7   Left rear wheel
    8   Right rear wheel.

6.2 Topping up the brake master cylinder

6.3 The brake bleeding jar and tube

6.4 A brake caliper bleed nipple being slackened

8 Brake master cylinder (vacuum brakes) - removal and replacement

1 Initially unscrew the connection at the rear of the master cylinder, which supplies the rear brake system, and collect the fluid in a clean container.

2 Ensure some clean dry rag is handy then remove the connection at the front of the master cylinder. Use the rag to soak up any fluid spillage and make sure that it does not contact the paintwork.

3 Carefully ease the brake pipes away, but do not bend them.

4 Pull off the stop light connections from the switch beneath the master cylinder.

5 Remove the two nuts which hold the master cylinder to the vacuum unit, them pull the master cylinder forwards and upwards.

6 Take care not to lose the seal ring which is fitted between the master cylinder and the vacuum unit. If damaged it must be renewed.

7 Refitting is the reverse of removal, following which the system must be bled.

9 Brake master cylinder (without vacuum unit) - removal and replacement

1 The procedure for removing and replacing the master cylinder is similar to that described in the previous section. Note that the stop light switch is on the extreme end of the master cylinder.

10 Brake master cylinder - overhaul

Note: The procedure given below is for master cylinders fitted to a vacuum unit. The master cylinder for non-vacuum brakes differs only in the respect of a different primary piston, only one boot is fitted to the secondary piston, there is no air compensating bore, the stop light switch is in a different position and a rubber cap is fitted at the operating rod end.

1 During the following operation cleanliness is of the utmost importance. Immediately before commencing, wash your hands.

2 Gather together a supply of clean, dry, non-fluffy rag, a quantity of brake fluid, and a container of methylated spirit. Make sure that you are working on a clean surface.

3 Before dismantling the master cylinder clean the outside. If necessary, a little methylated spirits can be used.

4 Firmly grip the fluid reservoir and pull it off the cylinder.

5 Unscrew the stop light switch, then remove the circlip at the pushrod end.

6 The master cylinder can now be fully dismantled but note that before removing the secondary piston the outer stop screw must be taken out.

7 Remove all the rubber seals etc and carefully clean each part in methylated spirit.

8 It is recommended that all rubber parts are renewed even though they may not appear to have deteriorated.

9 Carefully inspect all the internal metal parts such as springs, pistons, rings and the cylinder walls. A magnifying lens such as a watchmaker's glass can be very useful for this. Any parts which are obviously scored, worn or corroded should be renewed.

10 When checking the housing and pistons, the maximum

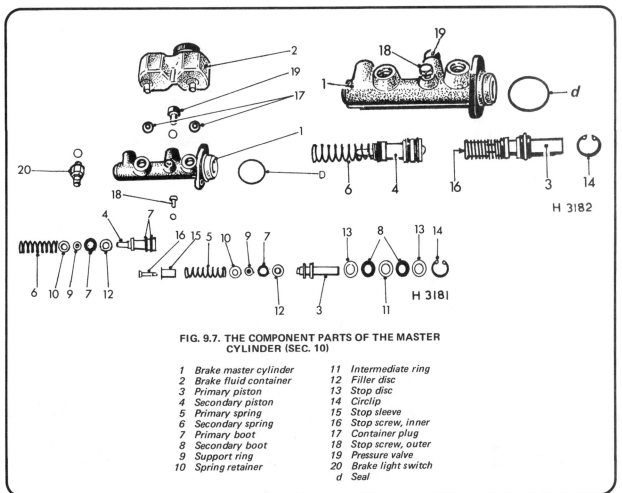

FIG. 9.7. THE COMPONENT PARTS OF THE MASTER CYLINDER (SEC. 10)

1	Brake master cylinder	11	Intermediate ring
2	Brake fluid container	12	Filler disc
3	Primary piston	13	Stop disc
4	Secondary piston	14	Circlip
5	Primary spring	15	Stop sleeve
6	Secondary spring	16	Stop screw, inner
7	Primary boot	17	Container plug
8	Secondary boot	18	Stop screw, outer
9	Support ring	19	Pressure valve
10	Spring retainer	20	Brake light switch
		d	Seal

permissible housing diameter is 0.817 in (20.75 mm) and the minimum permissible piston diameter is 0.807 in (20.50 mm).

11 Once the parts have been cleaned and inspected it is advisable to reassemble the master cylinder as soon as possible to prevent corrosion on the sealing surfaces.

12 When reassembling it is essential that all parts are 'wet assembled' using brake fluid. On no account should rubber seals be forced into dry parts as they will be damaged. Make sure that all parts are correctly assembled -- **your life could well depend on it.** Double check each operation.

13 To facilitate the fitting of the secondary boots it may well be necessary to use some stiff steel wire which is suitably bent to shape, but whatever you do, always make sure that there are no burrs. Paper clips can often be used for an exercise of this type.

14 When the pistons have been assembled, make sure that they operate freely in the cylinder and they return quickly to their original position under the spring action.

15 The assembly can now be completed in the reverse order to dismantling.

16 For master cylinders which are fitted to a vacuum unit, don't forget the O-ring seal between the two units.

11 Disc pad replacement

1 Disc pad replacement needs to be carried out from beneath the car due to the inboard location of the calipers. According to the particular facilities available it may be necessary to remove each front wheel in turn for access.

2 Using a pair of long nose pliers, initially remove the lock clips (photo).

3 Withdraw the retaining pins which hold the parts and cross springs in position (photo).

4 Using a suitably bent piece of steel rod of about 1/8 in (3 mm) diameter, hook out the brake pad using the holes at the top of the backplate.

5 It is now necessary to press both pistons back fully into the brake cylinder. A special tool is available for this but two thin steel straps suitably bent towards their ends will do the job. At the same time as doing this job it is essential that the brake fluid reservoir is not allowed to overflow. The fluid level will rise as the pistons are pushed back so it may be necessary to draw off some of the fluid.

6 Before the replacement pads can be fitted it is necessary to check the angular position of the pistons in their cylinders. They can easily have been rotated slightly during the previous operation. This will require the use of a special tool (see Fig.9.14) for checking the position (refer to caliper overhaul, later in this Chapter). Rotate the pistons as necessary (photo).

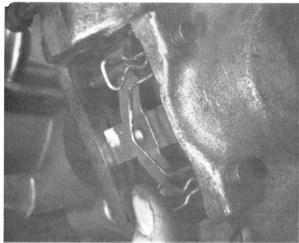
11.2 Removing the caliper lock clips

11.3 Withdrawing the retaining pins

11.6 The brake piston correctly orientated

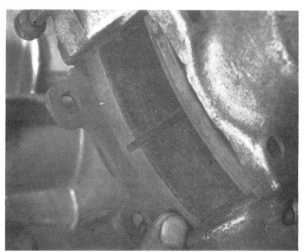
11.7 Fitting a brake pad

7 The disc pads can now be fitted (photo) but first make sure that there are no burrs on the backplates or dirt inside the caliper that could prevent them from seating properly.

8 The retaining pins can now be refitted but always use new cross springs and lock clips. Different types of lock clips are available so make sure the correct type for the Audi 100 are used; do not use copper plated lock clips.

9 Now pump the brake pedal several times to ensure that the pistons are correctly positioned and check the level of fluid in the reservoir. This is important.

10 Repeat the procedure for the other front wheel.

---

12 Caliper and brake disc -removal and refitting

---

1 Initially jack up the car and, if the right hand caliper and disc are to be removed, remove the front exhaust pipe.

2 If a pedal support is available it should be fitted to the brake pedal in such a way that the pedal is depressed approximately 1 3/16 in (3 cm). Otherwise the pedal should be supported by a wooden block which will permit the 1 3/16 in movement, then a wooden strut made to hold the pedal down against the block. The other end of the strut can be wedged against the seat frame or steering wheel. This operation is to block the compensation bore in the master cylinder and prevent loss of fluid from the reservoir.

3 Remove the brake pads as previously described.

4 Disconnect the brake line where it enters the caliper and blank the opening with the dust cap from the bleed nipple.

5 Using a suitable ring spanner remove the caliper nuts.

6 Now remove the hexagon headed screws which retain the drive shaft. Pull the drive shaft away and upwards and, if found more convenient, support it in this position. Do not lose the insulating washer between the flange and the brake disc.

7 Refitment is a reversal of the removal procedure. However, ensure that each caliper is positioned so that the bleed nipple is at the top. All bolts should be tightened to the correct torque (see specifications).

8 On completion, bleed the braking system and road test the car to check braking efficiency.

---

13 Caliper and brake disc, USA models with automatic transmission - removal and refitting

---

Note: It is important that the left and right caliper and/or brake disc are removed separately.

1 Initially remove the bolt which secures the steering damper to the holder then slacken the holder mounting bolts.

2 Compress the damper and pull it upwards.

3 Disconnect the temperature transmitter wire.

4 Depress the brake pedal approximately 1 3/16 in as described in paragraph 2 of the previous section.

5 Disconnect the brake line at the tee-piece.

6 Undo the flexible exhaust gas feedback line at the exhaust pipe then loosen the clip and remove the exhaust pipe mounting bolt.

7 Remove the front exhaust pipe and guard from the exhaust manifold connection.

8 Disconnect the drive shaft from the stub axle. Take care not to lose the insulating washer.

9 Remove the support joint mounting bolt and pull the wheel downwards. Prise off the steering knuckle from the support joint and swing the steering knuckle outwards.

10 Remove the disc brake pads as described earlier in this Chapter. Do not remove the spring with the break-off element

FIG. 9.8. REMOVING THE STEERING DAMPER (SEC. 13)

A   Holder
B   Temperature transmitter connector

Fig. 9.9. Disconnecting the brake line (Sec. 13)

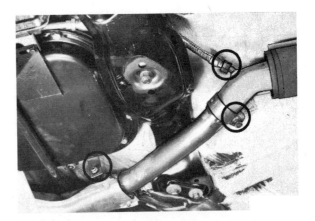

Fig. 9.10. The exhaust pipe and feedback connections (Sec. 13)

or the wire.

11 Remove the exhaust feedback filter.

12 Loosen the brake caliper. This is not very accessible and may require local manufacture of a suitable spanner or modification of an existing one.

13 It may be necessary to move the power unit slightly to one side to remove the caliper and brake disc. If this is required, a lever can be used against the engine mounting bracket.

14 Reassembly to the car can be carried out in the reverse order to removal, following which, it will be necessary to bleed the braking system and check braking efficiency.

14 Caliper and brake disc, USA models with manual transmission - removal and refitting

Note: It is important that the left and right caliper and/or brake disc are removed separately.

1 Depress the brake pedal approximately 1 3/16 in as described earlier in Section 12 of this Chapter.

2 Remove the temperature transmitter, front exhaust pipe and guard, drive shaft at the stub axle, support joint and disc brake pads as described in the previous section of this Chapter.

3 Disconnect the brake line at the caliper and blank the line with the dust cap from the bleed nipple. If the left brake line is to be disconnected it will also be necessary to unscrew the oil drain hose clip beforehand.

4 Loosen the brake caliper (refer to paragraph 12 of the previous section).

5 It may be necessary to move the power unit slightly to one side to remove the caliper and brake disc. If this is required, a lever can be used against the engine mounting bracket.

6 Reassembly to the car can be carried out in the reverse order to removal, following which it will be necessary to bleed the braking system and check braking efficiency.

15 Caliper overhaul

1 Clean the outside of the caliper using methylated spirit to remove road grime, but avoid getting it into the fluid passageways.

2 Carefully prise off the clamping ring then take off the cap.

3 Cut a piece of plywood to a suitable shape and fit it into the caliper together with a used or unserviceable brake pad as shown (see Fig.9.12).

4 Apply compressed air to the fluid inlet taking care that the piston does not fly out and cause damage.

5 Once the piston has moved, the plywood can be removed (but not the disc pad) and the piston removed by further application of the compressed air. Do not remove the second piston until the first one has been refitted after overhaul. On no account attempt to separate the two halves of the caliper.

6 Remove the seals from the piston taking extreme care that the ground surfaces are not scratched by sharp tools.

7 Clean all the parts carefully in methylated spirit, with the exception of rubber parts, which must be renewed.

8 Carefully inspect the piston and cylinder for scoring and corrosion. A magnifying glass and small mirror can usefully be employed on an operation of this type.

9 When reassembling always use new seals, caps and clamping rings. Wet assemble, (using hydraulic fluid), the seals to the piston and the piston to the caliper.

10 When the piston has been fitted to the cylinder it is necessary to align it correctly and for this purpose a small tool can be made as shown in the illustration (Fig. 9.14).

11 Only when the piston on one side has been reassembled, may the piston on the other side be removed.

16 Brake shoes - removal and refitting

1 Jack the car up with the wheels chocked and the handbrake

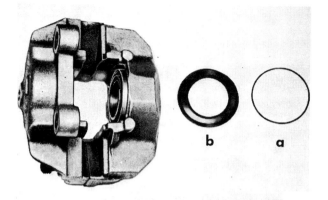

FIG. 9.11. THE BRAKE CALIPER (SEC. 15)

a   Clamping ring
b   Cap

FIG. 9.12. REMOVING THE PISTON (SEC. 15)

a   Disc pad
b   Plywood
c   Piston

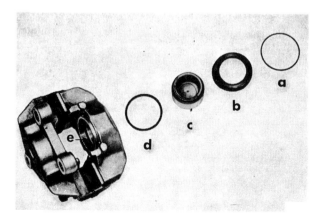

FIG. 9.13. THE PISTON AND SEALS (SEC. 15)

a   Clamping ring
b   Cap
c   Piston
d   Seal
e   Groove

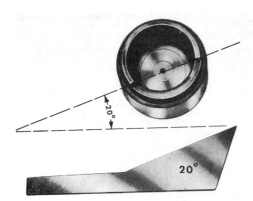

Fig. 9.14. Alignment tool for the piston (Sec. 15)

in the off position then remove the wheel.

2 Prise off the grease cap from the hub.

3 Take out the split pin from the stub axle, remove the castellated locking device and take off the nut and spacing washer.

4 Pull off the brake drum (photo), taking care that the washer and bearing race do not fall out, then turn back the brake adjuster nuts.

5 Remove the retaining/anti-rattle spring (photo) but take care that it does not fly out.

6 To remove the brake shoes, pull them off at the wheel cylinders then remove the retaining clip and springs (photos).

7 With the brake shoes off, disconnect the handbrake cable (photo) then use a stiff dry ½in paintbrush to remove any dust and dirt from the drum and backplate. Do not inhale the dust. Also inspect the wheel cylinder carefully for leaks.

8 When the brake shoes are refitted make sure that the long end of the coil spring is connected to the shoe with the handbrake lever. Align the slots in the piston with the ends of the shoes if necessary. Check that the projection on the brake cable guide is correctly aligned with the notch in the brake plate.

9 After fitting the retaining spring, put the brake drum on and refit the nut and spacing washer.

10 Now check the end float of the wheel bearing as described in Chapter 11.

11 Before fitting the grease cap it should be filled with approximately 10 gm of multi-purpose grease (eg Castrol LM). Do not damage the cap when refitting.

12 Now adjust the brakes and bleed the system as described earlier in this Chapter.

13 Finally road test the car and check the operation of the brakes.

16.4 The brake drum being removed

16.5 Removing the brake shoe retaining spring

16.16a The brake shoes withdrawn from the back plate

16.16b The brake shoes withdrawn from the back plate

16.7 The brake back plate showing the handbrake cable end

17 Wheel cylinder - removal and refitting

1 Initially remove the brake linings as described previously and fit the brake pedal support as described under 'Caliper and brake disc - removal and refitting'.
2 Disconnect the brake line at the wheel cylinder and blank the opening with the rubber cap from the bleed nipple.
3 Remove the two screws which retain the wheel cylinder. The cylinder can now be taken off.
4 After overhaul or repair of the cylinder (covered later in this Chapter) it can be refitted, following which brake adjustment, bleeding and testing will be required.

18 Handbrake cable - removal and refitting

1 Removal of the handbrake connection on the brake shoe lever is covered earlier in this Chapter with removal of the brake shoes.
2 Remove the cables from the mounting plates on the rear suspension arms.
3 Remove the brake rod/cable connection at the metal bridge pieces (compensator).
4 Prise out the plastic bushes on the mounting plates, then pull off the rubber caps and pull the cable in the direction of the brake drums.
5 The cable can now be removed by pulling it downwards from the slot in the mounting.
6 Replacement in the reverse of removal but care must be taken that the brake cable projection engages properly in the holder.
7 Finally adjust the handbrake as described in Section 5 of this Chapter.

19 Wheel cylinder overhaul

1 During the following operation cleanliness is of the utmost importance. Immediately before commencing work, wash your hands.
2 Gather together a supply of clean, dry, non-fluffy rag, a quantity of brake fluid and a container of methylated spirit. Make sure that you are working on a clean surface.
3 Initially clean the outside of the cylinder. If necessary, methylated spirit can be used.
4 Remove the dust caps and take out the pistons and spring.
5 Discard the rubber parts and clean all the remaining parts in

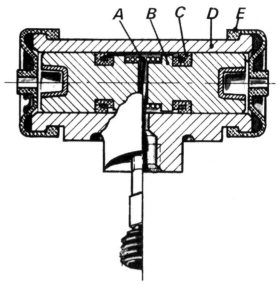

FIG. 9.15. SECTIONAL VIEW OF THE WHEEL CYLINDER (SEC. 19)

a Spring   d Wheel brake cylinder
b Piston   e Cap
c Grooved cup

methylated spirit.
6 Using a magnifying lens or watchmaker's glass, examine the parts carefully. Any parts which are corroded or scored must be renewed. The maximum permissible cylinder diameter is 0.6287 in (15.97 mm) and the minimum permissible piston diameter is 0.6197 in (15.74 mm).
7 When reassembling the rubber parts, they should be wet assembled using brake fluid. Never try to fit dry seals in the bores as they will become damaged.
8 When the assembly is complete the pistons should slide smoothly in the cylinder, and after being pressed in should slide out under the action of the spring.
9 Finally fit the dust caps on the ends and reinstall in the hydraulic system of the car.
10 After reinstallation, brake adjustment, bleeding and testing will be required.

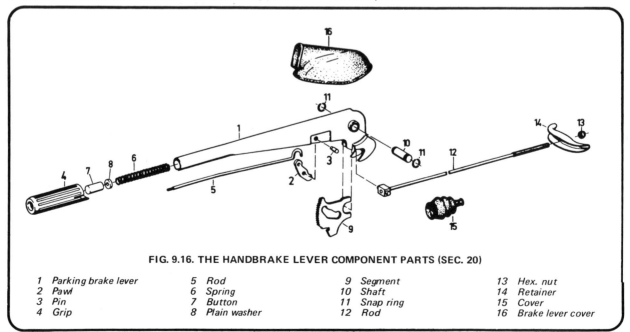

FIG. 9.16. THE HANDBRAKE LEVER COMPONENT PARTS (SEC. 20)

1 Parking brake lever	5 Rod	9 Segment	13 Hex. nut
2 Pawl	6 Spring	10 Shaft	14 Retainer
3 Pin	7 Button	11 Snap ring	15 Cover
4 Grip	8 Plain washer	12 Rod	16 Brake lever cover

20 Handbrake lever and footbrake pedal - removal

1 Removal of the handbrake lever is a straighforward operation. Firstly disconnect the pull rod at the metal handbrake cable holder.

2 Unhook the pull rod at the handbrake lever by sliding in the rod and turning it through 90°.

3 Pull at the sides of the handbrake pivot cover and slide the cover up the lever.

4 The circlip at the pivot can now be removed and the shaft pin pushed out.

5 Now move the lever rearwards (to disengage the ratchet segment) and remove it from the car.

6 If it is necessary to remove the handle, prise up the tab at the rear end and pull the handle off.

7 The moving parts can now be removed with the exception of the ratchet and segment which will entail removal of the rivet.

8 Removal of the footbrake pedal also requires removal of the clutch pedal and is covered in Chapter 5.

21 Vacuum unit - removal and refitting

1 To remove the vacuum unit, it will first of all be necessary to disconnect the brake pedal linkage and remove the brake master cylinder and reservoir. For the former it will be necessary to remove the knee padding (as described in Chapter 2 when removing the heater) and then disconnect the pedal linkage, (as described in Chapter 5 for clutch and brake pedal removal). Removal of the brake master cylinder is dealt with earlier in this Chapter.

2 Disconnect the hose from the vacuum unit.

3 The vacuum unit can then be withdrawn from the bracket on the bulkhead by removing the four securing nuts.

4 If the bracket also is to be removed from the bulkhead, it must be refitted with the centre punch indentation downwards and on the right hand side when viewed from the driving direction.

5 Replacement is a direct reversal of the removal procedure.

6 On completion adjust the brake pedal travel as detailed in Chapter 5, bleed the brakes and road test the car to check braking performance.

7 The vacuum unit check valve is situated on the manifold on early models and can be removed by first disconnecting the vacuum hose then removing the valve insert.

8 On later models the valve is fitted approximately halfway along the hose (photo). If it is to be removed, note that the arrow on the side points towards the inlet manifold.

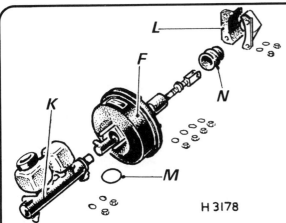

H 3178

FIG. 9.17. THE BRAKE SERVO ASSEMBLY (SEC. 21)

f   Brake servo   m   Seal
k   Brake master cylinder   n   Rubber boot
l   Adaptor

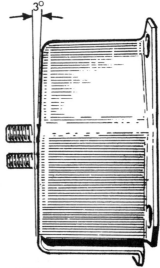

Fig. 9.18. The servo bracket showing the installation attitude (Sec. 21)

H 3179

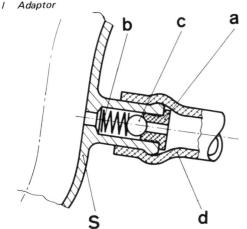

FIG. 9.19. SECTIONAL VIEW OF THE EARLY TYPE CHECK VALVE (SEC. 21)

a   Valve insert   d   Hose
b   Spring   S   Inlet manifold
c   Ball

21.8 The later type vacuum unit check valve

22 Brake lines and hoses

1   Brake hose renewal is an operation which is bound to be required from time to time. If the car is in your ownership for a long period, the flexible hoses should be renewed at least every 60000 miles (100000 km). Rigid brake lines are unlikely to need much attention but they should be checked carefully for security of fixing, and to ensure that there is no serious corrosion and/or damage.

2   Renewal of the flexible hoses is not difficult but as with all repairs which involve disconnecting the hydraulics, the pedal support is required to prevent loss of fluid. For instructions regarding fitment of the pedal support refer to paragraph 2 of Section 12.

3   Whenever pipes and hoses are disconnected take note of the relative clips and brackets used to prevent them rattling and vibrating.

4   When removing the flexible brake hoses first remove the rigid line connection at the fixing bracket before undoing the hose.

5   When any connections have been removed, blank the open pipe ends to prevent dirt entering the system.

6   Remember that cleanliness is very important. Never reuse the fluid which has drained or been bled from the system.

7   If in doubt about the condition of parts always renew them - **your life could well depend on it.**

8   After repairs to the system, always check the brake adjustment, bleed the system free of air and road test the car to check braking efficiency.

23 Brake caliper ventilation

1   Audi 100 GL models from Chassis No 8221 014 373 onwards

are fitted with brake caliper ventilation. This is due to the higher engine temperatures - caused by emission control system.

2   Manual transmission cars have only the right hand caliper ventilated. However, on automatics the calipers on both sides are ventilated.

3   Ventilation is via a hose (or hoses) from the radiator cooling fan. On USA versions which have electric fans a thermal switch is mounted on the right hand caliper which operates if the temperature is too high - regardless of radiator coolant temperature.

4   USA models which have the Volkswagen Product Corporation air conditioning equipment have a manual switch which can override both the brake caliper and radiator thermal switches.

Fig. 9.21. A brake caliper ventilation hose (Sec. 23)

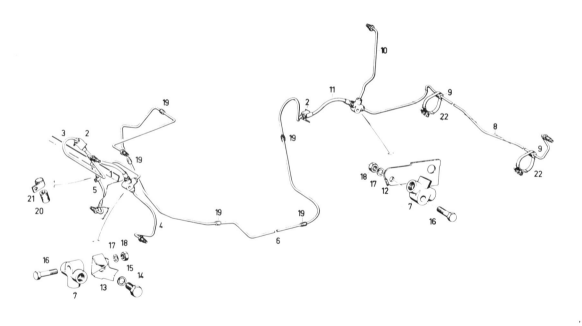

FIG. 9.20. THE COMPONENT PARTS OF THE BRAKE LINES (SEC. 22)

1 Brake hose, front	5 Brake pipe to trans-	7 T-joint	10 Brake pipe to rear axle, right
2 Retaining spring	mission, right	8 Brake pipe to rear axle,	11 Brake hose, rear
3 Brake pipe to brake	6 Brake pipe to brake	left	19 Protective hose
master cylinder, front	master cylinder, rear	9 Protective hose	20 Protective hose
			21 Clip
			22 Hose clip at rear axle

24 Modified braking system

1 In the modified braking system, full brake pressure is applied to the front brakes but a brake pressure regulator governs the rear brake system pressure to a predetermined setting. In order to improve braking performance, even at low brake pedal pressures, the rear brakes are operated slightly in advance of the front brakes. At heavier pedal pressures the front brake system pressure actuates the pressure regulator which then applies and releases pressure rapidly to the rear brakes.

2 In this system a different brake caliper is used which incorporates larger pads and a one piece lock clip. Models for the USA market also have a pad thickness transmitter mounted on the caliper cross spring. This will break after severe wear has occurred and thus operate the low brake fluid level warning light. Pads must then be renewed immediately (or the fluid level topped up).

3 To renew the pads, remove the lock clips, then pull out the retaining pins into the openings in the chassis member. Do not remove the grommets which protect the holes. The old pads can then be hooked out of the calipers but take note of the procedure given for pad renewal on other types of system given earlier in this Chapter.

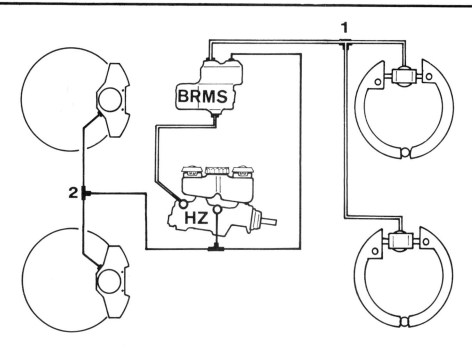

FIG. 9.22. SCHEMATIC DIAGRAM OF THE MODIFIED BRAKING SYSTEM (SEC. 24)

BRMS   *Regulator*
HZ   *Master cylinder*
1   *Rear wheel circuit*
2   *Front wheel circuit*

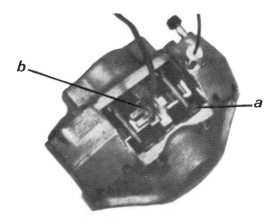

**FIG. 9.23. BRAKE CALIPER WITH THE CERAMIC
THICKNESS TRANSMITTER (SEC. 24)**

a   *One piece lock clip*
b   *Ceramic transmitter*

25 Fault finding table - Braking system

Symptom	Reason/s	Remedy
PEDAL TRAVELS ALMOST TO FLOOR BEFORE BRAKES OPERATE		
Leaks and air bubbles in hydraulic system	Brake fluid level too low	Top up master cylinder reservoir. Check for leaks.
	Wheel cylinder leaking	Dismantle wheel cylinder, clean, fit new rubbers and bleed brakes.
	Master cylinder leaking. (Bubbles in master cylinder fluid)	Dismantle master cylinder, clean, and fit new rubbers. Bleed brakes.
	Brake flexible hose leaking	Examine and fit new hose if old hose leaking. Bleed brakes.
	Brake line fractured	Replace. Bleed brakes.
	Brake system unions loose	Tighten as necessary. Bleed brakes.
Normal wear	Linings badly worn	Fit replacement shoes and brake linings.
Incorrect adjustment	Brakes badly out of adjustment	Jack up car and adjust brakes.
	Master cylinder push rod out of adjustment causing too much pedal free movement	Reset to manufacturer's specification.
BRAKE PEDAL FEELS SPRINGY		
Brake lining renewal	New linings not yet bedded-in	Use brakes gently.
Excessive wear or damage	Brake drums or discs worn or cracked	Fit new brake drums or discs.
Lack of maintenance	Master cylinder securing nuts loose	Tighten master cylinder securing nuts.
BRAKE PEDAL FEELS SPONGY AND SOGGY		
Leaks or bubbles in hydraulic system	Wheel cylinder leaking	Dismantle wheel cylinder, clean, fit new rubbers, and bleed brakes.
	Master cylinder leaking. (Bubbles in master cylinder reservoir)	Dismantle master cylinder, clean, and fit new rubbers and bleed brakes. Replace cylinder if internal walls scored.
	Brake pipe or flexible hose leaking	Fit new pipeline or hose.
	Unions in brake system loose	Examine for leaks, tighten as necessary.
EXCESSIVE EFFORT REQUIRED TO BRAKE VEHICLE		
Lining type or condition	Linings or pads badly worn	Fit replacement pads or linings.
	New linings recently fitted - not yet bedded-in	Use brakes gently until braking effort normal.
	Harder linings fitted than standard causing increase in pedal pressure	Remove linings and replace with normal units.
Oil or grease leaks	Drums or discs contaminated with oil, grease, or hydraulic fluid	Rectify source of leak, clean discs and drums, fit new linings.
Servo unit (if fitted)	Leaking vacuum hose	Fit new hose.
	Servo unit worn internally	Fit new servo unit or overhaul.
BRAKES UNEVEN AND PULLING TO ONE SIDE		
Oil or grease leaks	Brakes contaminated with oil, grease, or hydraulic fluid	Ascertain and rectify source of leak, clean brakes, fit new linings.
Lack of maintenance	Tyre pressures unequal	Check and inflate as necessary.
	Brake assembly loose	Tighten the nuts and bolts.
	Different type of linings fitted at each wheel	Fit the linings specified by the manufacturer's all round.
	Brake drums or discs worn or loose	Fit new brake drums or discs.
BRAKES TEND TO BIND, DRAG, OR LOCK-ON		
Incorrect adjustment	Brake shoes adjusted too tightly	Slacken off brake shoe adjusters, slightly.

Chapter 10 Electrical system

For modifications, and information applicable to later models, see Supplement at end of manual

Contents

Specifications

System type	12 volt, negative earth
Battery	12 volt, 45 amp hour (54 amp hour for 100 Sweden, 100LS Automatic, 100LS Sweden, 100LS USA, 100 Coupe' S
Battery location	Beneath rear seat squab
Starter	12 volt 0.8 HP
Alternator	K1/14V 35 A 20 (55 A 20 with built-in regulator for 100LS USA, 100GL and 100 Coupe' S)
Regulator	AD 1/14 V (except 100LS, USA and 100 Coupe' S)
Regulator voltage	13.9 to 14.8 volts
Headlights	Assymetrical 45/40 watt or double halogen if 55 A alternator is fitted. (Double sealed beam 50/37.5 W for 100LS USA. Double halogen 55 W for 100GL and Coupe' S)
Reverse lights	2 x 21 watt spherical
Sidelights	2 x 4 watt oblong
Turn indicators	4 x 21 watt spherical
Rear lights	2 x 5 watt spherical
Stop lights	2 x 21 watt spherical
Number plate lights	2 x 4 watt oblong
Heater control light	2 watt oblong
Interior light	10 watt festoon
Glove compartment light	3 watt oblong
Speedometer light	3 watt oblong
Combination instrument lamp	4 x 3 watt oblong
Charge warning light	3 watt oblong
Oil warning light	3 watt oblong
High beam warning light	3 watt oblong
Turn indicator warning light	3 watt oblong
Emergency warning light	1.2 watt oblong
Brake system warning light	3 watt oblong
Handbrake warning light	3 watt oblong
Tail fog light (optional)	21 or 35 watt spherical
Fog light warning light	1.2 watt oblong
Halogen fog light (optional)	55 watt YC
Halogen long range headlight (optional)	55 watt Y
Rear window heater warning light (optional)	2 watt oblong

Fuses

Fuse No.	Current rating	Circuit
1	8 amp	Turn indicators, emergency warning systems
2	16 amp	Windscreen washer, blower motor, horn, temperature gauge, fuel gauge, oil warning light, reverse lights
3	16 amp	Windscreen wipers, stop light, number plate lights, panel lights, glove compartment lights, cigarette lighter, clock, interior light
4	8 amp	Parking and tail lights right
5	8 amp	Main beam left
6	8 amp	Main beam right and warning light
7	8 amp	Dipped beam left
8	8 amp	Dipped beam right
9	8 amp	Parking and tail lights left

Temperature transmitter

Part No.	Voltage	Application
803 919 501	5.05 V	All 100 models up to chassis No. 11 017 508
815 919 501 (old)	10.0 V	All 100 models from chassis No. 11 017 509, including GL and Coupe' S
028 919 501 (new)	10.0 V	All 100 models from chassis No. 11 017 509, including GL and Coupe' S

1 General description

The electrical system of the Audi 100 series is 12 volt negative earth, charging current is supplied by a 14 volt alter-nator with integral rectification via silicon diodes. In general, a two contact regulator is fitted although some models in the range have a transistorized electronic regulator built into the alternator.

The advantages of an alternator, when compared with a dynamo, are: low weight, maintenance - free operation, simple voltage regulation and high current generation at very low engine speeds.

Note 1: Do not run, or attempt to run, the engine with the battery disconnected.

Note 2: During any maintenance operations on the electrical system (except bulb replacement etc), or when carrying out any operation with welding equipment, the battery MUST be disconnected.

2 Battery - checking specific gravity of electrolyte

1 The battery is located beneath the rear seat (photo). To remove the seal lift the front edge first; when replacing, fit the front edge first then press down the rear edge.

2 Before the battery cover can be removed it is necessary to fold back the triangular carpet flap and remove the plastic terminal cap.

3 Remove the battery cover, but do not take off the breather connection.

4 Check first that the electrolyte level is up to the base of the filler tubes.

5 Using a hydrometer, check the specific gravity of the battery. The correct values for a fully charged battery at 20°C (68°F) are given below:

For normal and cold climates:

Specific gravity	Degree of charge
1.285	fully charged
1.21	half charged
1.14	discharged

For tropical climates:

Specific gravity	Degree of charge
1.23	fully charged
1.16	half charged
1.09	discharged

Note: If the specific gravity is found to be above 1.28, the electrolyte should be diluted a little with distilled water.

3 Battery - checking the terminal voltage under load

1 The battery can be checked by using a tester which will short circuit it with a very low resistance. These testers are used by all reputable battery specialists and the cost of the operation is negligible.

2 An alternative method is to remove the coil to distributor HT lead, connect a voltmeter (suitable for 12 volts dc) across the battery terminals, place chocks in front of the wheels, put the handbrake on, engage fourth gear then energise the starter motor for two or three seconds. The battery voltage should not fall below 7 volts. If necessary the test may be repeated after a delay of about five minutes, but don't continually repeat it since the battery will eventually become discharged.

4 Battery charging

1 If the battery is to be charged from an external source it is

2.1 The battery location beneath the rear seat squab

preferable to remove it from the car. In addition to removal of the cover, unscrew both terminal lugs and the clamping strip at the base.

2 If the battery is not removed from the car, the earth strap **MUST** be removed before commencing to charge.

3 Initially remove the cell caps and then check the electrolyte level. Top up with distilled water, if necessary, to the bottom of the filler tubes only.

4 Do not exceed a charging rate of one tenth of the battery capacity for normal charging (ie 4½ amps per hour for a 45 amp hour battery).

5 After completing the charge do not replace the cell caps for at least one hour afterwards - when the gasing will have more or less stopped.

Note: During charging, and the period of heavy gasing afterwards, do not smoke or have naked lights near the battery, since an explosive gas is being given off. Always ensure that there is adequate ventilation.

6 If there is ever a need to give the battery a rapid "boost" charge always follow the instructions given with the particular charger being used. Under no circumstances exceed the ampere hour rate of the battery.

5 Battery terminal corrosion

1 Battery terminal corrision does not normally occur if the battery is maintained in a good condition and the terminals are lightly lubricated with petroleum jelly from time to time.

2 In cases of severe corrosion, remove the battery from the car, then scrape off the worst of the corrosion with an old penknife. Do the same with the connections on the leads but don't let the corrosion deposits contact the hands, car upholstery, carpeting or paintwork, since damage may occur.

3 Mix up a solution of hot water (about a pint) and a dessert-spoonful of bicarbonate of soda.

4 Pour a little of the solution into a jar and brush it on to the battery terminals. There will be a lot of fizzing and bubbling so take care. Wipe dry afterwards and repeat the operation until all the bubbling stops. Treat the connections on the leads in the same manner.

5 On completion wipe everything dry and lightly coat all the surfaces with petroleum jelly.

6 Finally refit all the terminals, tightly.

6 Removing the alternator

1 Disconnect the battery earth strap and the red lead at the starter motor.

2 Pull off the connector at the regulator (see next section) then disconnect the flat plug connection from this connector.

3 Remove the plastic cable clip and the screw on the adjustment bracket.

4 Swing the alternator outwards and remove the drive belt from the pulley.

5 Disconnect the earth strap then whilst supporting the weight of the alternator remove the long pivot bolt.

6 Replacement is the reverse of removal, but adjust the drive belt tension. Belt tension is correct when with a pressure of approximately 22 lb (10 kg) there is a deflection of the belt of approximately 0.4 in (10 mm).

7 Regulator (where fitted) - removal and replacement

1 Disconnect the battery earth strap.

2 Remove the connector from beneath the regulator (This is situated on the front right hand wheel housing, adjacent to the headlight assembly).

3 Remove the hexagon headed screws beneath the regulator then lift it away.

4 Replacement is the reverse of removal.

FIG. 10.1. THE ALTERNATOR WITH THE FAN BELT REMOVED (SEC. 6)

d   Earth strap
e,f   Pivot bolt and nut

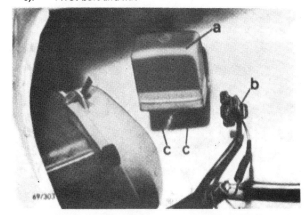

FIG. 10.2. THE REGULATOR (WHERE FITTED) (SEC. 7)

a Regulator   c Hex. head screws
b Triple point plug   d Flat plug connection

8 Charging system - fault finding

1 If trouble is experienced with the alternator, first check that it rotates when the engine is running and that the drive belt is correctly tensioned.

2 The alternator charge warning lamp should be extinguished at idling speeds or speeds slightly above idling.

3 If the lamp continues to be brightly illuminated, check the lead D+/61 for a short circuit to earth. If this is satisfactory a fault in the regulator is indicated.

4 If the lamp does not illuminate, check the bulb and associated leads to the ignition switch and alternator for an open circuit.

5 If the lamp illuminates at half brilliance regardless of engine speed check for an open circuit in the alternator lead DF. If this is satisfactory, a fault is indicated in either the regulator, alternator carbon brushes or alternator slip rings.

6 If the lamp illuminates brightly with the engine stationary and flickers with the engine running, there is either a defective alternator or a faulty connection in the charging circuit. This can be checked by connecting a 12 volt lamp of at least 2 watts rating between terminals D+ and B- on the alternator. If the lamp is more or less bright at moderate engine speeds, alternator fault is indicated; if the lamp flickers there is a faulty connection in the charging circuit.

7 If the test lamp is illuminated with the ignition switched off and is extinguished with the ignition switched on, a defective diode is indicated. In this instance the battery will discharge if

the car is not in use. Therefore, the earth strap must be disconnected until the alternator is repaired. If it is necessary to drive the car in an emergency, disconnect the B+ lead at the alternator which will permit the car to be used until the battery charge is exhausted.

9 Checking the alternator (and regulator) in the car

1 With the engine switched off, initially disconnect the battery earth strap.
2 Disconnect the red lead on terminal 30 of the starter motor, and which comes from terminal B+ of the alternator.
3 Make the connections to suitable test equipment as shown in the illustration (Fig. 10.4).

4 Reconnect the battery earth strap.
5 Now run the engine at a speed of 2050 rev/min to give an alternator speed of 4000 rev/min.
6 Whilst maintaining a constant engine speed, adjust the alternator load resistor until a current of 28 to 30 amps is obtained then check that a voltage of 13.9 to 14.8 volts is obtained.
7 If this voltage cannot be obtained, the only way of checking whether the alternator or regulator is at fault is to substitute items known to be serviceable. If these are not available consult a car electrical specialist for further advice.
8 Further checking to be carried out on an otherwise satisfactory alternator should produce the following results when the

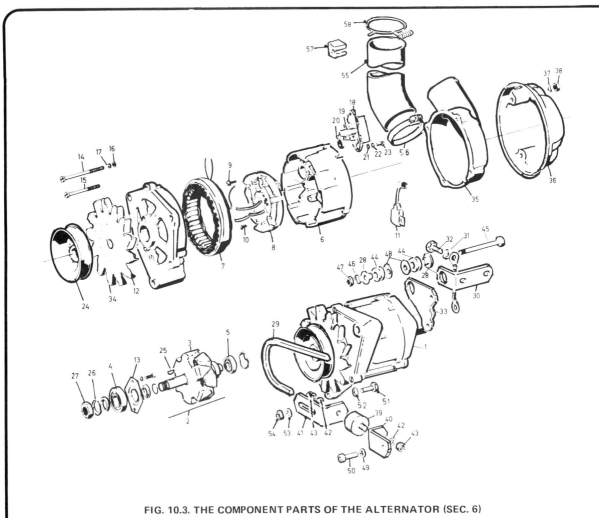

FIG. 10.3. THE COMPONENT PARTS OF THE ALTERNATOR (SEC. 6)

1	Alternator with governor	15	Screw	29	V belt	44	Sleeve
2	Set of rotor parts	16	Plain washer	30	Holder, alternator	45	Hex. head screw
3	Rotor	17	Lock washer	31	Washer	46	Washer
4	Annular grooved bearing 6	18	Governor	32	Hex. head screw	47	Hex. nut
5	Annular grooved bearing 6	19	Set of carbon brushes	33	Mounting plate, alternator	48	Disc
6	Slip ring bearing	20	Spring	34	Fan	49	Washer
7	Stator	21	Plain washer	35	Cap	50	Socket head screw
8	Diode plate	22	Lock washer	36	Cap	51	Hex. head screw
9	Socket head screw	23	Socket head screw	37	Washer	52	Plain washer
10	Socket head screw	24	Pulley	38	Hex. nut	53	Washer
11	Condenser	25	Woodruff key	39	Rubber bearing	54	Hex. nut
12	Drive bearing	26	Lock washer	40	Adjuster	55	Fresh air hose
13	Holder	27	Hex. nut	41	Adjuster	56	Clip
14	Screw	28	Sleeve	42	Washer	57	Rubber holder
				43	Hex. nut	58	Holder

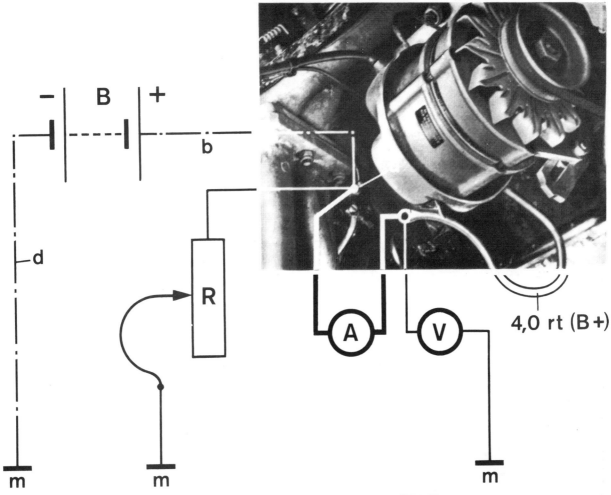

FIG. 10.4. TESTING THE ALTERNATOR (SEC. 9)

A   Ammeter (up to 40A d.c.)
V   Voltmeter (up to 20V d.c.)
R   Resistor (capable of carrying 40A loads)

B   Car battery
a   Starter terminal 30
b   Lead from battery to terminal 'a' on starter

d   Battery earth
m   Chassis earth
4.0 rt   Lead from alternator terminal 'b' (red)

alternator is warm.

Engine speed	current
1150 rev/min maximum	24 amps
2800 rev/min maximum	35 amps

9   During all the above tests the alternator charge warning light must be extinguished.
10 If the results of the aforementioned tests prove satisfactory, the test equipment may be removed and the original connections restored.

10 Starter motor - removal and replacement

1   Initially disconnect the battery earth strap.
2   Place a suitable container beneath the oil filter to catch any escaping oil, then unscrew the filter.
3   Disconnect the electrical leads at the starter motor.
4   Remove the nuts and bolts from the starter mounting then pull the starter forwards to remove.
5   Replacement should be carried out in the reverse order to removal.
6   When replacing the oil filter clean the seal and sealing face with a clean rag, then lightly lubricate both with a little oil or grease.
7   Screw the filter on, hand tight only then start the engine and check for oil leaks.

FIG. 10.5. THE STARTER MOTOR CONNECTIONS (SEC. 10)

a   Terminal 30
b   Terminal 50
c   Solenoid

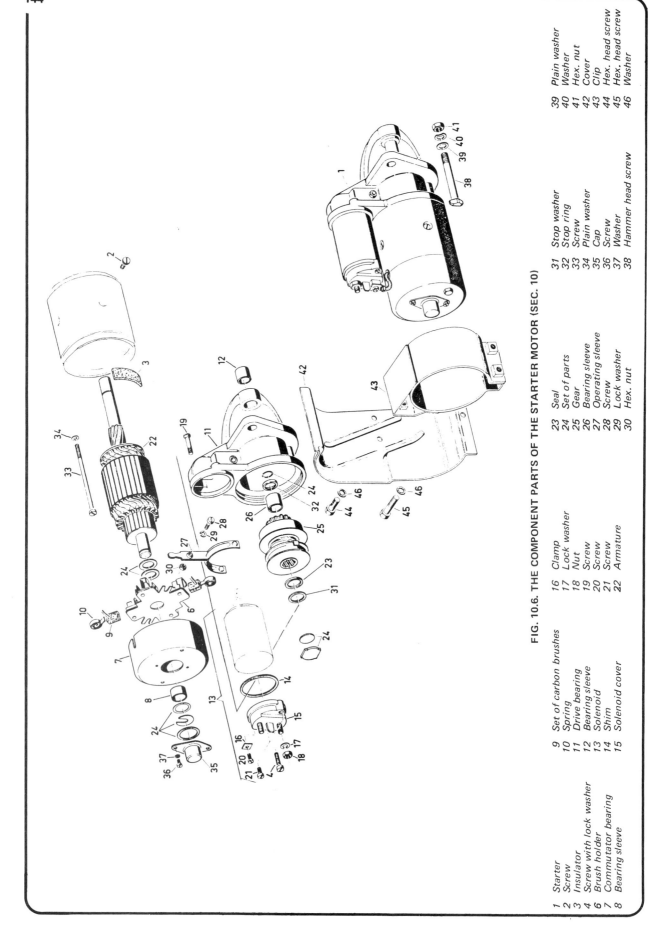

FIG. 10.6. THE COMPONENT PARTS OF THE STARTER MOTOR (SEC. 10)

1 Starter
2 Screw
3 Insulator
4 Screw with lock washer
6 Brush holder
7 Commutator bearing
8 Bearing sleeve

9   Set of carbon brushes
10 Spring
11 Drive bearing
12 Bearing sleeve
13 Solenoid
14 Shim
15 Solenoid cover

16 Clamp
17 Lock washer
18 Nut
19 Screw
20 Screw
21 Screw
22 Armature

23 Seal
24 Set of parts
25 Gear
26 Bearing sleeve
27 Operating sleeve
28 Screw
29 Lock washer
30 Hex. nut

31 Stop washer
32 Stop ring
33 Screw
34 Plain washer
35 Cap
36 Screw
37 Washer
38 Hammer head screw

39 Plain washer
40 Washer
41 Hex. nut
42 Cover
43 Clip
44 Hex. head screw
45 Hex. head screw
46 Washer

11 Checking the starter motor

1 There is no simple method for checking the starter motor unless a 'clip-on' type of dc ammeter is available.

2 If this is available, initially carry out the tests described for the battery at the beginning of this chapter then check the battery current. This should be between 250 and 300 amps.

3 If the current is low, and the battery is known to be satisfactory, one of the following faults is indicated:
a) A dirty or worn commutator.
b) Badly worn carbon brushes.
c) A faulty solenoid switch.
d) Broken or damaged brush springs.

4 If the current is high an internal short circuit of the starter motor is indicated.

12 Headlamp bulb renewal - double headlights

1 Pull off the rubber cap on the rear of the headlamp casing (photo).

2 Pull off the large flat spade connection.

3 Prise the spring clip out of its holder, fold it back then lift out the bulb.

4 When installing a bulb take great care not to handle the bulb glass with bare fingers, since any deposits of perspiration or grease will condense on the lens due to the heat of the bulb, and shorten the life of the bulb.

5 Reassembly is the reverse of removal.

12.1 The headlamp bulbs - double headlights

13 Sidelamp bulb renewal - double headlights

1 Initially proceed as for the headlamp bulb renewal but in addition pull out the sidelamp bulb after the headlamp bulb has been removed. **Note:** Sidelamp bulbs are fitted to the outer headlamps only.

14 Headlamp bulb renewal - single headlamps

1 Lift the spring on the rear of the headlamp which retains the cap, then pull the cap off.

2 Press in the locking ring at the rear of the bulb then turn it in an anticlockwise direction.

3 Pull out the bulb complete with the cable connector. Take out the bulb.

4 When installing a bulb take great care not to handle the bulb glass with bare fingers, since any deposits of perspiration or

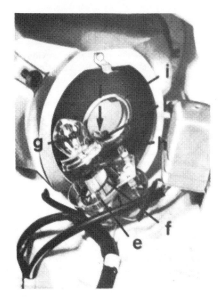

**FIG. 10.7. THE SINGLE HEADLAMP BULB ASSEMBLY
(SEC. 14)**

e	Tightening ring
f	Plug
g	Double filament bulb
h	Parking light bulb
i	Guide ring in reflector
k	Projection (must engage in guide ring cutout)
l	Cutout fork

**FIG. 10.8. THE DOUBLE HEADLAMP ASSEMBLY
SHOWING ADJUSTERS (SEC. 16)**

a	Vertical adjustment	c	Rubber guard with
b	Lateral adjustment	d	Flat plug connectors

grease will condense on the lens due to the heat of the bulb, and shorten the life of the bulb.

5 Reassembly is the reverse of removal, but make sure that the guide on the bulb holder locates in the groove in the lens aperture.

15 Sidelamp bulb renewal - single headlights

1 Initially proceed as for the headlamp bulb renewal but take out the sidelamp bulb instead of the double filament bulb.

16 Headlamp beam adjustment

1 Headlamp beam adjusting screws are provided for both horizontal and vertical alignment. However, adjustment of beam alignment should not be attempted without the appropriate beam setting equipment.

17 Headlamp - removal and replacement (double headlights)

1 Initially remove the headlamp bulbs as previously described but additionally disconnect the battery earth strap.
2 Remove the front grille. This is held in position by crosshead screws at the top and pressed into spring clips at the bottom.
3 Remove the headlamp assembly by unscrewing the retaining screws around the periphery of the lens (photo).
4 Reassembly is the reverse of removal.

18 Headlamp - removal and replacement (single headlamps)

1 Initially remove the headlamp bulb as described previously but additionally disconnect the battery earth strap.
2 Press the lamp cover ring downwards at the bottom edge, then outwards.
3 Slip a screwdriver between the cover ring and lens then press the cover ring upwards and off.
4 Remove the headlamp by unscrewing the retaining screws around the periphery of the lens.
5 To remove the lens, first prise off the clips which hold it in position. Caution - do not touch the reflective surface of the reflector.
6 Reassembly is the reverse of removal.

19 Front direction indicators

1 To remove the lens, simply unscrew the two retaining cross-head screws (photo).
2 The bulb is now accessible for removal. It is of the bayonet fixing type.
3 To remove the complete lamp assembly remove the two screws beneath the lamp on the underside of the bumper.
4 Reassembly is the reverse of removal, but make sure that the heavily ribbed side of the lens is facing outwards.

20 Rear light cluster

1 Working from inside the luggage boot remove the knurled nut on the transparent cover (photo).
2 Pull off the cover and bulb holder. The bulbs are now accessible (photo).
3 To remove the lamp assembly complete, remove the four hexagon nuts and one screw then pull off the assembly from outside the car.
4 Reassembly is the reverse of removal, but it is advisable to use a new seal between the lens assembly and the bodywork.

21 Number plate lamps

1 To remove the number plate lamp, unscrew the cross-head screws and pull the lamp downwards (photo).
2 The bulb can now be removed if necessary.

22 Interior lamp

1 Carefully prise out the lamp bezel from the roof frame. Replace the bulb if necessary.
2 When refitting the lamp it needs only to be pressed into position to allow the spring loaded ball to engage (photo).

23 Headlight and tail foglight switch

1 Remove the instrument panel trim and knee protection. The procedure for this is given in Chapter 2 with the instructions for removing the heater.

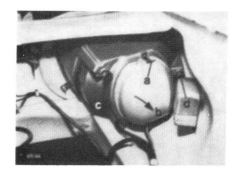

FIG. 10.9. THE SINGLE HEADLAMP ASSEMBLY SHOWING ADJUSTERS (SEC. 16)

a   *Cap release spring clip*
b   *Cap*
c   *Vertical adjustment*
d   *Lateral adjustment*

FIG. 10.10. SINGLE HEADLAMP REMOVAL (SEC. 18)

m, n   *Press downwards here*

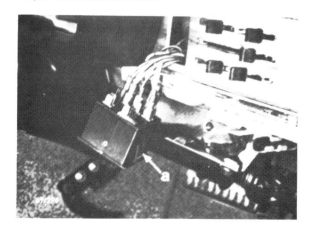

FIG. 10.11. REMOVING THE HEADLIGHT AND TAIL FOGLIGHT SWITCH (SEC. 23)

a   *Spring clip*

2 If not already carried out, remove the battery earth strap.
3 Press out the switch from behind the panel. It is held in by spring clips only.
4 Make a note of the various cable colours before pulling them off.
5 Replacement is the reverse of removal.

17.3 Headlamp assembly removal - double headlights

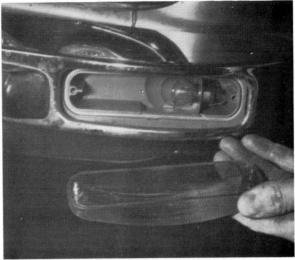

19.2 Front direction indicator bulb renewal

20.1 Removing the transparent rear light cluster cover

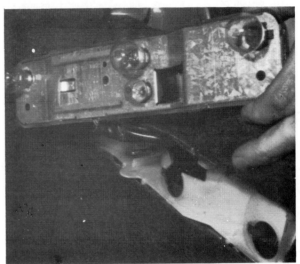

20.2 The rear light bulb holder and bulbs

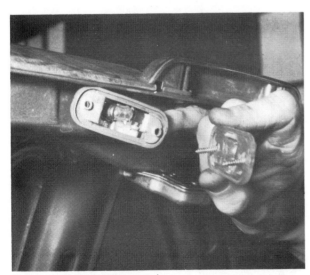

21.1 Number plate lamp renewal

22.2 The interior lamp

24 Windscreen wiper switch and warning light

1 Remove the instrument panel trim and knee protection padding. The procedure for this is given in Chapter 2 with the instructions for removing the heater.
2 If not already carried out, remove the battery earth strap.
3 Press out the switch from behind the panel, complete with the fresh air jet. They are held by spring clips only - take care not to damage the seal.
4 Note the colour of the various cables before pulling them off.
5 Using a screwdriver in the retangular holes, carefully prise the casing apart and press out the switch.
6 Replace the switch then refit the assembly in the reverse order to removal.

25 Horn contact plate and multi-function switch

1 Remove the battery earth strap.
2 Pull off the horn contact plate.
3 Remove the hexagon nut and pull off the steering wheel.
4 The carbon contacts, contact ring and earth lead can now be removed.
5 Remove the screws which retain the steering column casing (two at the steering wheel end and one below the ignition switch).
6 The multi-function switch can now be unscrewed, but before removing the cables make a note of the various colours.
7 Reassembly is the reverse of removal.

26 Door contact switch

1 Remove the battery earth strap.
2 The door contact switch is retained by one cross-head screw.
3 Once the switch has been removed, prise open the crimped connection.
4 Crimp the new cable/switch connection using a pair of pliers.

27 Fuse box, relay and flasher unit

1 Remove the battery earth strap.
2 To remove the fuse box, slide it towards the right to dis-engage it from the holders (the flasher unit and relay are incorporated in the fuse box).
3 To remove the slow action windscreen washer relay, simply slide it upwards clear of the holder.
4 Before removing any cable connections either make a note of the lead colours or refer to the appropriate wiring diagram.
5 Refitting of the various parts is the reverse of removal.

FIG. 10.12. REMOVING THE WINDSCREEN WIPER SWITCH AND WARNING LIGHT (SEC. 24)

a   Spring clips   c   Fresh air inlet
b   Seal

FIG. 10.13. THE HORN CONTACT PLATE AND MULTI-FUNCTION SWITCH (SEC. 25)

d   Contact ring
e   Screws for contact ring
f   Column casing
g   Screws for column casing
h   Earth lead

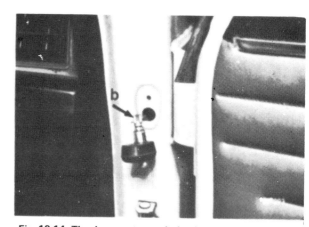

Fig. 10.14. The door contact switch crimped connection (b) (Sec. 26)

FIG. 10.15. THE FUSE BOX, RELAY AND FLASHER UNITS (SEC. 27)

a   Slow action relay
b   Flasher unit
c   Relay
d   Holder
e   Fuse box retaining slot

28 Windscreen wiper motor - removal and replacement

1 Disconnect the battery earth lead.
2 Remove the windscreen wiper switch as previously described.
3 Working from inside the engine compartment. pull out the rubber grommet on the windscreen wiper harness.
4 Pull out the harness, bending back the mated tabs as necessary.
5 Loosen the hexagon nut on the wiper motor drive end and prise off the connecting rod. Note the position of the operating lever for when replacement is carried out (photo).
6 Remove the three slotted head screws which hold the wiper to the base, then remove the wiper complete with its wiring harness.
7 Replacement is a reversal of the removal procedure.

29 Windscreen wiper arms - removal and replacement

1 To remove the wiper arms, prise off the plastic cap on the spindle then unscrew the hexagon nut (photo).
2 Mark the position of the arm on the spindle to facilitate positioning (unless new parts are to be fitted).
3 Pull off the arm.
4 Replacement is a reversal of the removal procedure. When refitting the arms do not exceed a torque of 7.23 lb ft (1 kgm) on the nut.

30 Windscreen wiper blade renewal

1 To renew the wiper blades, lift the arm away from the windscreen and swing out the blade (photo).
2 Press the spring towards the wiper arm, take out the blade and fit the replacement.

31 Windscreen wiper base - removal and replacement

1 Remove the wiper blades and motor as described previously in this section.
2 Remove the nut, washer and seal from beneath the wiper arm mounting on the spindle.
3 Working from the engine compartment, remove the two screws retaining the base to the horizontal surface and the two on the vertical bulkhead.
4 The base can now be lifted slightly and removed.
5 When replacing the parts ensure that the appropriate rubber mountings and washers are refitted, and that the nut on the spindle is fitted with the collar outwards.

32 Windscreen washer - removal and replacement

1 Remove the reservoir and motor by sliding them upwards out of the holder (photo).
2 Disconnect the plastic hose connection then slide the motor unit to one side to remove it from the bosses on the base of the reservoir.
3 If the jets need to be removed, pull off the plastic hose then working from below the jets press the two halves of the hook together. The jet and seal can then be removed from above.
4 Refitment is the reverse of removal, but make sure that all the hose connections are tight.

33 Combination instrument - removal and replacement

1 Remove the earth strap.
2 Remove the screws which retain the instrument panel padding.
3 Working from beneath the combination instrument, remove

28.5 The windscreen wiper motor

29.1 Windscreen wiper arm removal

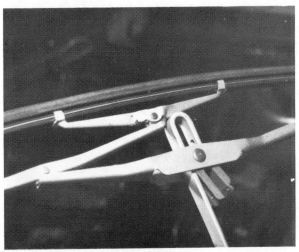
30.1 Windscreen wiper blade renewal

32.1 Windscreen washer reservoir and motor

the two fixing nuts and carefully pull the instrument forwards. Note the washers and rubber padding strips.

4 Disconnect the speedometer drive cable.

5 Pull off the multi-connection plug.

6 Pull off the remaining connections but make a note of the various cable colours since the connections vary with different models.

7 The combination instrument can now be fully removed.

8 Refitting is the reverse of removal.

Note: If it is required to remove any or all of the instruments, carefully make a sketch of the various parts before commencing and note the colours of the electrical leads.

34 Installing additional electrical equipment

1 Before installing any additional electrical equipment consult an Audi dealer. There are many approved accessories but care must be taken with the connections to prevent overloading of existing fuses. Additionally, some items require the addition of separate fuses.

2 If it is intended to fit items each as radios, aerials, tape players etc, always consult a specialist since some additional suppression of electrical equipment may be required.

35 Fault finding table - Electrical system

Symptom	Reason/s	Remedy
Starter motor fails to turn engine No voltage at starter motor	Battery discharged Battery defective internally Battery terminal leads loose or earth lead not securely attached to body Loose or broken connections in starter motor circuit Ignition switch or solenoid faulty	Charge battery. Fit new battery. Check and tighten leads Check all connections and tighten any that are loose. Test and replace faulty components with new.
Voltage at starter motor: faulty motor	Starter motor pinion jammed in mesh with flywheel gear ring Starter brushes badly worn, sticking, or brush wires loose Commutator dirty, worn, or burnt Starter motor armature faulty Field coils earthed	Disengage pinion by rocking car in fourth gear. Examine brushes, replace as necessary, tighten down brush wires. Clean commutator, recut if badly burnt. Overhaul starter motor, fit new armature. Overhaul starter motor.
Starter motor turns engine very slowly Electrical defects	Battery in discharged condition Starter brushes badly worn, sticking, or brush wires loose Loose wires in starter motor circuit	Charge battery. Examine brushes, replace as necessary, tighten down brush wires. Check wiring and tighten as necessary.
Starter motor operates without turning engine	Starter motor pinion sheared	Remove starter motor and repair motor drive.
Mechanical damage	Pinion or flywheel gear teeth broken or worn	Fit new gear ring to flywheel, and new pinion to starter motor drive.
Starter motor noisy or excessively rough engagement	Pinion or flywheel gear teeth broken or worn	Fit new gear teeth to flywheel, or new pinion to starter motor drive.
Lack of attention or mechanical damage	Starter drive broken Starter motor retaining bolts loose	Dismantle and repair, Tighten starter motor securing bolts. Fit new spring washer if necessary.
Battery will not hold charge Wear or damage	Battery defective internally Electrolyte level too low or electrolyte too weak due to leakage Plate separators no longer fully effective Battery plates severely sulphated	Remove and fit new battery. Top up electrolyte level to just above plates. Remove and fit new battery. Remove and fit new battery.
Insufficient current flow to keep battery charged	Drive belt slipping Battery terminal connections loose or corroded Alternator not charging properly Short in lighting circuit causing continual battery drain. Regulator unit not working correctly	Check belt for wear, replace if necessary, and tighten. Check terminals for tightness, and remove all corrosion. Remove alternator for repair. Trace and rectify. Check regulator and replace if necessary.
Ignition light fails to go out, battery runs flat Alternator not charging	Drive belt loose and slipping, or broken Alternator diode faulty Carbon brushes or slip rings faulty Faulty ignition light ot wiring	Check, replace, and tighten as necessary. Repair alternator. Check alternator and replace if necessary. Renew bulb and check wiring as necessary.

Failure of individual electrical equipment to function correctly is dealt with alphabetically, item by item, under the headings listed below.

Fuel gauge gives no reading	Fuel tank empty! Electric cable between tank sender unit and gauge earthed or loose Fuel gauge case not earthed Fuel gauge supply cable interrupted Fuel gauge unit broken	Fill fuel tank. Check cable for earthing and joints for tightness. Ensure case is well earthed. Check and replace cable if necessary. Replace fuel gauge.

Symptom	Reason/s	Remedy
Fuel gauge registers full all the time	Electric cable between tank unit and gauge broken or disconnected	Check over cable and repair as necessary.
Horn operates all the time	Horn push either earthed or stuck down	Disconnect battery earth. Check and rectify source of trouble.
	Horn cable to horn push earthed	Disconnect battery earth. Check and rectify source of trouble.
Horn fails to operate	Blown fuse	Check and renew if broken. Ascertain cause.
	Cable or cable connection loose, broken or disconnected	Check all connections for tightness and cables for breaks.
	Horn has an internal fault	Remove and overhaul horn.
Horn emits intermittent or unsatisfactory noise	Cable connections loose	Check and tighten all connections.
	Horn incorrectly adjusted	Adjust horn until best note obtained.
Lights do not come on	If engine not running, battery discharged	Push-start car, charge battery.
	Light bulb filament burnt out or bulbs broken	Test bulbs in live bulb holder.
	Wire connections loose, disconnected or broken	Check all connections for tightness and wire cable for breaks.
	Light switch shorting or otherwise faulty	By-pass light switch to ascertain if fault is in switch and fit new switch as appropriate.
	Blown fuse	Replace fuse and trace fault.
Lights come on but fade out	If engine not running battery discharged	Push-start car, and charge battery.
Lights give very poor illumination	Lamp glasses dirty	Clean glasses.
	Reflector tarnished or dirty	Fit new reflectors.
	Lamps badly out of adjustment	Adjust lamps correctly.
	Incorrect bulb with too low wattage fitted	Remove bulb and replace with correct grade.
	Existing bulbs old and badly discoloured	Renew bulb units.
	Electrical wiring too thin not allowing full current to pass	Re-wire lighting system.
Lights work erratically - flashing on and off especially over bumps	Light connections or earth faulty	Examine and rectify.
Wiper motor fails to work	Blown fuse	Check and replace fuse if necessary.
	Wire connections loose, disconnected, or broken	Check wiper wiring. Tighten loose connections.
	Brushes badly worn	Remove and fit new brushes.
	Armature or field coils faulty	Overhaul wiper motor or fit replacement unit.
Wiper motor works very slowly, and takes excessive current	Commutator dirty, greasy, or burnt	Clean commutator thoroughly.
	Linkage bent	Check and rectify as necessary.
	Armature bearings dry or unaligned	Replace with new bearings correctly aligned.
Wiper motor works slowly and takes little current	Brushes badly worn	Remove and fit new brushes.
	Commutator dirty	Clean commutator thoroughly.

**WIRING DIAGRAMS
FOLLOW ON PAGES
154 TO 173**

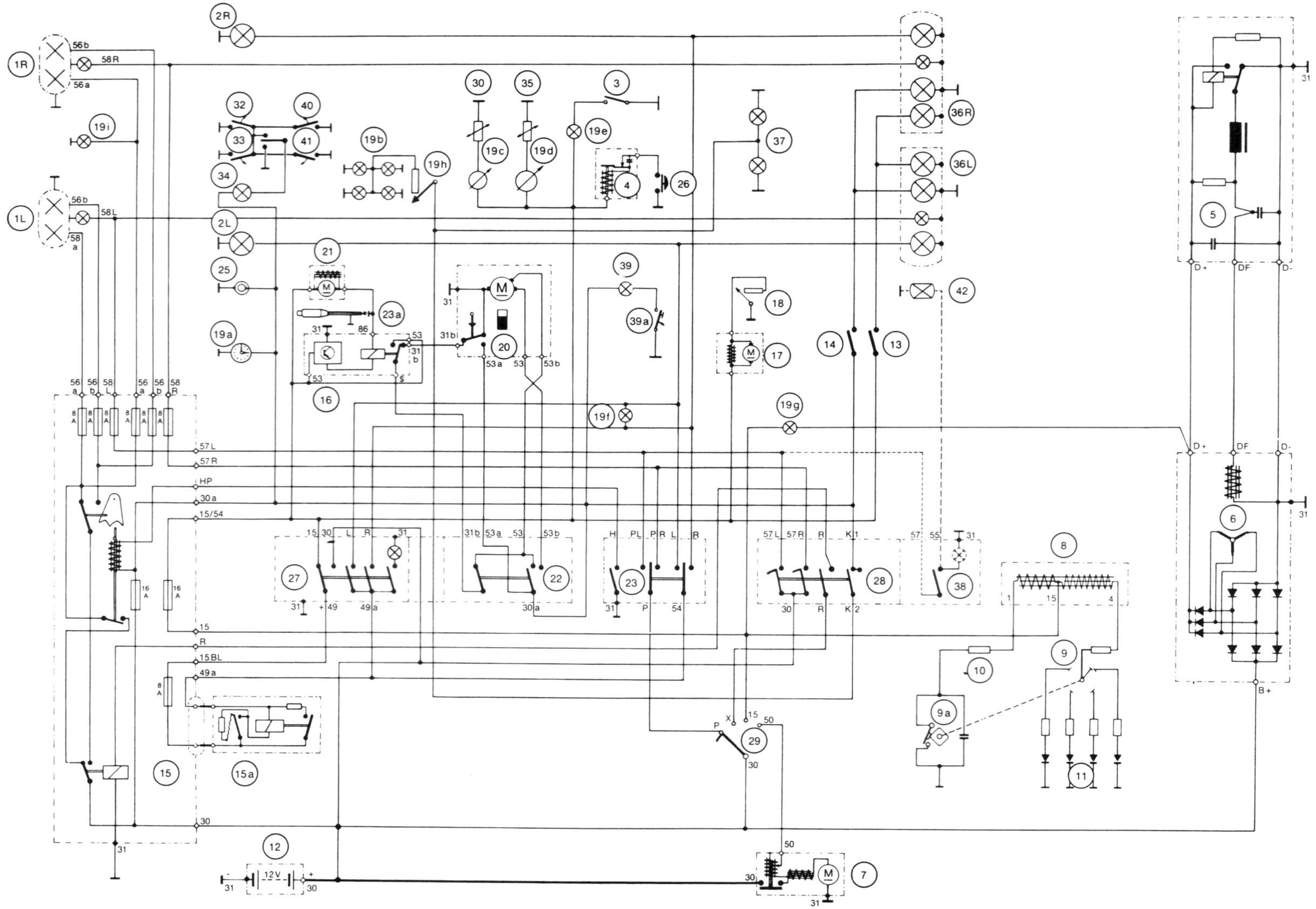

Fig. 10.16. Wiring diagram, early 1969 except N. America ('Key' on page 165)

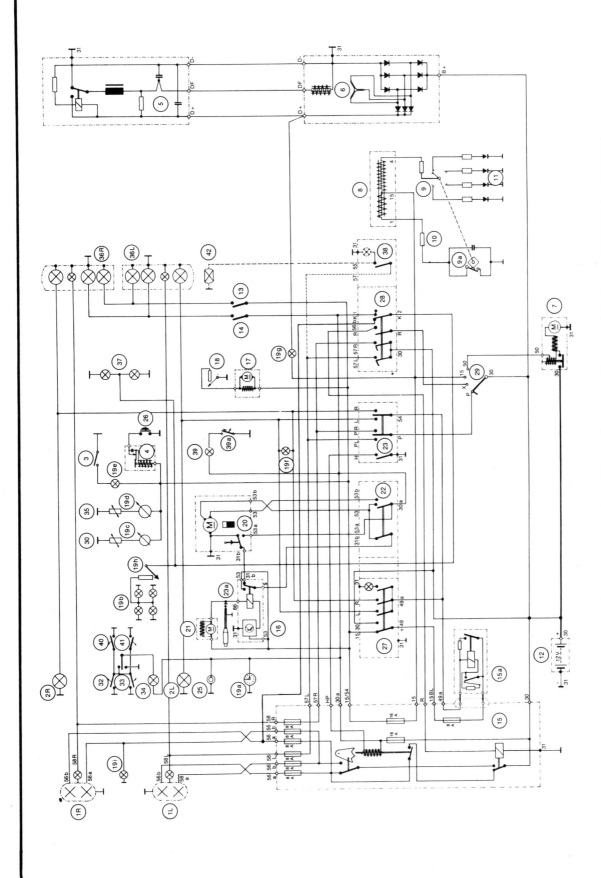

Fig. 10.17. Wiring diagram for combined operation of flasher, dip beams and license plate light, early 1969 ('Key' on page 165)

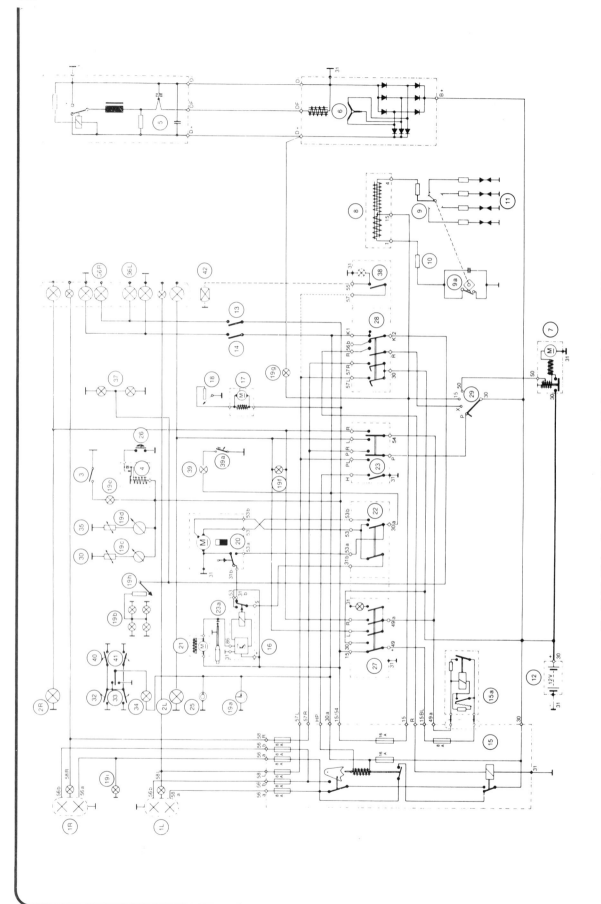

Fig. 10.18. Wiring diagram, late 1969 except N. America ('Key' on page 165)

157

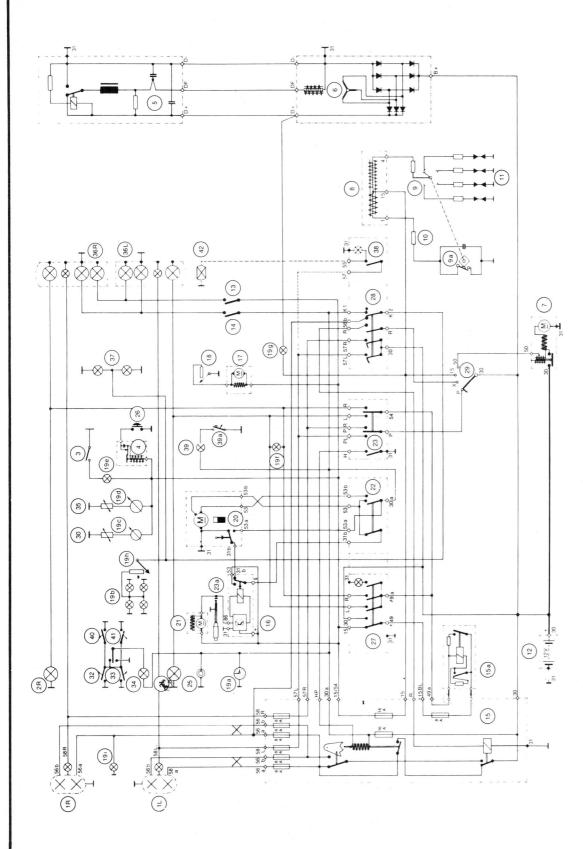

Fig. 10.19. Wiring diagram for combined operation of flasher, dip beam and license plate light, late 1969 ('Key' on page 165)

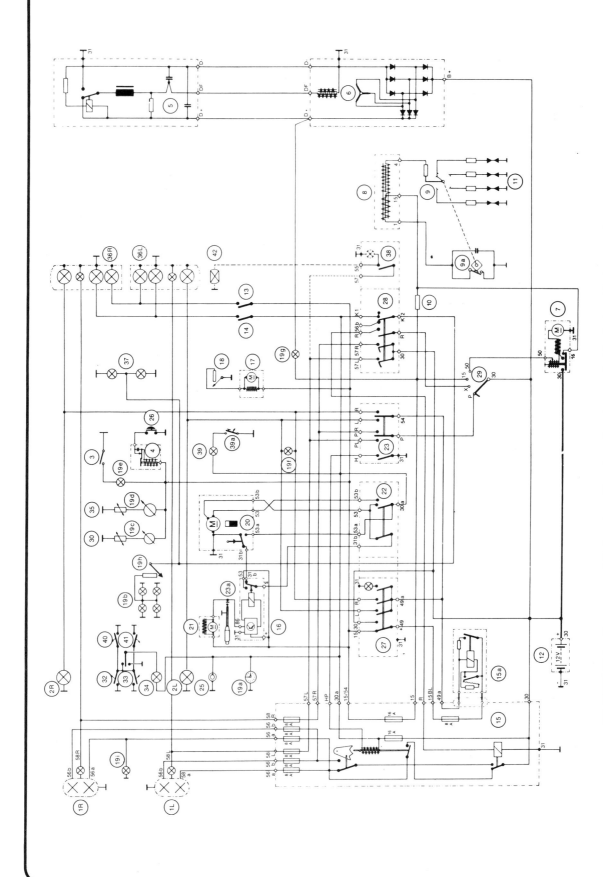

Fig. 10.20. Wiring diagram, except N. America, with series resistor between ignition lock and ignition coil ('Key' on page 165)

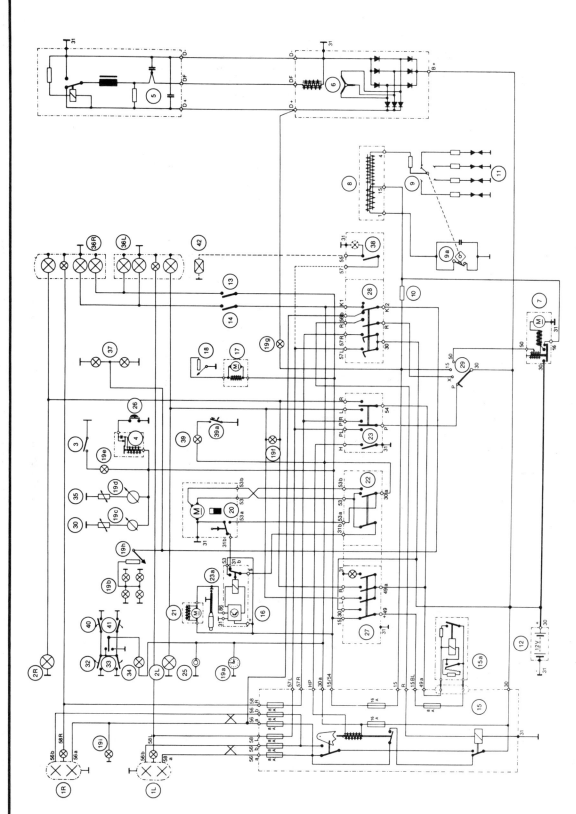

Fig. 10.21. Wiring diagram for combined operation of flasher, dip beam and license plate light, with series resistor between ignition lock and ignition coil, 1970–71 ('Key' on page 165)

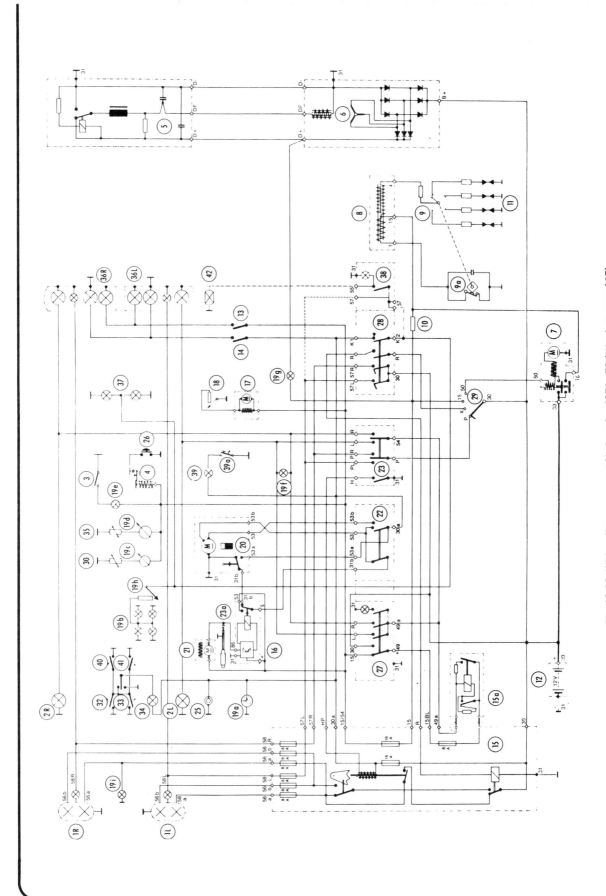

Fig. 10.22. Wiring diagram, except N. America 1971–72 ('Key' on page 165)

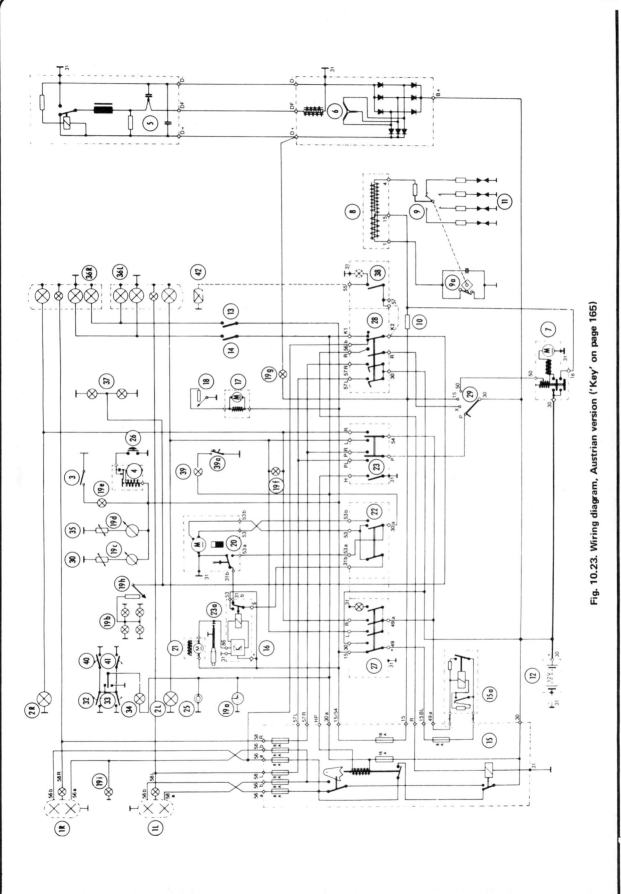

Fig. 10.23. Wiring diagram, Austrian version ('Key' on page 165)

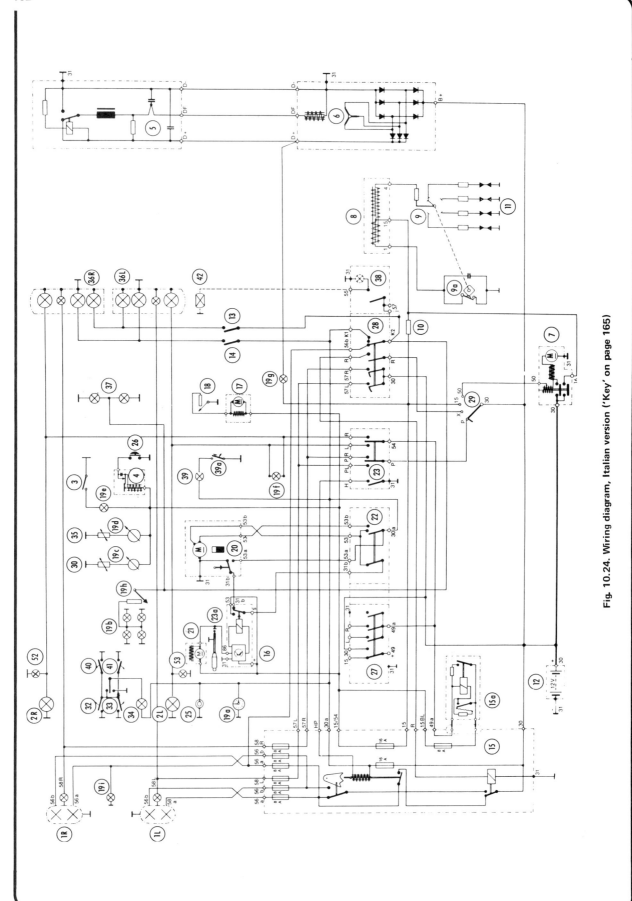

Fig. 10.24. Wiring diagram, Italian version ('Key' on page 165)

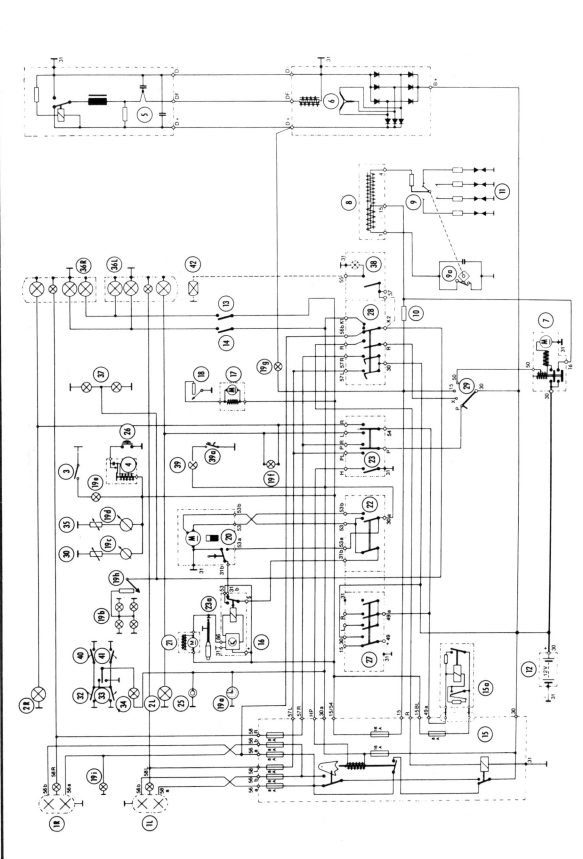

Fig. 10.25. Wiring diagram, French version ('Key' on page 165)

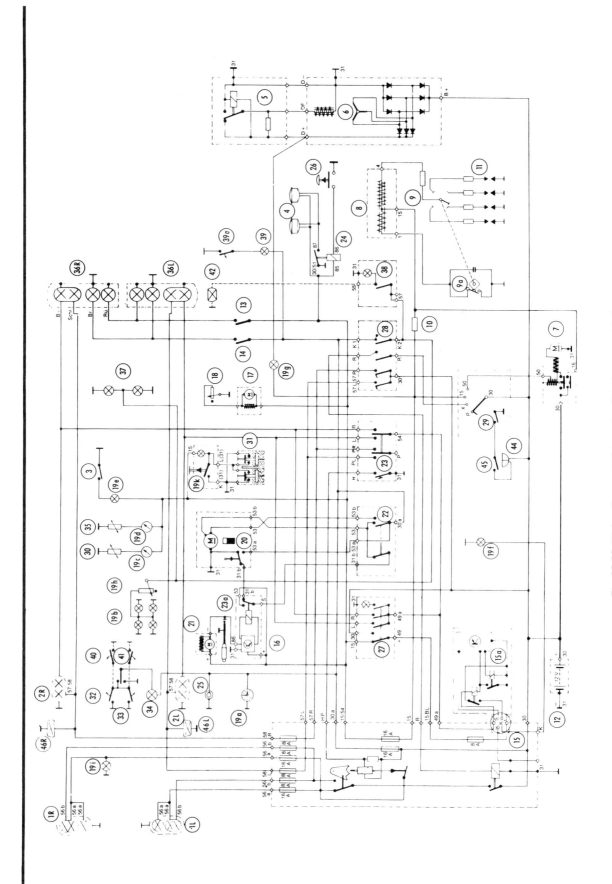

Fig. 10.26. Wiring diagram, USA version ('Key' on page 165)

KEY TO WIRING CIRCUITS – FIGURES 10.16 to 10.26 INCLUSIVE

1R	Headlight, right	23	Turn signal - dip beam switch	
1L	Headlight, left	23a	Washer impulse tracer	
2R	Turn signal, right	24	Multi-connector	
2L	Turn signal, left	25	Cigarette lighter	
3	Oil pressure switch	26	Horn button	
4	Horn	27	Emergency warning light switch	
5	Governor	28	Light switch	
6	Alternator	29	Steering - ignition lock	
7	Starter	30	Temperature transmitter	
8	Ignition coil	32	Door contact switch, front, right	
9	Distributor	33	Door contact switch, front, left	
9a	Contact breaker	34	Interior light and switch	
10	Series resistor for position 8	35	Fuel tank gauge	
11	Spark plugs	36R	Tail light, right	
12	Battery	36L	Tail light, left	
13	Reverse light switch	37	License plate light	
14	Brake light switch	38	Switch, tail fog light	
15	Combination relay	39	Glove compartment light	
15a	Flasher unit	39a	Switch for position 39	
16	Relay, windshield washer	40	Door contact switch, rear, right	
17	Blower motor	41	Door contact switch, rear, left	
18	Series resistor for position 17	42	Tail fog light (optional extra)	
19a	Clock			
19b	Instrument illumination	19k	Twin-circuit brake warning lamp	}
19c	Temperature gauge	24	Switching relay for position 4	} for
19d	Fuel gauge	31	Twin-circuit braking system	} USA
19e	Oil warning lamp	44	Audible buzzer	} only
19f	Turn signal warning lamp	45	Door contact switch for position 44	}
19g	Battery warning lamp	46R	Side marker lights	}
19h	Regulating resistor for position 19b	46L	Side marker lights	}
19i	High beam warning lamp			
20	Wiper motor	52	Additional turn signal, right	} for Italy
21	Washer motor	53	Additional turn signal, left	} only
22	Wiper switch			

KEY TO WIRING DIAGRAM, AUDI 100 WITH MANUAL TRANSMISSION, 1972 VERSIONS

1R	Headlight, right
1L	Headlight, left
2R	Turn signal, right
2L	Turn signal, left
3	Oil pressure switch
4	Electronic brake wear indicator control unit
5	Transistorized governor
6	Alternator
7	Starter
8	Ignition coil
9	Distributor with contact breaker
10	Resistor, ignition coil
11	Spark plugs
12	Battery
13	Backup light switch
14	Brake light switch
15	Combination relay
15a	Flasher
16	Automatic wiper/washer relay
17	Blower motor
18	Blower motor resistor
19	Combination instrument
19a	Electronic voltage stabilizer
19b	Instrument light
19c	Temperature gauge
19d	Fuel gauge
19e	Oil indicator
19f	Turn signal indicator
19g	Charger indicator
19h	Instrument light resistor
19i	High beam indicator
19j*	Clock
19k	Indicator and test button for 47, 41 R/L
20	Wiper motor
21	Washer motor
22	Wiper/washer switch
23	Turn signal/low beam switch
24	Horn relay
25	Socket (cigar lighter)
26	Horn button
27	Hazard warning light switch
28	Light switch

29	Steering wheel/ignition lock
30	Temperature transmitter
31a	Electromagnetic valve
31b	Enrichment valve
32	Door contact switch, front, right
33	Door contact switch, front, left
34	Interior light with switch
35	Fuel level transmitter
36R	Tail lights, right
36L	Tail, left
36h	Turn signal
36i	Tail light
36k	Brake light
36l	Backup light
37	Licence plate light
38*	Rear window defogger indicator
39	Glove compartment light
39a	Brake temperature control thermo switch
40R	Side marker, front, right
40L	Side marker, front, left
41R	Brake wear indicator 1
41L	Brake wear indicator 2
42*	Auxiliary fuse box
43*	Rear window defogger relay
44	Horn 1
45*	Horn 2
46*	Rear window defogger
46a*	Rear window defogger switch
47	Twin circuit brake indicator
48	Air conditioning diode
49	Buzzer
50	'Fasten seat belt' light
50a	Seat belt switch (driver's side)
50b	Seat belt switch (passenger's side)
50c	Seat contact switch (driver's side)
50d	Transmission switch
50e	Speed booster valve
50f	Speed booster transmission switch (4th gear)
51	Door contact switch, rear, right
52	Door contact switch, rear, left
53	Fan motor, coolant
54	Fan motor thermo switch
55	Fan motor relay

* For Audi 100LS only

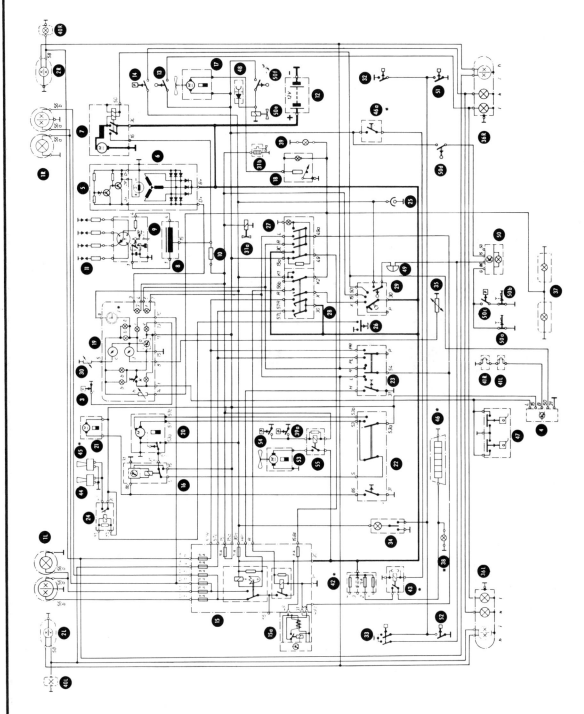

Fig. 10.27. Wiring diagram, Audi 100 with manual transmission, 1972 versions

KEY TO WIRING DIAGRAM, AUDI 100 WITH AUTOMATIC TRANSMISSION, 1972 VERSIONS

1R	Headlight, right
1L	Headlight, left
2R	Turn signal, right
2L	Turn signal, left
3	Oil pressure switch
4	Electronic brake wear indicator control unit
5	Transistorized governor
6	Alternator
7	Starter
8	Ignition coil
9	Distributor with contact breaker
10	Resistor, ignition coil
11	Spark plugs
12	Battery
14	Brake light switch
15	Combination relay
15a	Flasher
16	Relay, automatic wiper/washer
17	Fan motor
18	Resistor, fan motor
19	Combination instrument
19a	Electronic voltage stabilizer
19b	Instrument light
19c	Temperature gauge
19d	Fuel gauge
19e	Oil indicator
19f	Turn signal indicator
19g	Charger indicator
19h	Resistor, instrument light
19i	High beam indicator
19i*	Clock
19k	Indicator light and test button for 47, 41 R/L
20	Wiper motor
21	Washer/motor
22	Wiper/washer switch
23	Turn signal/low beam switch
24	Horn relay
25	Socket (cigar lighter)
26	Horn button
27	Hazard warning light switch
28	Light switch
29	Steering wheel/ignition lock
30	Temperature transmitter
31a	Electromagnetic valve
31b	Enrichment valve
32	Door contact switch, front, right
33	Door contact switch, front, left
34	Interior light with switch
35	Fuel level transmitter
36R	Tail lights, right
36L	Tail lights, left
36h	Turn signal
36i	Tail light
36k	Brake light
36l	Backup light
37	Licence plate light
38*	Rear window defogger indicator
39	Glove compartment light
39a	Brake temperature control thermo switch
40R	Side marker, front, right
40L	Side marker, front, left
41R	Brake wear indicator 1
41L	Brake wear indicator 2
42*	Auxiliary fuse box
43*	Rear window defogger relay
44	Horn 1
45*	Horn 2
46*	Rear window defogger
46a*	Rear window defogger switch
47	Twin circuit brake indicator
49	Buzzer
50	'Fasten seat belt' light
50a	Seat belt switch (driver's side)
50b	Seat belt switch (passenger's side)
50c	Seat contact switch (passenger's side)
50d	Selector lever
50e	Kickdown switch
50f	Solenoid
51	Door contact switch, rear, right
52	Door contact switch, rear, left
53	Fan motor, coolant
54	Fan motor thermo switch
55	Fan motor relay

* For Audi 100LS only

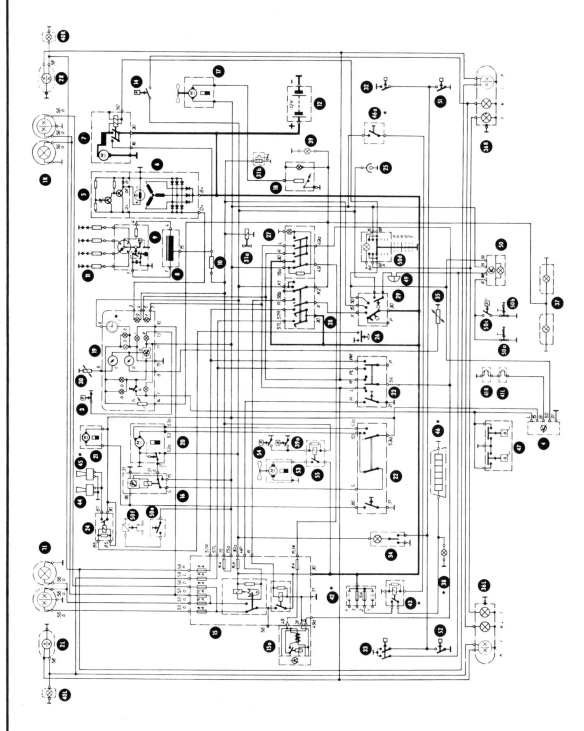

Fig. 10.28. Wiring diagram, Audi 100 with automatic transmission, 1972 versions

KEY TO WIRING DIAGRAM – AUDI 100GL, 1972/73 VERSIONS

1R	Right headlight
1L	Left headlight
2R	Right turn signal
2L	Left turn signal
3	Oil pressure switch
4	Relay for 1R and 1L
5	Transistorized governor
6	Alternator
7	Starter
8	Ignition coil
9	Distributor (contact breaker)
10	Resistor for 8
11	Spark plugs
12	Battery
13	Backup light switch
14	Brake light switch
15	Combination relay
15a	Flasher unit
16	Relay for interval, wiper and washer automatic
17	Blower motor
18	Resistor for 17
19	Combination instrument
19a	Electronic voltage governor
19b	Instrument illumination
19c	Temperature gauge
19d	Fuel gauge
19e	Oil warning light
19f	Turn signal warning light
19g	Charge warning light
19h	Resistor for 19b
19i	High beam warning light
19k	Transistorized tachometer
20	Wiper motor
21	Washer motor
22	Wiper/washer switch
23	Turn signal/low beam switch
24	Horn relay
26	Horn button
27	Emergency warning light switch
28	Light switch
29	Steering wheel/ignition lock
30	Temperature transmitter
31a	Solenoid
32	Door contact switch, front, right
33	Door contact switch, front, left
34	Interior light and switch
35	Fuel level transmitter
36R	Right tail light
36L	Left tail light
36h	Turn signal
36i	Tail light
36k	Brake light
36l	Backup lights
37	Licence plate light
39	Glove compartment light
42	Additional fuse box
44	Horn 1
45	Horn 2
50	Centre console
50a	Clock
50b	Clock and shift diagram light
50d	Cigarette lighter
51	Door contact switch, rear, right
52	Door contact switch, rear, left

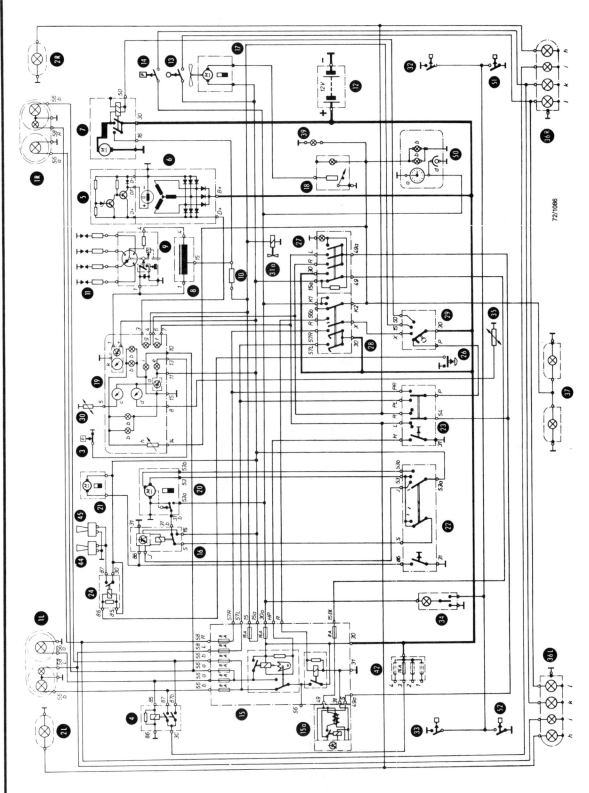

72/1086

Fig. 10.29. Wiring diagram, Audi 100GL, 1972/73 versions

KEY TO WIRING DIAGRAM, AUDI 100LS AND AUDI 100, 1972/73 VERSIONS

1R	Right headlight
1L	Left headlight
2R	Right turn signal
2L	Left turn signal
3	Oil pressure switch
5	Governor
6	Alternator
7	Starter
8	Ignition coil
9	Distributor
9a	Contact breaker
10	Resistor for 8
11	Spark plugs
12	Battery
13	Backup light switch
14	Brake light switch
15	Combination relay
16a	Flasher unit
16	Relay, windshield washer
17	Blower motor

18	Resistor for 17
19	Combination instrument
19a	Electronic voltage stabilizer
19b	Instrument illumination
19c	Temperature gauge
19d	Fuel gauge
19e	Oil warning light
19f	Turn signal warning light
19g	Charge warning light
19h	Resistor for 19b
19i	High beam warning light
19j	Clock
20	Wiper motor
21	Washer motor
22	Wiper switch
23	Turn signal/low beam switch
24	Horn relay
25	Cigar lighter
26	Horn button
27	Emergency warning light switch

28	Light switch
29	Ignition/steering lock
30	Temperature transmitter
31a	Solenoid
32	Front door contact switch, right
33	Front door contact switch, left
34	Interior light with switch
35	Fuel level transmitter
36R	Tail lights, right
36L	Tail lights, left
36h	Turn signal
36i	Tail light
36k	Brake light
36l	Backup light
37	Licence plate lights
38	Tail fog light switch
39	Glove compartment illumination
44	Horn 1
45	Horn 2 (Audi 100LS only)
51	Rear door contact switch, right
52	Rear door contact switch, left

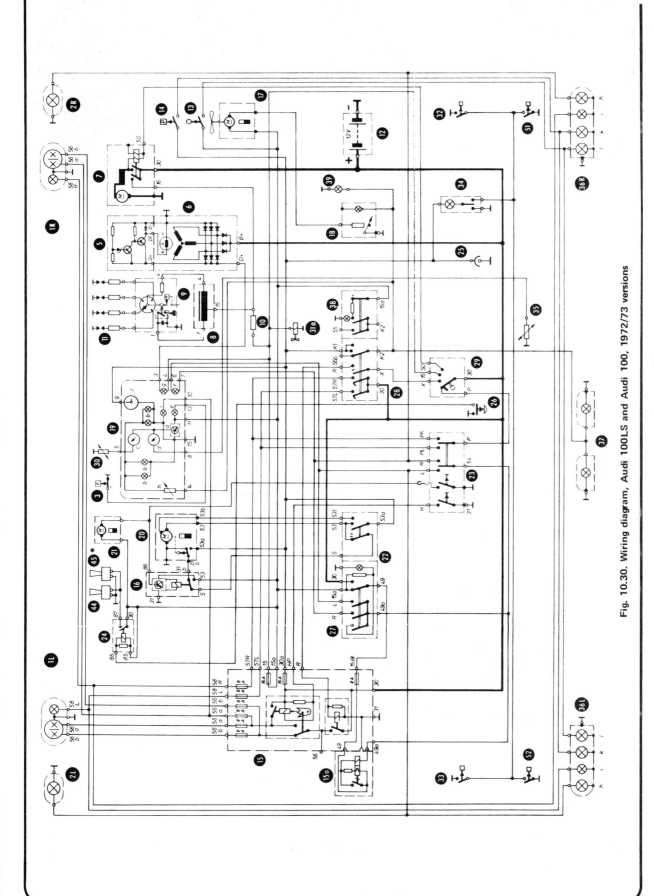

Fig. 10.30. Wiring diagram, Audi 100LS and Audi 100, 1972/73 versions

Chapter 11 Front and rear axles; suspension

For modifications, and information applicable to later models, see Supplement at end of manual

Contents

Specifications

Front suspension

Type	Independent coil spring, with double wishbones and transverse stabilizer
Shock absorbers	Telescopic, double acting
Maximum axle load	800 kg (1763.7 lb)
Track width	1420 mm (55.9 in.)
Coupe' S	1443.4 mm (56.82 in.)
Castor angle:	0° 6' $\pm$ 20', maximum difference left to right: 20'
Coupe' S	0° 30' $\pm$ 20', maximum difference left to right: 20'
Tropic and bad road versions	0° 4' $\pm$ 20', maximum difference left to right: 20'
Camber angle:	0° 11' $\pm$ 20'
Coupe' S	0° 9' $\pm$ 20'
Tropic and bad road versions	0° 4' $\pm$ 20'
Wheel bearing end play	0.04 to 0.07 mm (0.0016 to 0.0028 in.)
Coupe' S	0.04 to 0.06 mm (0.0016 to 0.0024 in.)
Toe-out	0° to $-20'$ (0 to 2 mm)

Rear suspension

Type	Trailing arm and torsion bar (coil spring on 1974 models - see Chapter 13), with stabilizing axle tube and Panhard rod
Shock absorbers	Telescopic, double acting
Maximum axle load	800 kg (1763.7 lb)
Coupe' S	700 kg (1543.2 lb)
Camber angle	-0° 30' $\pm$ 15'
Wheel bearing end play	0.02 to 0.04 mm (0.00 to 0.0016 in.)
Track width	1425 mm (56.1 in.)
Coupe' S	1440 mm (56.7 in.)

Wheel bearing lubrication

Lubricant	Multi purpose lithium based grease (eg. Castrol LM Grease)
Quantity	1.5 gm to wheel bearing, outer 3.0 gm to wheel bearing, inner 30.5 gm to hub, brake drum 10.0 gm to cap

Ground clearance

Front:	8.346 + 0.315 in. - 0.157 in.	(212 + 8 mm) - 4 mm)	Audi 100, 100S and 100LS up to chassis number 80 01 or 81 01 077 291
	7.283 + 0.315 in. - 0.157 in.	(185 + 8 mm) - 4 mm)	Up to chassis number 81 11 063 309
	8.070 + 0.315 in. - 0.157 in.	(205 + 8 mm) - 4 mm)	Audi 100, 100S and 100LS from chassis number 80 01 or 81 01 077 291
	7.007 + 0.315 in. - 0.157 in.	(178 + 8 mm) - 4 mm)	Audi 100, Coupe' S from chassis number 81 11 063 309
	8.31 + 0.315 in. - 0.157 in.	(211 + 8 mm) - 4 mm)	Bad road versions, measured from the lower edge of the power unit guard
	9.25 + 0.315 in. - 0.157 in.	(235 + 8 mm) - 4 mm)	Tropic version

Maximum permissible difference ... ...   5 mm
between left and right, (Tropic version only)

Rear:	0.708 + 0.197 in. - 0.078 in.	(18 + 5 mm) - 2 mm)	less than the front for Audi 100, 100S and 100LS up to chassis number 80 01 or 81 01 077 291
	0.433 + 0.197 in. - 0.078 in.	(11 + 5 mm) - 2 mm)	less than the front for Audi 100, Coupe' S up to chassis number 80 01 or 81 01 077 291
	0.472 + 0.197 in. - 0.078 in.	(12 + 5 mm) - 2 mm)	less than the front for Audi 100, 100S and 100LS from chassis number 80 01 or 81 01 077 291
	0.28 + 0.078 in. - 0.197 in.	(7 + 2 mm) - 5 mm)	higher than the front for bad road and tropic versions

Maximum permissible ... ...   7 mm
difference between left and right

Wheels

Rim size	4½ J x 14 H1/H2
Coupe' S	5 J x 14 H2 - B
Tyre size	165 SR 14
Coupe' S	185/70 HR 14
Tyre pressure	26 psi (1.8 atmospheres). For high speed driving the pressure should be increased by 3 psi (0.2 atmospheres)
Wheel bolt tightening torque	86.75 lb ft (12 kg)

Torque wrench settings (Front suspension)	lb ft	kg m
Upper wishbones to body	15.9 ± 1.8	2.2 ± 0.25
* Upper wishbone assembly	36.2 ± 3.6	5.0 ± 0.5
Lower wishbone to body, front	30.4 ± 3.6	4.2 ± 0.5
Lower wishbone to body, rear	15.9 ± 1.8	2.2 ± 0.25
* Lower wishbone assembly (M10)	30.4 ± 3.6	4.2 ± 0.5
* Lower wishbone assembly (M12)	36.2 ± 3.6	5.0 ± 0.5
Joint plate	86.8 + 14.5	12.0 + 2
Stabilizer to lower wishbone	15.9 ± 1.8	2.2 ± 0.25
Lower/upper wishbone to steering knuckle	30.4 ± 3.6	4.2 ± 0.5
Shock absorber to spring retainer	21.7 ± 3.6	3.0 ± 0.5
Coil spring to body	13.0 ± 1.8	1.8 ± 0.25
* Coil spring to upper wishbone	65.1 ± 3.6	9.0 ± 0.5
Drive shaft to stub axle	73.8 ± 3.6	10.2 ± 0.5

For items marked with an asterisk it is essential that new locknuts are fitted when re-assembling.

Torque wrench settings (Rear suspension)	lb ft	kg m
Shock absorber to body	21.7 + 3.6	3 + 0.5
Shock absorber to rear axle	50.6 ± 7.2	7 ± 1
Suspension arm to rear axle (nut and bolt)	30.4 ± 3.6	4.2 ± 0.5
Wishbone to rear axle (locknut and bolt)	47.0 ± 5.0	6.5 ± 0.7
Wishbone to cross tube	28.9 ± 0.7	4 ± 0.1
Suspension arm to cross tube	15.9 ± 1.4	2.2 ± 0.2
Cross tube to body	30.4 ± 3.6	4.2 ± 0.5
**Brake back plate and stub axle to rear axle	15.9 ± 1.4	2.2 ± 0.2

**21.7 lb ft (3.0 kg m) after chassis number 809 021 387

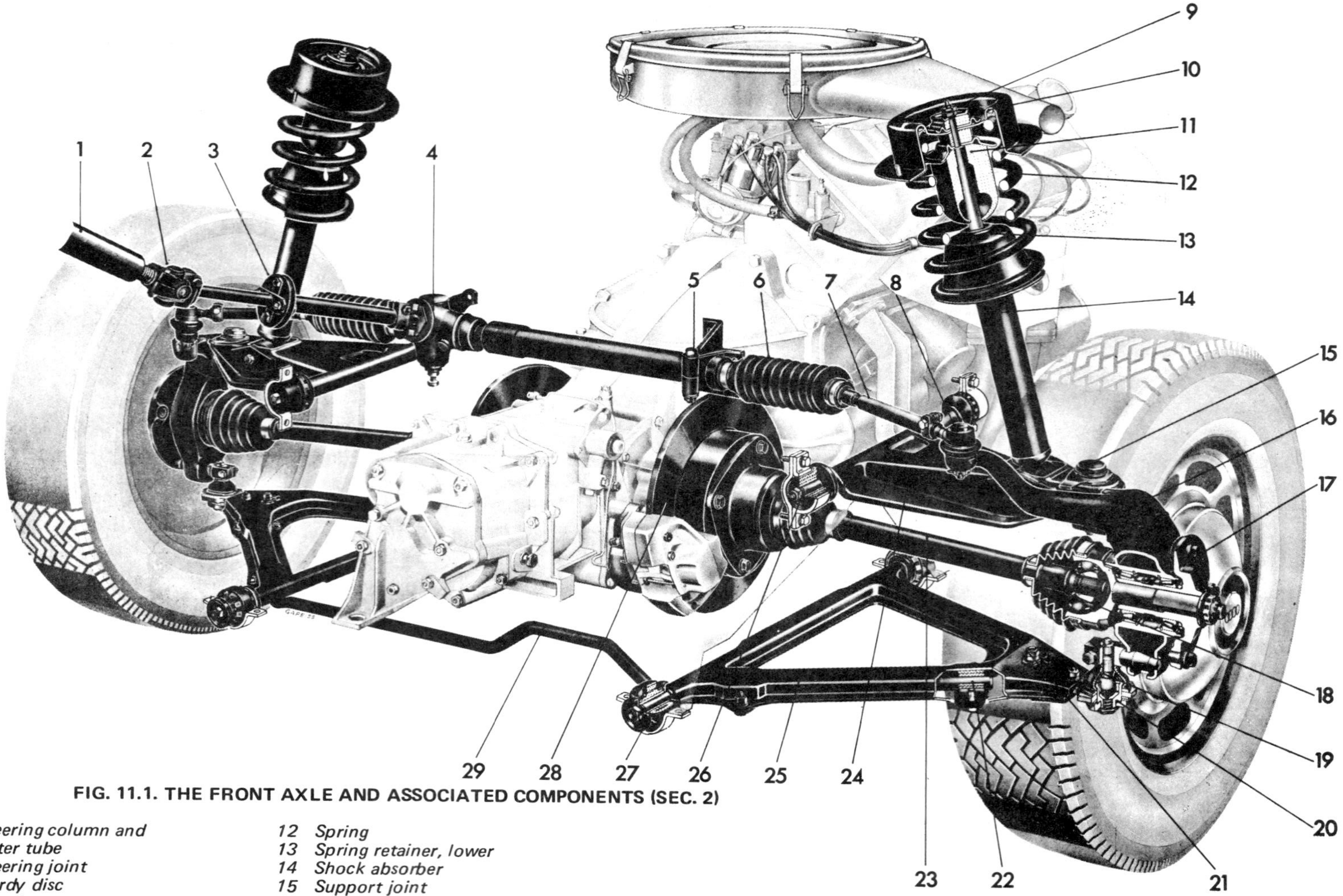

FIG. 11.1. THE FRONT AXLE AND ASSOCIATED COMPONENTS (SEC. 2)

1 Steering column and
  outer tube
2 Steering joint
3 Hardy disc
4 Steering gear
5 Mount
6 Boot
7 Track rod
8 Front ball and socket
  joint
9 Spring retainer, upper
10 Rubber ring
11 Stop pad

12 Spring
13 Spring retainer, lower
14 Shock absorber
15 Support joint
16 Steering knuckle and
   track rod arm
17 Wheel hub
18 Rzeppa joint (homokinetic)
19 Wishbone joint
20 Castor adjustment
21 Camber adjustment
22 Stabilizer bearing
23 Drive shaft

24 Wishbone, upper
25 Wishbone, lower
26 Wishbone bearing, upper
27 Wishbone bearing, lower
28 Brake disc
29 Stabilizer

68/720

1 General description

Front wheel drive with independent front suspension is a standard feature of the Audi 100 range. The double acting, double cylinder, hydraulic shock absorbers are mounted inside the springs and a transverse stabilizer, or anti-roll bar, is fitted to limit the side inclination during fast manoeuvres.

The drive shafts are each equipped with two Rzeppa synchronization joints which take up any lateral movement during springing action.

The rear axle tube is linked to a pair of trailing arms, the forward ends of which are attached to torsion arms mounted in a cross tube. Attachment to the underbody is at the cross tube itself and is, via two double acting hydraulic shock absorbers, fitted to the outer ends of the axle tube. A transverse stabilizer, (Panhard rod) provides lateral stability. The design of the rear suspension is such that the wheel position does not affect the camber during the application of unequal loads.

Note 1: It is most important that the car is not driven if shock absorbers have been removed, since there is a possibility of the brake hoses being fractured.

Note 2: Under no circumstances should a jack be placed beneath the rear axle tube since permanent deformation can occur (this restriction does not apply to the cross tube).

See Chapter 13 for coil spring type rear suspension.

2 Front spring leg and shock absorber - removal, overhaul and replacement

1 Remove the spring leg and shock absorber by removing the pivot bolt on the upper wishbone.

2 Remove the three nuts and washers securing the upper spring retainer to the wheel housing.

3 Ease the spring leg downwards a little then swing the top towards you. Rotate the complete spring leg through 90° about its major axis. If necessary, the steering ball joint may be pressed downwards.

4 Pull the spring leg completely out of the car.

5 To dismantle the assembly will require the use of a jig to restrain the spring whilst the two central nuts are being removed.

6 When the two nuts are removed the assembly is completely dismantled.

7 When replacement parts are required, note the number of yellow paint markings on the spring coil (ie. one, two or three). Right-hand drive vehicles are fitted with two or three rings only. Replacement parts must be of the same spring marking.

8 Early type springs are made from 14.5 mm (0.571 in) material and later types made from 14.8 mm (0.583 in) material. When new springs are fitted they must be matched with the springs that they are replacing.

9 When refitting the springs the correct thickness ring must be fitted between the top of the spring and the upper spring retainer. For right-hand drive cars, springs with three yellow marks require rings with two notches, these are 1.023 in (26 mm) thick. Springs with two yellow marks require rings with one notch, ie 0.709 in (18 mm). Left-hand drive cars require rings with 3 notches (1.339 in, 34 mm) for springs marked with three yellow marks, rings with two notches for springs with 2 yellow marks and rings with one notch for springs with 1 yellow mark. This is to compensate for the effects of road camber (rings with one notch are not fitted to right-hand drive vehicles).

10 During 1972 modified upper spring retainers were introduced. This does not affect removal or refitting but three grooves each 0.866 in (22 mm) wide have been ground in the 0.709 in (18 mm) ring to accommodate the fixing screw heads. This later type of ring can be used with earlier type spring retainers, but the converse is not true unless facilities are at hand to grind the three notches required. Rings of other thicknesses

FIG. 11.2. REMOVING THE SPRING LEG (SEC. 2)

a   Spring leg
Arrows 1, 2 and 3 show method of turning the assembly to remove it

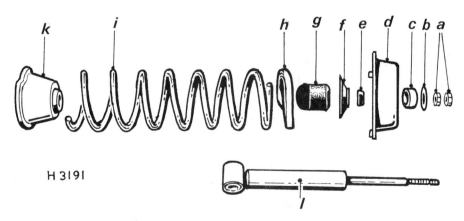

H 3191

FIG. 11.3. THE COMPONENTS OF THE SPRING LEG AND SHOCK ABSORBER (SEC. 2)

a *Hex. head nut*	d *Spring retainer*	g *Stop pad*	k *Spring retainer*
b *Plate*	e *Mounting pad*	h *Ring*	l *Shock absorber*
c *Mounting pad*	f *Plate*	i *Spring*	

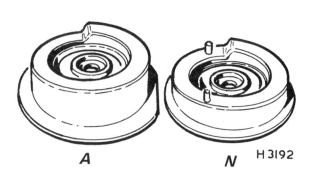

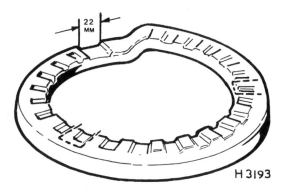

FIG. 11.4. THE SPRING RETAINERS (SEC. 2)

A   Old type
N   New type

Fig. 11.5. The three notches required to modify the spring retainer ring (Sec. 2)

Fig. 11.6. Removing the drive shaft using the special Audi extractor (Sec. 3A)

FIG. 11.7. WITHDRAWING THE WHEEL HUB (SEC. 3A)

x   Bolt
y   Packing piece
g   Knuckle

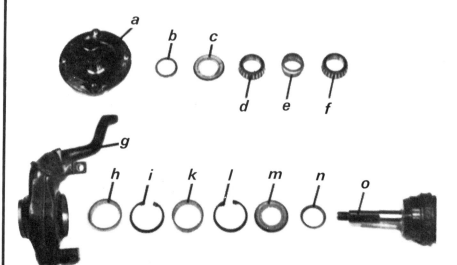

FIG. 11.8. COMPONENT PARTS OF THE KNUCKLE AND HUB (SEC. 3B)

a   Wheel hub
b   Spacer
c   Nilos ring
d   Ball bearing inner ring
e   Spacer bushing
f   Ball bearing inner ring
g   Steering knuckle, right
h   Outer ring of ball bearing
i   Retaining ring 68 x 2,5
k   Outer ring of ball bearing
l   Retaining ring 68 x 2,5
m   Nilos ring
n   Spacer
o   Drive shaft

have not been altered.

11 When reassembling, make sure that the step in the ring is aligned with the step in the upper spring retainer.

12 Fit the spring in such a way, that the spring end is correctly located in the ring.

13 Reassemble the spring leg and shock absorber; fitting the stop pad to the shock absorber after the latter has been fitted through the lower spring retainer.

14 The assembly can now be compressed and the nuts refitted to the end of the shock absorber spindle. Before fully tightening, ensure that a gap of at least 0.079 in (2 mm) is present between the upper spring retainer and the periphery of the spring. (The spring may be turned end-over-end if necessary). At the same time check that the flat on the upper spring retainer is parallel to the axis of the pivot bolt at the lower end of the shock absorber.

15 Now tighten the nuts fully and remove the assembly from the compressing jig.

16 The completely assembled unit can now be fitted to the car, taking care that the flat on the upper spring retainer is facing towards the centre of the vehicle.

17 When refitting the spring leg to the upper wishbone it is essential that a new nut is fitted to the 12 mm pivot bolt.

3 Drive shaft complete with steering knuckle

A Removing and dismantling

1 Remove the four hexagon headed screws and lock washers which secure the stub axle to the brake disc.

2 Take off the drive shaft, taking care not to lose the insulating washer fitted between the shaft and the disc.

3 Remove the two screws which retain the steering knuckle at the wishbone swivel joints.

4 Remove the track rod ball joint using a universal extractor.

5 Now take off the split pin, castellated nut, hexagon headed nut and spacer.

6 The next step is to drive out the drive shaft from steering knuckle. This may prove difficult without the use of the special Audi extractor but a three pronged universal extractor should prove to be satisfactory. The only alternatives are to purchase the special extractor or arrange for a properly equipped Audi garage to do the job.

7 Obtain two hexagon headed steel screws about 2½ in (60 mm) in length and relieve the outside diameter slightly at the end. This is to ensure that any burring of the end of the screw will not damage a thread or cause the screw to seize.

8 Obtain two mild steel packing pieces about 1 in (25 mm) square and about 3/16 in (3 mm) thick.

9 Fit the bolts to two opposite holes in the hub flange and use the packing pieces between the ends of the bolts and the shoulder of the steering knuckle.

10 Withdraw the wheel hub by tightening the bolts evenly and very carefully.

11 Take off the spacer, Nilos ring and the tapered roller bearing from the knuckle.

12 Place the steering knuckle over a suitable piece of tube and carefully drift out the outer ring of the tapered roller bearing.

13 Remove the internal circlips.

14 Now press out the second outer ring of the tapered roller bearing, Nilos ring and spacer backing from the hub. Two short pins will be required to fit into the two blind holes on the outer side of the hub, for the application of pressure. Note that it will only be possible to press out the bearing assembly a short distance.

15 Clamp the flange of the hub plate in a vice and fully extract the bearing assembly using a universal bearing extractor. Depending on the type of extractor used, it may be necessary to fit a pressure plate to the inner side of the hub tube.

B Reassembly

1 It is assumed that at least some of the parts which have been removed from the steering knuckle will be reused. Before

refitting parts, they must be very carefully examined for scoring, burrs and corrosion. All parts should be degreased before reassembly; if ultrasonic cleaning facilities are available the tapered roller bearings should be cleaned by this method after initial degreasing. All parts must be thoroughly dried before being refitted; the surfaces of the roller bearings and outer rings can be greased lightly with a multi-purpose wheel bearing grease such as Castrol LM. It is good engineering practice to automatically fit new split pins, circlips and locking washers once they have been removed.

2 Fit the two circlips to the steering knuckle.

3 Press in the two bearing outer rings using a hand press and suitable mandrel. Fill the space between the rings with a multi-purpose wheel bearing grease such as Castrol LM.

4 Fit the spacer and Nilos ring to the hub followed by the inner bearing (larger diameter first) and spacer bushing.

5 Assemble the hub to the steering knuckle and press in the remaining inner bearing.

6 Apply grease to the spacer and Nilos ring and press them firmly by hand on to the drive shaft. They will stay in position due to the surface tension of the grease.

7 Fit the drive shaft into the assembled hub.

8 Fit the spindle, bush and nut of the special tool and carefully draw the assembly together. Make sure that the spacer and Nilos ring are correctly in position.

9 The drive shaft and steering knuckle can now be refitted to the car, following which it will be necessary to check the wheel bearing end float as described later in this chapter.

4 Drive shaft rubber boots - renewal

1 Remove the drive shaft from the car as previously described.

2 Carefully clean the exposed outer surfaces of the drive shaft using methylated spirit.

3 Remove the band clips and slide the rubber boot away from the Rzeppa synchronization joint.

4 Clamp the drive shaft in a vice and spread open the snap ring in the Rzeppa joint. At the same time apply a heavy blow with a rubber headed mallet to the hub end of the shaft to overcome the pre-load of the spring discs within the joint.

Note: It may be necessary to grind down the tips of a pair of circlip pliers to spread the snap ring.

5 Having spread open the snap ring, drive off the joint housing from the shaft and remove the rubber boot. If the inner boot, only, requires replacement it is necessary to remove the outer boot first. In this case, unless the outer boot has only recently been replaced, it is worthwhile considering replacement of both.

6 Loosely fit the new or replaced boots to the shaft.

7 When reassembling, note the order of fitting the spring discs and pressure ring: (1) spring disc, concave face towards the spline end (2) spring disc, convex face towards the spline end (3) pressure ring, convex face towards the spline end.

8 Fit a new snap ring into the joint housing making sure that the tongues fit properly into the machined groove.

9 Fit the joint to the drive shaft so that the ring snaps home. If necessary the hub end of the shaft can be pounded against a wooden block until it is properly in position.

10 Fill each joint with 3.7 cu in (60 cc) of Molykote BR2 grease (or grease of similar specification).

11 Slide the boots into position and fit the clips. It is strongly recommended that only Audi approved clips are fitted. Under no circumstances must a 'hose-type'(eg Jubilee) clip be used for the largest joint since there is a possibility of it fouling the wishbone joint under certain conditions. When fitting the clips the slotted clip end should always be trailing when the direction of rotation is considered.

12 Tighten the clips by hand as much as possible, then finally pinch them tight by pressing the raised sides together with pincers. The boots should be fitted neatly so that the convolutions are equally spaced.

180

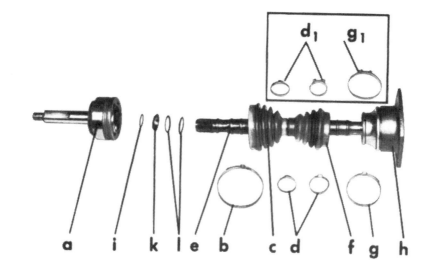

FIG. 11.9. THE DRIVE
SHAFT COMPONENTS
(SEC. 4)

a   Outer drive shaft
b   Clamp
c   Rubber boot
d   Clip
d1 Alternative clips
e   Inner drive shaft
f   Rubber boot
g   Clip
g1 Alternative clips
h   Rzeppa joint

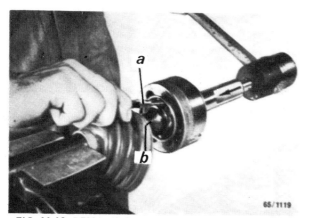

FIG. 11.10. REMOVING THE JOINT FROM THE HOUSING
(SEC. 4)

a   Seeger ring
b   Snap ring

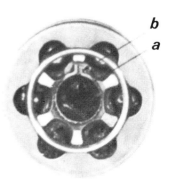

FIG. 11.11. THE RZEPPA JOINT (SEC. 4)

a   Snap ring
b   Machined groove

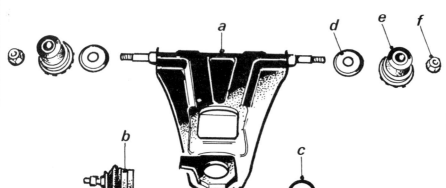

FIG. 11.12. THE UPPER
WISHBONE ASSEMBLY
(SEC. 5A)

b   Support joint
c   Retaining ring
d   Washer
e   Wishbone bearing, upper
f   Self-locking hex. head nut

H3190

5 Upper wishbone

A Removing and dismantling

Note: Before removing the upper wishbone it must be appreciated that an alignment tool (left and right versions) is required for when refitting is carried out (see paragraph B5 of this Section).

1 Initially remove the spring leg and shock absorber as previously described.

2 Remove the 10 mm screw (17 mm AF nut) securing the steering knuckle to the upper wishbone.

3 Remove the two saddle clamps which retain the wishbone pivots and bearings.

4 Remove the two nuts from the wishbone pivots and take off the bearings and spacers.

5 Remove the circlip from the support joint.

6 Obtain a piece of tubing which can be used as a support for the wishbone, then drive or press out the support joint. It is essential that the tubular support is a good match for the profile of the wishbone in order to avoid damage.

B Reassembly and refitting

1 When reassembling check that all jointing and mating surfaces are clean. When fitting a new support joint the contact faces may be lightly greased. If any wear is evident in the wishbone pivot bearings they should be renewed. It is essential that new self locking nuts are fitted to the 12 mm thread wishbone pivots.

2 Press in the support joint, using adequate tubular supports on the upper wishbone face and for pressing purposes. Take care not to damage the rubber bellows of the support joint.

3 Assemble both wishbone bearings (see sub-section C, following this Section).

4 In order to align the upper wishbone it is necessary to remove the lower wishbone (see following Section).

5 Fit the alignment tool with the long arm towards the front of the car. Raise the two arms and rest the upper wishbone pivots in the cradle ends of the special tool.

6 Raise the outer end of the wishbone arm to its installed position (approximately) and tighten the saddle bolts.

7 Remove the alignment tool.

C Modified upper wishbone bearings

1 A modified upper wishbone bearing is used from chassis number 809 020 690 onwards which is designed to prevent squeaking.

2 If a squeaking problem arises, a spacer can be fitted to the wishbone pivot between the bearing and the existing washer. The washer should be approximately 0.04 in (1 mm) thick.

3 The later type can be used as a replacement for the earlier type.

6 Stabilizer and lower wishbone

A Removing and dismantling

1 Remove the bolts, from the saddles which are used to secure the stabilizer to the lower wishbone. If necessary, detach the exhaust pipe at the manifold.

2 Remove the bolt securing the wishbone joint to the steering knuckle.

3 Detach the wishbone at the pivots and remove it from the car.

4 Unscrew the nuts on the ends of the pivots, and remove the bearings and cup washers. Note that the rear bearing is slightly larger than the front bearing.

5 Remove the circlip from the wishbone joint and remove the large (46 mm AF) nut.

6 Remove the disc springs and pull the wishbone joint out of

Fig. 11.13. The upper wishbone alignment tool in position (C)
(Sec. 5B)

FIG. 11.14. THE LOWER WISHBONE ASSEMBLY (SEC. 6A)

a *Wishbone, lower*
b *Wishbone bearing, rear - 52 dia.*
c *Wishbone bearing, front - 46 dia.*
d *Wishbone joint*
e *Joint plate*
f *Disc spring*
g *Hex. head nut*
h *Retaining ring*
i *Mounting screws, nuts and washers for 'e'*

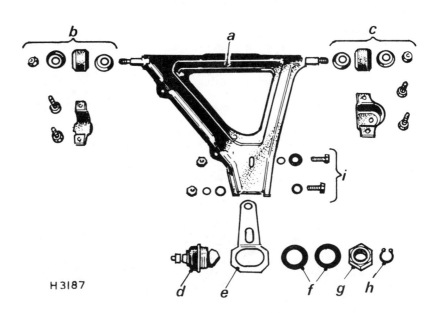

H 3187

the joint plate.

7 The joint plate can now be removed from the wishbone if necessary.

B Reassembly and refitting

1 Before reassembling check that all jointing and mating surfaces are clean. If any wear is evident in the wishbone pivot bearings or stabilizer bar bearings they should be renewed without hesitation. When reassembling, it is essential that new nuts are fitted to the wishbone pivot screw threads and joint plate bolts (if dismantled).

2 Fit the joint plate to the wishbone if previously removed.

3 Assemble the wishbone joint to the joint plate. The disc washers are to be fitted on the steering knuckle joint side with their convex surfaces against the joint plate.

4 Further assembly is now the reverse of removal.

5 Refer to Sections 17, 18 and 19 for castor, camber and toe-out alignment.

6 If it is necessary to replace the rubber bearings of the stabilizer they can be lubricated using a clean solution of soap and water. It is essential that they are correctly spaced on the stabilizer bar.

7 When fitting the wishbone to the car initially loosely assemble the wishbone bearings until it has been established that the rear bearing is seated equidistantly from each of the two notches in the rear saddle (photo). The bolts should then be lightly pinched up only to prevent movement. Only when the steering knuckle has been fitted may these bolts be fully tightened.

8 When the stabilizer is fitted ensure that the curved edges of the saddle brackets are facing towards the front of the car (photo).

---

7 Front wheel bearings - checking endfloat

---

1 Jack up the front of the car and remove the road wheels.

2 Clamp a suitable dial gauge to the hub flange, in such a way that its probe passes through one of the wheel bolt holes and contacts the steering knuckle directly above the castellated nut. This may require the manufacture of a bracket to hold the dial gauge.

3 Bolt a home-made lever to the opposite hub flange hole (ie directly below the castellated nut).

4 Move the lever backwards and forwards along the axis of the front axle and note the total deflection of the dial gauge pointer. The permitted play is 0.0016 to 0.0027 in (0.04 to 0.07 mm).

5 If the play is too great, remove the split pin, castellated nut and locknut, then carefully drive the hub further on to the drive shaft using a hide or plastic faced mallet.

6 When the correct end float is obtained, replace the locknut, castellated nut and fit a new split pin.

7 If the amount of play is too small, you will need to use the same extractor which was used for removing the drive shaft from the steering knuckle (earlier in this Chapter).

8 Remove the split pin, castellated nut, locknut and spacer, then withdraw the hub slightly. You will probably withdraw it too far, in which case the procedure detailed in paragraph 5 should be repeated.

---

8 Rear axle (with cross tube), suspension arms and transverse stabilizer rod (panhard rod) - removal

---

1 Remove the rear silencer.

2 If a pedal support is available, fit it to the brake pedal in such a way that the pedal is depressed approximately 1 3/16 in (3 cm). The pedal can otherwise be supported by a wooden block which will permit the 1 3/16 in movement, then a wooden strut used to hold the pedal down against the block. The other end of the strut can be wedged against the seat frame or steering wheel.

3 Remove the right-hand brake line at the brake drum back-plate.

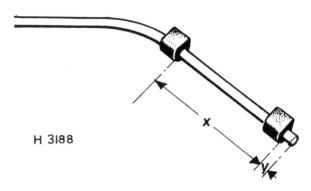

H 3188

FIG. 11.15. THE STABILIZER BAR RUBBER BEARINGS (SEC. 6B)

x = 8.15 in. (207 mm)
y = 0.492 in. (12.5 mm)

6B.7 Notches on rear wishbone bearing saddle

6B.8 Curved edge of saddle bracket

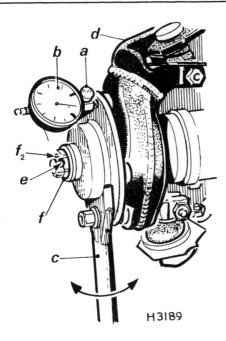

FIG. 11.16. CHECKING THE FRONT WHEEL BEARING
END FLOAT (SEC. 7)

a   *Dial gauge attachment*   d   *Steering knuckle*
   fixture   e   *Pin*
b   *Dial gauge*   f   *Castellated nut*
c   *Lever* f_2 *Nut*

4 Jack up the vehicle and remove both rear wheels.
5 Disconnect the handbrake linkage at the metal bridge piece
(compensator) (photo).
6 Pull out the nylon sleeves from the brackets, then pull out
the handbrake cables so that they can be removed with the axle
(photo).
7 Disconnect the flexible brake hose from the rigid pipe at the
fixing bracket (photo). Blank the rigid pipe with the dust cap
from the bleed nipple and use a suitable plastic or rubber plug to
blank the flexible hose.
8 Place supports under the cross tube to take the axle weight.
9 Remove the two nuts on each cross tube mounting plate
(photo).
10 For further dismantling the complete rear axle assembly can
be placed on a suitable work bench (see later Section in this
Chapter).

9 Rear axle (without cross tube) - removal

1 Initially carry out the procedure detailed in paragraphs
2,3,4,5 and 6 of Section 8.
2 Remove the left hand brake line at the T-piece on the right
hand suspension arm (photo). Blank the T-piece with a rubber or
plastic plug, and the brake line with the dust cap from the left
hand brake bleed nipple.
3 Remove the right-hand brake line at the brake drum back
plate. Suitably blank both open connections.
4 Unclamp the brake cables on each suspension arm. Slightly
prise open the clamps as necessary.
5 Remove the transverse stabilizer (Panhard rod) on the left-
hand suspension arm.
6 Remove the screws on each suspension arm which hold the
axle tube. Additionally on the right-hand side, the T-piece
bracket must be removed (photo).

8.5 Handbrake linkage compensator

8.6 Nylon sleeve for the handbrake cable

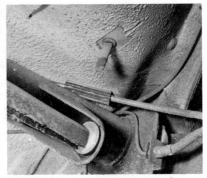

8.7 Disconnect the flexible hose at the
fixing bracket

8.9 Cross tube mounting plate nuts

9.2 The T-piece on the suspension arm

9.6 Axle tube fixing screws

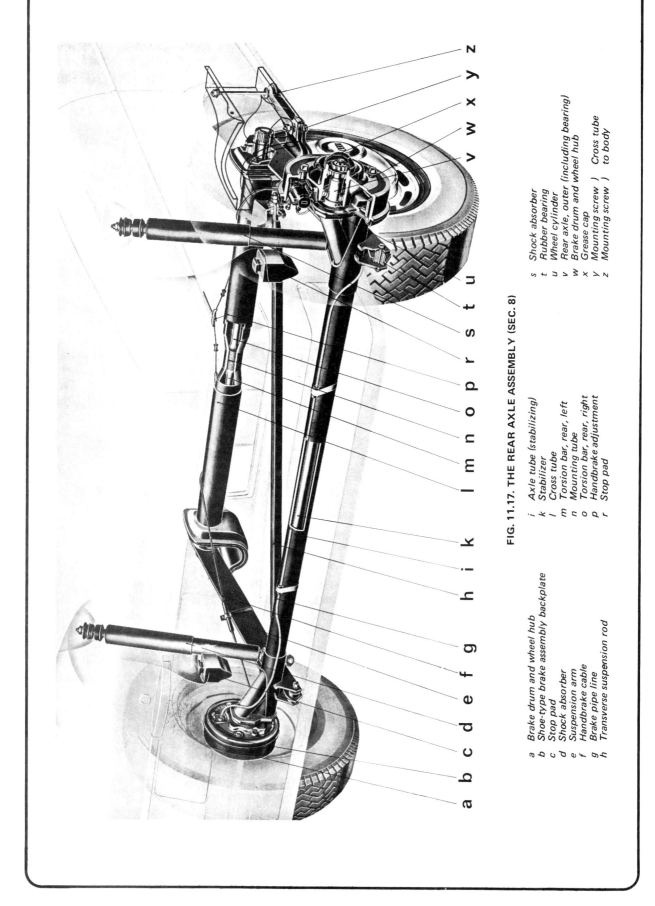

FIG. 11.17. THE REAR AXLE ASSEMBLY (SEC. 8)

a   Brake drum and wheel hub
b   Shoe-type brake assembly backplate
c   Stop pad
d   Shock absorber
e   Suspension arm
f   Handbrake cable
g   Brake pipe line
h   Transverse suspension rod

i   Axle tube (stabilizing)
k   Stabilizer
l   Cross tube
m   Torsion bar, rear, left
n   Mounting tube
o   Torsion bar, rear, right
p   Handbrake adjustment
r   Stop pad

s   Shock absorber
t   Rubber bearing
u   Wheel cylinder
v   Rear axle, outer (including bearing)
w   Brake drum and wheel hub
x   Grease cap
y   Mounting screw } Cross tube
z   Mounting screw } to body

7   The axle can now be removed and placed on a suitable work bench for further dismantling if required.

10 Cross tube (with suspension arm) - removal

1   Initially carry out the procedures detailed in paragraphs 1,2 and 4 of Section 8.
2   Disconnect the flexible brake hose from the brake line on the cross tube. Blank the brake line with the bleed nipple dust cap and the brake hose with a suitable rubber or plastic cap.
3   Disconnect the transverse stabilizer (Panhard rod) at both ends (photo) and remove it from the car.

10.3 Transverse stabilizer attachment point

4   Remove the screws on each suspension arm which hold the axle tube. Additionally, on the right-hand side, the brake line T-piece bracket must be removed.
5   Unclamp the brake cables on each suspension arm. Slightly prise open the clamps as necessary.
6   Remove the two bolts on each cross tube mounting plate.
7   The cross tube and suspension arms can now be removed to a suitable work bench for further dismantling if required.

11 Suspension arms - dismantling, reassembly and adjustment

1   Initially remove the cross tube with suspension arms as previously described.
2   Using a two pronged universal extractor drive out one torsion bar from the suspension arm. Note that the end face of each torsion bar is marked 'L' or 'R' as appropriate (If this mark is not visible, suitably mark the faces with paint to avoid mix-up).
3   Remove the suspension arm from the cross tube. There are three bolts at each end.
4   Now withdraw the torsion bar from the cross tube.
5   Again use the extractor to drive the other torsion bar clear of the suspension arm, then remove the suspension arm and withdraw the remaining torsion bar.
6   If it is necessary to replace the rubber bushes at the axle tube end of suspension arm, they can be driven out using a suitable press tool. When fitting new bushes they can be lubricated with a solution of soap and water. The rubber bushes at the cross tube end cannot be replaced.
7   When reassembling it is essential that the suspension arms are correctly set as detailed in the following paragraphs:
8   Loosely assemble the suspension arms to the cross tube.
9   Using a locally manufactured tool, check that dimension X is in accordance with the table. This dimension includes 0.73 in (18.5 mm) clearance.

10 When the required setting is achieved, tighten the three nuts. Repeat the operation for the other side.
11 Slide the torsion bars into the cross tube. Note the markings on the end face; although, the torsion bars have 40 splines on the inner end and 44 splines on the outer end, and cannot therefore be reversed in this way, it is extremely important that the correct bar is fitted to each side of the car.
12 Using a suitable tool, and having already set the suspension arm correctly, turn the torsion bar one spline at a time until it will slide smoothly into the splined sleeve of the cross tube and the splines in the suspension arm. Repeat the operation for the other side.

Fig. 11.18. The torsion bar markings (Sec. 11)

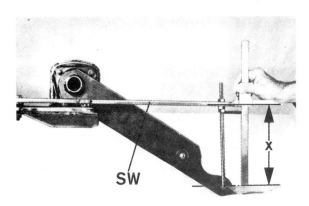

FIG. 11.19. CHECKING THE SUSPENSION ARM SETTING
(SEC. 11)

X   Setting dimension
SW   Setting gauge

12 Suspension arm settings

The following table includes the suspension arm adjusting dimension X for the various rear torsion bars

Torsion bar	Remarks	Rear torsion bar Part No.	diameter in mm.	Code on circumference	Dimension X LHD in. (mm)	RHD in. (mm)
L	standard	311 511 115B	22	—	8.464 ± 0.137 (215 ± 3.5) 8.189 ± 0.137 * (208 ± 3.5)	7.559 ± 0.137 (192 ± 3.5) 7.559 ± 0.137 * (192 ± 3.5)
R		311 511 116B	22		8.464 ± 0.137 (215 ± 3.5) 8.189 ± 0.137 * (208 ± 3.5)	8.464 ± 0.137 (215 ± 3.5) 8.189 ± 0.137 * (208 ± 3.5)
L	optional extra M 263 (harder rear spring)	311 511 115	23	1 white ring	7.559 ± 0.137 (192 ± 3.5) 7.834 ± 0.137 ** (199 ± 3.5)	6.771 ± 0.137 (172 ± 3.5) 6.496 ± 0.137 * (165 ± 3.5)
R		311 511 116	23		7.559 ± 0.137 (192 ± 3.5) 7.834 ± 0.137 ** (199 ± 3.5)	7.559 ± 0.137 (192 ± 3.5) 7.283 ± 0.137 * (185 ± 3.5)
L	optional extra M 103/M 6	361 511 115	24	2 white rings	7.834 ± 0.137 (199 ± 3.5)	7.165 ± 0.137 (182 ± 3.5)
R	(tropics and bad road)	361 511 116	24		7.834 ± 0.137 (199 ± 3.5)	7.834 ± 0.137 (199 ± 3.5)
L	Coupe' S standard	815 511 115	21.5	3 white rings	7.480 ± 0.137 (190 ± 3.5) 7.086 ± 0.137 * (180 ± 3.5)	
R		815 511 116	21.5		7.480 ± 0.137 (190 ± 3.5) 7.086 ± 0.137 * (180 ± 3.5)	
L	Coupe' S Italy	815 511 115	21.5	3 white rings	7.480 ± 0.137 (190 ± 3.5)	
R		815 511 116	21.5		7.480 ± 0.142 (190 ± 3.6)	

* The vehicle height was reduced by approximately 0.275 in. (7 mm) from Chassis No. 80 11/81 11 063 280
** The vehicle height was increased by 0.55 in. (14 mm) from Chassis No. 80 21/81 21 078 762

13 Rear stub axle

A Removing and dismantling

1 Set the brake pedal so that it is depressed approximately 1 3/16 in (3 cm) - as described in Section 8, paragraph 2.
2 Detach the brake line connection on the rear of each brake back plate. Blank the line with the bleed nipple dust cap, and fit a suitable rubber or plastic plug to the wheel cylinder connection.
3 Carefully prise off the grease cap from the centre of the drum (photo).
4 Remove the split pin, castellated locking cap, hexagon headed nut and the spacing washer.
5 Pull off the brake drum taking care that the inner ring of the tapered roller bearing does not fall out and become lost.
6 Take the inner ring out of the drum.
7 Prise out the spring clip which holds the brake shoes, but take care that it does not fly out.
8 Remove the brake shoes complete with pressure rod and spring. They should be removed at the bottom bracket first, but more information is given in Chapter 9 regarding removal and replacement of brake shoes.
9 Disconnect the handbrake cable from the brake shoe.
10 Remove the six hexagon headed bolts and washers then remove the backplate and stub axle from the axle.
11 Take out the grease seal from the brake drum and remove the taper roller bearing inner ring.
12 Remove the outer ring of the taper roller bearing on the grease seal side of the brake drum. This can be carefully driven out from the grease cap side of the drum; there are three cutaways for this purpose.
13 Working from the grease seal side of the brake drum, remove the circlip then carefully drive out the remaining outer bearing ring using an appropriate tool.

B Reassembly and refitment

1 When reassembling carefully examine any parts which are being reused. Any parts which are burred, chipped or corroded should be renewed. All parts should be degreased before

reassembly; if ultrasonic cleaning facilities are available the taper roller bearings should be cleaned by this method after initial degreasing. All parts must be thoroughly dried before being refitted. The surfaces of the roller bearings and outer rings can be greased lightly with a multi-purpose wheel bearing grease such as Castrol LM. It is good engineering practice to automatically fit new split pins, circlips and locking washers once they have been removed. Always renew the brake drum grease seal.

2   Fit the circlip to the brake drum.

3   Fit both tapered roller bearing outer rings.

4   Apply about 3 gm of multi-purpose wheel bearing grease to the surfaces of the taper roller bearing (grease seal side of brake drum) and fit it in position.

5   Carefully fit the grease seal in position, open side towards the bearing.

6   Fill the space between the taper roller bearings with

approximately 30 gm of multi-purpose grease (eg Castrol LM).

7   Smear the same type of grease on to the remaining taper roller bearing and fit it in position in the brake drum.

8   Refit the backplate and stub axle to the axle using new high tensile bolts on cars up to chassis number 809 021 387 (unless already modified). The stub axle is fitted with the groove uppermost.

9   Refit the brake shoes, handbrake cable and spring clip. Refer to Chapter 9 if necessary.

10 Fit the brake drum, then the spacing washer, to the stub axle (photo).

11 Refit the nut, castellated locking device and a new split pin, adjusting the wheel bearing end float as described in Section 15. Do not bend over the split pin until adjustment is made (photo).

12 Put about 10 gm of grease inside the grease cap then carefully drive into position. Do not damage the cap dome.

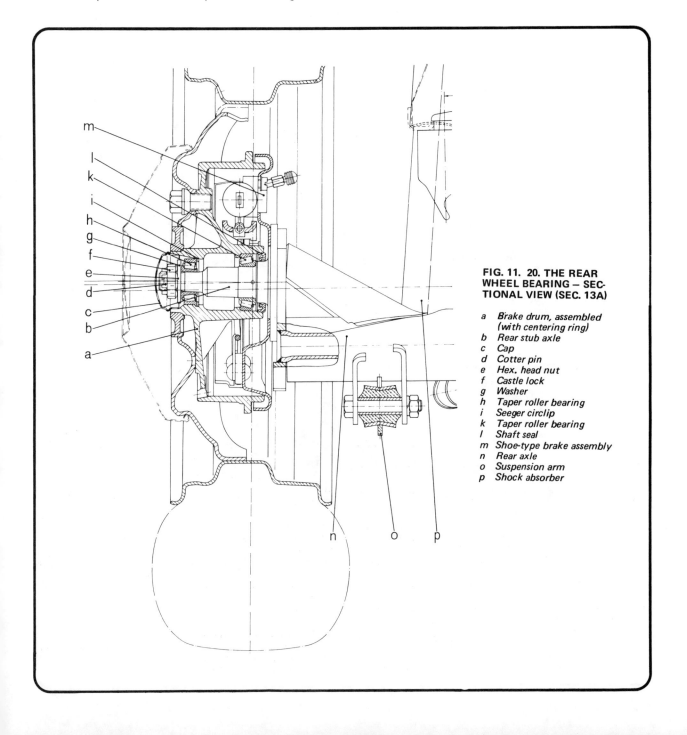

FIG. 11. 20. THE REAR WHEEL BEARING – SECTIONAL VIEW (SEC. 13A)

a   Brake drum, assembled (with centering ring)
b   Rear stub axle
c   Cap
d   Cotter pin
e   Hex. head nut
f   Castle lock
g   Washer
h   Taper roller bearing
i   Seeger circlip
k   Taper roller bearing
l   Shaft seal
m   Shoe-type brake assembly
n   Rear axle
o   Suspension arm
p   Shock absorber

13A.3 The grease cap on the brake drum

13B.10 The brake drum, bearing and spacing washer

13B.11 The split pin and castellated locking device

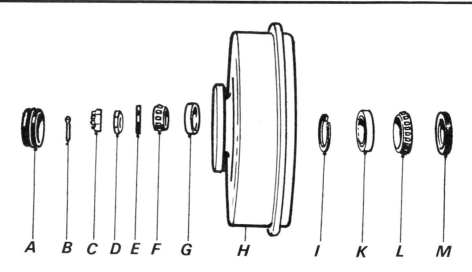

A   B   C   D   E   F   G   H   I   K   L   M

FIG. 11.21. THE BRAKE DRUM AND REAR WHEEL BEARINGS (SEC. 13A)

a	Cap	g	Outer ring - taper roller bearing
b	Cotter pin	h	Brake drum
c	Castle lock	i	Seeger circlip
d	Hex. head nut	k	Outer ring - taper roller bearing L
e	Washer	l	Inner ring - taper roller bearing L
f	Inner ring - taper roller bearing	m	Shaft seal

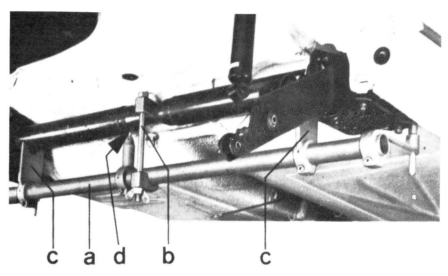

c   a   d   b   c

FIG. 11.22. ALIGNING THE REAR AXLE (SEC. 14)

a Centering gauge	b Clamp	c Support	d Centering bolt

14 Rear axle - installation

Note: When refitting the rear axle components to the car it is absolutely essential that the cross tube is correctly positioned. Alignment should be carried out, using the special tool, except where the cross tube position has not been disturbed.

1 Loosely assemble the cross tube to the underside of the car at the mounting plates.
2 Secure the centring gauge to the cross tube by means of the clamps.
3 Align the dowel on the spigot of the centring gauge with the hole in the axle tube and bring the two supports on the centring gauge up to the cross tube.
4 Tighten the wing nut in this position.
5 Move the cross tube laterally until the bolts in the arms of the centring gauge are aligned with the holes in the body. Do not use force.
6 When the bolts can be freely aligned with the holes, tighten the cross tube mounting bolts.
7 Remove the centring gauge.
8 Fit the axle tube to the suspension arms. Fit the bolt on the outer end first, then by using a lever rotate the axle tube about this point and fit the second bolt.
9 Replacement of the other parts can now take place, in the reverse order to removal.
10 When the replacement operation is completed, remove the brake pedal support and bleed the braking system as described in Chapter 9.

15 Rear wheel bearings - checking end float

1 Jack up the car up and remove the hub caps and wheel trims. Remove the grease caps.
2 Using a home-made bracket if necessary, mount a suitable dial gauge directly over the end of the stub axle with the bracket screwed into one wheel bolt hole as shown (Fig. 11.23).
3 Grasp the tyre in two opposite positions and check the total deflection on the dial gauge when the wheel is pulled and pushed. The permissible end float is 0.00078 to 0.00157 in (0.02 to 0.04 mm).
4 If the end float is above or below that permitted, the hexagon nut can be carefully tightened or loosened after removing the split pin and castellated locking device. Fit a new split pin.

16 Checking vehicle alignment - preparation

1 Check and correct the tyre pressures as necessary.
2 Check that the rear ground clearance, measured from the ground to the 0.393 in (10 mm) hole in the cross tube mounting plate, is in accordance with the specification requirements at the beginning of this Chapter. The method of adjustment is given in Section 11 of this Chapter.

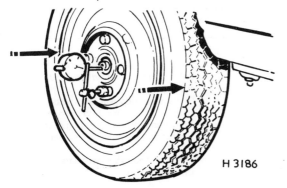

H 3186

Fig. 11.23. Checking the rear wheel bearing end float (Sec. 15)

3 Check that the front ground clearance, measured from the ground to the 0.315 in (8 mm) hole in the front lower wishbone bearing saddle, is in accordance with the specification at the beginning of this Chapter. Note the special method of measurement for rough road versions. If the clearance is too small, proceed as stated in the following paragraphs.
4 Remove the spring leg and shock absorber as described earlier in this chapter.
5 Compress the spring and remove the shock absorber.
6 Fit one or more spacers between the top of the shock absorber tube and the upper spring retainer (on the shock absorber shaft). The spacers are 0.393 in (10 mm) thick.
7 When refitting the spring leg and shock absorber remember to use a new nut to the pivot bolt.
8 Place the car on blocks, as detailed below (this is to simulate a car loaded with two people each weighing 143.3 lb (65 kg)).
9 Fit blocks or supports beneath the rear cross tube mounting plates. The block length must be 6.77 in (172 mm) for saloons up to chassis number 80 01/81 01 077 291 or 7.01 in (178 mm) for saloons from this number onwards. The block length for the Coupe' S is 6.063 in (154 mm).
10 Fit blocks or supports beneath the front lower wishbone bearing saddles. The block length must be 7,24 in (184 mm). For the rough road versions the block length must be such, that the distance from the power unit guard to the ground is 6.259 in (159 mm). Note: If rotary discs are used beneath the front wheels to enable the wheels to be turned more freely, packing pieces of the same height must be used beneath the rear wheels to keep the car on an even keel. This additional height must also be taken into consideration when setting the block length.

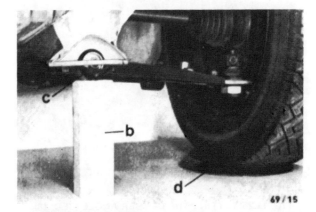

69/15

69/12

FIG. 11.24. PUTTING THE CAR ON BLOCKS (SEC. 16)

b   Block
c   Bearing saddle
d   Rotary disc

f   Block
g   Cross tube mounting plate

17 Castor angle

1 The castor angle is the angular difference between an imaginary vertical line running through the front wheel hub and an imaginary straight line running through the wheel suspension joints. The method of checking and adjusting is given below but before commencing it is essential that the procedure of the previous section has been carried out.
2 Using a suitable gauge, establish the point on each front wheel rim which has the least amount of run-out.
3 Turn the front wheels through an arc, from 20° left lock to 20° right lock and check that the castor angle meets the specification requirements. Adjustment can be made, if necessary, by slackening the large hexagon headed nut on the wishbone joint and turning the eccentric bolt (photo).
4 Positive castor is when the steering axis is inclined rearward.

18 Camber angle

1 The camber angle is the angular difference between an imaginary line perpendicular to the road surface and an imaginary straight line running through the radial axis of the wheel. Before checking and adjusting it is essential that the procedure of the previous two sections has been carried out.
2 To adjust the camber angle, set the wheels to the straight ahead position and slacken the nut and bolt.

FIG. 11.25. SETTING THE CAMBER ANGLE (SEC. 18)

a   Eccentric nut
b   Nut
c   Bolt

3 On cars up to chassis number 80/81 21 099 499 turn the eccentric bolt. From chassis number 80/81 21 099 499 onwards a hole is drilled in the lower wishbone where a pin can be inserted to apply leverage to the inner fixing bolt for the joint plates.
4 When the camber angle is correctly set, tighten the bolt and nut.
5 Positive camber is when the wheels are inclined outward at the top.

19 Toe-out

1 The toe-out is the difference in distance between the wheel rims measured at two opposite points in a horizontal plane. Before checking and adjusting it is essential that the three previous operations have been carried out.
2 Set the wheels to the straight ahead position and apply a load of approximately 22 lb (10 kg) to the front of the wheels to press them together, or the rear of the wheels to pull them apart.
3 Set up the gauge to measure the distance between the wheel rims at the rear at axle height.
4 Move the gauge forwards and measure the distance at the forward edge of the rim.
5 If the measurement at the front minus the measurement at the back does not meet the specification requirements, loosen the pinch bolt and hose clip on the track rod and rotate it. If large adjustments are to be made, both track rods should be adjusted to prevent differences in turning circles from arising.

17.3 Castor angle adjustment nut

20 Fault finding table - Front and rear axles; suspension *

Symptom	Reason/s	Remedy
Wheel wobble and vibration		
General wear or damage	Wheel nuts loose	Check and tighten as necessary.
	Front wheels and tyres out of balance	Balance wheels and tyres and add weights as necessary.
	Steering ball joints badly worn	Replace steering gear ball joints.
	Hub bearings badly worn	Remove and fit new hub bearings.
	Steering gear free play excessive	Adjust and overhaul steering gear.
	Front springs, weak or broken	Inspect and overhaul as necessary.
Excessive tyre wear	Tyres incorrectly inflated	Check and adjust as necessary
	Suspension geometry incorrect	Check and rectify.

* Also refer to the Fault finding table in Chapter 8.

Chapter 12 Bodywork

Contents

1 General description

The bodywork of the Audi 100 range is of unit construction and is welded to the frame/floor assembly - the bonnet, boot lid and front wings are bolted on separately to facilitate replacement following accident damage. The framework and panels are of deep drawn sheet steel with a high fatigue strength.

All inaccessible body cavities are foam filled which assists in noise reduction and prevention of rust corrosion. The underbody is sealed with a PVC compound.

A vinyl roof covering is available for all models except those which have the optional steel sunroof. The sunroof is not available for the Coupe' bodied cars.

Note 1: Where two coat metallic finishes (ie a metallic coat followed by a clear lacquer coat) require touch-up or major panel respraying is necessary, special paint finishes are supplied for this particular purpose by the car manufacturer. The advice of an Audi dealer should be sought where work of this type is to be carried out.

Note 2: In this chapter you will find information regarding fitment and removal of body trim and accessories, together with the replacement of bolt-on panels. Where major bodywork repair is necessary, a special alignment jig will be required together with cutting and welding tools, hydraulic jacks, etc. Here, it is essential that the work is carried out by a bodywork specialist.

Note 3: It is essential that the battery earth lead is disconnected during any operation where welding equipment is to be used, to prevent damage to the car's electrical equipment.

2 Maintenance - bodywork and underframe

1 The condition of your car's bodywork is of considerable importance as it is on this that the secondhand value of the car will mainly depend. It is much more difficult to repair neglected bodywork than to renew mechanical assemblies. The hidden portions of the body, such as the wheel arches, the underframe and the engine compartment are equally important, although obviously not requiring such frequent attention as the immediately visible paintwork.

2 Once a year or every 12 000 miles (19 000 km), it is a sound scheme to visit your local agent and have the underside steam cleaned. All traces of dirt and oil will be removed and the underside can then be inspected carefully for rust, damaged hydraulic pipes, frayed electrical wiring and similar maladies.

3 At the same time the engine compartment should be cleaned in a similar manner. If steam cleaning facilities are not available then brush a water soluble cleanser over the whole engine and engine compartment with a stiff paint brush, working it well in where there is an accumulation of oil and dirt. Do not paint the ignition system, and protect it with oily rags when the solvent is washed off. As the solvent is washed away it will take with it all traces of oil and dirt, leaving the engine looking clean and bright.

4 The wheel arches should be given particular attention as undersealing can easily come away here and stones and dirt thrown up from the roadwheels can soon cause the paint to chip and flake, and so allow rust to set in. If rust is found, clean down the bare metal with wet and dry paper, paint on an anti-corrosive coating and renew the paintwork and undercoating.

5 The bodywork should be washed once a week or when dirty. Thoroughly wet the car to soften the dirt and then wash the car down with a soft sponge and plenty of clean water. If the surplus dirt is not washed off very gently, in time it will wear the paint down as surely as wet and dry paper. It is best to use a hose if this is available. Give the car a final wash down and then dry with a soft chamois leather to prevent the formation of spots.

6 Spots of tar and grease thrown up from the road can be removed by a rag dampened with petrol.

7 Once every six months, give the bodywork and chromium

trim a thoroughly good wax polish. If a chromium cleaner is used to remove rust on any of the car's plated parts remember that the cleaner also removes part of the chromium, so use sparingly.

3 Minor body repairs

The photo sequences on pages 198 and 199 illustrate the operations detailed in the following sub-sections.

Repair of minor scratches in the car's bodywork

If the scratch is very superficial and does not penetrate to the metal of the bodywork, repair is very simple. Lightly rub the area of the scratch with a paintwork renovator, or a very fine cutting paste, to remove loose paint from the scratch and to clear the surrounding bodywork of wax polish. Rinse the area with clean water.

Apply touch-up paint to the scratch using a thin paintbrush; continue to apply thin layers of paint until the surface of the paint in the scratch is level with the surrounding paintwork. Allow the new paint at least two weeks to harden; then blend it into the surrounding paintwork by rubbing the paintwork, in the scratch area, with a paintwork renovator or a very fine cutting paste. Finally, apply wax polish.

An alternative to painting over the scratch is to use a paint transfer. Use the same preparation for the affected area, then simply pick a patch of suitable size to cover the scratch completely. Hold the patch against the scratch and burnish its backing paper; the patch will adhere to the paintwork, freeing itself from the backing paper at the same time. Polish the affected area to blend the patch into the surrounding paintwork.

Where the scratch has penetrated right through to the metal of the bodywork, causing the metal to rust, a different repair technique is required. Remove any loose rust from the bottom of the scratch with a penknife, then apply rust inhibiting paint to prevent the formation of rust in the future. Using a rubber or nylon applicator fill the scratch with bodystopper paste. If required, this paste can be mixed with cellulose thinners to provide a very thin paste which is ideal for filling narrow scratches. Before the stopper-paste in the scratch hardens, wrap a piece of smooth cotton rag around the top of the finger. Dip the finger in cellulose thinners and then quickly sweep it across the surface of the stopper-paste in the scratch; this will ensure that the surface of the stopper-paste is slightly hollowed. The scratch can now be painted over as described earlier in this Section.

Repair of dents in the car's bodywork

When deep denting of the car's bodywork has taken place, the first task is to pull the dent out, until the affected bodywork almost attains its original shape. There is little point in trying to restore the original shape completely, as the metal in the damaged area will have stretched on impact and cannot be reshaped fully to its original contour. It is better to bring the level of the dent up to a point which is about 1/8 in (3 mm) below the level of the surrounding bodywork. In cases where the dent is very shallow anyway, it is not worth trying to pull it out at all.

If the underside of the dent is accessible, it can be hammered out gently from behind, using a mallet with a wooden or plastic head. Whilst doing this, hold a suitable block of wood firmly against the impact from the hammer blows and thus prevent a large area of the bodywork from being 'belled-out'.

Should the dent be in a section of the bodywork which has double skin or some other factor making it inaccessible from behind, a different technique is called for. Drill several small holes through the metal inside the dent area — particularly in the deeper sections. Then screw long self-tapping screws into the holes just sufficiently for them to gain a good purchase in the metal. Now the dent can be pulled out by pulling on the protruding heads of the screws with a pair of pliers.

The next stage of the repair is the removal of the paint from the damaged area, and from an inch or so of the surrounding 'sound' bodywork. This is accomplished most easily by using a wire brush or abrasive pad on a power drill, although it can be done just as effectively by hand using sheets of abrasive paper. To complete the preparation for filling, score the surface of the bare metal with a screwdriver or the tang of a file, or alternatively, drill small holes in the affected area. This will provide a really good 'key' for the filler paste.

To complete the repair see the Section on filling and respraying.

Repair of rust holes or gashes in the car's bodywork

Remove all paint from the affected area and from an inch or so of the surrounding 'sound' bodywork, using an abrasive pad or a wire brush on a power drill. If these are not available a few sheets of abrasive paper will do the job just as effectively. With the paint removed you will be able to gauge the severity of the corrosion and therefore decide whether to renew the whole panel (if this is possible) or to repair the affected area. New body panels are not as expensive as most people think and it is often quicker and more satisfactory to fit a new panel than to attempt to repair large areas of corrosion.

Remove all fittings from the affected area except those which will act as a guide to the original shape of the damaged bodywork (eg headlamp shells etc). Then, using tin snips or a hacksaw blade, remove all loose metal and any other metal badly affected by corrosion. Hammer the edges of the hole inwards in order to create a slight depression for the filler paste.

Wire brush the affected area to remove the powdery rust from the surface of the remaining metal. Paint the affected area with rust inhibiting paint; if the back of the rusted area is accessible treat this also.

Before filling can take place it will be necessary to block the hole in some way. This can be achieved by the use of one of the following materials: Zinc gauze, Aluminium tape or Polyurethane foam.

Zinc gauze is probably the best material to use for a large hole. Cut a piece to the approximate size and shape of the hole to be filled, then position it in the hole so that its edges are below the level of the surrounding bodywork. It can be retained in position by several blobs of filler paste around its periphery.

Aluminium tape should be used for small or very narrow holes. Pull a piece off the roll and trim it to the approximate size and shape required, then pull off the backing paper (if used) and stick the tape over the hole; it can be overlapped if the thickness of one piece is insufficient. Burnish down the edges of the tape with the handle of a screwdriver or similar, to ensure that the tape is securely attached to the metal underneath.

Polyurethane foam is best used where the hole is situated in a section of bodywork of complex shape, backed by a small box section (eg where the sill panel meets the rear wheel arch on most cars). The usual mixing procedure for this foam is as follows: put equal amounts of fluid from each of the two cans provided in the kit, into one container. Stir until the mixture begins to thicken, then quickly pour this mixture into the hole, and hold a piece of cardboard over the larger apertures. Almost immediately the polyurethane will begin to expand, gushing out of any small holes left unblocked. When the foam hardens it can be cut back to just below the level of the surrounding bodywork with a hacksaw blade.

Bodywork repairs - filling and respraying

Before using this Section, see the Sections on dent, deep scratch, rust holes and gash repairs.

Many types of bodyfiller are available, but generally speaking those proprietary kits which contain a tin of filler paste and a tube of resin hardener are best for this type of repair. A wide, flexible plastic or nylon applicator will be found invaluable for imparting a smooth and well contoured finish to the surface of the filler.

Mix up a little filler on a clean piece of card or board — use the hardener sparingly (follow the maker's instructions on the pack) otherwise the filler will set very rapidly.

Using the applicator apply the filler paste to the prepared area: draw the applicator across the surface of the filler to achieve the correct contour and to level the filler surface. As soon as a contour that approximates the correct one is achieved, stop working the paste — if you carry on too long the paste will become sticky and begin to 'pick up' on the applicator. Continue to add thin layers of filler paste at twenty-minute intervals until the level of the filler is just proud of the surrounding bodywork.

Once the filler has hardened, excess can be removed using a Surform plane or Dreadnought file. From then on, progressively finer grades of abrasive paper should be used, starting with a 40 grade production paper and finishing with 400 grade wet-and-dry paper. Always wrap the abrasive paper around a flat rubber, cork, or wooden block — otherwise the surface of the filler will not be completely flat. During the smoothing of the filler surface the wet-and-dry paper should be periodically rinsed in water. This will ensure that a very smooth finish is imparted to the filler at the final stage.

At this stage the 'dent' should be surrounded by a ring of bare metal, which in turn should be encircled by the finely 'feathered' edge of the good paintwork. Rinse the repair area with clean water, until all of the dust produced by the rubbing-down operation has gone.

Spray the whole repair area with a light coat of primer — this will show up any imperfections in the surface of the filler. Repair these imperfections with fresh filler paste or body-stopper, and once more smooth the surface with abrasive paper. If bodystopper is used, it can be mixed with cellulose thinners to form a really thin paste which is ideal for filling small holes. Repeat this spray and repair procedure until you are satisfied that the surface of the filler, and the feathered edge of the paintwork are perfect. Clean the repair area with clean water and allow to dry fully.

The repair area is now ready for final spraying. Paint spraying must be carried out in a warm, dry, windless and dust free atmosphere. This condition can be created artificially if you have access to a large indoor working area, but if you are forced to work in the open, you will have to pick your day very carefully. If you are working indoors, dousing the floor in the work area with water will 'lay' the dust which would otherwise be in the atmosphere. If the repair area is confined to one body panel, mask off the surrounding panels; this will help to minimise the effects of a slight mis-match in paint colours. Bodywork fittings (eg chrome strips, door handles etc) will also need to be removed or masked off. Use genuine masking tape and several thicknesses of newspaper for the masking operations.

Before commencing to spray, agitate the aerosol can thoroughly, then spray a test area (an old tin, or similar) until the technique is mastered. Cover the repair area with a thick coat of primer; the thickness should be built up using several thin layers of paint rather than one thick one. Using 400 grade wet-and-dry paper, rub down the surface of the primer until it is really smooth. While doing this, the work area should be thoroughly doused with water, and the wet-and-dry paper periodically rinsed in water. Allow to dry before spraying on more paint.

Spray on the top coat, again building up the thickness by using several thin layers of paint. Start spraying in the centre of the repair area and then using a circular motion, work outwards until the whole repair area and about 2 inches of the surrounding original paintwork is covered. Remove all masking material 10 to 15 minutes after spraying on the final coat of paint.

Allow the new paint at least two weeks to harden, then, using a paintwork renovator or a very fine cutting paste, blend the edges of the paint into the existing paintwork.

Finally, apply wax polish.

4 Major body and underframe repairs

Major chassis and body repair work cannot be successfully undertaken by the average owner. Work of this nature should be entrusted to a competent body repair specialist who should have the necessary jigs, welding and hydraulic straightening equipment as well as skilled panel beaters to ensure a proper job is done.

5 Front door trim panel - removal and replacement

1 Prise off the chrome fitting in the armrest (photo). If a screwdriver or similar item is used, take care not to damage the armrest material or the chrome.
2 Remove the three cross-head screws retaining the armrest - there are two underneath the horizontal section, and one at the top end (photo).
3 Remove the armrest and the mounting plate.
4 Take off the plastic cover which is fitted to the window winder then remove the cross-head screw (photo). The winder can then be pulled off.
5 Unscrew the cross-head screw securing the door handle (photo), then pull the handle off.
6 Slide a lever or screwdriver between the trim panel and the door, and prise off the panel (photo). Take care that the implement used as a lever does not cause any damage to paint surfaces or trim material. Inspect the implement carefully, and remove any burrs that are evident.
7 Whilst the door panel is off check that the plastic film which is bonded to the surface of the door panel underneath the trim, and over the apertures in the door inner panels (inside the door cavity), is intact and undamaged. Replacement film and the correct adhesive is available from Audi dealers and it is recommended that, whenever possible, this is used for any repair operations (photo).
8 Replacement of the trim panel is the reverse of removal, but care must be taken that the snap fasteners are correctly aligned with their respective holes. They can be snapped home using the ball of the hand.

6 Front door exterior handle - removal and replacement

1 Remove the door trim panel as previously described.
2 Remove the nut and washers from the door handle stud.
3 Pull back the door sealing strip in the region of the handle then remove the exposed cross-head screw.
4 The door handle can now be pulled off from the outside.
5 Replacement is the reverse of removal but make sure that the plastic spacers are fitted between the ends of the handle and the door.

7 Rear door exterior handle - removal and replacement

1 Remove the door trim panel as described previously.
2 Remove the nut and washer from the door handle stud.
3 Remove the single cross-head screw adjacent to the lockplate.
4 The door handle can now be pulled off from the outside.
5 Replacement is the reverse of removal but make sure that the plastic spacers are fitted between the ends of the handle and the door.

8 Rear door panel trim - removal and replacement

1 Remove the two cross-head screws on the underside of the armrest, then pull the armrest off.
2 Take off the plastic cover which is fitted to the window

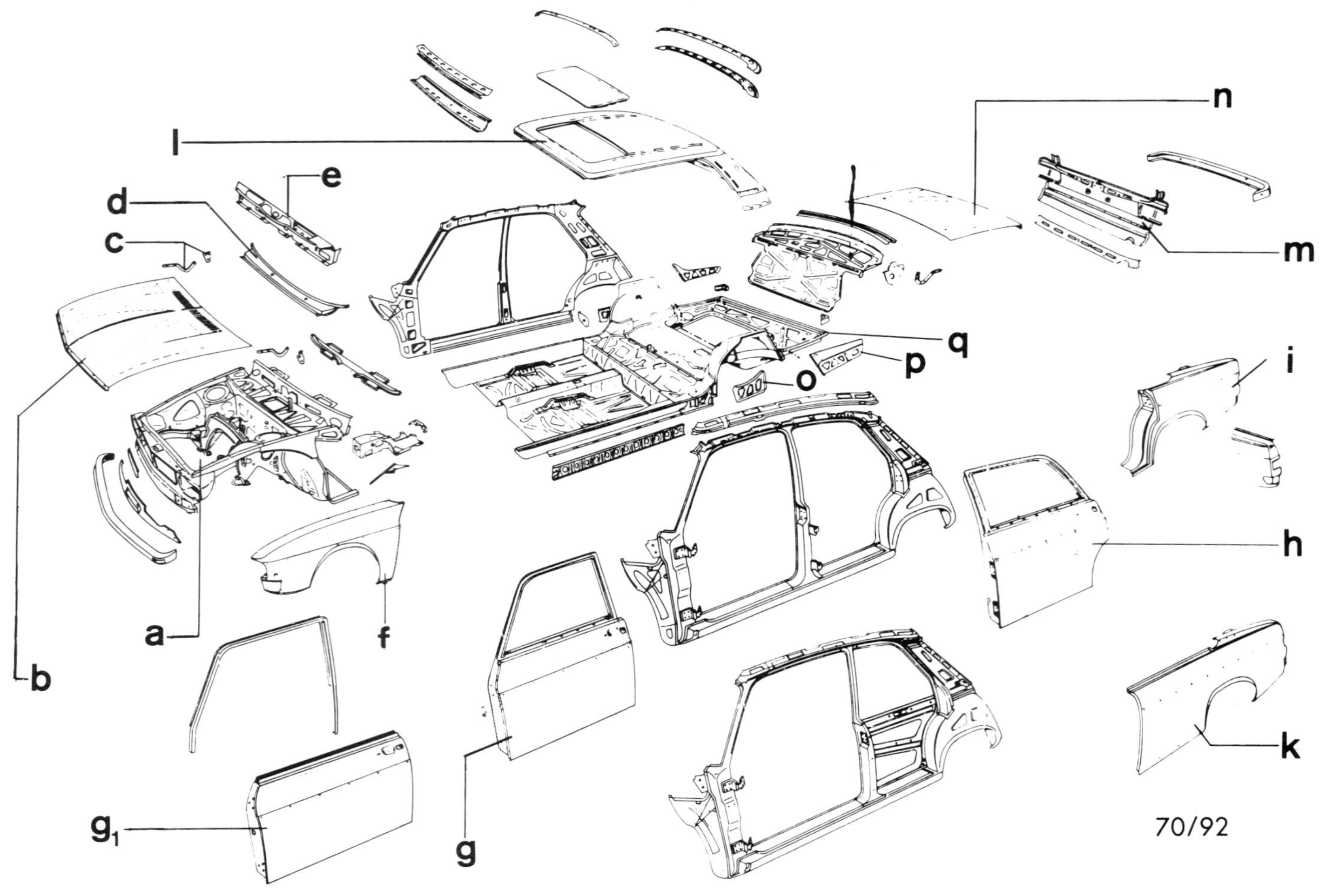

70/92

FIG. 12.1. THE MAJOR BODY PANELS OF THE SALOON (SEC. 1)

a   Front end assembly
b   Engine hood
c   Hinge
d   Apron

e   Instrument panel
f   Front fender
g   Front door, left, 4-door
g1 Front door, left, 2-door
    (Audi 100)

h   Rear door
i   Rear fender
k   Rear fender
l   Sun roof

m   Tail panel
n   Trunk lid
o   Plate
p   Joint
q   Floor pan

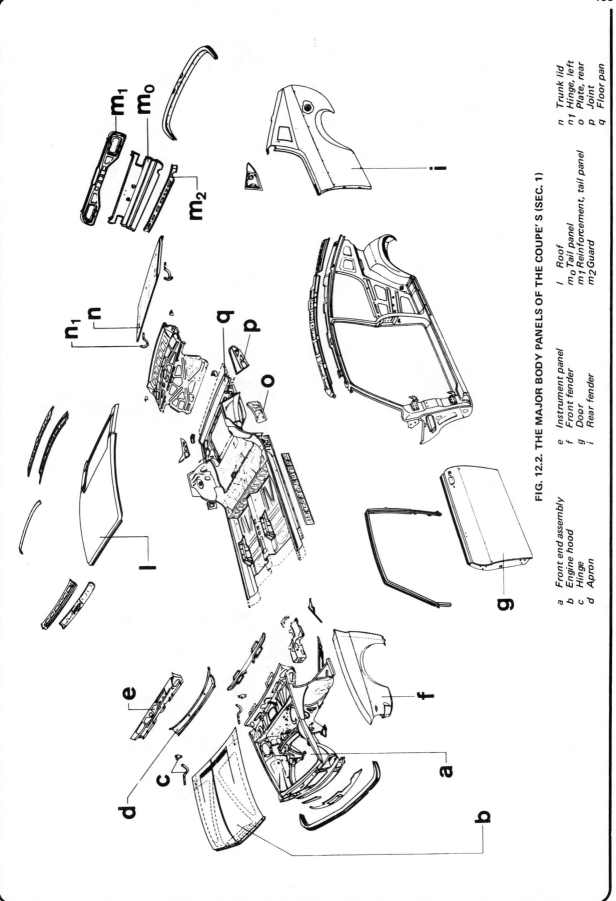

FIG. 12.2. THE MAJOR BODY PANELS OF THE COUPE' S (SEC. 1)

a Front end assembly	e Instrument panel	l Roof	n Trunk lid
b Engine hood	f Front fender	m_0 Tail panel	n_1 Hinge, left
c Hinge	g Door	m_1 Reinforcement, tail panel	o Plate, rear
d Apron	i Rear fender	m_2 Guard	p Joint
			q Floor pan

5.1 Chrome fitting on the arm rest

5.2 Removing the arm rest

5.4 Removing the window winder handle cross-head screw

5.5 Removing the door handle crosshead screw

5.6 Removing the door trim panel

5.7 The door panel after removal of the trim

winder then remove the cross-head screw. Pull off the winder.
3   Remove the cross-head screw securing the door handle and pull the handle off.
4   Slide a lever or screwdriver between the trim panel and the door, and prise off the panel. Take care that whatever is used as a lever does not cause damage to paint surfaces or trim material. As a precaution - remove any burrs before starting.
5   Check that the plastic film is intact (see paragraph 7 of previous section).
6   Replacement of the panel is the reverse of removal, but take

care that the snap fasteners are correctly aligned with their respective holes. The ball of the hand can be used to snap the fasteners home.

9   Front door lock - removal and replacement

1   Remove the trim panel and exterior door handle as previously described.
2   Remove the two hexagon headed screws which retain the

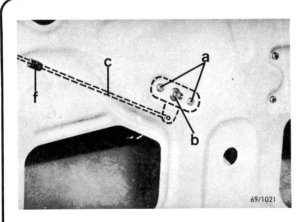

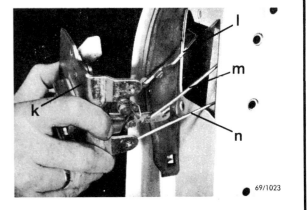

FIG. 12.3. FRONT DOOR LOCK REMOVAL (SEC. 9)

a Hex. head screws	c Control rod	k Door lock	m Locking rod
b Auxiliary lock	f Rubber holder	l Locking rod	n Control rod

auxiliary lock fitting.

3 Disconnect the remote control rod at the lock fitting and press in the rubber holder midway along the length of the control rod.

4 Unscrew the door lock button.

5 Unscrew the four screws which retain the lockplate (two on the lockplate and two on the door panel).

6 Pull out the door lock complete with the remote control rod and locking rod.

---

10 Rear door lock - removal and replacement

A Cable operated lock

1 Remove the trim panel and outer door handle as previously described.

2 Pull up the button in the window frame, hold the threaded adaptor with a pair of pliers then unscrew the button.

3 Remove the two hexagon headed screws which retain the auxiliary lock fitting.

4 Disconnect the remote control rod at the lock fitting and press in the rubber holder midway along the length of the control rod.

5 Loosen the cable adjustment nut at the lock and prise open the cable securing clamps.

6 Remove the four screws which retain the lockplate (two on the plate and two on the door panel), then pull out the lock mechanism.

7 When replacing, make sure that the mechanism is unlocked, and press the operating panel inwards. Tighten the cable clamps sufficiently to prevent the cable outer from moving.

B Linkage operated lock

1 Remove the trim panel and outer door lock as previously described.

2 Remove the screws which retain the auxiliary lock fitting to the door panel.

3 Unscrew the button in the window frame.

4 Remove the linkage rods at the auxiliary lock fitting and the bellcrank.

5 Remove the four screws which retain the lock plate (two on the plate and two on the door panel), then pull out the lock mechanism.

6 The bellcrank can be removed, by turning it, until the projection is opposite the cutaway in the bearing sleeve.

7 Replacement is the reverse of removal.

---

11 Door - removal and replacement

1 Remove the trim panel as previously described.

FIG. 12.5. THE LINKAGE OPERATED LOCK MECHANISM (SEC. 10B)

f   Bellcrank lever   k   Holder
h   Linkage

2 If the same door is to be replaced mark around the hinges on the door using a pencil or fine tipped ball point pen. This simplifies realignment of the door.

3 Remove the circlip from the pin in the door check link then tap the pin out, upwards.

4 Remove the hexagon headed hinge screws, from inside the door cavity, and lift away the door. There are three screws per hinge on the front doors and two per hinge on the rear doors.

5 Replacement is the reverse of removal. If the same door is to be refitted, use the alignment marks made before removal.

---

12 Door rattles - tracing and rectification

1 Door rattles can be caused by a number things, so some careful detective work will be required.

2 Loose or worn hinges can be detected by opening the door and attempting to lift it. The remedy for loose hinges is obvious, but excessively worn hinges will require replacement.

3 Worn or badly adjusted catches can be detected by pushing and pulling on the outside door handle when the door is closed. If slackness is detected tighten or adjust the lockplates and door pillar catches.

4 To check for window rattles, open the door and try to move the glass from side-to-side with the palms of the hands.

5 Door trim rattles on early cars can be rectified by using a piece of foam rubber on the inside of the trim panel. This is a standard fitment on later cars.

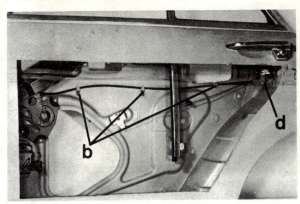

FIG. 12.4. THE CABLE OPERATED LOCK MECHANISM (SEC. 10A)

b   Clamps   d   Cable adjusting screw

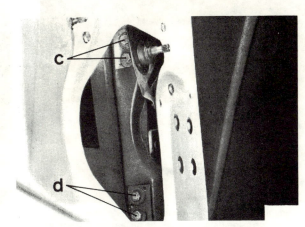

FIG. 12.6. REMOVING THE DOOR (SEC. 11)

c, d   Hinge screws

This sequence of photographs deals with the repair of the dent and paintwork damage shown in this photo. The procedure will be similar for the repair of a hole. It should be noted that the procedures given here are simplified – more explicit instructions will be found in the text

In the case of a dent the first job – after removing surrounding trim – is to hammer out the dent where access is possible. This will minimise filling. Here, the large dent having been hammered out, the damaged area is being made slightly concave

Now all paint must be removed from the damaged area, by rubbing with coarse abrasive paper. Alternatively, a wire brush or abrasive pad can be used in a power drill. Where the repair area meets good paintwork, the edge of the paintwork should be 'feathered', using a finer grade of abrasive paper

In the case of a hole caused by rusting, all damaged sheet-metal should be cut away before proceeding to this stage. Here, the damaged area is being treated with rust remover and inhibitor before being filled

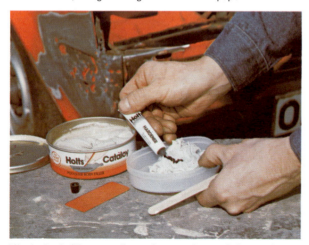

Mix the body filler according to its manufacturer's instructions. In the case of corrosion damage, it will be necessary to block off any large holes before filling – this can be done with aluminium or plastic mesh, or aluminium tape. Make sure the area is absolutely clean before ...

... applying the filler. Filler should be applied with a flexible applicator, as shown, for best results; the wooden spatula being used for confined areas. Apply thin layers of filler at 20-minute intervals, until the surface of the filler is slightly proud of the surrounding bodywork

Initial shaping can be done with a Surform plane or Dreadnought file. Then, using progressively finer grades of wet-and-dry paper, wrapped around a sanding block, and copious amounts of clean water, rub down the filler until really smooth and flat. Again, feather the edges of adjoining paintwork

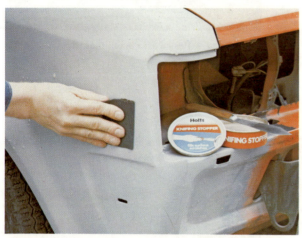

Again, using plenty of water, rub down the primer with a fine grade wet-and-dry paper (400 grade is probably best) until it is really smooth and well blended into the surrounding paintwork. Any remaining imperfections can now be filled by carefully applied knifing stopper paste

The top coat can now be applied. When working out of doors, pick a dry, warm and wind-free day. Ensure surrounding areas are protected from over-spray. Agitate the aerosol thoroughly, then spray the centre of the repair area, working outwards with a circular motion. Apply the paint as several thin coats

The whole repair area can now be sprayed or brush-painted with primer. If spraying, ensure adjoining areas are protected from over-spray. Note that at least one inch of the surrounding sound paintwork should be coated with primer. Primer has a 'thick' consistency, so will find small imperfections

When the stopper has hardened, rub down the repair area again before applying the final coat of primer. Before rubbing down this last coat of primer, ensure the repair area is blemish-free — use more stopper if necessary. To ensure that the surface of the primer is really smooth use some finishing compound

After a period of about two weeks, which the paint needs to harden fully, the surface of the repaired area can be 'cut' with a mild cutting compound prior to wax polishing. When carrying out bodywork repairs, remember that the quality of the finished job is proportional to the time and effort expended

13 Sunroof - removal and replacement

1 Open the sunroof to approximately the mid position, then, carefully prise off the trim.

2 Slide the trim panel back, then pull the roof panel forward to within an inch or two of the closed position.

3 Remove the slotted nut from the front guides; ease the roof upwards and take off the guides. Note the left and right-hand guides for when replacement is required.

4 Turn the rear guide springs inwards and remove them, then remove the hexagon headed screws from the guide plates.

5 Pull the guide plates inwards, away from their brackets.

6 Lift the sunroof upwards and off of the car.

7 Replacement is the reverse of removal but care must be taken when installing the front guides that the locking spigot has aligned with the hole in the roof panel. When the spigots are engaged in the holes, the guides should be pushed outwards to engage in the guide rails and tightened.

8 If it is required to adjust the height of the sunroof proceed as follows.

9 Adjustment at the front: Take off the front guides as previously described and remove the locking key.

10 Temporarily refit the guide and adjust the roof height by turning the outer part of the guide.

11 Refit the key in the guide ensuring that the hook in the key is below the step in the inner part.

12 Adjustment at the rear: Remove the trim panel as previously described and fully close the sunroof.

13 Loosen the shouldered screw and adjust the roof height as necessary. Finally tighten the shouldered screw.

14 Windscreen - removal and replacement

1 Loosen the windscreen by pressing outwards with the palm of the hand. If a laminated windscreen is fitted carefully prise off the inner rubber lip.

2 Once the windscreen has been loosened it can be removed from outside the car.

3 For replacement, smear the grooves in the sealing strip with a rubber lubricant or glycerine.

4 Fit the rubber strip to the windscreen then fit the chrome strips.

5 Obtain a length of heavy cord (a plastic clothes line would be suitable) of about 3/16 in (5 mm) diameter and 16½ ft (5 m) length. Fit it into the body seam groove on the rubber strip around the complete periphery.

6 With an assistant, fit the windscreen at the bottom edge with the cord inside the car.

7 Use the cord to pull the inner sealing lip over the body seam at the same time as pressing the windscreen against the body. Light hand blows may be required but take great care if a laminated windscreen is fitted since they shatter very easily.

8 Finally seal the windscreen and bodywork against the rubber strip using a proprietary sealant such as Seelastik.

15 Rear window - removal and replacement

1 The procedure is identical to that given for the windscreen.

16 Windscreen - removal and replacement, Audi 100 LS USA

1 Remove the windscreen wiper arms (see Chapter 10).

2 Remove the chrome strip from the windscreen rubber sealing strip.

3 Cut the inner lip of the sealing strip along the length of the chrome trim groove.

4 Tear off the lip around the windscreen.

5 Carefully remove the windscreen then the remains of the sealing strip.

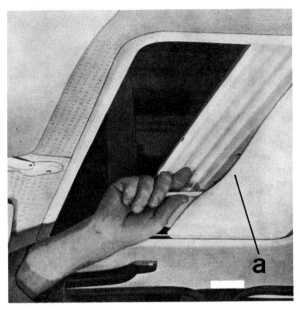

Fig. 12.7. Prising off the sun-roof trim (a) (Sec. 13)

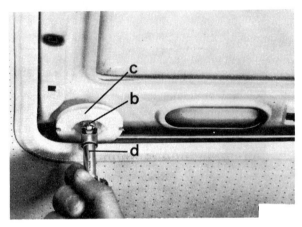

FIG. 12.8. REMOVING THE FRONT GUIDES (SEC. 13)

b   Slotted nut   d   Special spanner
c   Front guide

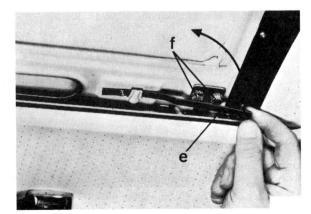

FIG. 12.9. REMOVING THE REAR GUIDES (SEC. 13)

e   Spring   f   Screws

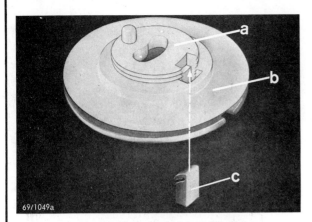

FIG. 12.10. THE FRONT GUIDE (SEC. 13)

a   Inner part   c   Key
b   Outer part

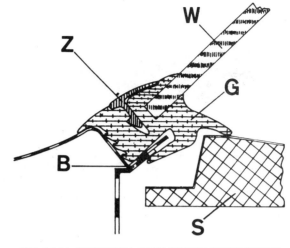

FIG. 12.11. SECTIONAL VIEW OF THE WINDSCREEN SEAL (SEC. 14)

B   Edge of body   W Windscreen
G   Rubber frame   Z Chrome strip
S   Instrument panel padding

Fig. 12.12. Pulling the seal lip over the body seam using a cord (Sec. 14)

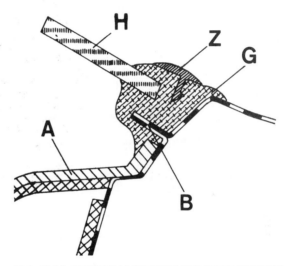

FIG. 12.13. SECTIONAL VIEW OF THE REAR WINDOW SEAL (SEC. 15)

A   Hat rack   G Rubber frame
B   Edge of body   H Rear window
                        Z Chrome strip

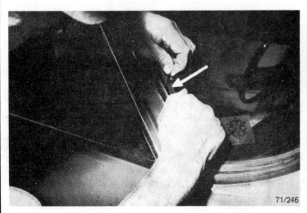

Fig. 12.14. Windscreen replacement, USA models (Sec. 16)

6   Remove any sealant from the windscreen frame using a petrol soaked cloth.

7   Liberally coat the cleaned windscreen frame with an adhesive such as Teroson Terokal 3212/10.

8   Fit the rubber strip and chrome trim to the windscreen and fit it to the car as described for European models, but do not apply any rubber lubricant. Note that a special rubber strip is provided for USA models.

Note: From chassis number 81 11 103 584 USA safety regulations require the windscreen to be held in by clamping plates and strips. Removal of this type of windscreen, or modification from the previous type is not straighforward and it is essential that the work is carried out by an Audi dealer.

17 Window winder mechanism - removal and replacement

A   Front door (four door model)

1   Close the window fully and tape the glass in position.

2   Remove the door trim as previously described.

3   Remove the four hexagon headed screws which retain the winder mechanism and pull the winder arm out of the guide rail in a direction towards the door hinge.

4   Remove the winder mechanism through the aperture below its installed position.

5   Replacement is the reverse of removal but make sure that the slides are fitted to the ball on the winder arm.

B   Front door (two door model)

1   Lower the window completely and remove the trim panel as previously described.

2   Remove the three screws which ssecure the winder mechanism then slide the winder arm out of the guide rail in a direction away from the door hinge.

3   Raise the window fully and tape the glass to the door frame.

4   Remove the winder mechanism through the oblong aperture near the base of the door.

5   Replacement is the reverse of removal.

C   Rear door

1   The procedure is identical to that for the front doors of four door models with the mechanism being withdrawn through the large aperture in the door panel.

18 Door windows - removal and replacement

1   Remove the trim panel and regulator as previously described.

2   Unscrew the button in the window frame (see Section 10A where cable operated lock mechanisms are fitted).

3   Fully lower the window then prise the window guide strip from the frame at the quarter light side.

4   Remove the frame fixing screw and the two screws in the door panel (in line with frame) which hold the frame in position.

5   Remove the two clips in a downward direction then ease the frame downwards slightly.

6   Now pull the frame upwards out of the door cavity in such a way that it is withdrawn from the inner side of the door.

7   Loosen the quarter light by running a blunt knife or similar tool around the rubber sealing strip. Remove the quarter light from the door complete with the rubber.

8   Remove the inner recess chrome strip then the outer from the lower edge of the window frame by prising upwards (both these strips are on the inner side of the door).

9   For cable operated two door models the cross-head screw, beneath the rectangular aperture near the bottom of door, must be removed and the cable disconnected at the forward end of the lifting rail.

10   The window and lifting rail are removed by lifting them upwards out of the window recess.

11   When replacing a window it is important that dimension X is as follows: (see Fig.12.20A, B and C)

Front window, four door model X = 5.87 in (149 mm)

Rear window, four door model X = 2.32 in (59 mm)

Two door model X = 0.59 in (15 mm)

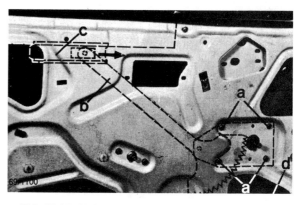

FIG. 12.15. FRONT WINDOW WINDER MECHANISM (FOUR DOOR MODEL) (SEC. 17A)

a	Fixing screws	c	Guide rail
b	Regulator arm	d	Aperture

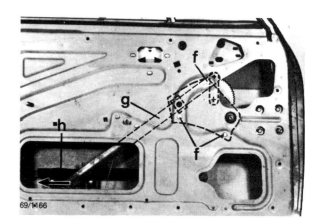

FIG. 12.16. FRONT WINDOW WINDER MECHANISM (TWO DOOR MODEL) (SEC. 17B)

f	Fixing screws	h	Guide rail
g	Regulator arm		

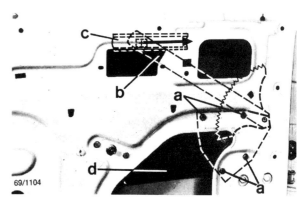

FIG. 12.17. REAR WINDOW WINDER MECHANISM (SEC. 17C)

a	Fixing screws	c	Guide rail
b	Regulator arm	d	Aperture

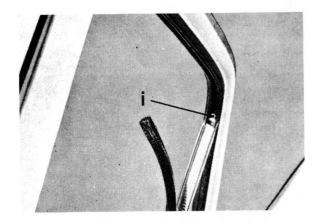

FIG. 12.18. DOOR WINDOW REPLACEMENT (SEC. 18)

i   Frame fixing screw

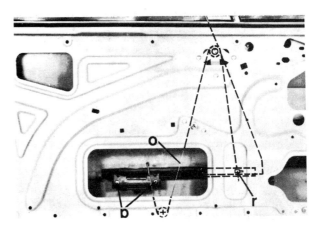

FIG. 12.19. CABLE OPERATED REGULATOR ON TWO DOOR MODEL (SEC. 18)

o   Cable
p   Screws
r   Disconnect the cable here

69/1179

FIG. 12.20. DIMENSIONS FOR FITTING THE LIFTING RAIL (SEC. 18)

X 5.866 in.	(149 mm)	Front door, four door model (above left)
X 2.32 in.	(59 mm)	Rear door - four door model (above right)
X 0.59 in.	(15 mm)	Two door model (left)

19 Rear side window (two door models) - removal and replacement

1   Prise off the rubber seal from inside the car.
2   Remove the four cross-head screws which retain the window and frame, then remove the window and frame from outside the car.

3   To remove the frame from the window remove the screws at the top and bottom corners and remove the short straight strip.
4   The glass and sealing strip can now be pulled out of the frame.
5   When replacing, lubricate the rubber parts with a rubber lubricant or glycerine, and initially slide the window inwards towards the rear of the car.

20 Opening quarter lights - removal and replacement

1 To remove the knurled wheel it will be necessary to make a tool as shown (Fig. 12.22).

2 Insert the end of the tool into the rear of the wheel at the point marked near the circumference to prise off the cap.

3 Remove the screw and knurled wheel.

4 Remove the trim panel as previously described.

5 Remove the drive coupling screw at the top of the pentagonal shaped aperture, and slacken the three remaining screws.

6 Remove the quarter light at the hinge, taking care not to lose the plastic washer. Ease the quarter light downwards if necessary.

7 Lift out the quarter light.

8 Replacement is the reverse of removal but after tightening the drive coupling screw make sure that the window will shut properly before tightening the remaining screws.

21 Window guide and rubber frame - removal and replacement

1 Prise out the existing sealing strip using a screwdriver. If the vertical guides are to be removed, the frame must be removed as described in Section 18.

2 New window guides can be fitted to the door frame using a rubber mallet.

3 If it is required to replace the plastic flange cover, it can be prised off with a screwdriver. New strips are supplied in straight lengths and it will be necessary to apply heat locally to bend the strip as required. The excess at the ends can be snipped off afterwards.

22 Bonnet - removal and replacement

1 Initially raise the bonnet and support it on its stay.

2 Pull off the windscreen washer connecting tube (photo).

3 With the help of an assistant, remove the nuts from the hinge lugs at each side, pull out the lugs slightly and lift away the bonnet (photo).

4 When replacing any adjustment should be made at the elongated slots in the hinge lugs.

23 Boot lid - removal and replacement

1 Remove the electrical connections to the number plate lamps at the connector near the hinge where they are attached to the bodywork.

2 With the help of an assistant remove the nuts from the hinge lugs at each side (photo), pull out the lugs slightly and lift away the panel.

24 Front grille - removal and replacement

1 Remove the cross-head screws at the top of the grille, then pull it outwards clear of the lower edge spring clips (photo).

25 Paintwork - touch-up

1 On any modern car with an all steel body, the greatest enemy of all is rust. This is most likely to start under the wings or along the sills where the road wheels have thrown up mud, water and stones.

2 Small chip marks are unavoidable and if attended to, in good time the paintwork can be touched up and the marks will be undectable.

3 A complete range of Audi paints and laquers is available in the form of touch-up tubes or pencils, small tins, or aersol cans. See Note 1, in the General Description Section at the beginning

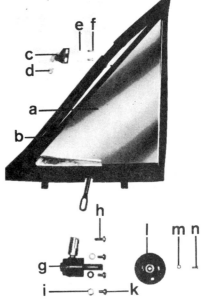

FIG. 12.21. THE COMPONENT PARTS OF OPENING QUARTER LIGHTS (SEC. 20)

a Vent window, left
b Rubber frame, left
c Holder, upper part, left
d Plastic washer
e Lock washer
f Oval head screw
g Pivot, left
h Oval head screw
i Washer
k Oval head screw
l Knob
m Lock washer
n Oval head countersunk screw

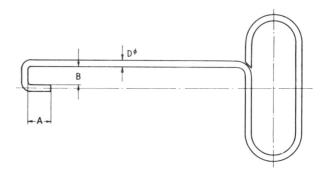

FIG. 12.22. A TOOL FOR REMOVING THE KNURLED WHEEL CAP (SEC. 20)

A = 0.629 inch (16 mm)
B = 0.512 inch (13 mm)
D = 0.157 inch (4 mm) dia.

FIG. 12.23. THE KNURLED QUARTER LIGHT OPENING WHEEL (SEC. 20)

The point for inserting the tool is arrowed.

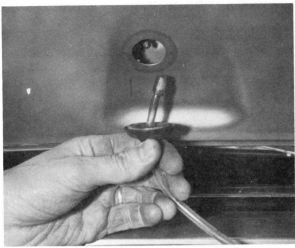

22.2 Removing the windscreen washer connection

22.3 The bonnet hinge

23.2 The boot lid hinge

24.1 Removing the front grille

of this Chapter, regarding two-coat metallic finishes.

4 To make good small scratches and chip marks, a touch-up pencil or tin and brush are best, but it is important to prepare the surface before starting.

5 First use a silicone solvent to remove all traces of polish from the paint surface, and should there be signs of rusting or paint lifting, the surface should then be scraped with a penknife and the affected area treated with Kurust. When dry the surplus should be wiped away using a cloth soaked in methylated spirit.

6 Initially, a very thin layer of touch-up paint should be applied and then allowed to dry.

7 Further layers can be applied at intervals to bring the new surface up to the level of the original paintwork - with a little time and patience the touch-up will be undetectable.

8 Where larger areas are to be treated, again the silicone solvent will be required but it will then be necessary to rub down the area with wet or dry paper, grade 400, using plenty of water, until the area is smooth. Again any rust should be neutralised with Kurust or a similar preparation.

9 For these larger areas it is best to use an aerosol spray, initially applying a primer. It is most important that the instructions on the canister be followed carefully, and it is always preferable to do paint jobs of this type on a warm, dry day.

10 If this is your first attempt at spraying, it is a good idea to practise first on an old piece of metal just to get the feel of the thing. The jet should be held 8 to 12 inches away from the working surface, and at right angles to it.

11 Where a large section is to be sprayed, the work should be commenced at the centre and then progressively moved outwards.

12 A period of several hours should be allowed for the primer to dry and it should then be rubbed down again with wet or dry paper. Any faults can then be rectified by applying a further coat of primer.

13 When you are satisfied with the finish give a final rub down before applying the undercoat. Here again, the same spraying technique should be adopted, but remember not to apply the paint too thickly.

14 The top coat can now be applied in the same way. If more than one coat is required, the first coat should be allowed to dry overnight before any reapplication.

15 If you are spraying near chromework, tyres or glasswork make sure that these are properly masked with tape and newspaper.

16 After applying new paint finishes it is recommended that a period of, at least, two weeks is allowed to pass before body-work polish is applied.

Chapter 13 Supplement:
Revisions and information on later models

Contents

1 Introduction

Since its introduction, the Audi 100 has had a number of modifications in order to keep pace with current technical advancement. The major changes covered by this Supplement are the introduction on 1975 models of outboard front brakes and a diagonal dual braking circuit, a different gearbox on 1976 models, and on USA models only, the introduction of the Continuous Injection System (CIS) for 1976 and 1977 models.

As with all other Chapters of this manual, the Supplement only covers side cam (OHV) engines.

In order to use the Supplement to the best advantage it is suggested that it is referred to before the main Chapters of the manual; this will ensure that any relevant information can be collected and accommodated into the procedures given in Chapters 1 to 12. When using the Supplement it is helpful to remember that the model year commences in August of the previous year, for example, 1975 models are manufactured as from August 1974.

2 Specifications

The Specifications given here are revised or supplementary to the original Specifications given at the beginning of each Chapter.

Engine

Audi 100, 1974 on ...   .   As Audi 100, with emission control (1972/73)

Audi 100 USA, 1974 on

Engine code
  Manual transmission... ... ...   ZG
  Automatic transmission ... ...   ZH
  For other specifications refer to Audi 100 USA (1973)

Audi 100 GL and Coupe S, 1974... ... ...   As Audi 100 GL (1972/73)

Audi 100 LS, 1974 ... ...   As Audi 100 LS (1972/73)

Audi 100 LS, 1975 on ... ...   As Audi 100 LS (1972/73) except for a compression ratio of 9.7 : 1

Audi 100 GL and Coupe S, 1975 on ... ...   As Audi 100 GL (1972/73) except for the following

Compression ratio ... ...   9.7 : 1
Valve timing (1 mm valve stroke/0.0 in (0.0 mm) tappet clearance)
  Inlet opens ... ...   14° BTDC on crankshaft
  Inlet closes ... ...   46° ABDC on crankshaft
  Exhaust opens ... ...   36° BBDC on crankshaft
  Exhaust closes ... ...   6° ATDC on crankshaft

Audi 100 USA, 1975

Engine code
  Manual transmission, 49 states ... ...   YA
  Automatic transmission, 49 states ... ...   YB
  Manual transmission, California and some 49 states ... ...   YC
  Automatic transmission, California and some 49 states ... ...   YD
Fuel grade... ... ...   Regular (91 RON/87 pump), unleaded fuel where catalytic converter fitted
Compression ratio ... ...   8.0 : 1 ± 0.3
Horsepower
  49 states ... ...   DIN 98 PS at 5500 rpm, SAE 95 bhp at 5500 rpm
  California ... ...   DIN 96 PS at 5200 rpm, SAE 93 bhp at 5200 rpm
Torque
  49 states ... ...   DIN 116 lbf ft (16 kgf m) at 3200 rpm, SAE 118 lbf ft (16.3 kgf m) at 3200 rpm
  California ... ...   DIN 108 lbf ft (15 kgf m) at 3000 rpm, SAE 109 lbf ft (15 kgf m) at 3000 rpm
Oil pressure
  Maximum ... ...   85 lbf/in^2 (5.97 kgf/cm^2)
  Minimum ... ...   8.5 lbf/in^2 (0.597 kgf/cm^2)
Maximum engine speed ... ...   6200 rpm
Tappet clearance, warm
  Inlet ... ...   0.006 in (0.15 mm)
  Exhaust ... ...   0.015 in (0.40 mm)
  For other specifications refer to Audi 100 USA (1973)

Audi 100 USA, 1976 and 1977 models with CIS fuel injection

Engine code
  Automatic transmission ... ...   YD
  Manual transmission, 49 states and Canada ... ...   YR
  Manual transmission, California ... ...   YC
Horsepower
  49 states and Canada ... ...   SAE 92 bhp at 5500 rpm
  California ... ...   SAE 90 bhp at 5500 rpm
Torque (all models) ... ...   SAE 106.3 lbf ft (14.7 kgf/m) at 3300 rpm
  For other specifications refer to Audi 100 USA, (1975)

All engines

Main bearing journal size
  Standard ... ...   2.520 in (64.0 mm) from chassis no. 8061 077 760

Fuel system

Carburettor application

Audi 100, 1974 on	As Audi 100, with emission control (1972/73)
Audi 100 USA, 1974/75	As Audi 100 USA (1972/73)
Audi 100 LS, 1974	As Audi 100 LS, with emission control (1972/73)
Audi 100 GL and Coupe S, 1974	As Audi 100 GL and Coupe S with emission control (1972/73)

Audi 100 LS, 1975

Carburettor model	32/35 TDID
Venturi, stage 1/2	24/27
Main jet, stage 1/2	X125/X140
Air correction jet, stage 1/2	150/100
Idle fuel jet in cut-off valve...	g50
Idle air jet bore	1.9
Injection rate/stroke (cc)	
Fast	0.87 + 0.1 (automatic transmission)
Slow	1.35 $\pm$ 0.15 (automatic transmission)
Choke valve gap	3.5 + 0.15 mm (0.14 $\pm$ 0.006 in)
Throttle valve gap	0.9 $\pm$ 0.06 mm (0.035 $\pm$ 0.002 in)
Float level	15.5 to 17.5 mm (0.6 to 0.68 in)
Float needle valve	2.0 mm (0.078 in)
CO% at idle	1.5

Audi 100 GL and Coupe S, 1975

Carburettor model	32/35 TDID
Venturi, stage 1/2	24/28 (GL), 24/24 (Coupe S)
Float needle valve	2.0 mm (0.078 in)
Main jet	
Manual transmission	X127.5/X140
Automatic transmission...	X127.5/X135
Air correction jet, stage 1/2	140/100
Idle fuel jet in cut-off valve...	g50
Idle air jet	1.9
Float level	15.5 to 17.5 mm (0.6 to 0.68 in)
Injection rate/stroke (cc)	
Fast	0.87 $\pm$ 0.1 (automatic transmission)
Slow	1.35 $\pm$ 0.15 (GL manual), 1.6 $\pm$ 0.15 (automatic and Coupe S)
Choke valve gap	3.5 $\pm$ 0.15 mm (0.14 $\pm$ 0.006 in)
Throttle valve gap	0.9 $\pm$ 0.06 mm (0.035 $\pm$ 0.002 in)
CO% at idle	1.5

Audi 100 LS, GL and Coupe S, 1976

Carburettor model	32/35 TDID
Venturi, stage 1/2	24/27 (LS), 24/28 (GL and Coupe S)
Main jet, stage 1/2	X125/X140 (LS), X127.5/X137.5 (GL and Coupe S)
Air correction jet, stage 1/2	150/100 (LS), 130/100 (GL and Coupe S)
Idle jet in cut-off valve	g52.5
Pump injection tube....	50
Injection rate/stroke (cc)	
Fast	1.45 to 1.6
Slow	0.87 to 0.97
Choke valve gap	2.0 to 5.0 mm (0.078 to 0.196 in)
Throttle valve gap	
Manual transmission	0.95 to 1.15 mm (0.037 to 0.045 in)
Automatic transmission...	1.15 to 1.35 mm (0.045 to 0.053 in)
Float level	15.5 to 17.5 mm (0.6 to 0.68 in)
Float needle valve	2.0 mm (0.078 in)
CO% at idle	1.0 to 2.0

Fuel system - 1976 Audi 100 USA

Type	Continuous Injection System (CIS)
Fuel pump delivery rate (min)	750 cc/30 sec
Control pressure (oil at 50 to 70°C)	48 to 54 lbf/in^2 (3.3 to 3.7 kgf/cm^2)
System pressure	64 to 74 lbf/in^2 (4.5 to 5.2 kgf/cm^2)
Injector spring pressure	35 to 50 lbf/in^2 (2.4 to 3.5 kgf/cm^2)
Maximum pressure difference between injectors	8.5 lbf/in^2 (0.59 kgf/cm^2)

Air cleaner

Type (from chassis no. 61 000 051)	Temperature controlled (as fitted to GL and Coupe S from 1972)

Fuel octane requirement

Audi 100, 1974	88 octane
Audi 100 USA, 1974	91 octane (pump 87)
Audi 100, 1975 on	98 octane

Audi 100 USA, 1975 on
  Catalytic converter models ... ...   Unleaded
  Non catalytic converter models ... ...   Regular (including low-lead or unleaded fuels)

Ignition system
Type
UK models, 1974 to 1976 ... ...   As previous models, but with BHCI system as optional extra
   (now termed CDI - Capacitor Discharge Ignition)

USA models, 1974 to 1977 ... ...   As 1973 model with CDI system

Dwell angle
1975 to 1977 models ... ... $47° \pm 3°$ ($53° \pm 3\%$)

Ignition timing
UK models, 1975 to 1977 ... ...   As for previous models
USA models, 1975 ... ... $6°$ ATDC at 925 ± 75 rpm, vacuum hose connected
USA models, 1976/77 fitted with CIS ... ... $6°$ ATDC at idle, vacuum hoses connected

Spark plugs
UK models, 1975 and 1976
  Audi 100 LS ... ...   Bosch W215 T30 or Champion N7Y
  Audi 100 GL and Coupe S ... ...   Bosch W230 T30, W225 T30 or Champion N6Y
USA models, 1974 to 1977 ... ...   Bosch W225 T2, W225 T30 or Champion N7Y
Spark plug gap ... ...   As for previous models

Manual transmission
Gear teeth
UK models, 1975 ... ...   As for previous models
USA models, to 1975 ... ...   As Audi 100
(Gearbox type reference 088, from August 1975)
Gear teeth
  First gear ... ...   36 : 10
  Second gear ... ...   34 : 16
  Third gear ... ...   34 : 25
  Fourth gear ... ...   29 : 30
  Reverse gear ... ...   42 : 12

Final drive
Audi 100 LS ... ...   35 : 9
Audi 100 GL and Coupe S ... ...   37 : 10
Audi 100 USA ... ...   37 : 9

Lubricant capacity (total) ... ...   4.6 Imp pt (2.6 litres/5.5 US pt). Note that this transmission is
   filled-for-life (ie maintenance free)

Automatic transmission
Final drive unit, 1975 Audi 100 USA
Crownwheel ... ...   43 teeth
Pinion ... ...   11 teeth
Ratio ... ...   3.909 : 1

Lubricant capacity ... ...   1.8 Imp pt (1.0 litre/2.1 US pt)

**Transmission type reference from August 1975 to
February 1977**...   010

Transmission type reference from February 1977   087

Gear ratios

		Overall ratio
Final drive	3.73 : 1	
First gear	2.55 : 1	9.51 : 1
Second gear	1.45 : 1	5.40 : 1
Third gear	1.00 : 1	3.73 : 1
Reverse gear	2.46 : 1	9.17 : 1

Transmission fluid

Type	Dexron ATF
Total capacity	10.5 Imp pt (6 litres/12.7 US pt) approx
Fluid change capacity	5.3 Imp pt (3 litres/6.3 US pt) approx

Final drive capacity ... ...   1.8 Imp pt (1 litre/2.1 US pt)

Power steering
Power steering fluid ... ...   ATF Dexron 'B'

Braking system
Type, 1975 models on ... ...   Diagonal dual hydraulic circuit with outboard front discs

Front brakes, 1974 models

Disc diameter	
Audi 100, 100 LS, 100 GL	279.2 mm (11.0 in)
All other models	291.0 mm (11.45 in)

Front brakes, 1975 models on

Disc diameter	257 mm (10.12 in)
Disc thickness	13 mm (0.51 in)
Pad thickness	14 mm (0.55 in)

Electrical system
Bulbs   **Wattage**

1975/76 Audi 100 L/LS	As for previous models
1975/76 Audi 100 GL	
Headlights	55
Rear window heater warning	1..2
1975 Audi 100 USA	
Headlights	55
Brake warning	3
1976/77 Audi 100 USA	
Headlights (inner)	37.5
Headlights (outer)	37.5/60
Brake warning	3

Fuses (as for previous models except for the following additions)

	Amp	Circuit
1976 Audi 100 Automatic		
No 2	16	Engine speed step up valve
1975 Audi 100 USA		
Auxiliary fuse panel	16	Radiator fan motor
	16	Rear window heater, clock
1976 (early) Audi 100 USA		
No 3	16	As previous plus electric fuel pump
Auxiliary fuse panel	16	Radiator fan motor
	16	Rear window heater, clock
1976 (late) and 1977 Audi 100 USA		
Auxiliary fuse panel	16	Radiator fan motor
	16	Rear window heater, clock, cigarette lighter
	16	Electric fuel pump

Alternator regulator voltage

1975/76 models	13.6 to 14.2 watts at 5 to 30 amp load

Front suspension
Up to and including 1974 models

Camber angle	$+0^o$ 15' $\pm$ 30'
Maximum difference, side to side	0° 20'
Track	$0^o \pm$ 15' (0 $\pm$ 1.5 mm)
Castor angle, without power steering	
Audi 100	-0° 10' $\pm$ 15'
Audi 100, Coupe S	$+0^o$ 10' $\pm$ 15'
Tropic and bad road version	-0° 35' $\pm$ 15'
Castor angle, with power steering	
Audi 100	$+0^o$ 20' $\pm$ 15'
.Audi 100 Coupe S	$+0^o$ 40' $\pm$ 15'
Tropic and bad road version	-0° 5' $\pm$ 15'

1975 on models
Camber angle
Audi 100	$0^o \pm 30'$
Audi 100 Coupe S	$0^o 10' \pm 30'$
Tropic and bad road version	$0^o 10' \pm 30'$
Maximum difference, side to side	$0^o 20'$

Toe-out
Audi 100	$0^o 25' \pm 15'$ (1.0 to 4.0 mm)
Audi 100 Coupe S	$0^o 35' \pm 15'$ (2.0 to 5.5 mm)
Tropic and bad road version	$0^o 30' \pm 15'$ (1.5 to 5.0 mm)

Castor angle, without power steering
Audi 100	$0^o 30' \pm 15'$
Audi 100 Coupe S	$0^o 30' \pm 15'$
Tropic and bad road version	$0^o 20' \pm 15'$

Castor angle, with power steering
Audi 100	$0^o \pm 15'$
Audi 100 Coupe S	$0^o \pm 15'$
Tropic and bad road version	$0^o 10' \pm 15'$

Rear suspension
Up to and including 1974 models
Camber angle	$- 0^o 30' \pm 30'$

1975 on models
Camber angle	$- 0^o 30' \pm 30'$

Ground clearance
Up to and including 1974 models
Front
Audi 100	7.87 to 8.43 in (200 to 214 mm)
Audi 100 (tropical)	8.66 to 9.21 in (220 to 234 mm)
Bad road version	7.68 to 8.27 in (195 to 210 mm)
Audi 100 Coupe S	
To 1973	6.85 to 7.32 in (174 to 186 mm)
From 1974	7.0 to 7.56 in (178 to 192 mm)

Rear
Audi 100	
To 1973	7.52 to 7.80 in (191 to 198 mm)
1974 models	9.72 to 10.0 in (247 to 254 mm)
1975 on models	10.03 to 10.31 in (255 to 262 mm)
Audi 100 (tropical)	
To 1973	7.99 to 8.27 in (203 to 210 mm)
1974 models	10.31 to 10.59 in (262 to 269 mm)
1975 on models	10.63 to 10.91 in (270 to 277 mm)
Audi 100 Coupe S	
To 1973	6.50 to 6.77 in (165 to 172 mm)
1974 models	8.93 to 9.21 in (227 to 234 mm)
1975 on models	8.93 to 9.21 in (227 to 234 mm)

Wheels
1975 models on
Rim size (steel)	5J x 14 H2-B
Rim size (alloy)	5½J x 14 H2-B
Tyre size	
Audi 100 Automatic Coupe	185/70 SR 14

Kerb weight
Manual transmission
100 GL	1100 kg (2425 lb)
100 LS	1090 kg (2403 lb)
100	1075 kg (2370 lb)
Coupe S	1100 kg (2425 lb)
100 USA - 4 door	1185 kg (2612 lb)

Automatic transmission
100 GL	1120 kg (2469 lb)
100 LS	1110 kg (2447 lb)
Coupe S	1120 kg (2469 lb)
100 USA - 4 door	1196 kg (2637 lb)
Maximum trailer load	
Without brakes	550 kg (1212 lb)
With brakes	1100 kg (2425 lb)

Dimensions
Width ... ...   68.1 in (1728 mm)

Height (unladen) ... ...   56.0 in (1421 mm)

Length (total)
UK models ... ...   182.0 in (4636 mm)
USA models ... ...   188.0 in (4774 mm)

---

3 Engine

Valve clearance adjustment - general

1 To ensure correct adjustment of the valve clearances, the engine should be lukewarm with the coolant temperature at approximately 35°C (95°F).

2 After. removal and refitting the cylinder head, the valve clearances should be checked after 600 miles (1000 km).

Cylinder head bolt - tightening sequence

3 The cylinder head bolt tightening sequence has been revised as shown in Fig.13.1.

4 The tightening sequence should be reversed when removing the bolts.

Engine/transmission assembly - removal and refitting

5 The modifications described in this Supplement, in particular the electric radiator fan and the installation of the CIS fuel injection system (USA models), have resulted in different procedures being necessary for the removal and refitting of the engine/transmission unit. The method remains the same as described in Chapter 1, but reference should be made to the relevant sections of this Supplement where the modified components are fitted. When outboard brakes are fitted, disconnect the driveshafts as described in Section 12.

Engine/transmission assembly - checking alignment

6 A revised alignment procedure has been introduced for models produced in 1975 and successive years, and the procedure must be carried out before refitting the radiator and exhaust system.

7 Refer to Fig.13.2 and install 2 shims (part no. 803 199 347) where indicated on all models except 1976 manual transmission models where 1 shim should be fitted.

8 Refer to Fig.13.3 and install 2 shims (part no. 803 199 347 C) where indicated on all models except 1976 manual transmission models where 1 shim should be fitted. If necessary, remove 1 shim (only where 2 have been fitted) to provide clearance from the stabilizer or tunnel.

9 With the number plate and front apron removed, measure the distance from the crankshaft pulley to the chassis side members; the difference between the left and right dimensions must not exceed 0.118 in (3.0 mm).

10 If adjustment is necessary, loosen the engine/transmission mountings and reposition the unit, then tighten the mountings.

11 The engine/transmission height must now be checked. To do this, position a length of straight wood between the two front wheels as shown in Fig.13.5. Measure the height of each inner driveshaft joint; the difference between left and right dimensions must not exceed 0.118 in (3.0 mm). If necessary, loosen the centre front mounting and the upper locknut of the left-hand side mounting. Turn the lower nut to realign the unit, then tighten the upper nut and the centre mounting; make sure that the mounting rubbers are free of any torsional stress.

12 Note that when installing new mountings, the full weight of the engine/transmission unit must be allowed to bear on the mountings for approximately ten minutes prior to making any adjustments.

Camshaft - identification

13 The camshaft for 1.9 litre engines can be distinguished from the one for the 1.8 litre engine by two rings located between the second and third cams (see Fig.13.7).

Crankshaft main bearing journal - modification

14 From chassis no. 8061 077 760 the main bearing journal diameter has been increased (see Specifications) and the timing chain guide rail modified. The previous type guide rail can only be used in the modified engine if it is altered as shown in Fig. 13.8.

---

4 Cooling system and exhaust system

Water pump - modification

1 As from chassis no. 21 145 027, the water pump installed

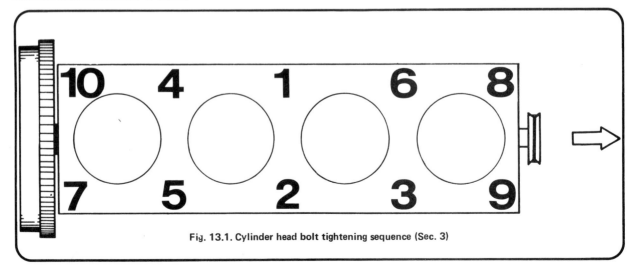

Fig. 13.1. Cylinder head bolt tightening sequence (Sec. 3)

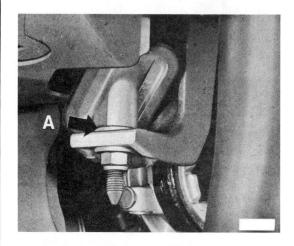

Fig. 13.2. Right-hand side engine mounting, and shim location 'A' (Sec. 3)

Fig. 13.3. Rear engine mounting, and shim location 'B' (Sec. 3)

Fig. 13.4. Engine centralisation checking dimension (Sec. 3)

Fig. 13.5. Engine/transmission height checking dimension using a length of straight wood (Sec. 3)

Fig. 13.6. Engine/transmission left-hand side mounting showing locknut (1) and adjustment nut (2) (Sec. 3)

Fig. 13.7. Identification of camshaft for 1.9 litre engine - arrowed (Sec. 3)

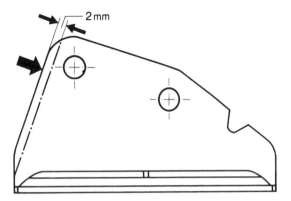

Fig. 13.8. Timing chain guide rail modification (Sec. 3)

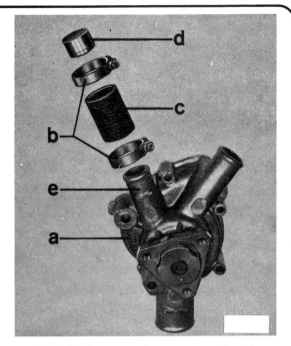

Fig. 13.9. Water pump plug components (Sec. 4).

a   Water pump   d   Plug
b   Clips   e   Outlet
c   Hose

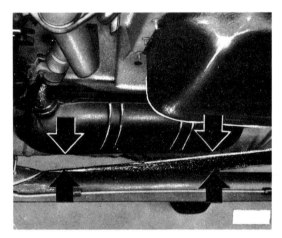

Fig. 13.10. Exhaust main silencer alignment (Sec. 4)

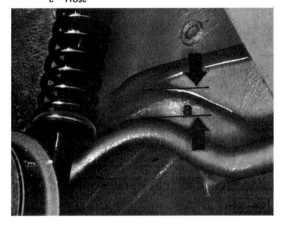

Fig. 13.11. Exhaust tailpipe to underframe. For dimension (a)
see text. (sec. 4)

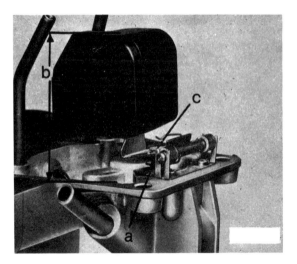

Fig. 13.12. Checking float level on 32/35 TDID carburettor
(Sec. 5)

a   Needle valve   c   Adjusting tab
b   Dimension (see text)

Fig. 13.13. Automatic choke thermal switch fitted to late models
(Sec. 5)

on Audi 100 USA models has been modified. When installing the modified water pump on earlier models it will be necessary to block the outlet with a plug as shown in Fig.13.9.

Cooling system - draining
2 The drain plug is no longer fitted in the base of the radiator, and to drain the system, the lower hose must be disconnected from the radiator outlet.

Radiator (Audi 100 USA) - removal and refitting
3 Drain the coolant and remove the radiator cap.
4 Disconnect the top and bottom hoses from the radiator.
5 Unscrew and remove the bottom mounting nut.
6 Remove the front grille and apron, then unscrew the left-hand side shroud retaining screws and withdraw the shroud.
7 Loosen the left-hand side radiator mounting nut.
8 Disconnect the fuel line clamps and identify the screws for correct refitting.
9 Remove the right-hand side shroud retaining screws and push in the shroud, at the same time slide the bonnet lock rod through the slot.
10 Unscrew and remove the remaining mounting screws and nuts, tilt the radiator and remove it sufficiently to withdraw the right-hand shroud.
11 Disconnect the electric fan wiring plug and lift out the radiator leaving the air ducts in position.
12 Refitting is a reversal of removal.

Exhaust system - alignment
13 When refitting the exhaust system, make sure that it is aligned correctly. The main silencer must be horizontal and in line with the rear axle (see Fig.13.10).
14 The distance between the tailpipe and the body underframe as shown in Fig.13.11, must be in accordance with the following chart:

All Audi 100 GL models	1.9 to 2.1 in (48 to 53 mm)
All Audi 100 Coupe S models	1.8 to 2.0 in (46 to 51 mm)
Other pre 1974 models	1.9 to 2.1 in (48 to 53 mm)
Other post 1973 models	1.97 to 2.2 in (50 to 55 mm)

---

5 Fuel system

32/35 TDID carburettor - checking the float level
1 The needle valve of the 32/35 TDID carburettor for models produced in 1975 onwards incorporates a spring tensioned damper ball in the end of the needle. When checking the float level, the carburettor cover must be tilted at an angle of 45° to prevent the weight of the float from depressing the damper ball.
2 It may be found easier to check the float height from the carburettor cover to the upper edge of the float. If this method is used the dimension 'b' (Fig.13.12) is 38.0 ± 1 mm.

Automatic choke - description and testing
3 From chassis no. 61 000 051 the bi-metallic spring of the automatic choke is heated electrically as well as by the engine coolant. The electrical heating is supplied by a thermal switch located in the coolant by-pass circuit, and the switch supplies current at temperatures below 25 to 30°C (77 to 86°F); this has the effect of reducing harmful emissions during the initial engine warm-up period.
4 The switch may be tested with an ohmmeter after removing it. At temperatures below 25°C (77°F) the ohmmeter must register zero resistance; at temperatures above approximately 30°C (86°F) infinity resistance must be registered. If an ohmmeter is not available a 12 volt testlamp and leads may be used.

Temperature controlled air cleaner - description
5 As from chassis no. 61 000 051, the thermo control valve fitted to UK Audi 100 models closes the warm air intake at temperatures above 48°C (144°F).

Continuous Injection System (CIS) - description
6 1976 and 1977 Audi 100 USA models are fitted with the CIS fuel supply system. Fuel is continuously metered to the engine by injection valves and the quantity delivered depends on the volume of air passing through the air intake. A sensor plate in the air intake moves a lever which in turn moves the control plunger. Shoulders on the control plunger communicate with metering ports in the fuel distributor, and the fuel then passes to the injection valves located in the cylinder head. The main components of the system are shown in Fig.13.15.
7 Before removing a CIS component, the surrounding area should be thoroughly cleaned to prevent the ingress of dirt. The seals and gaskets must always be renewed after being removed; this is particularly important for the intake manifold, injection valve seals, and the cold start valve flange, where an air leak will result in a weak mixture.

CIS - adjusting idle and CO%
8 Run the engine until the normal operating temperature is reached.
9 Connect a tachometer and exhaust gas analyser in accordance with the manufacturer's instructions. On pre 1977 models fitted with a catalytic converter it will also be necessary to obtain an exhaust probe, since the CO% reading must be measured ahead of the converter.
10 Adjust the idle speed screw located in the throttle housing until the engine is running at 850 to 1000 rpm.
11 Turn the headlights on main beam and make sure that the air conditioner, if fitted, is not running.
12 Check the reading on the gas analyser which should be a maximum of 0.9% (49 states and Canada) or 0.3% (California) measured at the tailpipe and 1.2% (California) measured ahead of the converter.
13 If adjustment is necessary, remove the plastic plug from the fuel distributor and turn the idle control screw clockwise to increase the CO% reading (enrich) or anti-clockwise to decrease the reading (weaken).
14 If necessary, readjust the idle speed and check the CO% again.

CIS sensor plate - adjustment
15 Temporarily run the engine at idle speed, then with the air duct disconnected, use a magnet to lift the sensor plate slowly; the movement must be smooth and even. On returning the plate, no resistance must be felt.
16 Make sure that the sensor plate is centred in the air cone. To do this, loosen the retaining bolt and run a 0.004 in (0.10 mm) feeler gauge around the plate, then tighten the bolt.
17 If the control plunger is sticking, it must be removed and cleaned after removing the fuel distributor.
18 To check the sensor plate rest position, first loosen the fuel union on the fuel distributor from the control pressure regulator.
19 The upper surface of the sensor plate must be flush with the edge of the air cone or not more than 0.019 in (0.5 mm) lower. If adjustment is necessary, remove the air cleaner and sensor, and bend the wire bracket.
20 Adjust the idle and CO% after reassembling the sensor plate.

CIS fuel pump delivery rate - testing
21 The fuel pump is located beneath the boot on the right-hand side of the fuel tank. If fuel pressure at the fuel distributor is suspected of being low, first check that the fuel filter located in the engine compartment is not clogged; it should be renewed every 15 000 miles (24 000 km).
22 If the fuel pump does not run, check the fuses and relays for good connections.
23 Temporarily remove the ignition distributor cap, and disconnect the fuel return line in the engine compartment.
24 Hold the fuel line into a calibrated beaker and have an assistant operate the starter motor for exactly 30 seconds. The quantity of fuel delivered must be at least 750 cc. If not, the fuel pump is faulty and should be renewed.

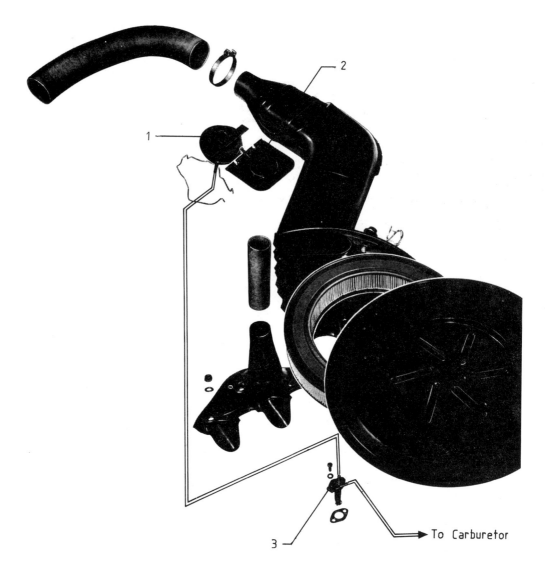

Fig. 13.14. Temperature controlled air cleaner components (Sec. 5)

1   Vacuum unit   *2   Control flap*   *3   Thermo-valve*

CIS fuel injectors - removal, testing and refitting

25 Pull the injectors from the cylinder head leaving the fuel lines connected, and position them in suitable containers for testing.

26 Temporarily remove the distributor cap to prevent the engine starting, then operate the starter for approximately 15 seconds. The spray from each injector must be cone-shaped and even.

27 With the ignition switched off, hold each injector horizontally and check that no drops of fuel form on the tips.

28 If an injector is faulty, disconnect the fuel lines and renew all four injectors.

29 To refit the injectors, first soak the rubber O-rings in fuel then install them and press the injectors firmly into their seats.

CIS cold start valve - removal, testing and refitting

30 Disconnect the wiring plug from the cold start valve, remove the valve, and position it in a suitable container.

31 Disconnect the wiring plugs to the air flow sensor, control

pressure regulator, and the auxiliary air regulator.

32 Connect a wire between the auxiliary air regulator and cold start valve terminals.

33 Switch on the ignition and check that the spray from the cold start valve is cone-shaped and even.

34 With the ignition still on, disconnect the temporary wire and wipe the nozzle dry; if the cold start valve is serviceable, no drops of fuel will form on the nozzle within a period of one minute.

35 If the cold start valve is proved faulty, disconnect the fuel line and renew it.

36 Refitting is a reversal of removal, but always fit a new gasket and fuel line seal.

CIS thermo-time switch - testing

37 With the engine cold (coolant temperature below 35°C (95°F)), disconnect the wire from the thermo-time switch and inter-connect a 12 volt test lamp and leads.

38 Temporarily remove the distributor cap, then operate the

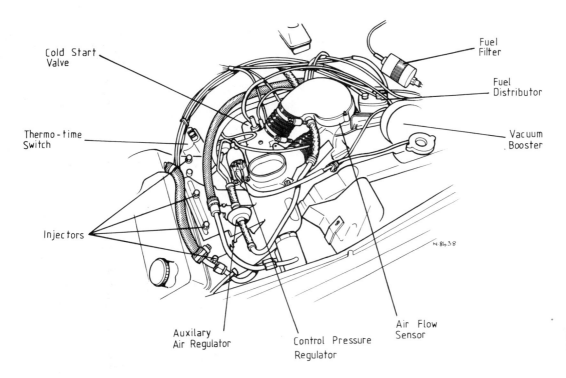

Fig. 13.15. The CIS system (Sec. 5)

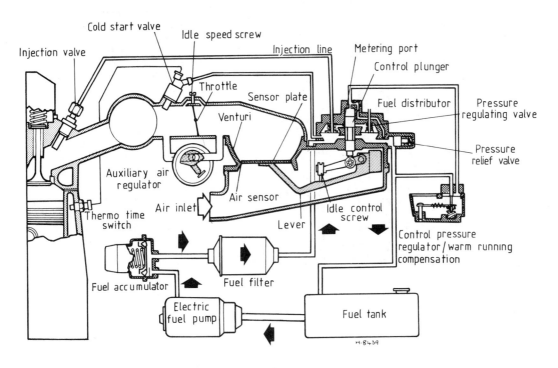

Fig. 13.16. Diagram of the CIS system components (Sec. 5)

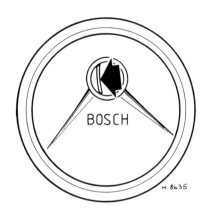

Fig. 13.17. CIS auxiliary air regulator gate valve - arrowed (Sec. 5)

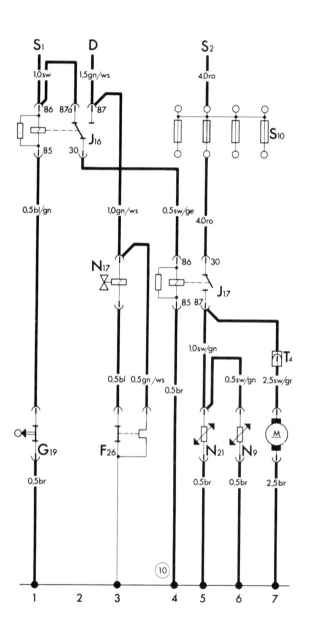

Fig. 13.18. CIS current flow diagram (Sec. 5)

Symbol	Description	Current track
D	Starter terminal 50	2, 3
F26	Thermo-time switch	3
G19	Air flow sensor	1
J16	Current supply relay	1, 2
J17	Fuel pump relay	4, 5
N9	Control pressure regulator	6
N17	Cold start valve	3
N21	Auxiliary air regulator	5
S1	Fuse terminal 15	
S2	Fuse terminal 30	5
S10	Fuse box (auxiliary)	4-7
T4	Wire connector 4 points (behind dashboard)	7
V14	Electric fuel pump	7
10	Ground connection	4

Colour code

ro — red
sw — black
gn — green
ge — yellow
bl — blue
ws — white
br — brown

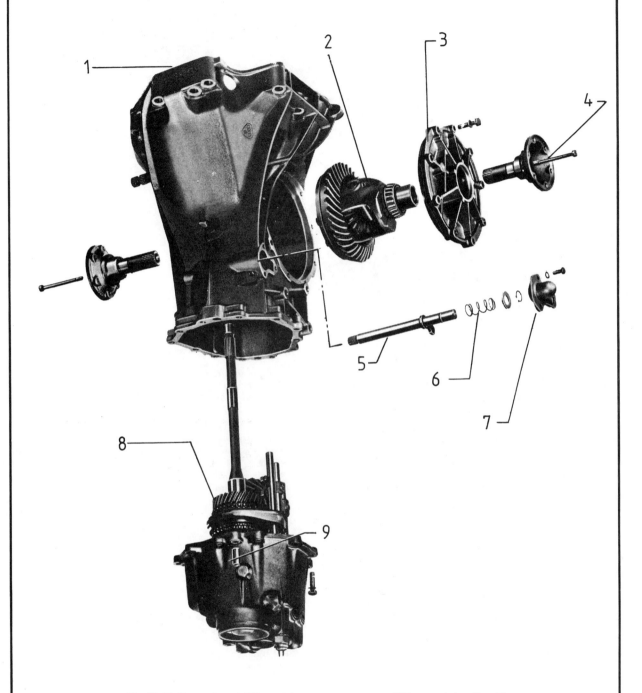

Fig. 13.19. Geartrain and differential components on type 088 transmission (Sec. 7)

1 Main casing	4 Drive flange	6 Spring	8 Geartrain
2 Differential unit	5 Selector shaft	7 Cap	9 Dowel
3 Final drive cover			

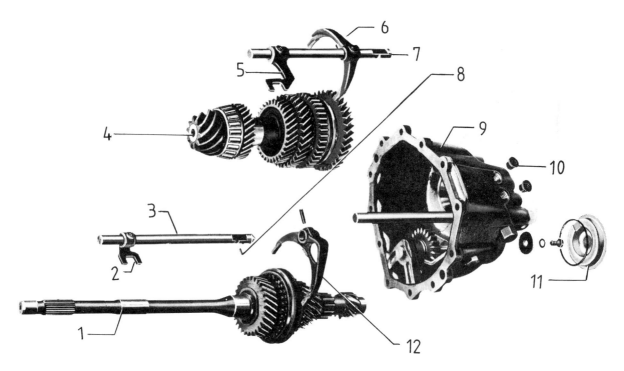

Fig. 13.20. Geartrain components on type 088 transmission (Sec. 7)

1 Mainshaft	4 Pinion shaft	7 1st/2nd shift rod	10 Plug
2 Lever	5 Lever	8 Interlock plunger	11 End cap
3 3rd/4th shift rod	6 1st/2nd selector fork	9 Geartrain housing	12 3rd/4th selector fork

starter. The test lamp should glow for 1 to 8 seconds if the thermo-time switch is serviceable.

CIS auxiliary air regulator - testing

39 Temporarily remove and plug the inlet hose from the auxiliary air regulator.

40 Allow the engine to idle from cold for a period of 5 minutes after which time the internal gate valve must be closed; if not, the regulator is faulty.

Air injection system - description

41 Late Audi 100 USA models are fitted with an air injection system which oxidizes exhaust gases as they leave the combustion chambers, thus reducing the emission of harmful gases from the exhaust system.

42 The system comprises an air pump, check valve, air filter, control valve, injection nozzles, and anti-back fire valve.

---

6 Ignition system

Tachometer - installation

1 When installing a tachometer on a car fitted with the CDI system having a chassis number after 61 054 901, the tachometer terminal 1 must be connected to terminal 7 of the CDI control unit. Prior to this chassis number, terminal 4 must be used.

---

7 Manual transmission

Drive flange and oil seal (type 088) - removal and refitting

1 Remove the driveshaft as described in Section 12, then

place a suitable container beneath the drive flange to accept any spilt oil.

2 Hold the flange stationary and unscrew the retaining bolt.

3 Remove the drive flange and lever out the oil seal.

4 Refitting is a reversal of removal, but fill the seal with grease before driving it into the casing.

Geartrain and differential (type 088) - removal and refitting

5 Remove the transmission and drain the oil.

6 Remove the drive flanges as previously described.

7 Remove the selector shaft cap, circlip, washer and spring.

8 Unscrew the geartrain casing retaining bolts and drive out the location dowels.

9 Push the selector shaft in as far as possible and withdraw the geartrain and casing from the main casing.

10 Mark the final drive cover in relation to the casing, unscrew the retaining bolts, and remove the cover.

11 Withdraw the differential from the casing.

12 Refitting is a reversal of removal, but coat the surfaces of the casings with sealant before assembling them. Note that the magnet on the final drive cover should be at the bottom. Wipe it clean from swarf. Finally, refill the transmission with oil.

Geartrain (type 088) - dismantling and reassembling

13 With the geartrain removed as previously described, hold the mainshaft in a soft jawed vice.

14 Prise out the end cap and seal, and unscrew the retaining bolt.

15 Unscrew the shift rod stop screws.

16 Using a suitable punch, drive out the 3rd/4th gear fork retaining roll pin while supporting the shift rod, then slide out the rod leaving the fork in position.

17 Using a bearing extractor, press the mainshaft through the bearing.

Fig. 13.21. Removing the 3rd/4th selector fork roll pin (Sec. 7)

18 Remove the mainshaft, selector rod and fork, and swing the pinion shaft so that it clears the reverse gear.
19 Reassembly is a reversal of dismantling, but the following additional points should be noted:-

   (a) Make sure that the selector shaft interlock plungers are located as shown in Fig.13.22
   (b) Pull the mainshaft into the bearing using an M8 bolt, nut and washer
   (c) Fit new washers on the plugs
   (d) Make sure that the recess in the end cap points towards the oil drilling in the housing

Transmission main housing (type 088) - overhaul
20 The drive flange, selector shaft, and mainshaft oil seals must be renewed at every major overhaul. To remove them, lever them out with a screwdriver. Make sure that they are refitted the correct way round.
21 If the mainshaft bush is worn, remove it with a suitable drift. When installing a new bush, drive it in to a depth of 0.45 in (11.5 mm) from the casing surface.
22 To remove the pinion bearing outer race, use a slide hammer and a suitable adaptor. Before installing a new race, heat the casing locally in boiling water, fit the race, and allow 1 to 2 minutes for the casing to contract onto the race.
23 The mainshaft needle roller bearing is also removed with a slide hammer and adaptor. When installing it, the lettering on the bearing must face out of the open end of the casing and the bearing must be flush with the casing surface.
24 To remove the differential bearing outer races a suitable extractor will be required, but since a dial gauge and special tools are required to determine the correct shims to provide the necessary pre-load, renewal of these components is best left to the local Audi garage.

Geartrain casing (type 088) - overhaul
25 Renewal of the pinion bearing outer race is not recommended for the home mechanic as special instruments are required to determine the correct pre-load.
26 To remove the mainshaft bearing, first extract the circlip then using a suitable drift, drive the bearing from the casing. When refitting the bearing, make sure that the closed side is towards the casing.
27 After reassembling the geartrain casing components, the reverse relay lever must be adjusted in the following manner. First, screw in the adjustment bolt until it just touches the

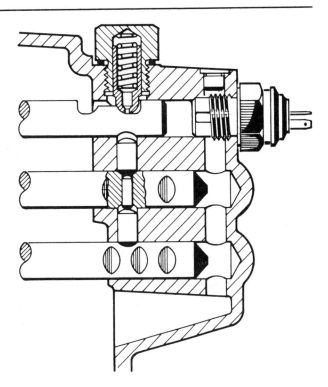

Fig. 13.22. Cross sectional view of the interlock plungers on the type 088 transmission (Sec. 7)

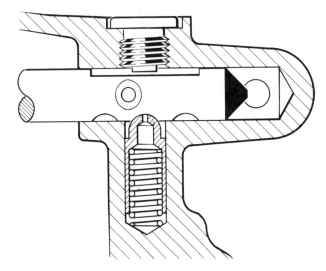

Fig. 13.23. Cross sectional view of the detent plunger on the type 088 transmission (Sec. 7)

relay lever. With the lever pressed against the bolt, turn the bolt until the threads just engage, now tighten the bolt to 25.3 lbf ft (3.5 kgf m).

Mainshaft (type 088) - dismantling and reassembly
28 Extract the circlip from the mainshaft.
29 Remove the thrust washer, 4th speed gear, 4th gear needle roller cage, 4th speed synchro ring, and the 3rd/4th synchro hub retaining circlip.

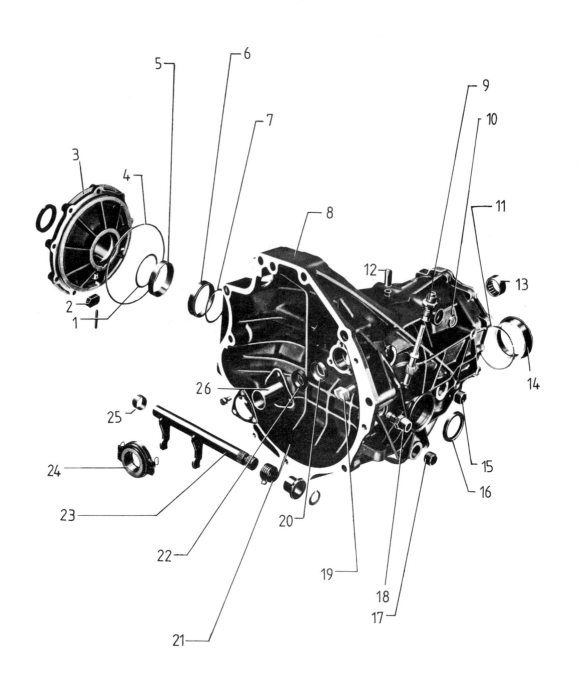

Fig. 13.24. Main housing components on type 088 transmission (Sec. 7)

1 Shim	7 Shim	14 Pinion bearing outer
2 Magnet	8 Main housing	race
3 Cover	9 Speedo drive gear	15 Filler plug
4 O-ring	10 Sealing ring	16 Drive flange oil
5 Differential bearing outer	11 Shim	seal
race	12 Breather	17 Drain plug
6 Differential bearing outer	13 Main shaft needle	18 TDC sensor
race	bearing	19 Stop

20 Bush
21 Return spring
22 Main shaft seal
23 Clutch release shaft
24 Release bearing
25 Bush
26 Sleeve

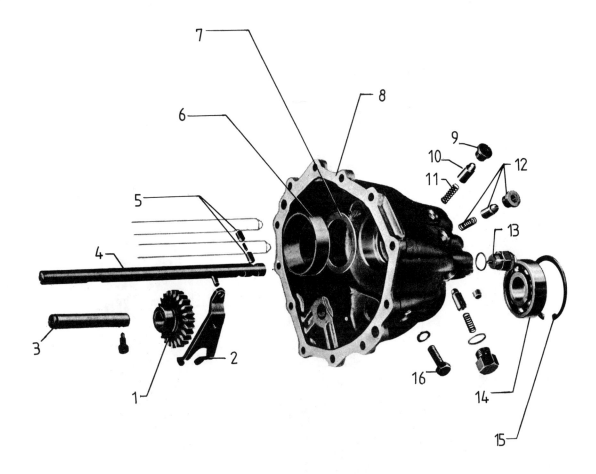

Fig. 13.25. Geartrain casing components on type 088 transmission (Sec. 7)

1	Reverse gear	6	Pinion shaft bearing
2	Relay lever		outer race
3	Reverse gear shaft	7	Shim
4	Reverse selector rod	8	Casing
5	Interlock plungers	9	Plug

10	Bush
11	Spring
12	Detent
13	Reverse light switch
14	Bearing

15	Circlip
16	Relay lever bolt

30 Support the 3rd speed gear and press the mainshaft through it. Keep the synchro ring with the 3rd speed gear for correct reassembly. Remove the needle bearing cage from the mainshaft.
31 Clean all component parts and examine them for deterioration and damage. To check the synchro rings for wear, check the gap between the engagement dogs as shown in Fig.13.27. If the gap is less than the minimum wear limit, the rings must be renewed. If it is found necessary to dismantle the synchro hub, make sure that the hub and sleeve are first marked in relation to each other to ensure correct reassembly. The sliding key springs must be fitted as shown in Fig.13.28 with the angled ends in the hollow key. The springs must run in opposite directions when both sides of the synchro unit are compared and their angled ends must not engage in the same keys.
32 Reassembly of the mainshaft is a reversal of dismantling, but the following additional points should be noted:-

(a) The annular groove in the synchro hub must face the 4th speed gear
(b) The slots in the synchro rings must engage with the sliding keys of the synchro unit

(c) The synchro hub retaining circlip must be selected to give an endfloat of between 0 and 0.002 in (0 and 0.05 mm)
(d) The running clearance between 2nd and 3rd speed gears must be between 0.004 and 0.014 in (0.1 and 0.35 mm). If necessary, the circlip selected in (c) must be changed
(e) The endfloat of the 4th speed gear must be between 0.008 and 0.014 in (0.20 and 0.35 mm) when measured with a feeler gauge. If necessary, the retaining circlip must be selected to give the correct endfloat

Pinion shaft (type 088) - dismantling and reassembly
33 Should any component part of the pinion shaft require renewal, the bearing pre-load will require adjusting and this work is best entrusted to an Audi garage having the necessary equipment. However, if the main components are serviceable, as would be the case in renewal of the synchro rings, proceed as follows.
34 Mount the shaft in a soft jawed vice and unscrew the end bolt.
35 Remove the washer, then support the 1st speed gear and press the shaft through.

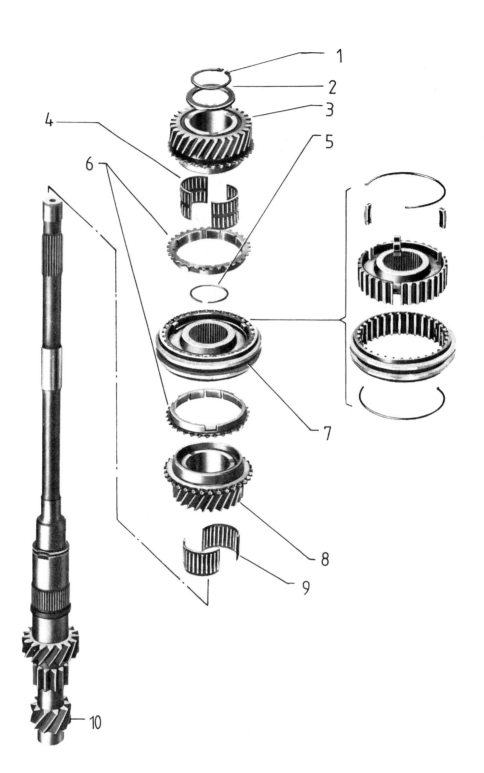

Fig. 13.26. Mainshaft components on type 088 transmission (Sec. 7)

1	Circlip	4	Needle bearing	7	3rd/4th synchro	9	Needle bearing
2	Thrust washer	5	Circlip		unit	10	Mainshaft
3	4th speed gear	6	3rd/4th synchro rings	8	3rd speed gear		

Fig. 13.27. Synchro ring wear. For dimension (a) see text. (Sec. 7)

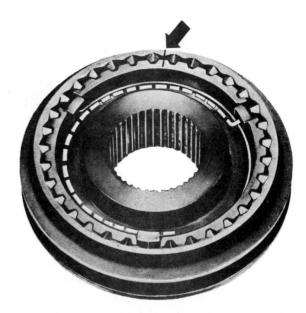

Fig. 13.28. Synchro unit spring location and alignment marks - arrowed (Sec. 7)

Fig. 13.29. Synchro unit annular groove (arrowed) (Sec. 7)

Fig. 13.30. Checking clearance between 2nd and 3rd speed gears (Sec. 7)

36 Remove the 1st gear needle bearing, 1st gear synchro ring, and 1st/2nd synchro hub retaining circlip.

37 Support the 2nd speed gear and press the shaft through.

38 Remove the 2nd gear needle bearing and the 3rd speed gear retaining circlip.

39 Press off the 3rd speed gear.

40 Remove the 4th speed gear retaining circlip, then press off the 4th speed gear followed by the pinion bearing.

41 Clean all component parts and examine them for deterioration and damage. Check the synchro rings as described in paragraph 31. Dismantling and reassembly of the synchro unit is identical to that described in paragraph 31.

42 Reassembly of the pinion shaft is a reversal of dismantling, but the following additional points should be noted:-

(a) Since the pinion is matched to the crownwheel, it cannot be renewed separately

(b) Heat the 4th speed gear to approximately 120°C (248°F) before pressing it onto the pinion shaft with the shoulder towards the 3rd speed gear

(c) The 4th speed gear endfloat must be between 0.0 and 0.001 in (0.0 and 0.02 mm). If necessary, select a circlip to give the correct clearance

(d) Heat the 3rd speed gear to approximately 120°C (248°F) before pressing it onto the pinion shaft with the larger shoulder towards the 2nd speed gear

(e) The 3rd speed gear endfloat must be between 0.0 and

Fig. 13.31. Checking the 4th speed gear endfloat on type 088 transmission (Sec. 7)

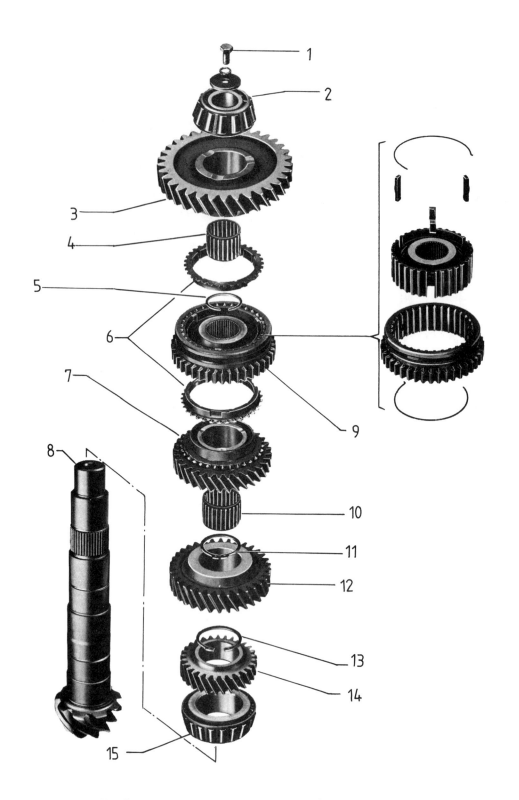

Fig. 13.32. Pinion shaft components on type 088 transmission (Sec. 7)

1	Bolt	5	Circlip	9	1st/2nd synchro unit	13	Circlip
2	Bearing inner race	6	1st/2nd synchro rings	10	Needle bearing	14	4th speed gear
3	1st speed gear	7	2nd speed gear	11	Circlip	15	Bearing inner race
4	Needle bearing	8	Pinion shaft	12	3rd speed gear		

0.002 in (0.0 and 0.04 mm). If necessary, select a circlip to give the correct clearance
(f) The teeth on the synchro unit must face the 2nd speed gear
(g) The slots in the synchro rings must engage with the sliding keys of the synchro unit
(h) The synchro hub retaining circlip must be selected to give an endfloat of between 0.0 and 0.002 in (0.0 and 0.04 mm)
(i) The 1st speed gear endfloat must be between 0.004 and 0.016 in (0.10 and 0.40 mm). If necessary, the circlip selected in (h) must be changed
(j) Tighten the end bolt to 18.1 lbf ft (2.5 kgf m)

Gearshift linkage (type 088) - adjustment

43 Slacken the clamp bolt in the central linkage frame.
44 Slacken the clamp bolt on the gearbox end of the selector lever.
45 With the selector shaft in neutral, the distance (a) in Fig. 13.33 must be 3.307 in (84 mm). If not, reposition the lever.
46 With the selector lever in neutral and in the 1st-2nd gear plane, the distance (b) in Fig.13.34 must be 0.236 in (6.0 mm) with the shift rod disconnected.
47 Refit the shift rod and loosen the locknuts on the cross bar. Turn the adjusting nut until the base of the shift rod is parallel with the upper face of the selector lever, then tighten the nuts.
48 With the selector lever in neutral, the distance (c) in Fig. 13.35 must be 1.614 in (41.0 mm). When the gear lever is set to this position, tighten the clamp bolt in the central linkage frame.
49 After adjusting the linkage, lubricate all the friction surfaces with a little grease.

8 Automatic transmission

Gearshift mechanism - description and adjustment

1 1975 Audi 100 models onwards are fitted with a modified gearshift as shown in Fig.13.37.
2 To adjust the gearshift, first remove the console and move the selector lever to position 'P'.
3 Loosen the adjustment nut ('a' in Fig.13.38) and pull the selector cable to the rear with a pair of grips, applying a tension of approximately 33 lbf (15 kg). Attach a spring balance to check this.
4 Tighten the nut and check that the selector lever functions correctly.

Automatic transmission - installation

5 It is important that the pump shaft remains in the oil pump when assembling the transmission to the engine, otherwise the drive dog will be broken.
6 To check that the shaft is fully engaged, use a straight edge across the bellhousing and check that the dimension 'a' Fig. 13.39 is approximately 0.4 in (10.0 mm).

Accelerator linkage – description and adjustment

7   Models having a chassis number from 61 000 051 on are fitted with a modified accelerator linkage as shown in Fig. 13.40.
8 To adjust the linkage, first slacken the locknut (a) and move the throttle valve (h) to the idle position.
9 Remove the clip (d) and detach the rod (b) from the lever (c).
10 Rotate the rod adjustment until rod (b) aligns with the hole in the lever (c), then refit the clip (d).
11 To check the adjustment, turn the lever (c) fully clockwise and make sure that the kickdown resistance can be felt.
12 The accelerator cable (f) must now be adjusted. Slacken the screw (g) and, with the accelerator pedal in the idle position, take up any slack in the cable then tighten the screw.
13 After adjusting the cable check that the throttle valve (h) operates fully from idle to full throttle, and that the full

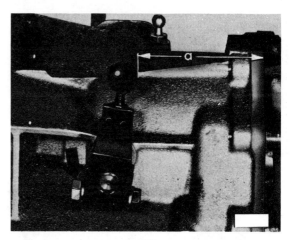

Fig. 13.33. Selector lever setting. For dimension (a) see text (Sec. 7)

A   Splined shaft

Fig. 13.34. Selector lever setting. For dimension (b) see text. (Sec. 7)

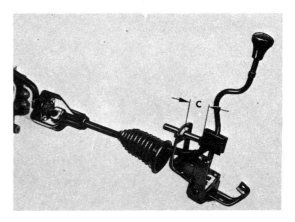

Fig. 13.35. Selector lever setting. For dimension (c) see text. (Sec. 7)

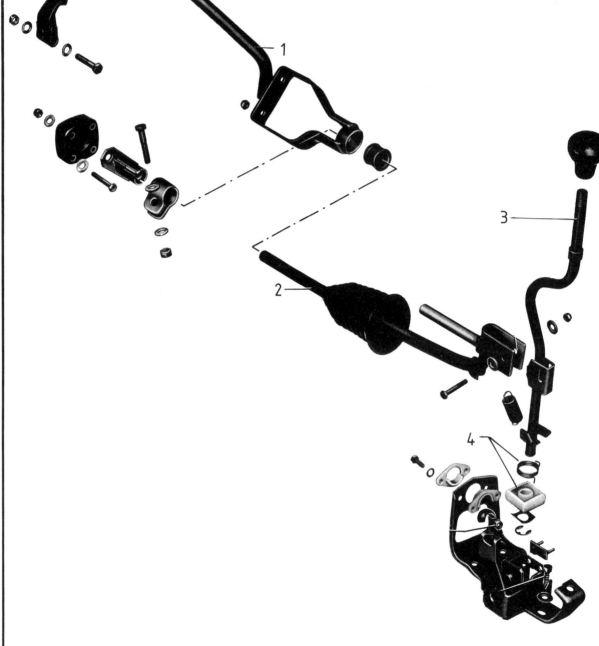

Fig. 13.36. Gearshift linkage components on type 088 transmission (Sec. 7)

| 1 | Front shift rod | 2 | Rear shift rod | 3 | Gear lever | 4 | Friction pad and spring |

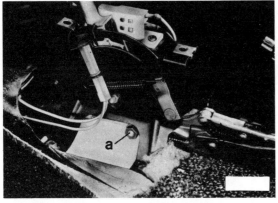

Fig. 13.38. Automatic transmission gearshift cable adjustment nut (a) location (Sec. 8)

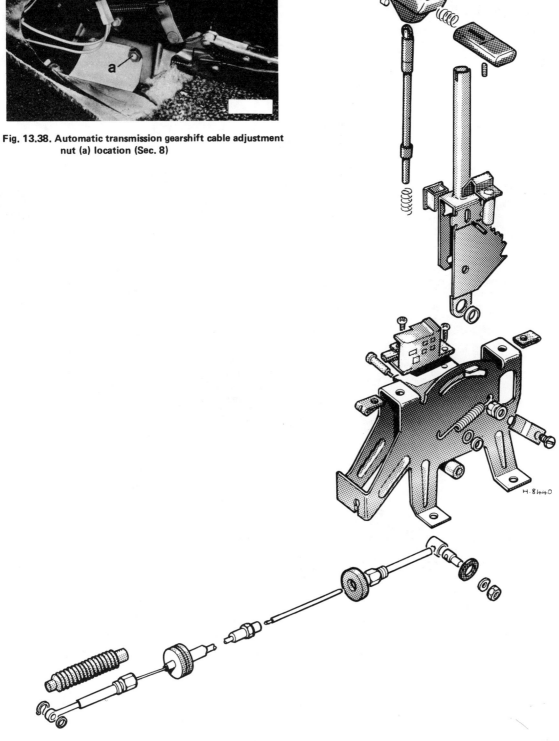

Fig. 13.37. Gearshift mechanism fitted to 1975 automatic transmission models onwards (Sec. 8)

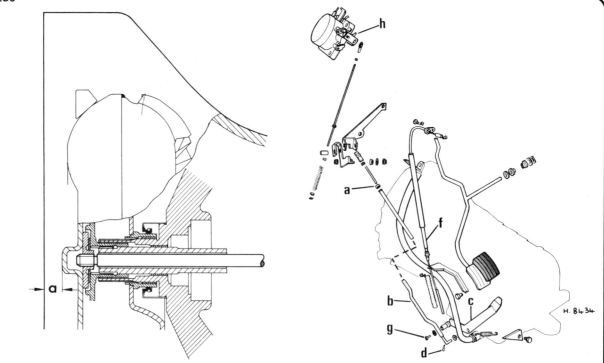

Fig. 13.39. Torque converter to bellhousing dimension (a) when checking for oil pump shaft engagement (Sec. 8)

Fig. 13.40 Accelerator linkage fitted to later models. For key see text (Sec. 8)

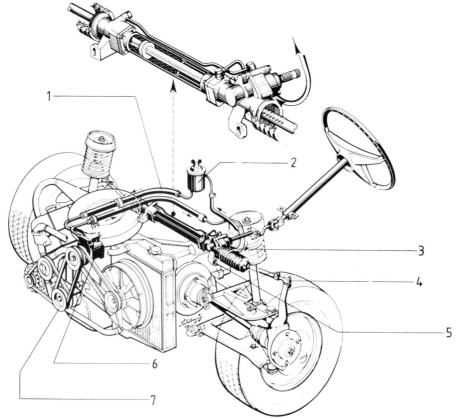

Fig. 13.41. Power steering layout (Sec. 9)

1 Suction line	3 Steering gear	5 Mounting	7 Two part
2 Oil reservoir	4 Track rod end	6 High pressure pump	pulley

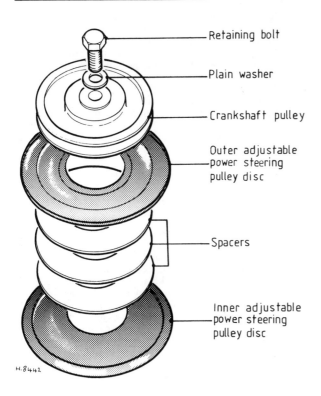

Fig. 13.42. Power steering pulley components (Sec. 9)

accelerator pedal movement is between 2.95 and 3.15 in (75 and 80 mm).

9 Steering

Power assisted steering - description
1 Power assisted steering may be fitted as an optional extra on models manufactured after 1974. The system comprises a high pressure oscillating pump, belt driven from the crankshaft, a steering gear incorporating a rotary piston valve, and an oil reservoir.

Power assisted steering - checking the oil level
2 With the engine idling, remove the reservoir lid and check that the oil is up to the level mark. If necessary, top it up with the specified fluid.
3 If the system has been drained for any reason, first fill the reservoir and run the engine briefly until the level reaches the bottom of the reservoir. Repeat this procedure until the system is full, then turn the steering wheel quickly from one lock to the other; this action will force any trapped air out of the steering gear. Top-up the system again if necessary.

Power steering gear - removal and refitting
4 Disconnect the hydraulic hose beneath the reservoir and drain the fluid into a suitable container, at the same time move the steering wheel from lock to lock.
5 Where inboard front brake discs are fitted, cover them with polythene sheeting to prevent contamination by the steering fluid.
6 Disconnect the hoses from the steering gear and plug the open ends to prevent ingress of dirt.
7 Separate the track rod ends from the steering knuckles.

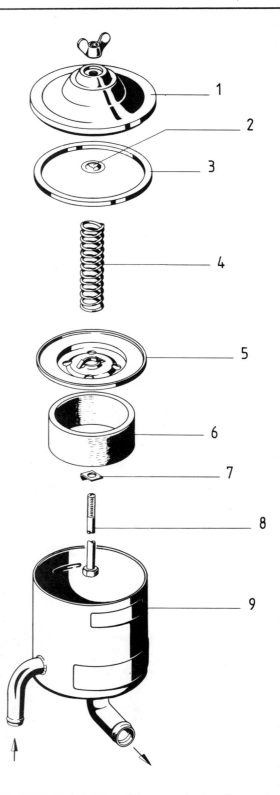

Fig. 13.43. Exploded view of the power steering oil reservoir (Sec. 9)

1	Lid	6	Filter
2	Lockwasher	7	Retainer
3	Seal	8	Bolt
4	Spring	9	Reservoir
5	Cover		

Fig. 13.44. Diagram of the diagonal circuit braking system (Sec. 10)

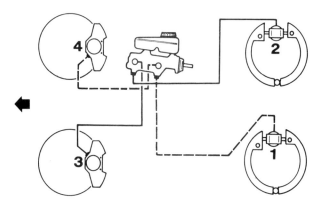

Fig. 13.45. Sequence for bleeding the diagonal circuit braking system - arrow indicates front of vehicle (Sec. 10)

8 Detach the steering column from the steering gear.
9 Where necessary on USA models, remove the brake vacuum servo unit and emission control hoses.
10 Where air conditioning is fitted, remove the evaporator and place on one side; do not, however, disconnect the hoses.
11 Disconnect the accelerator linkage, then detach the steering gear from the crossmember.
12 On Audi 100 USA models manufactured before 1974 it will be necessary to disconnect the brake hoses from the transmission, remove the anti-roll bar, and lower the engine in order to remove the steering gear.
13 Move the steering gear into the right-hand side wheel arch and then lift it out of the engine compartment.
14 Refitting is a reversal of removal, but it will be necessary to bleed the power steering system as described earlier, and, where the brake hoses have been disconnected, bleed the brake hydraulic system.

Power steering pump drivebelt - adjusting tension
15 Remove the engine front apron.
16 Check the drive belt play which should be approximately 0.5 in (13 mm) under firm thumb pressure half way between the pump pulley and the crankshaft pulley. If not, the quantity of spacers on the crankshaft pulley must be varied.
17 Unscrew the retaining bolt and remove the two part pulley together with the spacers. If the tension was insufficient, remove one spacer and refit it in front of the outer pulley, and vice versa. If the crankshaft pulley bolt is hard to remove, jam the starter ring gear to prevent the crankshaft turning.
18 Reassemble the pulley, at the same time turn the engine in alternate directions to ensure that the belt seats correctly. Finally tighten the pulley retaining bolt.

Power steering filter - renewal
19 The filter in the oil reservoir should be renewed periodically. Noisy steering operation may be caused by a clogged filter.
20 To remove the filter, remove the reservoir lid and seal followed by the lockwasher, spring and filter cover. The filter can now be removed.
21 Refitting is a reversal of removal, but top-up the oil level as necessary.

10 Braking system

Diagonal circuit braking system - description
1 1975 models are equipped with a diagonal hydraulic circuit

Fig. 13.46. Outboard front brake disc and caliper (Sec. 10)

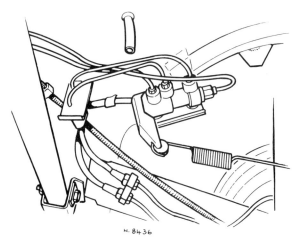

Fig. 13.47. Rear brake pressure regulator location - 1975 models on (Sec. 10)

Fig. 13.48. Coupe S modified number plate lights (Sec. 11)

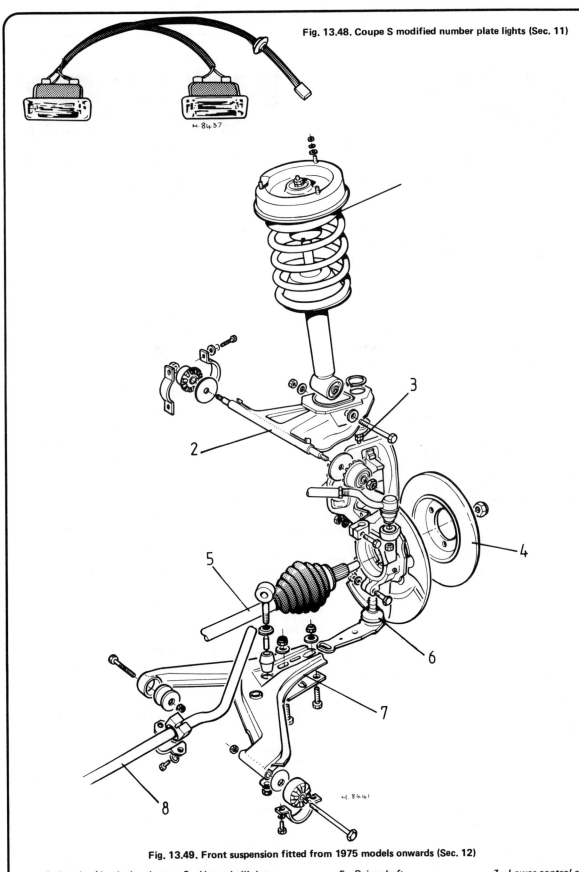

H.8437

H.8441

Fig. 13.49. Front suspension fitted from 1975 models onwards (Sec. 12)

1	Coil spring/shock absorber assembly	3	Upper balljoint	5	Drive shaft	7	Lower control arm
2	Upper control arm	4	Brake disc	6	Lower balljoint	8	Anti-roll bar

Fig. 13.50. Using tool no. 3007 'C' (arrowed) to set the front suspension upper control arm bush retainers '9' (Sec. 12)

Fig. 13.51. Front suspension upper mounting nut location - arrowed (Sec. 12)

connected to a tandem master cylinder. The system operates in a similar manner to the system described in Chapter 9, but if one circuit fails, one front and one rear brake will still be operative.

Diagonal circuit braking system - bleeding
2   The brake hydraulic system is bled in the same manner as described in Chapter 8, but the sequence is different. Refer to Fig.13.45 and note that the left-hand side rear wheel cylinder must be bled first, followed by the right-hand side rear wheel cylinder, left-hand side front caliper, and right-hand side front caliper.

Outboard front brake discs - description
3   The outboard front brake system fitted to 1975 models onwards incorporates single piston floating calipers. Removal and refitting the disc pads and calipers is similar to the procedure described in Chapter 9, although the caliper overhaul is different.

Rear brake pressure regulator - description
4   The pressure regulator fitted to models equipped with the diagonal hydraulic system is attached to the rear underframe and is controlled by a spring connected to the rear axle. The amount of pressure allowed through the regulator to the rear brakes depends on the weight being carried by the rear suspension, and therefore the position of the rear axle.
5   If the regulator develops a fault, it should be checked by an Audi garage equipped with the special spring tensioners and pressure gauges necessary.
6   The regulator retains a certain amount of pressure in the rear hydraulic fluid lines and therefore, before adjusting the rear brakes, the regulator lever should be pressed towards the rear axle as far as possible.

11 Electrical system

Headlight washers - fluid replenishment
1   As from chassis number 51 009 366, the quantity of headlight cleaner fluid in the reservoir is 4.4 Imp pt (2.5 litres/5.28 US pt). The solution of water and antifreeze must be mixed at a ratio of 4 to 1.

Number plate lights - bulb renewal
2   As from chassis number 51 002 943 the number plate lights are retained in the rear bumper by spring clips on Coupe S models only.
3   The light units are only obtainable in pairs owing to the integral wiring.

12 Front and rear axles

Front suspension - description
1   1975 Audi 100 models onwards are equipped with outboard brakes as shown in Fig.13.49. The following procedures are different from those given in Chapter 11.

Suspension upper control arm - removal and refitting
2   Jack-up the front of the car and support it on axle-stands.
3   Unscrew and remove the upper balljoint clamp bolt, and the coil spring/shock absorber mounting bolt. Support the suspension on a trolley jack.
4   Unscrew the bolts and remove the pivot bush retaining clamps. The upper control arm can now be lifted away from the car.
5   With the control arm removed, the upper balljoint can be pressed out after removing the retaining circlip.
6   Refitting is a reversal of removal, but it will be necessary to obtain the alignment gauge (tool no. 3007) in order to set the bush retainers in their correct position. The gauge is fitted over the lower pivot bolts (with nuts removed) and the bush retainers moved as necessary.

Suspension lower control arm - removal and refitting
7   Jack-up the front of the car and support it on axle-stands.
8   Unscrew and remove the lower balljoint clamp bolt.
9   Detach the anti-roll bar from the lower control arm.
10 Unscrew the rear pivot bush retaining clamp bolts and the brake line guard plate retaining bolt.
11 Unscrew and remove the front pivot bolt, and withdraw the lower control arm from the car.
12 With the lower control arm removed, the front flexible bearing can be pressed from its location and a new bearing fitted. Dip the bearing in soapy water to facilitate installation.

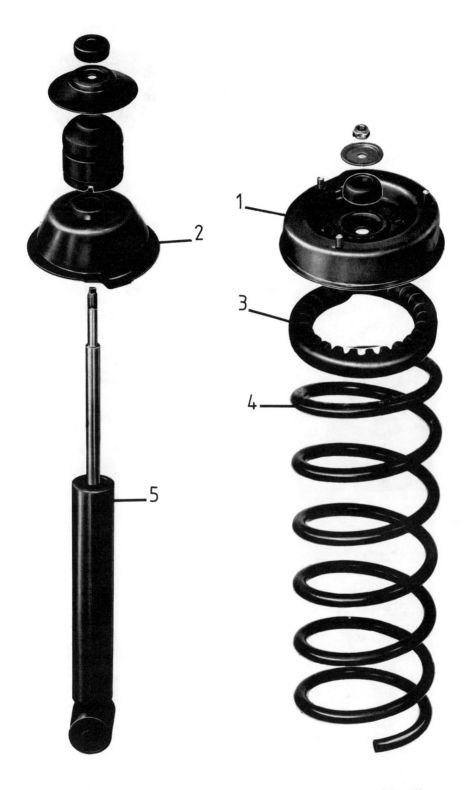

Fig. 13.52. Front suspension coil spring and shock absorber components (Sec. 12)

1 Upper seat	3 Rubber bearing	4 Coil spring	5 Shock absorber
2 Lower seat			

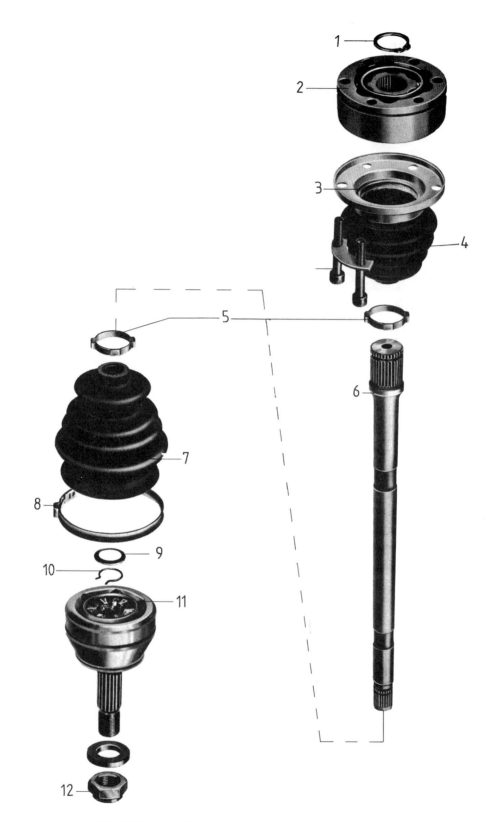

Fig. 13.53. Driveshaft components - 1975 models onwards (Sec. 12)

1 Circlip	4 Bellows	7 Bellows	10 Circlip
2 Inner joint	5 Clamp	8 Clamp	11 Outer joint
3 Cap	6 Shaft	9 Washer	12 Axle nut

Fig. 13.54. Driveshaft outer joint retaining circlip location 'A', 'B' indicates joint outer end (Sec. 12)

Fig. 13.55. Checking the rear wheel bearing adjustment with a screwdriver (Sec. 12)

13 Refitting is a reversal of removal, but make sure that the rear flexible bearing is located correctly between the tabs of the retaining clamp.

Front suspension anti-roll bar - removal and refitting
14 Jack-up the front of the car and support it on axle-stands. Additionally, support the weight of the suspension beneath both balljoints.
15 Unscrew the retaining nuts from the centre of each lower control arm and recover the washers.
16 Unscrew the retaining bolts and detach the bush clamps from the underframe.
17 Withdraw the anti-roll bar from the car noting the location of the bush, sleeve, and washer on the lower control arm.
18 Examine the bushes for deterioration and damage, and renew them if necessary.
19 Refitting is a reversal of removal, but tighten the clamp bolts with the full weight of the car on the suspension.

Front coil spring - removal and refitting
20 Jack-up the front of the car and support it on axle-stands. Support the weight of the suspension with a trolley jack.
21 Unscrew and remove the upper mounting nuts from inside the engine compartment.
22 Unscrew and remove the shock absorber lower mounting bolt, then lower the suspension on the trolley jack.
23 Swivel the assembly from under the car and withdraw it.
24 A coil spring compressor will be required in order to separate the coil spring from the shock absorber. Note the location of the various components as shown in Fig.13.52.
25 Refitting is a reversal of removal, but dust the rubber seating with talcum powder to prevent any subsequent operational noise. Tighten the spring retaining nut to 18 lbf in (2.5 kgf m).

Driveshaft - removal, overhaul and refitting
26 Jack-up the front of the car and support it on axle-stands. Remove the roadwheel.
27 Unscrew and remove the axle nut and washer while an assistant depresses the footbrake pedal. If the nut is very tight, refit the roadwheel and lower the car with the handbrake applied.
28 Using a hexagon key, unscrew the bolts retaining the driveshaft to the transmission drive flange and pull away the driveshaft.
29 Turn the steering to full lock then extract the driveshaft from the steering knuckle; use an extractor if necessary.
30 To dismantle the driveshaft, first remove the circlip from the inner joint.

31 Using a small punch, drive the metal cap from the joint. Remove the clamp and slide the rubber bellows away from the joint.
32 Support the joint hub and press the driveshaft through it.
33 Remove the rubber bellows from the driveshaft.
34 Remove the clamps and slide the rubber bellows from the outer joint.
35 Using circlip pliers, open the joint retaining circlip while tapping the outer end of the driveshaft with a wooden or plastic mallet.
36 Mount the driveshaft in a vice and drive the outer joint off the splines. Remove the bellows.
37 Wash all the component parts in paraffin and examine them for deterioration and damage. The joints and shaft can be renewed separately.
38 Reassembly and refitting is a reversal of dismantling and removal, but the following additional points should be noted:-

(a) Install the inner joint with the groove facing away from the driveshaft
(b) Use only the special grease available in 90 gram tubes to lubricate the joints, working the grease well into the joints. Use one tube for each joint
(c) Tighten the inner flange bolts to 28.9 lbf ft (4.0 kgf m), and the axle nut to 253 lbf ft (35 kgf m)

Rear wheel bearings - adjustment
39 Jack-up the rear of the car and remove the wheel cap (if fitted) and hub grease cap.
40 Remove the split pin and castle locknut.
41 With the handbrake fully released, tighten the bearing nut while turning the wheel, then loosen it.
42 Tighten the nut again until the washer behind it can just be rotated with the tip of a screwdriver without exerting any leverage.
43 Fit the castle locknut, split pin and grease cap and lower the car to the ground.

Rear suspension - description
44 Audi 100 models built from 1974 are fitted with coil springs mounted on the rear shock absorbers in place of torsion bars. The component parts are shown in Fig.13.56, but the protective sleeve was not fitted to early models.
45 When installing the rear upper mounting rubbers, dust them with talcum powder to prevent any operational noises such as squeaking.
46 The rear coil springs and shock absorbers must only be renewed in pairs.

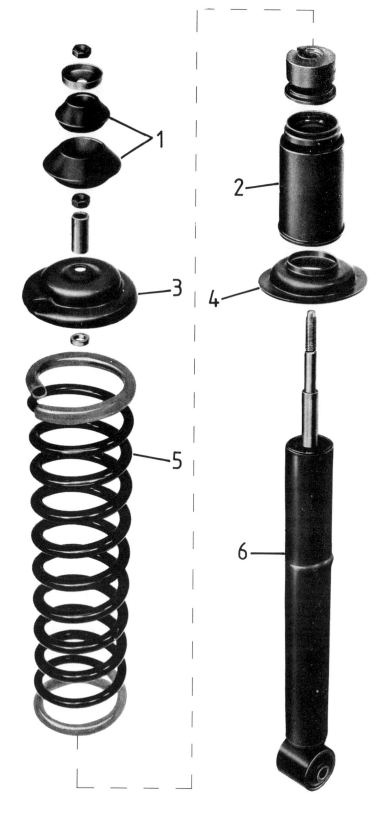

Fig. 13.56. Rear suspension components (Sec. 12)

| 1 Mounting rubbers | 3 Upper seat | 4 Lower seat | 5 Coil spring |
| 2 Protection sleeve | | | 6 Shock absorber |

Fig. 13.57. Key to wiring diagram for 1975 UK models

Designation		In current path	Designation		In current path
A	Battery	7	T3c	Plug connector, three-pole, engine compartment, left	
B	Starter	3	T3d	Plug connector, three-pole, behind instrument panel	
C	Alternator	2			
C1	Voltage regulator	1	T3e	Plug connector, three-pole, behind instrument panel	
D	Ignition/starter switch	4			
E2	Turn signal switch	41	T3f	Plug connector, three-pole, behind instrument panel	
E3	Hazard light switch	37			
E13	Heater switch	11	T4	Plug connector, four-pole, behind instrument panel	
E15	Rear window defogger switch	14			
F1	Oil pressure switch	28	T7	Plug connector, seven-pole, in engine compartment near ignition coil	
G	Fuel level transmitter	30			
G1	Fuel gauge	30	T15	Plug connector, fifteen-pole, for instrument panel insert	
G2	Coolant temperature transmitter	29			
G3	Coolant temperature gauge	29	T20	Central socket	44
G5	Tachometer	34	Y	Clock	16
G7	TDC sensor	10	Z1	Rear window defogger	13
J1	Turn signal/hazard light flasher unit	42	E	Windshield wiper switch	56
J6	Voltage stabilizer	32	E1	Light switch	48
J9	Rear window defogger relay	13	E4	Headlight dip switch and headlight flasher switch	54
J33	Low beam and high beam relay	20			
K1	High beam indicator light	31	E20	Instrument light control/instrument panel insert	48
K2	Alternator charge indicator light	2			
K3	Oil pressure indicator light	28	F	Brake light switch	60
K5	Turn signal indicator light	33	F2	Front left door contact switch	52
K6	Hazard light indicator light	35	F3	Front right door contact switch	53
K10	Rear window defogger indicator light	16	F	Reversing light switch	65
L1	Low beam headlight bulb, left	22	F10	Rear left door contact switch	51
L2	Low beam headlight bulb, right	20	F11	Rear right door contact switch	54
L8	Clock light bulb	18	H	Horn control	61
L13	High beam headlight bulb, left	23	H1	Horn	62
L14	High beam headlight bulb, right	21	H2	Horn	63
L19	Gearshift diagram light bulb	18	J4	Horn relay	61
L21	Heater control light bulb	42	J25	Main light relay	48
L28	Cigar lighter light bulb	19	J31	Wipe/wash and intermittent wiper relay	57
M1	Overnight light bulb, left	24			
M2	Tail light bulb, right	27	L10	Instrument panel light bulb	48
M3	Overnight light bulb, right	26	M9	Left brake light bulb	60
M4	Tail light bulb, left	25	M10	Right brake light bulb	59
M5	Front turn signal bulb, left	37	M16	Left reversing light bulb	65
M6	Rear turn signal bulb, left	38	M17	Right reversing light bulb	64
M7	Front turn signal bulb, right	39	N3	Solenoid cut-off valve	66
M8	Rear turn signal bulb, right	40	S	Fuses in fusebox	
N	Ignition coil	9	T1c	Plug connector, single pole, cigar lighter connection behind instrument panel	
N6	Series resistance	8			
O	Distributor	9			
P	Spark plug connector	9	T1i	Plug connector, single-pole, behind instrument panel	
Q	Spark plugs	9			
S	Fuses in fuse box		T2a	Plug connector, two-pole, on trunk lid, left	
T1a	Plug connector, single pole, engine compartment, left				
			T2b	Plug connector, two-pole, behind instrument panel	
T1b	Plug connector, single pole, behind instrument panel				
			T3f	Plug connector, three-pole, behind instrument panel	
T1c	Plug connector, single pole, cigar lighter connection behind instrument panel				
			T3e	Plug connector, three-pole, behind instrument panel	
T1d	Plug connector, single pole, radio connection behind console				
			T4	Plug connector, ten-pole, fog light connection behind instrument panel	
T1e	Plug connector, single pole, twin circuit brake indicator light connection behind console				
			T7	Plug connector, eight-pole, behind instrument panel	
T1f	Plug connector, single pole, twin circuit brake indicator light connection behind console		T15	Plug connector, fifteen-pole for instrument panel insert	
			T20	Central socket	44
T1g	Plug connector, single pole, behind instrument panel		V	Windshield wiper motor	56
			V5	Windshield washer pump	59
T3	Plug connector, three-pole, engine compartment, right		W6	Glove compartment light	49
			W7	Interior light	50
T3a	Plug connector, three-pole, engine compartment, left		X	License plate light	45
T3b	Plug connector, three-pole, engine compartment, right				

The circles mark the connections of the test circuit leads which go directly to the connections of the central socket (T20). The numbers in the circles correspond with the connections in the central socket.

Key to additional current flow diagram for automatic transmission

Designation		In current path	Designation		In current path
B	Starter	2	T1l	Plug connector, single-pole, behind instrument panel	
D	Ignition/starter switch	2			
E17	Starter cut-out and reversing light switch	2	T1m	Plug connector, single-pole, main harness/terminal 15a connection, behind instrument panel	
F8	Kickdown switch	3			
F21	Brake pressure balance switch 1	7	T1n	Plug connector, single-pole, behind instrument panel	
F22	Brake pressure balance switch 2	6			
K20	Brake pressure balance indicator light	9	T1o	Plug connector, single-pole, behind instrument panel	
L19	Gear selector light bulb	3			
M9	Left brake light bulb	6	T1p	Plug connector, single-pole, instrument panel harness/terminal 15a connection, behind instrument panel	
M10	Right brake light bulb	7			
M16	Left reversing light bulb	4			
M17	Right reversing light bulb	5	T2e	Plug connector, two-pole, behind instrument panel	
N5	Control solenoid	5			
N16	Electric control switch for raising engine speed	1	T2f	Plug connector, two-pole, in engine compartment near ignition coil	
N14	Electronic control unit for parking brake and twin circuit brake system	8, 9	T3	Plug connector, three-pole, in engine compartment, left	
T1j	Plug connector, single-pole, behind instrument panel		T6	Plug connector, six-pole, behind instrument panel	
T1k	Plug connector, single-pole, fuse box connection, terminal 15a, behind instrument panel				

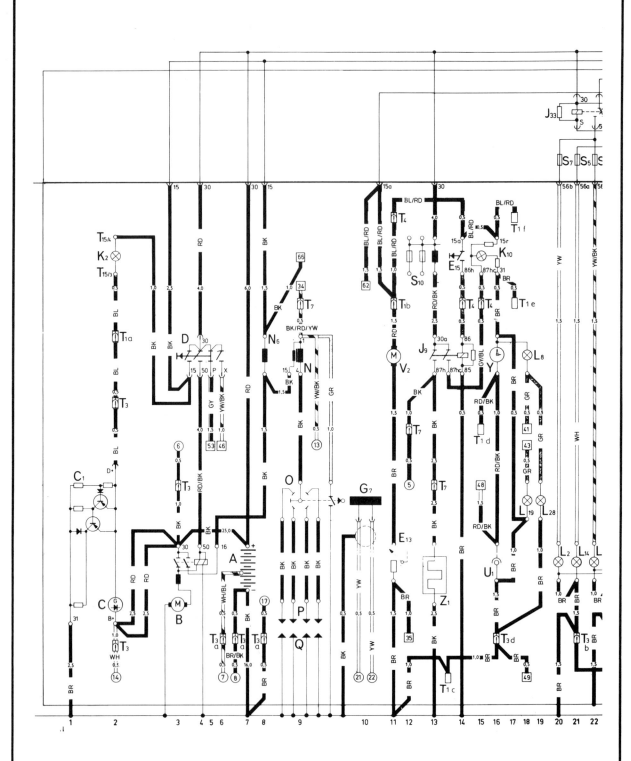

Fig. 13.57A Wiring diagram for 1975 UK models

Colour Code

Pink	= PI	Red	= RD	Green	= GR	Grey	= GY
Black	= BK	Orange	= OR	Blue	= BL	White	= WH
Brown	= BR	Yellow	= YW	Violet	= VI	Purple	= PU

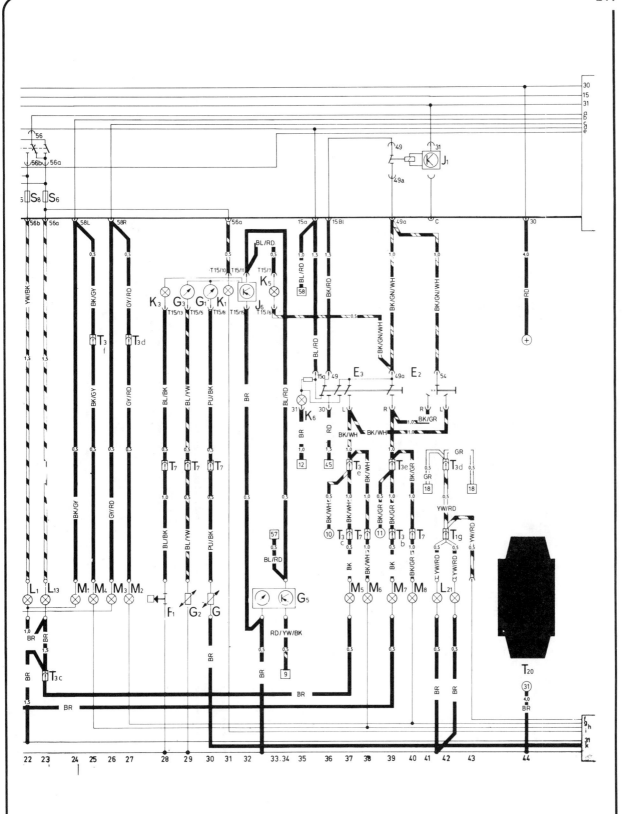

Fig. 13.57B Wiring diagram for 1975 UK models (contd)

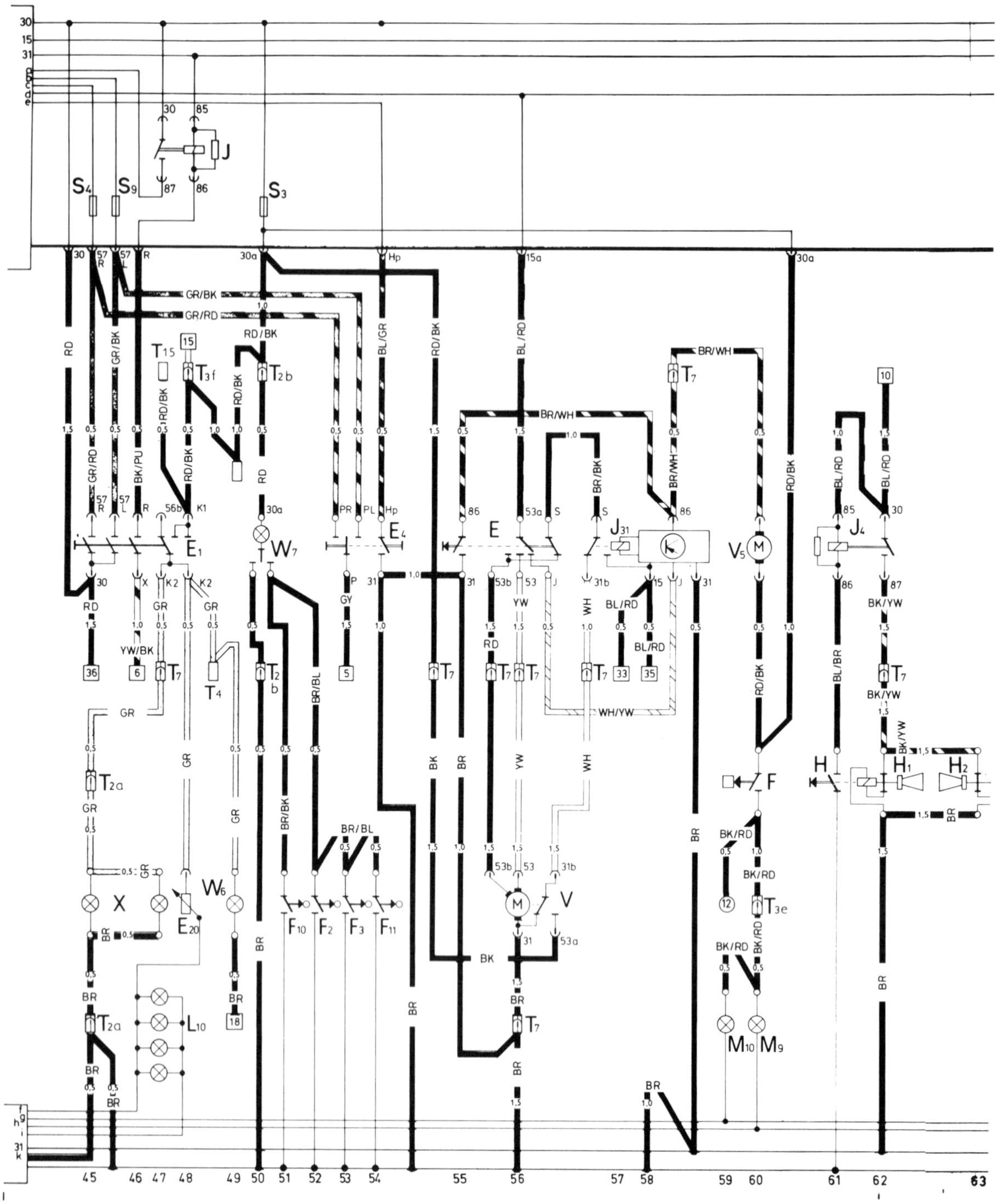

Fig. 13.57C Wiring diagram for 1975 UK models (contd)

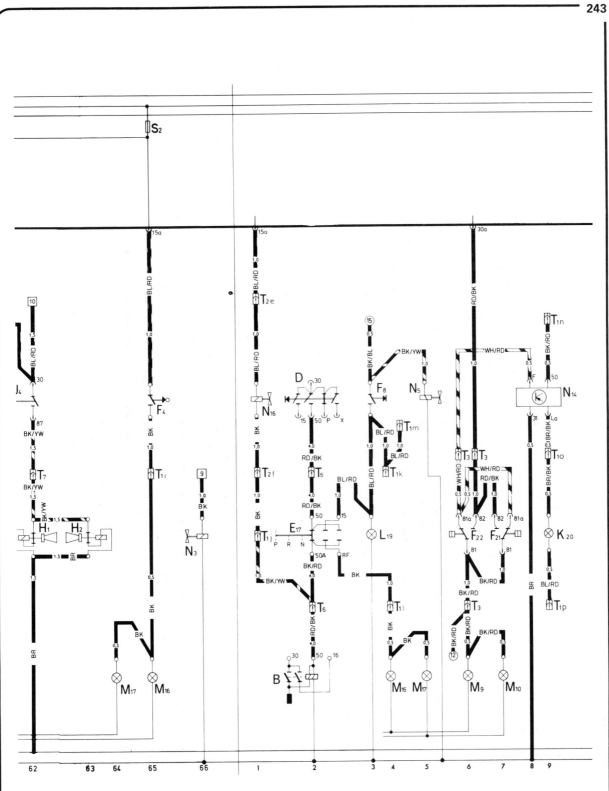

Fig. 13.57D Wiring diagram for 1975 UK models (contd)

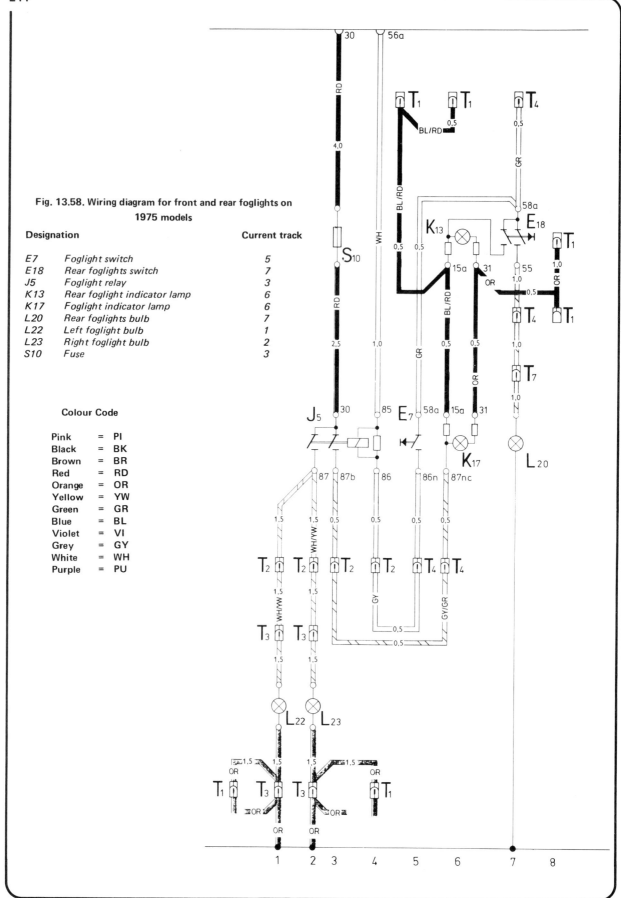

Fig. 13.58. Wiring diagram for front and rear foglights on 1975 models

Designation		Current track
E7	Foglight switch	5
E18	Rear foglights switch	7
J5	Foglight relay	3
K13	Rear foglight indicator lamp	6
K17	Foglight indicator lamp	6
L20	Rear foglights bulb	7
L22	Left foglight bulb	1
L23	Right foglight bulb	2
S10	Fuse	3

Colour Code

Pink	=	PI
Black	=	BK
Brown	=	BR
Red	=	RD
Orange	=	OR
Yellow	=	YW
Green	=	GR
Blue	=	BL
Violet	=	VI
Grey	=	GY
White	=	WH
Purple	=	PU

Fig. 13.59. Key to wiring diagram for 1975 USA models

Description		Current track	Description		Current track
A	Battery	7	E4	Headlight dimmer switch	72
B	Starter	4	E6	Interior light switch	54
C	Alternator	3	E13	Heater fan switch	65
C1	Regulator	2	E20	Instrument panel lighting control switch	51
D	Ignition/starter switch	5			
E2	Turn signal switch	47	E24	Safety belt lock contact, left	59
E3	Emergency flasher switch	42	E25	Safety belt lock contact, right	62
E15	Rear window defogger switch	15	E31	Contact in driver's seat	60
F1	Oil pressure switch	32	E32	Contact in passenger's seat	62
F18	Radiator fan thermo switch	12	F2	Door contact and buzzer alarm switch, left front	57
G	Fuel gauge sender unit	34			
G1	Coolant temperature gauge sender unit	33	F3	Door contact switch, right front	56
			F4	Reversing light switch	79
G3	Coolant temperature gauge	33	F9	Parking brake control light	58
G7	TDC marker unit	8	F10	Door contact switch, left rear	54
J1	Turn signal relay	45	F11	Door contact switch, right rear	55
J6	Voltage vibrator	35	F21	Brake light switch 1	78
J9	Rear window defogger relay	14	F22	Brake light switch 2	77
J29	Blocking diode for CDI system	3	F26	Cold start thermo switch	82
J33	Headlight low and high beam relay	22	G6	Fuel pump	87
K1	Headlight high beam warning light	35	G19	Air flow sensor	81
K2	Alternator charging warning light	3	H	Horn button	73
K3	Oil pressure warning light	32	H1	Dual horns	74/75
K5	Turn signal warning light	37	H6	Buzzer alarm system contact in steering lock	59
K6	Emergency flasher warning light	39			
K10	Rear window defogger warning light	18	J4	Dual horn relay	73/74
K20	Dual circuit brake warning light	31	J10	Fuel pump switch (activated by air flow sensor)	81, 82
K22	EGR warning light	28			
L1	Headlight sealed beam units, left	22	J17	Fuel pump relay	84, 85
L2	Headlight sealed beam units, right	19	J25	Headlight relay	51
L21	Heater operating lever illumination	37/38	J30	Windshield washer/wiper relay	69
L28	Cigarette lighter illumination	17	J34	Safety belt warning system relay	57
M1	Sidemarker, left rear	27	J42	Catalytic converter control relay	83
M2	Tail light, left	26	K19	Safety belt warning system warning light	64
M3	Sidemarker, right rear	28			
M4	Tail light, right	29	K21	Catalytic converter warning light	85
M5	Turn signal and parking light, left front	25/42	L10	Instrument panel illumination	49
			M9	Brake light, left	77
M6	Turn signal, left rear	43	M10	Brake light, right	78
M7	Turn signal and parking light, right front	31/45	M16	Reversing light, left	80
			M17	Reversing light, right	79
M8	Turn signal, right rear	46	N9	Warm running compensation switch	86
M11	Sidemarkers, front	25/30	N12	Brake pad wear indicator, right side	76
N	Ignition coil	10	N13	Brake pad wear indicator, left side	76
N15	CDI system control unit	10	N14	Brake wear control unit	75/76
O	Ignition distributor	10	N17	Cold start valve	83
P	Spark plug connectors	11	N21	Auxiliary air regulator	85
Q	Spark plugs	11	S2	Fuse in fuse box	76
S1	Fuse in fuse box	41	S3	Fuse in fuse box	54
S5	Fuse in fuse box	23	S4	Fuse in fuse box	49
S6	Fuse in fuse box	20	S9	Fuse in fuse box	49
S7	Fuse in fuse box	24	T	Wire connector	61, 62
S8	Fuse in fuse box	21	T1	Wire connector, single	60, 65, 79
S10	Fuse in fuse box	13	T2	Wire connector, double	52, 54, 60, 62, 76
T1	Wire connector, single	8, 37, 42, 45			
T3	Wire connector, 3 point	3, 4, 6, 12, 25, 30	T7	Wire connector, 7 point	52, 53, 64, 69, 70, 77, 85, 87
T4	Wire connector, 4 point	9, 11			
T7	Wire connector, 7 point	15, 18, 26, 29, 30, 37	T12	Wire connector, 12 point	58, 59, 60, 62, 63, 66, 67, 74, 82, 83
T12	Wire connector, 12 point	3, 14, 32, 33, 34, 42, 43, 45, 46			
			T20	Test network, test socket	74
U1	Cigarette lighter	18	V	Windshield wiper motor	70
V7	Radiator fan	12	V4	Heater fan	65
W6	Glove compartment light	40	V5	Windshield washer pump	67
Z1	Rear window defogger heating element	14	W7	Interior light	54
			X	License plate light	53
E	Windshield wiper switch	70	Y	Clock	48
E1	Light switch	49			

The circles mark the connections of the test circuit leads which go directly to the connections of the central socket (T20). The numbers in the circles correspond with the connections in the central socket.

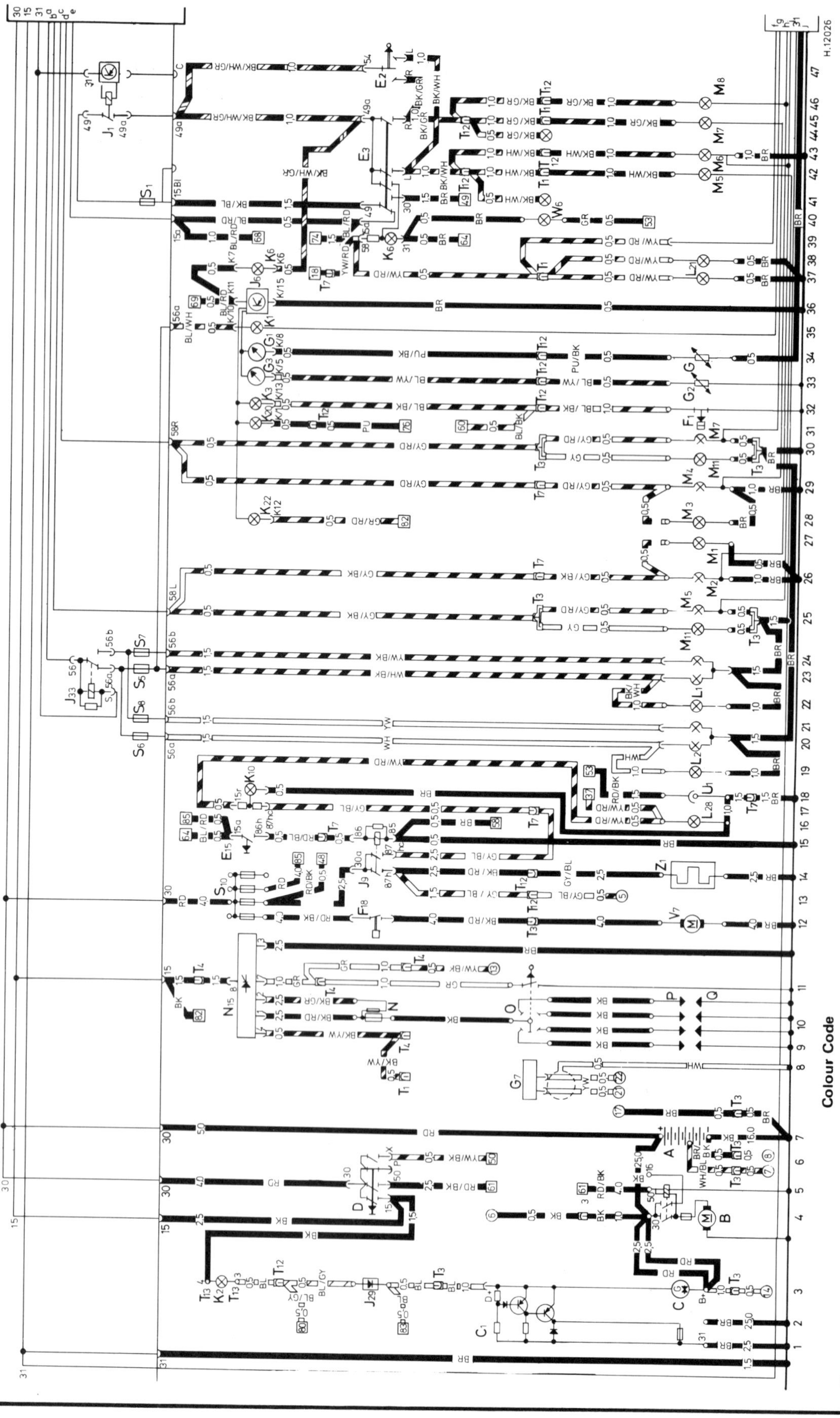

Fig. 13.59A Wiring diagram for 1975 USA models

Colour Code

Pink	=	PI	Red	=	RD	Green	=	GR	Grey	=	GY
Black	=	BK	Orange	=	OR	Blue	=	BL	White	=	WH
Brown	=	BR	Yellow	=	YW	Violet	=	VI	Purple	=	PU

H.12026

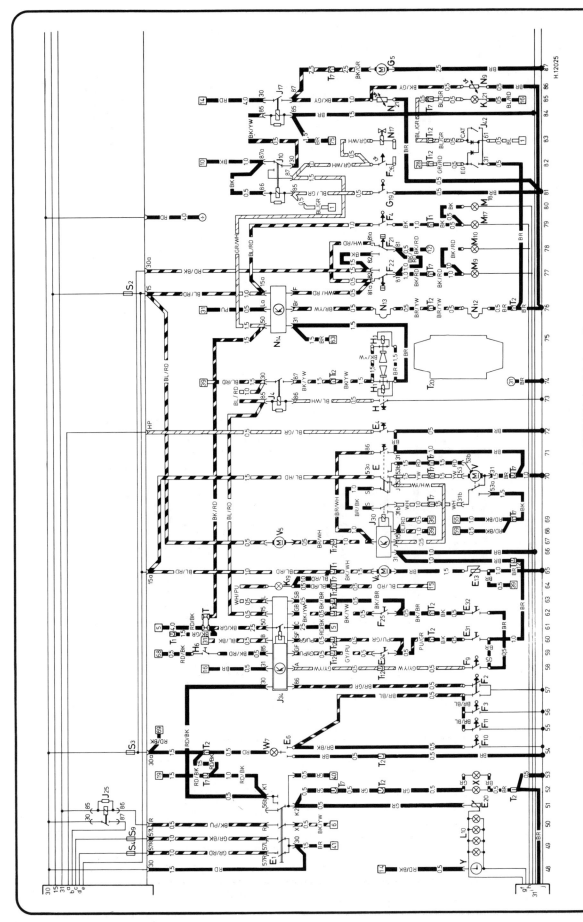

Fig. 13.59B Wiring diagram for 1975 USA models (contd)

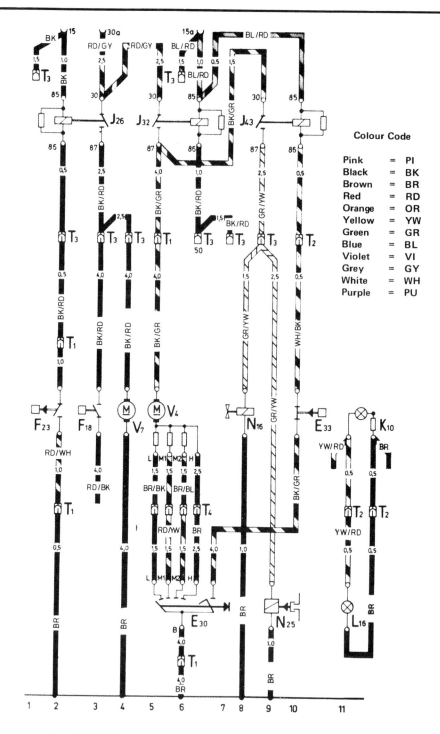

Colour Code

Pink	=	PI
Black	=	BK
Brown	=	BR
Red	=	RD
Orange	=	OR
Yellow	=	YW
Green	=	GR
Blue	=	BL
Violet	=	VI
Grey	=	GY
White	=	WH
Purple	=	PU

Fig. 13.60A. Wiring diagram for air conditioning system (1975 USA models)

Description		Current track	Description		Current track
E30	Air conditioner switch	6	N16	Check valve for increasing	
E33	Air conditioner thermo switch	10		engine RPM	8
F18	Thermo switch for radiator fan	3	N25	Relay for magnetic clutch	9
F23	Pressure switch	2	T1	Wire connector, single	2, 5, 6
F26	Radiator fan	2	T2	Wire connector, double	10, 11
J32	Air conditioner relay	5, 6	T3	Wire connector, 3 point	1, 2, 3, 4,
J43	Blocking diode for CIS	8, 9, 10			6, 7, 8, 9
K10	Rear window defogger warning		T4	Wire connector, 4 point	5, 6
	light	11	V4	Heater fan	5
L16	Heater operating lever light	11	V7	Coolant fan	4

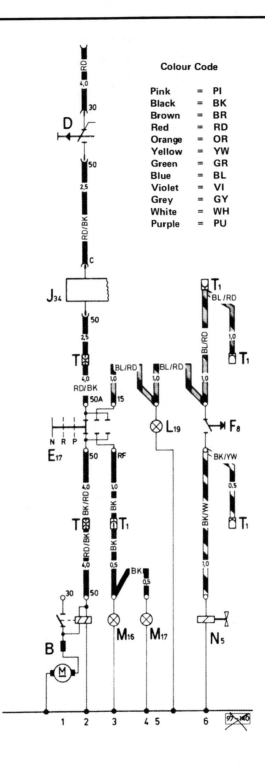

Colour Code

Pink	=	PI
Black	=	BK
Brown	=	BR
Red	=	RD
Orange	=	OR
Yellow	=	YW
Green	=	GR
Blue	=	BL
Violet	=	VI
Grey	=	GY
White	=	WH
Purple	=	PU

Fig. 13.60B. Wiring diagram for safety belt warning system for cars with automatic transmission up to chassis number 805 1 015 109 (relay J34 with starter cut-out switch) (1975 USA models)

Description		Current track	Description		Current track
B	Starter	1, 2	L19	Shift console light	5
D	Ignition/starter switch	2	M16	Reversing light, left	3
E17	Starter cut-out and reversing light switch	2	M17	Reversing light, right	4
			N5	Control solenoid	6
F8	Kickdown switch	6	T	Wire connector	2
F34	Safety belt warning system relay	2	T1	Wire connector, single	3, 6

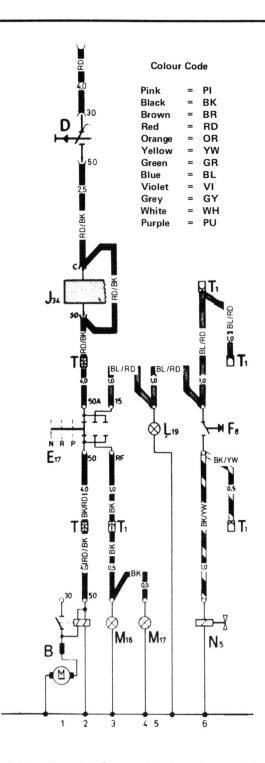

Colour Code

Pink	=	PI
Black	=	BK
Brown	=	BR
Red	=	RD
Orange	=	OR
Yellow	=	YW
Green	=	GR
Blue	=	BL
Violet	=	VI
Grey	=	GY
White	=	WH
Purple	=	PU

Fig. 13.60C. Wiring diagram for safety belt warning system for cars with automatic transmission from chassis number 805 1 105 110 to 805 1 032 564 (relay J4 bridged between terminals 50 and C) (1975 USA models)

Description		Current track	Description		Current track
B	Starter	1	L19	Shift console light	5
D	Ignition starter switch	2	M16	Reversing light, left	3
E17	Starter cut-out and reversing light		M17	Reversing light, right	4
	switch	2	N5	Control solenoid	6
F8	Kickdown switch	6	T	Wire connector	2
J34	Safety belt warning system relay	2	T1	Wire connector, single	3, 6

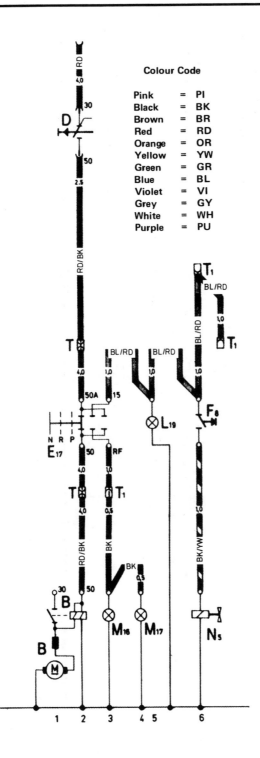

Colour Code

Pink	=	PI
Black	=	BK
Brown	=	BR
Red	=	RD
Orange	=	OR
Yellow	=	YW
Green	=	GR
Blue	=	BL
Violet	=	VI
Grey	=	GY
White	=	WH
Purple	=	PU

Fig. 13.60D. Wiring diagram for safety belt warning system for cars with automatic transmission from chassis number 805 1 032 565 (relay J34 with starter cut-out switch) (1975 USA models)

Description		Current track	Description		Current track
B	Starter	1, 2	M16	Reversing light, left	3
D	Ignition/starter switch	2	M17	Reversing light, right	4
E17	Starter cut-out and reversing light switch	2	N5	Control solenoid	6
F8	Kickdown switch	6	T	Wire connector	2
L19	Shift console light	5	T1	Wire connector, single	3, 6

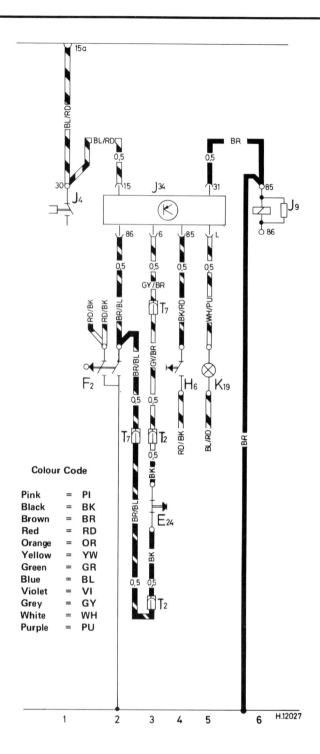

Colour Code

Pink	=	PI
Black	=	BK
Brown	=	BR
Red	=	RD
Orange	=	OR
Yellow	=	YW
Green	=	GR
Blue	=	BL
Violet	=	VI
Grey	=	GY
White	=	WH
Purple	=	PU

Fig. 13.60E. Wiring diagram for safety belt warning system for cars with manual transmission from chassis number 805 1 302 565 (relay J34 without starter cut-out switch) (1975 USA models)

Description		Current track	Description		Current track
E24	Safety belt lock with contact, left	3	J9	Rear window defogger relay	6
F2	Door contact and alarm switch	2	K19	Safety belt warning system warning	
H6	Buzzer alarm system contact in			light	5
	steering lock	4	T2	Wire connector, double	3
J4	Dual horn relay	1	T7	Wire connector, 7 point	3
J34	Safety belt warning system relay	3			

Fig. 13.61. Key to wiring diagram for 1976/77 UK models

Designation		In current path	Designation		In current path
A	Battery	8	T3f	Plug connector, three-pole, behind instrument panel	
B	Starter	3–7	T3g	Plug connector, three-pole, behind instrument panel	
C	Alternator	1			
C1	Voltage regulator	1	T4	Plug connector, four-pole, behind instrument panel	
D	Ignition/starter switch	4–7	T4a	Plug connector, four-pole, behind instrument panel	
E2	Turn signal switch	46			
E3	Hazard light switch	39–45	T7	Plug connector, seven-pole, behind instrument panel	
E15	Rear window defogger switch	18	T7a	Plug connector, seven-pole, behind instrument panel	
F	Brake light switch	49			
F1	Oil pressure switch	30	T15	Plug connector, fifteen-pole, central plug for combination instrument	
F26	Thermo switch for automatic choke	12			
G	Fuel level transmitter	32	U1	Cigar lighter	19
G1	Fuel gauge	32	V5	Windshield washer pump	50
G2	Coolant temperature transmitter	31	Y	Clock	20
G3	Coolant temperature gauge	31	Z1	Rear window defogger	14
G5	Tachometer	36, 37	E	Windshield wiper switch	65–67
G7	TDC sensor	15–17	E1	Light switch	54
J1	Turn signal flasher unit	43–45	E4	Headlight dip switch and flasher switch	61–63
J6	Voltage stabilizer	34	E13	Heater switch	75
J9	Rear window defogger relay	14–16	E20	Instrument light control	54
J33	Low beam and high beam relay	22–25	F2	Front left door contact switch	60
K1	High beam indicator light	33	F3	Front right door contact switch	61
K2	Alternator charge indicator light	1	F4	Reversing light switch	72
K3	Oil pressure indicator light	30	H	Horn control	74
K5	Turn signal indicator light	36	H2	Two-tone horn	73, 74
K6	Hazard light indicator light	38	J4	Relay, two-tone horn	73, 74
K10	Rear window defogger indicator light	16	J25	Main light relay	54
L1	Twin filament bulb, left headlight	24	J31	Wipe/wash and intermittent wiper relay	68–70
L2	Twin filament bulb, right headlight	22	L10	Instrument panel insert light bulb	51–53
L8	Clock light bulb	21	L21	Heater control light bulb	69, 70
L13	High beam headlight bulb, left	25	M16	Reversing light bulb, left	72
L14	High beam headlight bulb, right	23	M17	Reversing light bulb, right	71
L19	Gearshift diagram light bulb	20	S2, S4, S9	Fuses in relay plate with fuse holder	67, 51, 52
L28	Cigar lighter light bulb	21			
M1	Overnight light bulb, left	26	T1b	Plug connector, single-pole, behind instrument panel	
M2	Tail light bulb, right	29	T1c	Plug connector, single-pole, behind instrument panel	
M3	Overnight light bulb, right	28			
M4	Tail light bulb, left	27	T1d	Plug connector, single-pole, behind instrument panel	
M5	Front turn signal bulb, left	41	T1e	Plug connector, single-pole, engine compartment, left, only for twin circuit brake indicator light (optional extra)	
M6	Rear turn signal bulb, left	43			
M7	Front turn signal bulb, right	45			
M8	Rear turn signal bulb, right	46			
M9	Brake light bulb, left	49			
M10	Brake light bulb, right	47	T2	Plug connector, two-pole, behind console, only for twin circuit brake indicator light (optional extra)	
N	Ignition coil	10			
N1	Automatic choke (carburettor)	12			
N3	Fuel cut-off valve	13	T2c	Plug connector, two-pole, behind instrument panel	
N6	Series resistance	9	T2d	Plug connector, two-pole, trunk	
O	Distributor	10	T3g	Plug connector, three-pole, behind instrument panel, only for twin circuit brake indicator light (optional extra)	
P	Spark plug connectors	10			
Q	Spark plugs	10			
SO	Auxiliary fuse box	14, 15			
S3, S5, S6, S7, S8	Fuses in relay plate with fuse holder	49, 23, 25, 22, 24	T4	Plug connector, four-pole, behind instrument panel	
T1	Plug connector, single-pole, engine compartment, near ignition coil		T4a	Plug connector, four-pole, behind instrument panel	
T1a	Plug connector, single-pole, behind instrument panel		T7	Plug connector, seven-pole, behind instrument panel	
T2	Plug connector, two-pole, behind console		T7a	Plug connector, seven-pole, behind instrument panel	
T2a	Plug connector, two-pole, behind console		T7b	Plug connector, seven-pole, behind instrument panel	
T3	Plug connector, three-pole, behind instrument panel		T20	Central socket	78
T3a	Plug connector, three-pole, engine compartment, right		V	Windshield wiper motor	66, 67
T3c	Plug connector, three-pole, behind instrument panel		V2	Blower motor	75
T3d	Plug connector, three-pole, engine compartment, right		W6	Glove compartment light	52
			W7	Interior light	59
T3e	Plug connector, three-pole, engine compartment, left		X	License plate light	56, 57

The circles mark the connections of the test circuit leads which go directly to the connections of the central socket (T20). The numbers in the circles correspond with the connections in the central socket.

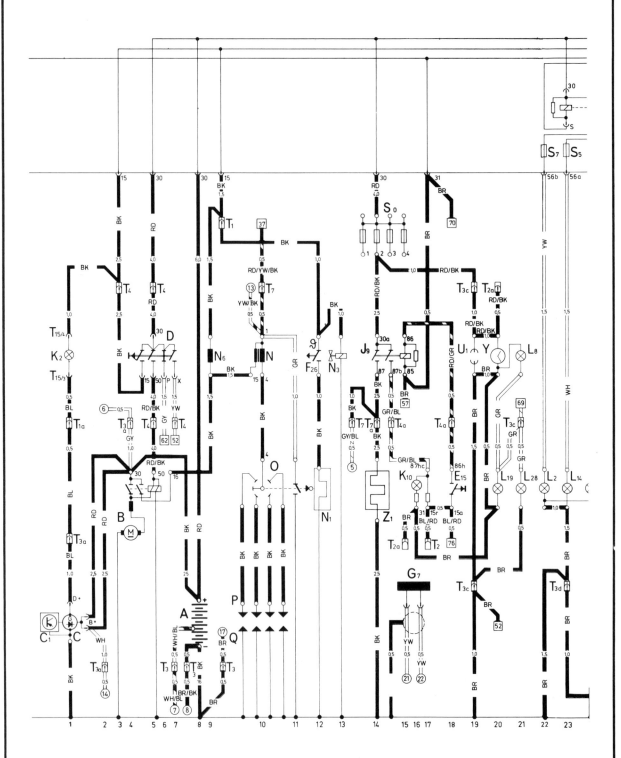

Fig. 13.61A Wiring diagram for 1976/77 UK models

Colour Code

Pink	= PI	Red	= RD	Green	= GR	Grey	= GY
Black	= BK	Orange	= OR	Blue	= BL	White	= WH
Brown	= BR	Yellow	= YW	Violet	= VI	Purple	= PU

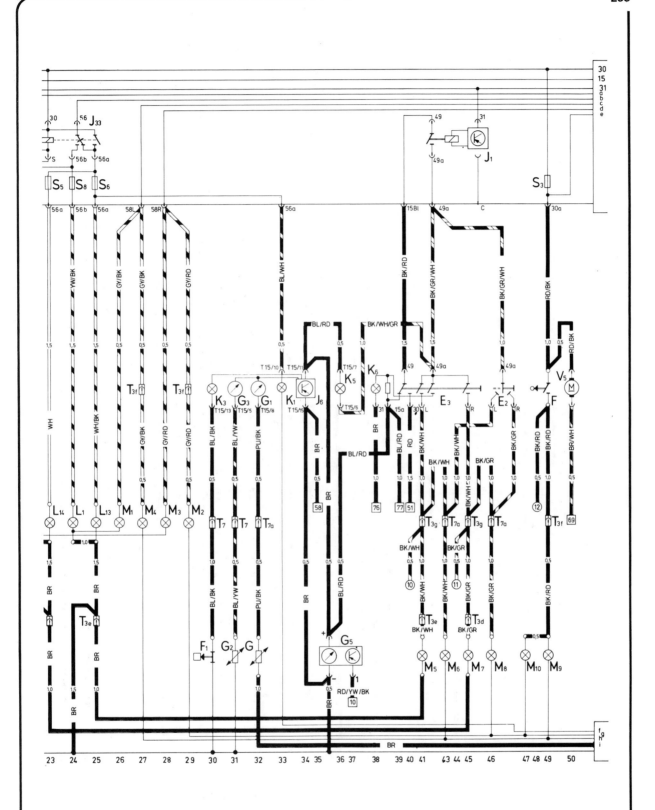

Fig. 13.61B Wiring diagram for 1976/77 UK models (contd)

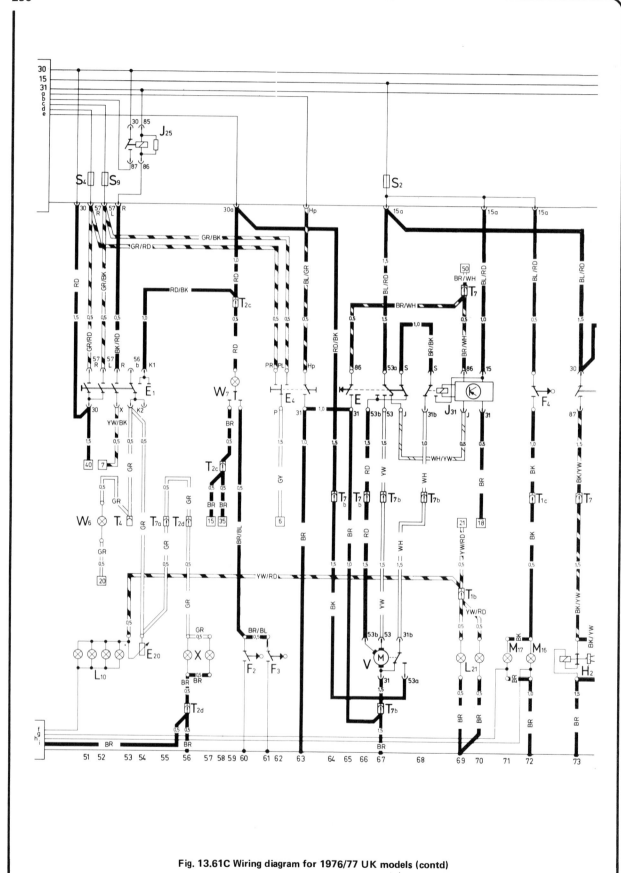

Fig. 13.61C Wiring diagram for 1976/77 UK models (contd)

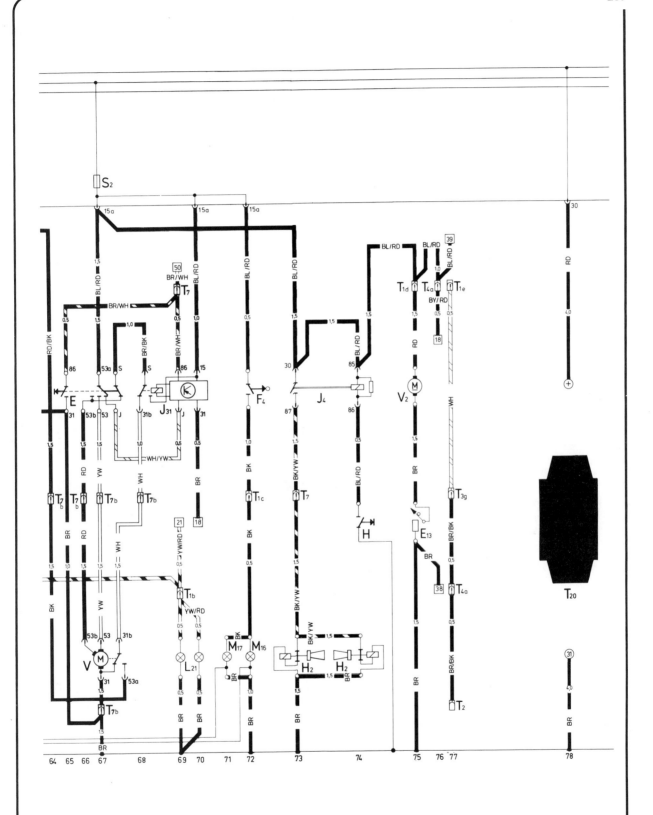

Fig. 13.61D Wiring diagram for 1976/77 UK models (contd)

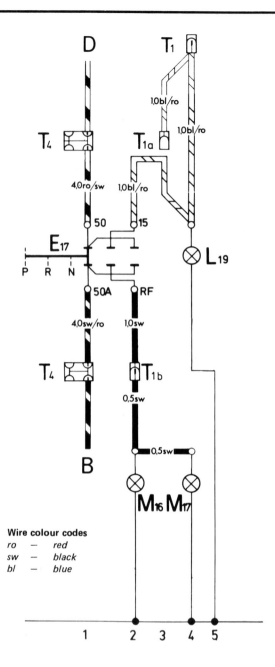

Fig. 13.62. Wiring diagram for automatic transmission models 1976 and 1977

Designation		In current path	Designation		In current path
B	To starter, terminal 50	1	T1b	Plug connector, single-pole, (tail light harness connection) behind instrument panel	
D	To ignition/starter switch, terminal 50	1			
E17	Starter inhibitor switch and reversing light switch	1	T4	Plug connector, four-pole (adaptor) behind instrument panel	
L19	Bulb, gearshift diagram illumination	4	*Italy		
M16	Bulb, left reversing light	2	T1	Plug connector, single-pole (light switch, terminal K2)	
M17	Bulb, right reversing light	4			
*T1	Plug connector, single-pole, (heater controls, terminal 15a) behind instrument panel		T1a	Plug connector, single-pole (instrument panel harness connection, terminal 58) behind instrument panel	
*T1a	Plug connector, single-pole (instrument panel harness connection, terminal 15a) behind instrument panel				

Fig. 13.63. Key to wiring diagram for 1976 USA models

	Description	Current track
A	Battery	7
B	Starter	4, 5, 6
C	Alternator	2
C1	Regulator	1
D	Ignition/starter switch	4, 5, 6
E2	Turn signal switch	47
E3	Emergency flasher switch	41, 42, 43, 44, 45, 46
E15	Rear window defogger switch	15
F1	Engine oil pressure switch	33, 34
F9	Parking brake warning light switch	32
F18	Radiator cooling fan thermo switch	11
G	Fuel gauge sender unit	36
G1	Fuel gauge	36
G2	Coolant temperature gauge sender unit	35
G3	Coolant temperature gauge	35
J1	Turn signal relay	45, 46, 47
J6	Voltage stabilizer	38
J9	Rear window defogger relay	13, 14, 15
J33	Headlight low and high beam relay	22, 23, 24
K1	Headlight high beam warning light	37
K2	Alternator charging warning light	2
K3	Engine oil pressure warning light	34
K5	Turn signal warning light	39
K6	Emergency flasher warning light	39
K10	Rear window defogger warning light	16
K20	Dual circuit brake warning light	32
K22	EGR warning light	33
L1	Sealed beam unit, left, low beam	22, 23
L2	Sealed beam unit, right, low beam	19, 20
L17	Sealed beam unit, left, high beam	21
L18	Sealed beam unit, right, high beam	18
L21	Heater lever light	40, 41
L28	Cigarette lighter light	18
M2	Tail light, right	29
M4	Tail light, left	27
M5	Turn signal and parking light, front left	25, 43
M6	Turn signal, rear left	44
M7	Turn signal and parking light, front right	31, 45
M8	Turn signal, rear right	46
M11	Side marker lights, front	24
M12	Side marker lights, rear	28
N	Ignition coil	8, 9
N15	CDI system control unit	8, 9, 10
O	Ignition distributor	8, 9, 10
P	Spark plug connectors	8, 9
Q	Spark plugs	8, 9
SO	Additional fuse box	12, 13
	Fuses S5, S6, S7, S8 in fuse box	19, 20, 22, 23
T1	Wire connector, single, behind dashboard	
T1a	Wire connector, single, in engine compartment left	
T1b	Wire connector, single, in engine compartment right	
T2	Wire connector, double, behind console (for CAT warning light)	
T2f	Wire connector, double, behind console (for air conditioner operating light)	
T3	Wire connector, 3 point, in engine compartment, front right	
T3a	Wire connector, 3 point, in engine compartment, left	
T3b	Wire connector, 3 point, in engine compartment, left	
T3c	Wire connector, 3 point, in engine compartment, right	
T3d	Wire connector, 3 point, behind dashboard	
T4	Wire connector, 4 point, behind dashboard	
T4a	Wire connector, 4 point, in engine compartment, right	
T7	Wire connector, 7 point, behind dashboard	
T7b	Wire connector, 7 point, behind dashboard	
T12	Wire connector, 12 point, behind dashboard	

	Description	Current track
T12a	Wire connector, 12 point, behind dashboard	
T15	Wire connector, 15 point, in instrument cluster	
U7	Radiator cooling fan	11
V1	Cigarette lighter	16
Z1	Rear window defogger heating element	13
E	Windshield wiper switch	61
E1	Light switch	48, 49, 50, 51
E4	Headlight dimmer switch	58
E13	Heater fan switch	90
E20	Instrument panel lighting switch	51
E24	Safety belt lock contact, driver's seat	80
F2	Door contact and buzzer alarm switch, front left	57
F3	Door contact switch, front right	58
F4	Reversing light switch	72
F21	Dual circuit brake system switch I	69, 70
F22	Dual circuit brake system switch II	67, 68
F26	Cold start thermo switch	83
G6	Electric fuel pump	88
G19	Air flow sensor	81
H	Horn button	75
H2	Dual horns	76, 78
H5	Buzzer alarm system contact in steering lock	77
J4	Dual horns relay	75
J10	Fuel pump switch (activated by air flow sensor)	81, 82, 83
J17	Fuel pump relay	85, 86
J25	Headlight relay	51
J31	Windshield washer/wiper and intermittent relay	62, 63, 64, 65, 66
J34	Safety belt warning system relay	78, 79, 80
J42	CAT relay	76, 77
K19	Safety belt warning system warning light	79, 80
L10	Instrument panel lights	50, 51, 52, 53
M9	Brake light, left	69, 70
M10	Brake light, right	67
M16	Reversing light, left	72
M17	Reversing light, right	73
N9	Warm running compensation switch	87
N12	Brake pad wear indicator, right	74
N13	Brake pad wear indicator, left	74
N14	Brake wear control unit	71, 72
N17	Cold start valve	84
N21	Auxiliary air regulator	86
	Fuses S3, S4, S9 in fuse box	
T1c	Wire connector, single, behind dashboard	
T1d	Wire connector, single, behind dashboard	
T2a	Wire connector, double, in luggage compartment, left	
T2b	Wire connector, double, behind dashboard	
T2c	Wire connector, double, in engine compartment, left	
T2d	Wire connector, double, in engine compartment, right	
T2e	Wire connector, double, behind dashboard	
T7	Wire connector, 7 point, behind dashboard	
T7a	Wire connector, 7 point, behind dashboard	
T7b	Wire connector, 7 point, behind dashboard	
T12	Wire connector, 12 point, behind dashboard	
V	Windshield wiper motor	61
V4	Heater fan	90
V5	Windshield washer pump	67
W6	Glove compartment lights	50
W7	Interior light	56
X	License plate light	52, 54
Y	Clock	48

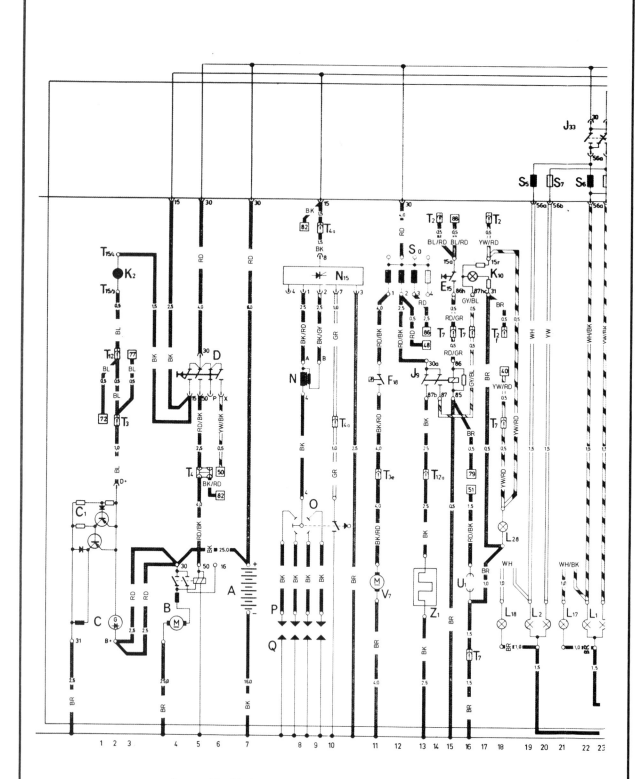

Fig. 13.63A Wiring diagram for 1976 USA models

Colour Code

Pink	= PI	Red	= RD	Green	= GR	Grey	= GY
Black	= BK	Orange	= OR	Blue	= BL	White	= WH
Brown	= BR	Yellow	= YW	Violet	= VI	Purple	= PU

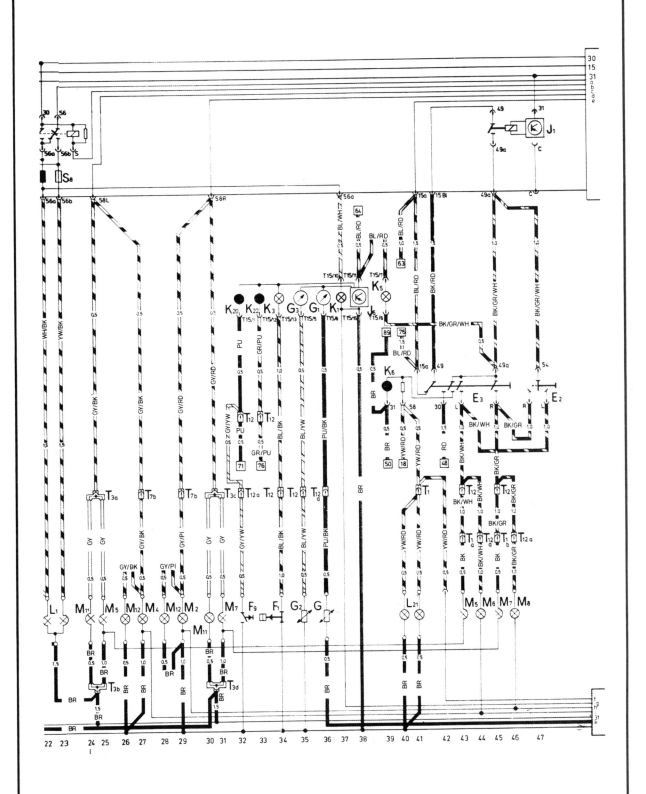

Fig. 13.63B Wiring diagram for 1976 USA models (contd)

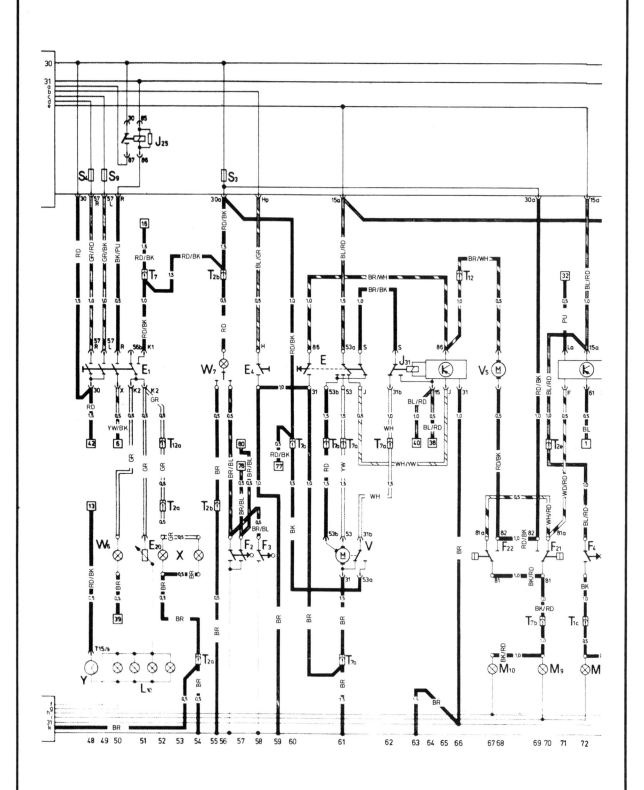

Fig. 13.63C Wiring diagram for 1976 USA models (contd)

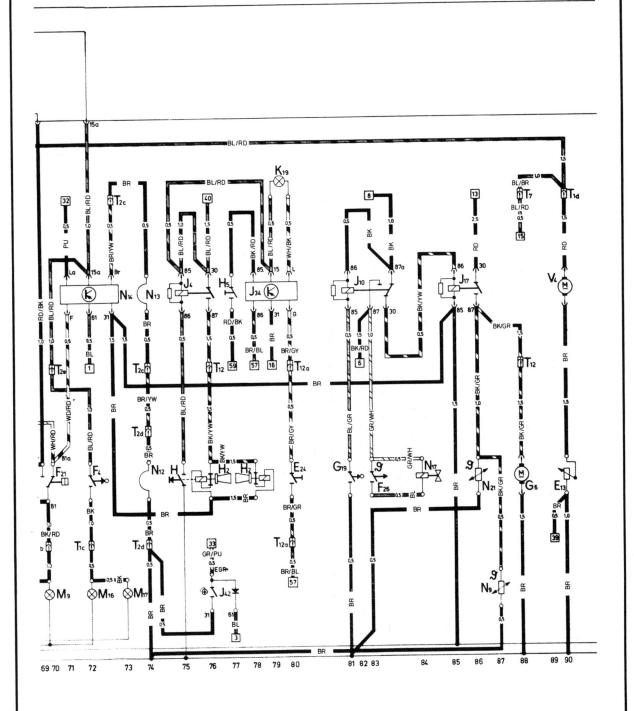

Fig. 13.63D Wiring diagram for 1976 USA models (contd)

Safety first!

Professional motor mechanics are trained in safe working procedures. However enthusiastic you may be about getting on with the job in hand, do take the time to ensure that your safety is not put at risk. A moment's lack of attention can result in an accident, as can failure to observe certain elementary precautions.

There will always be new ways of having accidents, and the following points do not pretend to be a comprehensive list of all dangers; they are intended rather to make you aware of the risks and to encourage a safety-conscious approach to all work you carry out on your vehicle.

Essential DOs and DON'Ts

DON'T rely on a single jack when working underneath the vehicle. Always use reliable additional means of support, such as axle stands, securely placed under a part of the vehicle that you know will not give way.

DON'T attempt to loosen or tighten high-torque nuts (e.g. wheel hub nuts) while the vehicle is on a jack; it may be pulled off.

DON'T start the engine without first ascertaining that the transmission is in neutral (or 'Park' where applicable) and the parking brake applied.

DON'T suddenly remove the filler cap from a hot cooling system – cover it with a cloth and release the pressure gradually first, or you may get scalded by escaping coolant.

DON'T attempt to drain oil until you are sure it has cooled sufficiently to avoid scalding you.

DON'T grasp any part of the engine, exhaust or catalytic converter without first ascertaining that it is sufficiently cool to avoid burning you.

DON'T allow brake fluid or antifreeze to contact vehicle paintwork.

DON'T syphon toxic liquids such as fuel, brake fluid or antifreeze by mouth, or allow them to remain on your skin.

DON'T inhale dust – it may be injurious to health (see *Asbestos* below).

DON'T allow any spilt oil or grease to remain on the floor – wipe it up straight away, before someone slips on it.

DON'T use ill-fitting spanners or other tools which may slip and cause injury.

DON'T attempt to lift a heavy component which may be beyond your capability – get assistance.

DON'T rush to finish a job, or take unverified short cuts.

DON'T allow children or animals in or around an unattended vehicle.

DO wear eye protection when using power tools such as drill, sander, bench grinder etc, and when working under the vehicle.

DO use a barrier cream on your hands prior to undertaking dirty jobs – it will protect your skin from infection as well as making the dirt easier to remove afterwards; but make sure your hands aren't left slippery.

DO keep loose clothing (cuffs, tie etc) and long hair well out of the way of moving mechanical parts.

DO remove rings, wristwatch etc, before working on the vehicle – especially the electrical system.

DO ensure that any lifting tackle used has a safe working load rating adequate for the job.

DO keep your work area tidy – it is only too easy to fall over articles left lying around.

DO get someone to check periodically that all is well, when working alone on the vehicle.

DO carry out work in a logical sequence and check that everything is correctly assembled and tightened afterwards.

DO remember that your vehicle's safety affects that of yourself and others. If in doubt on any point, get specialist advice.

IF, in spite of following these precautions, you are unfortunate enough to injure yourself, seek medical attention as soon as possible.

Asbestos

Certain friction, insulating, sealing, and other products – such as brake linings, brake bands, clutch linings, torque converters, gaskets, etc – contain asbestos. *Extreme care must be taken to avoid inhalation of dust from such products since it is hazardous to health.* If in doubt, assume that they *do* contain asbestos.

Fire

Remember at all times that petrol (gasoline) is highly flammable. Never smoke, or have any kind of naked flame around, when working on the vehicle. But the risk does not end there – a spark caused by an electrical short-circuit, by two metal surfaces contacting each other, by careless use of tools, or even by static electricity built up in your body under certain conditions, can ignite petrol vapour, which in a confined space is highly explosive.

Always disconnect the battery earth (ground) terminal before working on any part of the fuel or electrical system, and never risk spilling fuel on to a hot engine or exhaust.

It is recommended that a fire extinguisher of a type suitable for fuel and electrical fires is kept handy in the garage or workplace at all times. Never try to extinguish a fuel or electrical fire with water.

Fumes

Certain fumes are highly toxic and can quickly cause unconsciousness and even death if inhaled to any extent. Petrol (gasoline) vapour comes into this category, as do the vapours from certain solvents such as trichloroethylene. Any draining or pouring of such volatile fluids should be done in a well ventilated area.

When using cleaning fluids and solvents, read the instructions carefully. Never use materials from unmarked containers – they may give off poisonous vapours.

Never run the engine of a motor vehicle in an enclosed space such as a garage. Exhaust fumes contain carbon monoxide which is extremely poisonous; if you need to run the engine, always do so in the open air or at least have the rear of the vehicle outside the workplace.

If you are fortunate enough to have the use of an inspection pit, never drain or pour petrol, and never run the engine, while the vehicle is standing over it; the fumes, being heavier than air, will concentrate in the pit with possibly lethal results.

The battery

Never cause a spark, or allow a naked light, near the vehicle's battery. It will normally be giving off a certain amount of hydrogen gas, which is highly explosive.

Always disconnect the battery earth (ground) terminal before working on the fuel or electrical systems.

If possible, loosen the filler plugs or cover when charging the battery from an external source. Do not charge at an excessive rate or the battery may burst.

Take care when topping up and when carrying the battery. The acid electrolyte, even when diluted, is very corrosive and should not be allowed to contact the eyes or skin.

If you ever need to prepare electrolyte yourself, always add the acid slowly to the water, and never the other way round. Protect against splashes by wearing rubber gloves and goggles.

When jump starting a car using a booster battery, for negative earth (ground) vehicles, connect the jump leads in the following sequence: First connect one jump lead between the positive (+) terminals of the two batteries. Then connect the other jump lead first to the negative (–) terminal of the booster battery, and then to a good earthing (ground) point on the vehicle to be started, at least 18 in (45 cm) from the battery if possible. Ensure that hands and jump leads are clear of any moving parts, and that the two vehicles do not touch. Disconnect the leads in the reverse order.

Mains electricity

When using an electric power tool, inspection light etc, which works from the mains, always ensure that the appliance is correctly connected to its plug and that, where necessary, it is properly earthed (grounded). Do not use such appliances in damp conditions and, again, beware of creating a spark or applying excessive heat in the vicinity of fuel or fuel vapour.

Ignition HT voltage

A severe electric shock can result from touching certain parts of the ignition system, such as the HT leads, when the engine is running or being cranked, particularly if components are damp or the insulation is defective. Where an electronic ignition system is fitted, the HT voltage is much higher and could prove fatal.

Conversion factors

Length (distance)
Inches (in)	X	25.4	= Millimetres (mm)	X	0.0394	= Inches (in)
Feet (ft)	X	0.305	= Metres (m)	X	3.281	= Feet (ft)
Miles	X	1.609	= Kilometres (km)	X	0.621	= Miles

Volume (capacity)
Cubic inches (cu in; in^3) X 16.387 = Cubic centimetres (cc; cm^3)   X 0.061 = Cubic inches (cu in; in^3)
Imperial pints (Imp pt) X 0.568 = Litres (l)   X 1.76 = Imperial pints (Imp pt)
Imperial quarts (Imp qt) X 1.137 = Litres (l)   X 0.88 = Imperial quarts (Imp qt)
Imperial quarts (Imp qt) X 1.201 = US quarts (US qt)   X 0.833 = Imperial quarts (Imp qt)
US quarts (US qt) X 0.946 = Litres (l)   X 1.057 = US quarts (US qt)
Imperial gallons (Imp gal) X 4.546 = Litres (l)   X 0.22 = Imperial gallons (Imp gal)
Imperial gallons (Imp gal) X 1.201 = US gallons (US gal)   X 0.833 = Imperial gallons (Imp gal)
US gallons (US gal) X 3.785 = Litres (l)   X 0.264 = US gallons (US gal)

Mass (weight)
Ounces (oz) X 28.35 = Grams (g)   X 0.035 = Ounces (oz)
Pounds (lb) X 0.454 = Kilograms (kg)   X 2.205 = Pounds (lb)

Force
Ounces-force (ozf; oz) X 0.278 = Newtons (N)   X 3.6 = Ounces-force (ozf; oz)
Pounds-force (lbf; lb) X 4.448 = Newtons (N)   X 0.225 = Pounds-force (lbf; lb)
Newtons (N) X 0.1 = Kilograms-force (kgf; kg)   X 9.81 = Newtons (N)

Pressure
Pounds-force per square inch (psi; lbf/in^2; lb/in^2) X 0.070 = Kilograms-force per square centimetre (kgf/cm^2; kg/cm^2)   X 14.223 = Pounds-force per square inch (psi; lbf/in^2; lb/in^2)

Pounds-force per square inch (psi; lbf/in^2; lb/in^2) X 0.068 = Atmospheres (atm)   X 14.696 = Pounds-force per square inch (psi; lbf/in^2; lb/in^2)

Pounds-force per square inch (psi; lbf/in^2; lb/in^2) X 0.069 = Bars   X 14.5 = Pounds-force per square inch (psi; lbf/in^2; lb/in^2)

Pounds-force per square inch (psi; lbf/in^2; lb/in^2) X 6.895 = Kilopascals (kPa)   X 0.145 = Pounds-force per square inch (psi; lbf/in^2; lb/in^2)

Kilopascals (kPa) X 0.01 = Kilograms-force per square centimetre (kgf/cm^2; kg/cm^2)   X 98.1 = Kilopascals (kPa)

Torque (moment of force)
Pounds-force inches (lbf in; lb in) X 1.152 = Kilograms-force centimetre (kgf cm; kg cm)   X 0.868 = Pounds-force inches (lbf in; lb in)

Pounds-force inches (lbf in; lb in) X 0.113 = Newton metres (Nm)   X 8.85 = Pounds-force inches (lbf in; lb in)

Pounds-force inches (lbf in; lb in) X 0.083 = Pounds-force feet (lbf ft; lb ft)   X 12 = Pounds-force inches (lbf in; lb in)

Pounds-force feet (lbf ft; lb ft) X 0.138 = Kilograms-force metres (kgf m; kg m)   X 7.233 = Pounds-force feet (lbf ft; lb ft)

Pounds-force feet (lbf ft; lb ft) X 1.356 = Newton metres (Nm)   X 0.738 = Pounds-force feet (lbf ft; lb ft)

Newton metres (Nm) X 0.102 = Kilograms-force metres (kgf m; kg m)   X 9.804 = Newton metres (Nm)

Power
Horsepower (hp) X 745.7 = Watts (W)   X 0.0013 = Horsepower (hp)

Velocity (speed)
Miles per hour (miles/hr; mph) X 1.609 = Kilometres per hour (km/hr; kph)   X 0.621 = Miles per hour (miles/hr; mph)

Fuel consumption*
Miles per gallon, Imperial (mpg) X 0.354 = Kilometres per litre (km/l)   X 2.825 = Miles per gallon, Imperial (mpg)
Miles per gallon, US (mpg) X 0.425 = Kilometres per litre (km/l)   X 2.352 = Miles per gallon, US (mpg)

Temperature
Degrees Fahrenheit = (°C x 1.8) + 32   Degrees Celsius (Degrees Centigrade; °C) = (°F - 32) x 0.56

*It is common practice to convert from miles per gallon (mpg) to litres/100 kilometres (l/100km),
where mpg (Imperial) x l/100 km = 282 and mpg (US) x l/100 km = 235

Index

Printed by
J H Haynes & Co Ltd
Sparkford Nr Yeovil
Somerset BA22 7JJ England